TROUT
FISHING

Near American Cities

D1279939

0 11557 02958 1

TROUT
FISHING
NEAR AMERICAN CITIES

Ann McIntosh

STACKPOLE
BOOKS

Published by
STACKPOLE BOOKS
5067 Ritter Road
Mechanicsburg, PA 17055
www.stackpolebooks.com

Printed in the United States

10 9 8 7 6 5 4 3 2 1

First edition

Cover photo by Douglas Lees
Cover design by Wendy A. Reynolds

Library of Congress Cataloging-in-Publication Data

McIntosh, Ann.
    Trout fishing near American cities/Ann McIntosh.—1st ed.
        p. cm.
    ISBN 0-8117-2958-3 (pbk.)
    1. Trout fishing—United States—Guidebooks. I. Title.
SH688.U6 M3874 2002
799.1'757'0973—dc21
                                                        2001034384

To my mother,
who made this book possible

Contents

Foreword

A lot of things can be said about a person, but no one can say that Ann McIntosh isn't serious about her fishing. It came through loud and clear in her first book, *Mid-Atlantic Budget Angler*, and she follows suit here with an impressive selection of favorites stretching from east to west, and north to south across the country.

Readers will find that Ann's book is a good reference to use in visiting not only the specific watersheds mentioned, but the general areas as well. She has done an incredible amount of work herself and has called upon the invaluable knowledge and assistance of local guides, authors, and regional authorities to complement her research. You'll find everything you need, from directions, hatches, and fly shops to restaurants and lodging. And if that's not enough, she gives readers a list of resources in each area for additional local information.

The one thing that kept occurring to us as we read Ann's manuscript is the number of streams and rivers across America that have made a dramatic comeback from years of pollution and devastation. Any number of culprits—logging, industrial waste, poor sewage treatment facilities, agricultural runoff, mine drainage, and development—can be blamed. The old saying "history repeats itself" should be a warning to all of us that we have to continue to be vigilant to protect and conserve our natural resources. Our environment will never be what it once was, but it can be a whole lot better than it once was, too. The moment we drop our guard, another precious jewel of bright water will succumb to the side effects of man's impact on his surroundings.

We share Ann's concern for the stocking programs in some of the states visited in the book, ours included. It's a tough job for fish commissions everywhere to try to please everyone who purchases a fishing license. Some anglers want to keep a creel full of fish, others like one or two for the campfire, still others return all fish caught. Some are happy with stocked fish, while others extol the experience of catching and releasing a wild trout.

We believe it's important for all of us to let our politicians know how we feel. If we want the wild trout fisheries carefully managed and protected, in the best interests of the trout, not the fishermen (or the voters), we must educate our elected officials. There will always be plenty of fisheries that are suited for stocked trout, and we'll all enjoy those as well. It's been proven in many watersheds that it's possible to have it both ways.

We didn't start reading at the beginning of the manuscript; we started with the Henry's Fork section, one of our favorite places. When Wood Road 16 came up, we selfishly thought, "Come on, Ann, don't enough people know about this spot already? Don't give it all away." But then later we came to the Frankstown Branch in the Pittsburgh chapter, where one conservationist comments, "A river can't have too many friends! Friends develop a stake in the resource and are there to help save it when disaster threatens," and we felt guilty. This, friends, is how we must all look at every piece of water that holds trout today. Thinking back to Henry's Fork, there is no river anywhere more vulnerable or sensitive.

So the next time we get to Wood Road 16 and find you there in our favorite spot, let's greet each other, share our thoughts about the fishing, and be thankful that it's there for us—all of us.

Barry and Cathy Beck
Benton, Pennsylvania, March 2001

Acknowledgments

My first thank you goes to my fellow contributors, who have provided much invaluable information throughout this book. They have cooperated with me completely, tolerated my not infrequent disorganization, and put in many hours for little reward. Thank you one and all. I hope we succeed.

Many of the individuals recognized below are conservationists and members of Trout Unlimited (TU). Without the inspiration of TU, this book would not have come to pass. When *Trout* magazine editor Pete Rafle and chief operating manager Ken Mendez invited me to write the quarterly column "The Budget Angler," research for the column involved fishing far beyond my home waters in the Mid-Atlantic region. The series became the inspiration for this book. I would also like to thank Charles Gauvin and Christine Arena, also TU folks, for their enthusiasm and help along the way.

There are so many guides, anglers, and other individuals who have helped me obtain the information available in these pages, that I have no doubt I will omit someone. I hope he or she will forgive me; I apologize in advance.

Starting with the beginning of the book, Fred and Marilyn Moran were invaluable informants on the Deerfield River in western Massachusetts. I had fished that river many times alone, but Fred brought my experience into focus. I would also like to thank Michael Flach of RiverRun in Great Barrington, Massachusetts, for his help reviewing the information about the Housatonic and the Farmington Rivers.

The New York City chapter, which includes the Catskill streams and the upper Delaware River, was enhanced by information from three veteran anglers: Dick Smith, of Battenkill Anglers in Roscoe, New York; Sara Crewes, at Al's Wild Trout fly shop on the East Branch of the Delaware; and Jim Serio, owner of Gray Ghost Flies in Hancock, New York. Thanks to Al Caucci for his ongoing wisdom and to Pat Schuler for travel information on the upper Delaware.

I was honored to have master angler and author Ed Koch review the material I wrote about south-central Pennsylvania limestone creeks. I was further assisted by Mary Kuss, a respected fly-fishing instructor and co-founder of the Delaware Valley Women's Fly Fishers.

I've fished central Pennsylvania most of my fly-fishing life. I am on the Little Juniata, Spruce Creek, Penns Creek, and Spring Creek many times each season. I list here only the folks that helped with this book: Alan Bright, owner of Spruce Creek Outfitters; Harry Redline, master guide and former staff member of the Pennsylvania Fish & Game Commission; Dave Rothrock; and Skip the Stalker, a master guide with Spruce Creek Outfitters.

My home water, Maryland's Gunpowder River, has changed dramatically from when I described it in my first book, *Mid-Atlantic Budget Angler.* I continue to love the river and fish it whenever I can. The guides that have helped me with this chapter include Phil Gay, Stacey Smith, and Wally Vait.

For the western Maryland chapter, my sources have remained the same since I published *Mid-Atlantic Budget Angler,* but there are many changes in the fisheries. I thank Ken Pavol, Western Maryland Fisheries manager with the Maryland Department of Natural Resources, for his updated information. I acknowledge Allan Noland and Harold Harsh as the best guides on western Maryland rivers.

Photographer/angler Douglas Lees deserves the credit for keeping me abreast of developments in Virginia's Shenandoah National Park. Alec Burnett at the Shenandoah Lodge was also helpful.

Frank Smith, owner of Hunter Banks Outfitters in Asheville, North Carolina, and Squeak Smith, a member of Trout Unlimited's Resource Board of Directors for the Southeast, proved that the state's reputation for hospitality is deserved. I thank them both for showing me a very good time and getting me into some pretty trout. Kevin Howell at Davidson River Outfitters also provided reliable information.

Thanks to Jeff and Bill, the fellows at the Fish Hawk in Atlanta; Steve Southard, owner of the Fly Factory in Grayling, Michigan; and Bill Schrieber at Laacke & Joys in Milwaukee for their advice and information.

Scott Graham, president of the Guadalupe River Trout Unlimited chapter, is largely responsible for my success on the Guadalupe—even when it was mostly unfishable. He showed me Texas trout, Texas bass, and Texas redfish, turning a rainy week into a delight.

In the Rocky Mountains, Greg Tolefson reviewed the material on Clark Fork and other rivers near Missoula, Montana. He provided many valuable suggestions. I am fortunate that Rene Harrop agreed to review the section about Henry's Fork. He is a wonderful new friend and a generous angler. My three wonderful guides are acknowledged in the chapter itself, but I want to thank my longtime friend Sue McDowell for getting me on the Fork in the first place.

In Colorado near Denver, Nick Doperalski and Greg Ward each showed me a good time on and gave detailed information about the Blue River. Ken Neubecker was the first to take me on the Eagle and show me stream restoration projects there. I also want to thank Anne Wentz, my lifelong friend and recent angling companion, for being a fabulous hostess and fishing partner.

Joe Evans, an avid and experienced angler, reviewed my text about the Provo and Green Rivers in Utah. His contribution to my original text is invaluable. I cannot omit Stu Asahina, who I believe has the best sense of humor and attitude of any guide anywhere. Pete Idstrom took me on good water on the middle Provo, and Stu Handy was a fine guide on the Green.

I know that all the contributors have people that helped them with their assignments. Together, we thank you all.

In closing, I'd like to recognize the individuals at Stackpole Books who stayed with me through this long endeavor: Judith Schnell, senior editor; Jon Rounds, her able second-in-command; and Caroline Stover, who is responsible for the maps.

Contributors

THE AUTHOR

Ann McIntosh is the author of *Mid-Atlantic Budget Angler* (Mechanicsburg, Pennsylvania: Stackpole Books, 1998). She has written for the major fly angling periodicals and published the series "The Budget Angler" in *Trout* magazine.

McIntosh has been a fly fisher since 1979, learning on her own in Vermont's Northeast Kingdom, refining her skills at home on the Gunpowder River and in central Pennsylvania. Ann makes an annual trip west and spends lots of time saltwater fly fishing on the Chesapeake Bay.

OTHER CONTRIBUTORS

Stephen M. Born (chapter thirteen—Chicago) is a longtime Trout Unlimited leader, having served in local leadership positions and then as chair of the National Resources Board and vice-chair of the Board of Trustees. He is co-author of *Exploring Wisconsin Trout Streams: The Angler's Guide*. Born is a professor of Planning and Environmental Studies at the University of Wisconsin-Madison, and a nationally recognized expert in water resources and watershed planning and management.

Ralph Cutter (chapter twenty-three—Reno, Nevada), along with his wife Lisa, operates the California School of Fly Fishing in Truckee, California. Cutter is the author of *Sierra Trout Guide*. Many of his articles have appeared in *American Angler, Fly Fisherman, Cal Trout,* and other fly-fishing magazines.

Michael Furtman (chapter fifteen—Namekagon and Bois Brule Rivers section) is a freelance author and Trout Unlimited member living in Duluth, Minnesota. He is the conservation editor for *Midwest Fly Fishing* and the author of ten books, one of which is *Trout Country* (NorthWord Press, 1995), an authoritative text on the natural history of North American trout and char. For more information on this and his other books, visit his website at: http://ourworld.compuserve.com/homepages/mfurtman.

Becky Garrison (chapter two—Hartford, Connecticut) is a freelance writer specializing in outdoor sports and comedy. Her selected writing credits include work for the *New York Times, American Angler, Fly Fishing in Saltwaters, Game & Fish Magazine, Sailing Magazine, Saltwater Flyfishing,* and the *Tonight Show.* Since 1996, she has served as a contributing editor to *The Door* (the nation's largest, oldest, and only religious satire magazine). She is a member of the Dramatists Guild, the Junior League, and Julianna Berners Anglers (a New York City–based women's fly-fishing group).

George Grant (chapter eleven—South Holston and Watauga Rivers section) is a native of eastern Tennessee currently living in Johnson City. He writes that he is too old for MTV, too young for bingo, so he does a lot of fly fishing. For the past decade Grant has sold tackle in a local shop, written articles for a local paper, and taught fly-tying classes.

Jim Matthews (chapter twenty-seven—Deep Creek section) lives in San Bernardino, where he writes a syndicated newspaper outdoor package and publishes *Western Birds,* a newsletter for upland and waterfowl bird hunters in Southern California. You can reach Matthews on the Internet at 72010.3541@compuserve.com.

Jeff Mayers (chapter fourteen—Milwaukee) lives in Monona, Wisconsin. He is co-author (with Stephen Born) of *Exploring Wisconsin Trout Streams,* and he frequently writes magazine articles about outdoor recreation and travel. Mayers was editorial consultant for *Catching Big Fish on Light Fly Tackle* by Tom Wendelburg (University of Wisconsin Press, 2001).

David Nolte (chapter twenty-five—Portland, Oregon) until recently worked for the Theodore Roosevelt Conservation Alliance as the Pacific Northwest field coordinator, bringing together hunters and anglers to have a voice in management of our national forests. Married (to Janice) and now residing in the Boston area, Nolte also shares his house with two ancient Siamese cats and one whitish Labrador retriever, Salmo, who is one of his favorite fishing buddies.

Eric W. Peper (chapter four—Streams of the Catskills section, and chapter ten—Atlanta) is the former editor of the *Field & Stream* Book Club. A native of Rockland County, New York, Peper recorded the audio tape *Fly Fishing the Beaverkill River* with Gary LaFontaine. The information is now also available in book form from Greycliff Press. Peper has published in *Fly Fisherman, Trout Fly Tyer,* and *Field & Stream.*

Ti Piper (chapter twenty—Albuquerque and Santa Fe, New Mexico) is the author of *Fishing in New Mexico* (University of New Mexico Press, 1989) and lives in the mountains of New Mexico with his wife, three dogs, and a cat. For the last ten years he has taught aquatic education and fishing skills workshops to thousands of children and adults for the New Mexico Department of Game & Fish.

Leroy Powell (chapter ten—Atlanta) was the co-host of *Georgia Outdoors* for Georgia Public Television for a number of years. He co-authored *Scenic Driving Georgia* (Falcon Press). Powell passed away in the late 1990s.

Conrad L. Ricketts (chapter twenty-seven—Piru Creek section) lives in Los Angeles and has produced ten California trout stream fishing maps. He writes, "When I was a child, the word *hyperactive* had yet to be invented, but my grandfather had cured many in his family with fly fishing. My family owned radio and television stations, and today I celebrate both my father and my grandfather. Both taught me the balance of life through fishing." When he is not fishing or writing about fishing, Ricketts makes movies and television shows.

John Rohmer (chapter twenty-two—Phoenix) has fished for Arizona trout for more than thirty-five years. He co-authored the first book on fly fishing in Arizona, *Arizona Trout Streams and Their Hatches*, with Charles Meck. He runs a fly-tying materials business and is co-owner of Arizona Flyfishing, a shop and outfitter in Tempe, Arizona.

Cindy Scholl (chapter nineteen—South Platte River section) is a guide on many western waters, including the Green River in Wyoming and Idaho. She lives near the Eagle River, her home waters. Scholl was an early leader in the formation of the International Women's Fly Fishing Association (IWFFA).

Bill Shogren (chapter fifteen—Kinnickinnic River, Hay Creek, Trout Run, and Whitewater River section) has lived most of his life in Wisconsin and Minnesota. He has been active in Trout Unlimited, serving as president of the Twin Cities chapter and chairman of the Minnesota State Council. Shogren is co-author, with Jim Humphrey, of *Wisconsin & Minnesota Trout Streams: A Fly Anglers Guide*.

Adem Tepedelen (chapter twenty-four—Seattle) is a Seattle-based freelance writer and former editor of *Canoe & Kayak* magazine. His work has appeared in *Trout, Wine X, Canoe & Kayak,* and other specialty magazines. He rang in the new millennium fishing a spring creek in eastern Washington amid snow flurries and temperatures in the twenties.

John Thurman (chapter eleven—Clinch River section) lives in Norris, Tennessee, about two miles from Norris Dam and the Clinch River. He was born and raised in southwestern Wisconsin, where he learned to fish for trout on the spring creeks. John fishes the Clinch year-round when he is not bird hunting or fishing in the West. He is retired and has a fly-tying business, Spring Creek and Tailwater Flies.

Stephen D. Trafton (chapter twenty-six—San Francisco) has been an avid fly fisherman since he was seven years old. He lives in El Cerrito, California, and is the California policy coordinator for Trout Unlimited. Prior to working for Trout Unlimited, Trafton was an infantry officer in the U. S. Marine Corps.

Stephen and Kim Vletas (chapters seventeen and eighteen—Missoula, Montana; and Jackson Hole, Wyoming, and Idaho Falls, Idaho), along with Reynolds Pomeroy, began their professional guiding careers in Jackson Hole, Wyoming, in the early 1980s. They founded Westbank Anglers in 1986. In 1988, they started the Westbank Anglers travel division. For the past decade, the Vletases have spent six to eight weeks each year traveling around the Bahamas. Their book, *Fly-fisher's Guide to the Bahamas*, was published by Lyons Press in 2000.

Jerry Warrington (chapter twelve—Pere Marquette River section) has been a freelance outdoor writer for more than twenty years. He has written about fly fishing, waterfowl hunting, the shooting sports, and travel. He currently lives in southern Michigan, where a good roll cast from the front steps of his house will touch the waters of a productive Michigan lake.

Introduction

Trout Fishing Near American Cities has a wide scope. I succumbed to the challenge of writing it because I have an unending wanderlust to fish challenging trout rivers and streams wherever they are. Every time I fish a new location I learn something new about the fish and angling strategies.

Reading my contributors' narratives about the many waters I have yet to fish makes me look forward to great fishing wherever I go. The prospect of fishing my contributors' rivers and streams is exciting.

More than a decade ago, Trout Unlimited asked me to write a quarterly feature for *Trout* magazine called "The Budget Angler." Because we had to narrow the choice of rivers we would include, we decided to focus on quality water near American cities. This decision resulted in the happy event of my going on assignment far beyond my familiar Mid-Atlantic streams. I traveled to metro areas as disparate as Portland, Oregon; Manchester, Vermont; San Antonio, Texas; and Denver, Colorado. And on every trip I had fun and met new friends.

This book is geared toward the traveling angler who wishes to fish near a city in which he or she has other business. I hope these stop-over anglers, with limited time to explore, will find this book a starting point.

Trout Fishing Near American Cities first describes the best trout streams within three or four hours (or less) of the designated city, and second, points to additional worthy waters. The "Also Worth Noting" category is intended to alert anglers to waters equally fine as those described in detail, but not as close or as accessible as the featured streams.

In no event should the streams listed in "Also Worth Noting" be considered secondary to those featured. For example, in the Denver chapter, most of the narrative is about the South Platte, the Blue, and the Eagle Rivers. In this instance, "Also Worth Noting" includes Gore Creek, the Frying Pan, and the Roaring Fork—better quality waters than those described in detail, albeit farther away from Denver.

There is not a single river noted in this book that is a secret—all are well-known waters. There are lesser known streams and secret spots that can be found through guides, local anglers, and by walking a mile or two. I believe there are very few really "secret" waters left in our country. The "secrets," for the most part, consist of good spots that require a bit of a walk in.

THE CONTRIBUTORS

I selected my contributors not only on their writing ability, but also for their intimate knowledge of their home waters. Every contributor shares with readers specific angling advice, including access, primary hatches, effective flies, and travel information useful to modern anglers. I hope we have all served the reader well.

I am sure some will wonder why I call the Au Sable River in Michigan a trout fishery "near an American city." The fact is that one can leave metropolitan Detroit at five o'clock and be in Grayling by nine o'clock, traffic permitting, and it's an easy drive. On the other hand, the Shenandoah National Park is only an hour and a half from Washington, D.C., but the stress and congestion can make one feel just as tired compared with a four-hour drive on an open interstate.

My criteria for choosing the fisheries included here is simple: quality water first (wild trout waters when possible), and distance (within a four-hour drive of the city) second.

ABOUT THIS BOOK

The book is divided into seven parts, representing seven major regions of the nation: the Northeast, the Mid-Atlantic, the Southeast, the Midwest, Texas and the Northern Rockies, the Southern Rockies and the Southwest, and the West Coast. I take a serpentine course, beginning with Boston, moving south to Georgia and Tennessee, then swinging up to the Midwest, then south and north again, finally coming to rest in Los Angeles after a tour from Seattle to San Francisco.

CHAPTER ORGANIZATION

While contributors loosely followed the suggested format, all made the chapters their own. In each chapter, the reader will find information about the character of the water, most productive times to fish it, important hatches and flies, maps, and text showing how to get to the water and where to access it, as well as other travel information.

I believe it is very helpful to include directions to the fisheries, access points, and amenities such as guides and destination fly shops, lodging, restaurants, and additional resources such as books, maps, and public agencies that may facilitate a wandering angler's trip. I apologize in advance for any mistakes.

HIRING A GUIDE

I believe that anyone fishing new water for the first time should hire a guide if he or she can afford one. In short order, you will learn the way the river works (the kinds of places its fish hide and why), effective patterns, presentation, and productive reaches. If you hire a guide for even half a day, your chances of improving your catch in the ensuing hours improve exponentially.

SAFETY

It's better to be safe than sorry. I'm always respectful of new and unfamiliar waters. I wear felt-soled boots, with studs when advised. I've had my share of stream dunkings and I don't like them very much. I carry a wading staff, a whistle, extra water, and food for sustenance. I don't carry a cell phone, but if I were to do so, I would fish with it in the "Off" position and use it only for dire emergencies.

MANNERS

As more and more anglers populate our better known waters, we need to respect one another.

- Never step into a pool that is being fished by another angler, unless invited to do so.
- Give other anglers wide berth: Pass them well away from the riverbanks.
- Keep quiet when you fish. Don't take your dog along, or if you do, make sure it stays out of the water unless you're the only angler within a hundred yards or so.
- If another angler asks advice, offer it freely. Helping another angler enriches the angling day.

MAPS, DIRECTIONS, AND ACCESS

The maps should help you reach the trout. In some instances, the narrative will provide more detail than the maps are able to include. I suggest that an angler unfamiliar with an area he or she wants to fish purchase a stream map from a local fly shop or invest in a DeLorme Atlas & Gazetteer for the state. Also, please check directions with the nearby fly shops.

REGULATIONS

These are provided in many chapters. Where they are not in the narrative they are available where you buy your local trout license. Regulations change annually, and often more frequently: Please do not use this book as the final word in rules and regulations on any of the waters included herein.

"IF YOU GO" INFORMATION

These listings are the most sensitive, frequently changing items in this book. Although I've listed many venerable tackle shops and guides that have plied their trade for more than two decades, there are others that will not endure so well. I wish this were not true, but not every establishment can be successful. Please check the information before you embark on a trip. Make sure you have your local source identified before you leave home.

PRICING CATEGORIES

The following list indicates the key I've used to designate lodging and restaurants as inexpensive, moderate, or expensive.

Lodging—Where to Stay
Inexpensive: Single—less than $45; double—$65 or less
Moderate: Single—$46–$70; double—$66–$90
Expensive: Single—more than $70; double—$91 and up
Restaurants—Where to Eat
Inexpensive: Under $20
Moderate: Dinner entrees $15–$25
Expensive: Dinner entrees beginning at $25

WEBSITES AND E-MAIL ADDRESSES

In every instance where the information was provided, I have listed website locations (URLs) and e-mail addresses. Because this book is written just as many sportfishing destinations, shops, lodging, etc. are going online, the list is not complete. I apologize in advance for this limitation, and I hope anyone who can provide information about electronic addresses will do so. Write to Stackpole Books at the address provided in the front of this book.

CORRECTIONS

It is nearly impossible that a book of this scope can be error-free. I invite anyone with information that corrects errors to get in touch with Stackpole.

PART ONE

The Northeast

CHAPTER ONE

BOSTON

Ann McIntosh

I'm an East Coast native who learned to fish for trout in New England, and until I discovered better wild trout opportunities in the Mid-Atlantic and out west, I had good times in Massachusetts. Some of the more memorable ones were on the Deerfield. (I knew nothing of saltwater fly fishing at the time and was unaware of what I was missing. If you enjoy fishing in the salt, opportunities near Boston abound. Contact the fly shops listed at the end of this chapter for information.)

Located about two and a half hours west of Boston, the Deerfield is often considered the best trout stream in the state. It is a very pretty tailwater, set in the northern Berkshire Mountains 50 miles north of the towns of Lenox and Stockbridge, Massachusetts. The stream is about 50 feet wide with a slippery stone bottom. Felt soles are a must. The water stays cool throughout the year, shaded by hardwoods and cooled by water released from Fife Brook Dam.

I've fished the Deerfield many times but never really understood it until recently, when I spent an August day with guide Fred Moran, the undisputed expert on this water. Moran invited me to meet him at the Charlemont Inn to "fish the tides" of the Deerfield. The "tides" here are artificial, created by the large quantities of water released twice daily from Fife Brook Dam. Twice a day the water rises 3 feet in five minutes. You need to exercise caution during the releases. Keep your eye on the top of a rock; if it disappears, get off the water as fast as you can. This is not a flow to be taken lightly. An angling friend nearly drowned when she didn't move as soon as she felt the river rise.

When and where you fish are also dictated by the dam schedule. You can begin fishing before the morning release in the upper catch-and-release area, then, when the water begins to rise, drive down to the lower

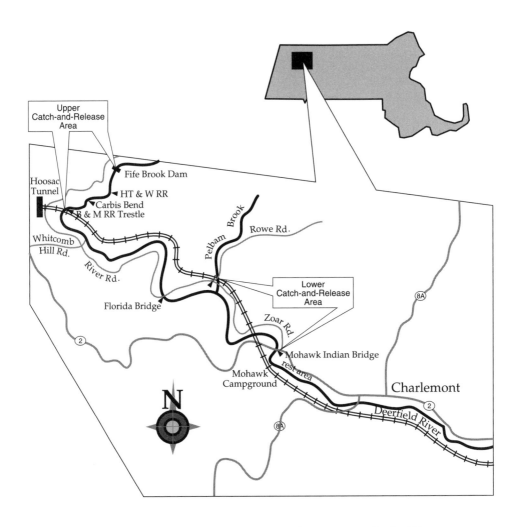

catch-and-release area. The water takes about one and a half hours to move from the dam to Pelham Brook.

In high water, the fish hole up in nooks and crannies out of the current; they are looking for safe havens, not food. Between releases, the water subsides, and educated trout begin to prowl. There are brook, brown, and rainbow trout in the river, both annual stocks and holdover fish. There are long, flat pools, eddies, riffles, and runs—all easily accessible from the many pulloffs on River Road.

When the river subsides, the fish turn on immediately; Moran likes the first half hour of "low tide" the best. He emphasizes the value of casting flies into the foam on the eddies and at the sides of the main current. Fish will nose up for dry flies placed in the foam or in the little patches of clear water in the foam.

There are some huge fish in the Deerfield, but I've never been lucky enough to meet one. Fred Moran, with his wife, Marilyn, as witness, took a 30-inch brown on a bamboo rod using a #16 tan Elk Hair Caddis. The average Deerfield fish is 14 to 16 inches, but there are many over 20 inches.

HATCHES, FLIES, AND BEST TIMES TO FISH

Since the Deerfield remains cool year-round, it can be fished at any time. However, it gets very cold (around 32 degrees F) in the winter, and the fish are sluggish. The best times to fish are between April and October, until the first real frost. Generally, rainbows feed most actively in the morning, before the sun hits the water, and the browns feed in the evening before and after dark.

In the spring during the runoff weeks, streams and nymphs are most effective. Popular patterns include the Gray Ghost, Mickey Finn, Muddler Minnow, and Black-Nose Dace.

In the late spring and summer, match the apparent hatches, which include Hendricksons, march browns, cahills, and sulphurs from June to early July. Deerfield anglers use standard attractors such as Adamses, Light Cahills, Royal Coachmen, and a variety of hairwing patterns in the faster, rougher water.

From mid-July, or whenever summer gets consistently hot, ants, beetles, and hoppers produce rises. A #12 Stimulator is one of Moran's favorite patterns. He also likes Deer Hair Caddis patterns from #12 to #16 in various colors: black, gray, tan, brown, olive.

ALSO WORTH NOTING

Swift River (East Branch)

The East Branch of the Swift River is located about an hour and a half west of Boston. Take Route 2 west to Route 32 south to Petersham. (Detailed directions appear in *An Angler's Guide to Trout Fishing in Massachusetts*, listed under Resources, below.)

The East Branch of the Swift flows into Quabbin Reservoir. It is stocked with rainbow and brown trout, some of which grow to mammoth proportions and have Ph.D.s in what *not* to eat. There are a number of regulars who frequent the banks of the Swift daily. Politely solicit their advice, and you may luck into a lunker.

Westfield River

This stream flows from the Berkshire Hills to the Connecticut River near Springfield. The East, West, and Middle Branches all have native brook trout, and the main stem has large (5- to 6-pound) stocked rainbow and brown trout. For information, contact B&G Sporting Goods at (413) 568-7569.

IF YOU GO
To reach the Deerfield River from Boston, take Route 2 west to Charlemont. Follow local directions from there. (See chapter map.)

Tackle Shops and Guides
Marla Blair. Ludlow. Instructor and guide on the Deerfield, Farmington, Swift, and Westfield Rivers. (413) 583-5141. www.marlablair.com. E-mail: marlablair@yahoo.com.

Orvis Company Store. Boston. (617) 742-0288.

Points North Outfitters. Adams. Fred Moran has guided on the Deerfield River for eighteen years. He and his wife, Marilyn, are the undisputed experts on this fishery. (413) 743-4030. E-mail: marilynmoran @hotmail.com.

River's Edge. Beverly. A good source of information for saltwater fly fishing north of Boston, as well as for the Swift and the Deerfield. (978) 921-8008.

RiverRun. Great Barrington. An Orvis store. Michael and Barbara Flach, owners. Michael specializes in fishing for trout on the Housatonic River in Massachusetts. (413) 528-9600.

Jack Smola. Enfield, Connecticut. Fly-fishing guide. (860) 763-1856. www.jacksmola.com.

Where to Stay
Charlemont Inn. On Route 2 (the Mohawk Trail) in Charlemont. Old-fashioned hotel with modest rooms and shared baths. Inexpensive. (413) 337-4321.

River House B&B. On Zoar Road, with access to one of the best pools on the river. Moderate. (413) 337-4321.

The Oxbow Resort. A motel with recreational facilities on Route 2 east of Charlemont. Moderate. (413) 625-6011.

Camping
Historic Valley Campground. Windsor Lake Road, North Adams. (413) 662-3198.

Mohawk Trail State Forest. Charlemont. (413) 339-5504.

Where to Eat
Charlemont Inn. Charlemont. Decent, basic food. Serves until 9 P.M. Moderate. (413) 337-4321.

The Copper Angel. Shelburne Falls. One of the best restaurants in an attractive, renovated Victorian village on the lower Deerfield. Moderate to expensive. No reservations. (413) 625-2727.

Warfield House. Charlemont. Stunning view atop a mountain. Serves Thursday through Sunday. Moderate. (413) 339-6600.

RESOURCES

Fife Brook Dam release schedule. (888) FLO-FONE.

Adams Chamber of Commerce. (413) 743-1881. Additional information on lodging and dining facilities.

Shelburne Falls Village Information Center. (413) 625-2544.

Ames, Thomas Jr. *Hatch Guide for New England Streams.* Portland, OR: Frank Amato Publications, 2000.

Blaisdell, Harold. *Trout Fishing in New England.* Lexington, MA: Stone Wall Press, 1977.

Raychard, Al. *Trout and Salmon Fishing in Northern New England.* Thorndike, ME: Thorndike Press, 1982.

Ross, John. *Trout Unlimited's Guide to America's 100 Best Trout Streams.* Helena, MT: Falcon Press, 1999.

Tucholke, Brian, ed. *An Angler's Guide to Trout Fishing in Massachusetts.* Published by the Massachusetts–Rhode Island Council of Trout Unlimited, c/o John Teahan, P.O. Box 1837, Westfield, MA 01086.

Massachusetts Atlas & Gazetteer. Yarmouth, ME: DeLorme Mapping Company. (207) 846-7000.

CHAPTER TWO

HARTFORD, CONNECTICUT

FARMINGTON RIVER

Becky Garrison

The Farmington River, the second-largest trout fishery in the state of Connecticut, enables fly fishers to angle year-round in the regulated trout management area (TMA) for a wide range of species. This river is stocked with brown, brook, and rainbow trout, as well as Atlantic salmon fry and other freshwater fish. The entire river is accessible from the road starting below Goodwin Dam in Hartland, Connecticut, to its intersection with the Connecticut River.

The Upper River section of the Farmington, which stretches from West Hartland to Canton, Connecticut, is a tailwater fishery with a wide range of riffles and pools. This portion of the Farmington harbors a good selection of stocked trout and Atlantic salmon fry, as well as an occasional wild brown trout. As the water is released from the bottom of Goodwin Dam, water temperatures remain favorable for many miles downstream throughout the year.

Many fly fishers flock to the TMA on the upper river. This 2½-mile stretch of the river was established in 1988 to create and maintain a top-quality cold-water fishery. This area, managed under catch-and-release regulations, has the greatest concentration of fish, the highest percentage of holdover fish, and some of the largest fish in the entire river. The TMA between Pleasant Valley (Route 318) and New Hartford (Route 219) is bounded by natural, undeveloped land with an abundance of beavers, ducks, deer, and other wildlife.

Although there are a few isolated spots along the TMA stretch of the river, the intersection of West River Road with Route 318 is nicknamed the Social Pool because of the crowded conditions along this popular fishing spot. (Its formal name is the Church Pool.) Another well-fished spot is the West Branch Reservoir at the intersections of West River Road and Route 219 and Dowd Avenue and Route 179.

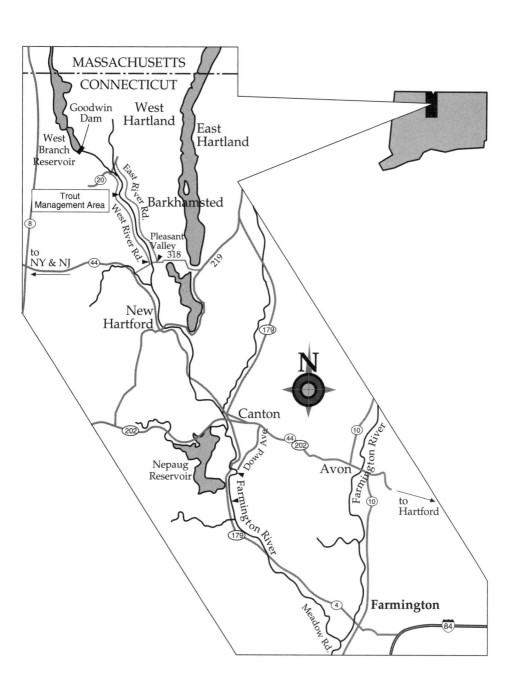

Even though stocked trout dominate the middle river from Canton to Farmington, the river begins to shift from a cold-water to a warm-water fishery. Here you can also catch largemouth bass, smallmouth bass, American eels, Atlantic salmon, and yellow perch. Bear in mind that anglers are only permitted to fish from the banks around Meadow Road and Route 10.

The middle river from Farmington to Rainbow Dam, east of Sinsbury (not on map), offers minimal trout habitat due to its sandy bottom and shallow depth. In this warm-water fishery, you can catch the occasional bass or panfish. Fishermen tend to have the best luck fishing from canoes. Rainbow Reservoir supports bass, panfish, and shad.

The fishing in the lower river from Rainbow Dam to the Connecticut River is influenced by the Rainbow Dam's hydropower generator release schedule. Much depends on the migration of American shad, alewives, blueback herring, and Atlantic salmon into the Farmington River from the Connecticut.

HATCHES, FLIES, AND BEST TIMES TO FISH

Even though the Farmington can be fished year-round with dry flies, the most productive times for fly fishers are from April to October. During a winter warm spell, you can also catch trout on dry flies.

The most popular hatch on the river is the Hendrickson. These insects arrive in mid-April and stay through mid-May. Sulphurs are also a strong hatch, emerging from late May into early July. Fish take ants and beetles in the summer. (See the Housatonic River, below, for a detailed list of major hatches.)

For up-to-date information on river conditions or recent hatch activity, check with the local fly shops or call the Farmington River Anglers' Association (FRAA) River Hotline, listed under Resources, below. The FRAA publishes *A Guide to Fishing the Farmington River*, which offers fly fishers very detailed descriptions of each pool and other pertinent information needed to fish this river. This association serves as an advocate to ensure that recreational fishing will continue on the river into the future.

IF YOU GO

From New York or New Jersey, take the Henry Hudson Parkway to the Saw Mill Parkway to I-684 north to I-84 east to Connecticut Route 8 north to U.S. Route 44 east, to its junction with Route 318 at Pleasant Valley.

From Albany, New York, take I-90 (the Massachusetts Turnpike) east to Massachusetts Route 8 south. Follow Route 8 several miles into Connecticut, then pick up U.S. Route 44 east.

From Boston, take the Massachusetts Turnpike (I-90) west to U.S. Route 44 west.

Tackle Shops and Guides

Marla Blair. Ludlow, Massachusetts. Fly-fishing instructor. (413) 583-5141. www.marlablair.com.

Alan Bump. Enfield, Connecticut. Fly-fishing guide. (860) 763-4803.

Classic and Custom Fly Shop. New Hartford. Full-service fly shop. Guides available. Does not sell licenses. (860) 738-3597.

Fred Jeans. New Hartford. Guide. (860) 693-6642.

Drake Rod Company. New Hartford. Custom rod building and repair. (860) 379-4371.

Dick Lowrey. Barkhamsted. Guide. (860) 738-0322.

Quiet Sports Flyfishing. Collinsville. Full-service fly shop, fly-tying and guide service. Does not sell licenses. (860) 693-2214.

Jack Smola. Enfield. Experienced fly-fishing guide. (860) 763-1856. www.jacksmola.com.

Upcountry Sports Fishing. New Hartford. Fly and tackle store. Sells fishing licenses. (860) 379-1952. www.FarmingtonRiver.com. E-mail: upcountry@farmingtonriver.com.

Where to Stay

Alcove Motel. New Hartford. Inexpensive. (860) 693-8577.

Hillside Motel. Canton. Moderate. (860) 693-4951.

Old Riverton Inn. Riverton. Authentic Colonial inn with restaurant. Expensive. (860) 379-8678.

Other Hotels. There are numerous hotels in East Hartford, Hartford, and West Hartford.

Camping

American Legion. Pleasant Valley. Has 30 sites. (860) 379-0922.

Connecticut Campground Owners Association. (860) 521-4704.

Where to Eat

Log House Restaurant. Barkhamsted. Family restaurant. Inexpensive. (860) 379-8937.

Old Riverton Inn. Riverton. Authentic Colonial inn with restaurant. Expensive. (860) 379-8678.

Riverton General Store. Pleasantville. Sandwiches and fishing licenses. Inexpensive. (860) 379-0811.

Saybrook Fish House. Canton. Upscale family restaurant. Moderate. (860) 693-0034.

RESOURCES

FRAA River Hotline. (860) 738-7327.

State of Connecticut Department of Environmental Protection. Fishing licenses and regulations. (860) 424-FISH.

Connecticut Vacation Center. (800) CT-BOUND.

Farmington Valley Visitor's Association. (860) 651-6950.

Connecticut Atlas & Gazetteer. Yarmouth, ME: DeLorme Mapping Company. (207) 846-7000.

A Guide to Fishing the Farmington River. Farmington River Anglers Association, P.O. Box 147, Riverton, CT 06065. An extremely worthwhile publication if you are going to fish the Farmington thoroughly.

Fuller, Tom, and Patricia Fuller. *Trout Streams of Southern New England: An Angler's Guide to the Watersheds of Massachusetts, Connecticut, and Rhode Island.* Woodstock, VT: Countryman Press, 1999.

HOUSATONIC RIVER

Becky Garrison

Housatonic is an Indian name meaning "river beyond the mountains." This river begins its 149-mile journey to Long Island Sound at a small pond in Washington, Massachusetts. Fishing opportunities exist for a wide variety of species along the entire length of this river in both Connecticut and Massachusetts.

The stretch of the Housatonic favored by avid fly fishers is the trout management area (TMA), which comprises the area of northwestern Connecticut that includes Salisbury, Canaan, Sharon, and Cornwall from the bridge at Routes 112 and 7 downstream to the bridge at Routes 4 and 7. These reaches receive a lot of pressure, due to their proximity to New York City. The first 3 miles of the TMA are regulated as catch-and-release and restricted to fly fishing.

During the spring and fall, the Connecticut Department of Environmental Protection stocks the Housatonic River with 9- to 11-inch brown trout. Holdover trout sustain themselves from year to year, and it's not uncommon to land a brown or rainbow trout more than 16 inches long.

While fly fishers can fish the majority of the pools along this area year-round, the portions within 100 feet of the tributary streams are closed to all fishing from June 15 to August 31. The early-spring runoff usually brings high water flow, often obscuring identification of pools, pocket water, and runs that would enable you to locate trout and feeding areas. Generally, the peak times for landing a brown, brook, or rainbow trout are from mid-May to mid-June and during the month of October. From June through September the smallmouth bass fishing is excellent. Fly fishers should be mindful of the numerous paddlers and tubers that float down the river all summer long.

Check with the local fly shops for current hatches, as well as up-to-date information about the Falls Village Hydroelectric Power Dam's

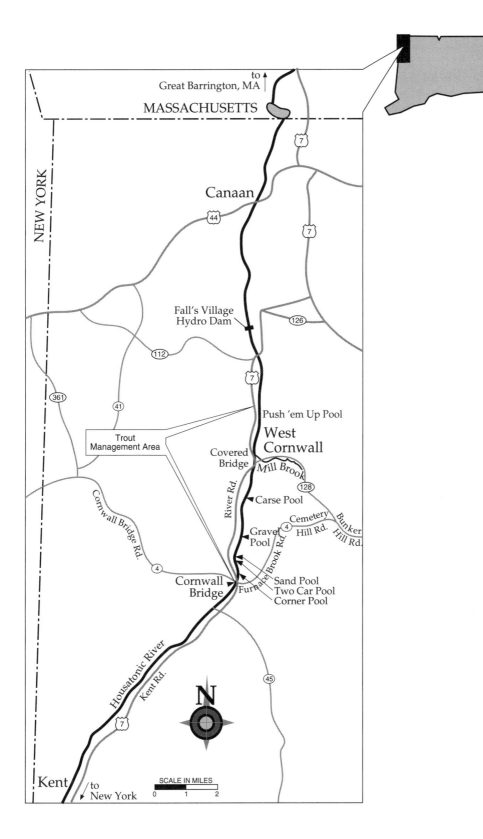

schedule for regulating the water flows. When the dam releases, the water comes in a slow, steady stream, and anyone wading in one of the pools needs to be mindful of the gradual rise of the river. As a rule of thumb, you should pick out a rock that is about 4 inches above water. When the rock becomes submerged, it's time to seek the shallows. A wading staff is recommended on the Housatonic.

Each pool along the TMA has its own character; thus choosing a favorite fishing spot can be difficult. Some anglers prefer to concentrate on fishing one or perhaps two pools for a period of time, until they have come to know them well. For an introduction to the Housatonic, check out Carse Pool; its combination of flats, riffles, and deep pools typifies the character of the river. Sand Hole and Corner Hole offer some of the easiest wading areas. Other favorite holes include Gravel Hole and Two Car Hole.

Housatonic Fly Fishermen's Association, a group dedicated to preserving and protecting the river, publishes *Fishing the Housatonic River Trout Management Area.* This book provides detailed information about each pool along the TMA, as well as other information of interest to those wishing to fish this area.

Connecticut's Housatonic River Valley area is also renowned for over a hundred antique shops scattered along Route 7. Nonangling partners will find lots to do on a relaxing weekend.

While the TMA remains the most popular stretch for fly fishing, many large brown trout can also be found above and below. Moreover, the Housatonic River near Great Barrington, Massachusetts, gives up a great number of large browns (16 inches and up) every year. You will often find yourself alone on this water. Contact Michael Flach at RiverRun (see Tackle Shops and Guides, below) in Great Barrington for more information on this overlooked fishery. Also, there are good opportunities for smallmouth bass in the Massachusetts sections of the river.

HATCHES, FLIES, AND BEST TIMES TO FISH

Major hatches on the Farmington and the Housatonic are similar to hatches on other eastern freestoners. Check with local fly shops before you set out, but some of the major hatches and effective patterns are as follows:

April–May. Hendricksons, Quill Gordons, tan and dark brown caddis, march browns, Gray Foxes, green caddis, blue-winged olives, green drakes, brown drakes, sulphurs, weighted nymphs, and streamers.

June. Blue-winged olives, green drakes, brown drakes, black caddis, light cahills, sulphurs, yellow stonefly nymphs.

July–August. Cream Variants, Tricos, ants.

September–October. Blue-winged olives, Dun Variants, streamers, Woolly Buggers, crayfish imitations, stonefly nymphs, any nymphs with peacock herl bodies.

IF YOU GO

From Boston, take the Massachusetts Turnpike (I-90) west to Exit 1 to Route 102 (West Stockbridge) to U.S. Route 7 south to Great Barrington. Fish the Housatonic there, or continue down Route 7 into Connecticut to Cornwall Bridge and the trout management area.

From New York or New Jersey, take the Henry Hudson Parkway to the Saw Mill Parkway to I-684 north to I-84 east. Pick up U.S. Route 7 north in Connecticut and follow to the TMA in Cornwall Bridge or continue north to Great Barrington, Massachusetts.

From Albany, New York, take I-90 (the Massachusetts Turnpike) east to Massachusetts Exit 1 to Route 102 (West Stockbridge) to U.S. Route 7 south to Great Barrington or Cornwall Bridge.

Tackle Shops and Guides

Housatonic Anglers. Sharon. (860) 672-4457.

Housatonic Meadows Fly Shop. Cornwall Bridge. Full-service Orvis shop and guide service. (860) 672-6064. http://flyfishct.com. E-mail: tight lines@mohawk.net.

Housatonic River Outfitters. West Cornwall. Full-service fly shop, guide service, and outfitters. (860) 672-1010. www.dryflies.com. E-mail: hflyshop@aol.com.

RiverRun. Great Barrington, Massachusetts. Michael and Barbara Flach, owners. Orvis shop and guide service. Michael specializes in fishing for big trout on the Housatonic in Massachusetts. He and his wife can provide lodging information near Great Barrington. (413) 528-9600.

Where to Stay

Lodging in this area ranges on the expensive side. Below are selected listings within reasonable proximity to the river.

Althea House. New Preston. Expensive. (860) 355-7387.

Constitution Oak Farm. Kent. Private or shared baths. Moderate. (860) 354-6495.

Fast Tracks Cabins. South Falls Village. Moderate. (860) 824-7886.

Fife and Drum Restaurant and Inn. Kent. Country inn and restaurant. Expensive. (860) 927-3509.

Hitching Post Country Motel. Cornwall Bridge. Moderate. (860) 672-4880.

7C Herb Gardens Bed & Breakfast. New Preston. Full breakfast. Expensive. (860) 868-7760.

Hopkins Inn. New Preston. Moderate. (860) 868-7295.

Rosewood Meadow Bed & Breakfast. Kent. Full breakfast. Also has an efficiency unit. Expensive. (800) 600-4334.

Camping

Hemlock Hill Camp Resort. Litchfield. Has 125 units. (860) 567-2267.

Housatonic Meadows Campground State Park. One mile north of Cornwall Bridge on Route 7, Connecticut. Two-mile stretch of water on Housatonic limited to fly fishing. Has 95 sites. (877) 668-2267.

Looking Glass Hill Campground. Litchfield. Has 50 sites. (860) 567-2050.

Macedonia Brook State Park. Kent. Has 83 sites. (877) 668-2267.

Lake Warmaug State Park. New Preston. Has 78 sites. (877) 668-2267.

White Pines Campsites. Winsted. Has 209 sites. (860) 379-0124.

Where to Eat

American Grill. Kent. Moderate. (860) 435-0030.

Bulls Bridge Inn. Kent. (860) 927-1000.

The Cannery. Canaan. Contemporary American. Moderate. (860) 824-7333.

Cafe Lally. West Cornwall. Italian. Moderate. (860) 672-1003.

Oliva. New Preston. Mediterranean. Moderate. (860) 868-1787.

Pub & Restaurant. Norfolk. American. Moderate. (860) 542-5716.

RESOURCES

Litchfield Hills Visitors Bureau. (860) 567-4506. www.litchfield hills.com.

Fishing the Housatonic River Trout Management Area. Housatonic Fly Fishermen's Association, P.O. Box 5092, Hamden, CT 06518.

Passante, Jeff. *Housatonic River Fly Fishing Guide.* Portland, OR: Frank Amato Publications, 1997.

Hickoff, Steve, and Rhey Plumley. *Flyfisher's Guide to Northern New England.* Gallatin Gateway, MT: Wilderness Adventures Press, 1999.

Fuller, Tom, and Patricia Fuller. *Trout Streams of Southern New England: An Angler's Guide to the Watersheds of Massachusetts, Connecticut, and Rhode Island.* Woodstock, VT: Countryman Press, 1999.

Massachusetts Atlas & Gazetteer. Yarmouth, ME: DeLorme Mapping Company. (207) 846-7000.

Ross, John. *Trout Unlimited's Guide to America's 100 Best Trout Streams.* Helena, MT: Falcon Press, 1999.

Tucholke, Brian, ed. *An Angler's Guide to Trout Fishing in Massachusetts.* Published by Massachusetts-Rhode Island Council of Trout Unlimited, c/o John Teahan, P.O. Box 1873, Westfield, MA 01086.

CHAPTER THREE

SOUTHWESTERN VERMONT

BATTENKILL RIVER, METTAWEE RIVER, OTTER CREEK, AND BIG BRANCH

Ann McIntosh

Two of Vermont's finest trout rivers, the Battenkill and the Mettawee, are located in the southwestern part of the state within four hours of Boston and New York City. These freestone streams provide classic eastern trout fishing: gentle, sparkling water coursing through meadows bordered by hemlock in the foothills and hardwoods streamside. Without question, this is some of the prettiest angling in the East. The Mettawee and the Battenkill are also two of the few rivers Vermont manages as wild trout waters.

Other streams in southwestern Vermont, such as Otter Creek and its tributary, Big Branch, provide excellent, less well-known opportunities. The Walloomsac near Bennington is a sleeper. It produces brown trout in the 12-inch range. And don't ignore the dozens of wild brook trout streams in the mountains.

I've fished Vermont mostly during the summer—the toughest time. During droughts, many streams dry up and turn into damp puddles flanking parched rocks. The majority of the state's public trout water fishes best in the late spring and again in the fall. If you plan a trip, go between mid-May and mid-June, or for leaf-peeking fall weekends in late September and October.

BATTENKILL RIVER

A wild brook and brown trout stream, the Battenkill (originally "Batten Kill," from the Dutch, meaning "watery stream") is the most famous Vermont trout water. It originates northwest of Manchester near the village of East Dorset. From there, it flows through Manchester and Arlington into New York State. Not stocked since 1975, some reaches produce trophy browns exceeding 16 inches.

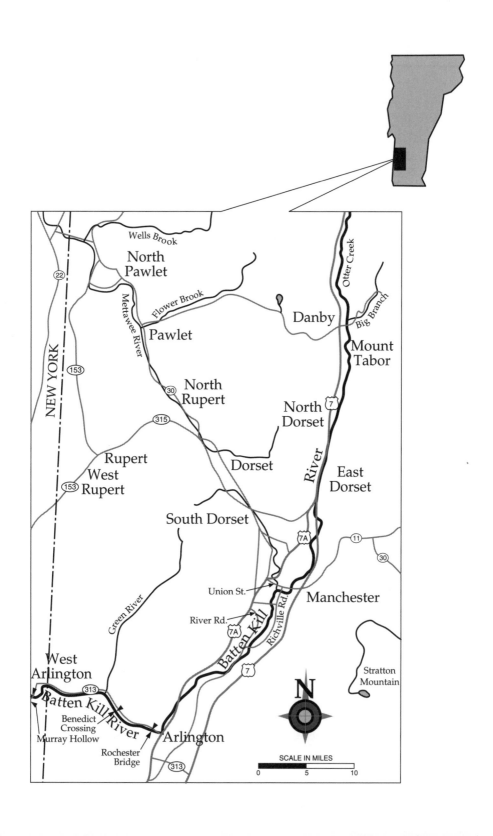

Fishing on the Battenkill has been on the decline in the past decade. At this writing, although hookups are limited and stream improvements have been initiated, the fish are not reproducing well. If you fish the Battenkill, fish with tender loving care. This "watery stream" was once one of the treasures of American fly fishing. One can only hope and pray that it will be restored to a shadow of its former glory.

Upstream from Arlington, the Battenkill ranges from the overgrown stretch along Route 30 north of Manchester to the slow, deep, soft-bottom pools between Richville Road and the Arlington Recreation Center. This section is where many of the remaining trophy fish may hold. It's not easy to access or to fish. I advise using a guide, a canoe, or both. There is a put-in at Richville Road and a take-out at the recreation field.

The most popular fly fishing on the Battenkill is along Route 313 between Arlington and the Vermont–New York state line. Here the river is 60 to 80 feet wide. Anglers will find riffles, shallow flats, deep pools, and—most fun of all—rapid runs where wary fish take well-presented wet flies. Since the trout are fished over frequently and are very educated and few and far between, be content with one or two fish. The footing is stable, but use felt soles and chest waders in spring and fall.

Access the lower Battenkill at pulloffs along Route 313. *Whatever you do, do not park on or beside posted private property!*

From the Rochester (West Mountain) bridge to Benedict Crossing, special regulations apply: All brook and brown trout between 10 and 14 inches must be released. The daily creel limit is three trout.

In the summer the Battenkill gets very low, but refreshing springs usually save it from fish kills. If you can tolerate canoeists and tubers, and refrain from fishing when the water temperature exceeds 70 degrees F, the river will produce. I used to enjoy memorable Trico hatches from late July through August.

The Battenkill is an outstanding fall fishery. In late September and October, after water temperatures have dropped and trout begin their spawning migrations, you will fish under the most colorful foliage of the year for the most colorful trout in the water. Cast at the mouth of the Green River or Benedict Hollow Brook, and you may be surprised at the size of the spawning brown that takes your fly.

Fly fishers should take advantage of the 21 miles of fine Battenkill water in New York State. The New York Department of Environmental Conservation has purchased easements for the sole purpose of providing fishing access. These points are marked with bright yellow signs. From the Vermont–New York line to the covered bridge at Eagleville, only artificial flies and lures are permitted. Fishing the New York Battenkill is a good way to avoid the pressure in Vermont and maintain quality sport.

Trout Unlimited has three chapters that help protect the Battenkill in New York: the Homewaters chapter in Troy, the Clearwater chapter in

Albany, and the Adirondack chapter in Glens Falls/Saratoga. Members have planted willows to stabilize banks, installed water deflectors, and helped in many other ways to enhance the fishery.

METTAWEE RIVER

The Mettawee is my personal favorite Vermont wild trout stream. Dairy farms and cattle and sheep pastures border the water as it wends its way gently from Dorset Mountain into New York State.

I taught myself to read water by studying Art Lee's *Fishing Dry Flies for Trout on Rivers and Streams* a chapter at a time, carefully applying Lee's methods as I fished the postcard-perfect Mettawee day after day. Most of the fish I caught were in the 10- to 12-inch range, but larger trout hide in deep pools away from the road.

The Mettawee has not been stocked since 1972. It supports rainbows and browns. Pocket water, riffles, long pools, and deep holes alternate along its length. The stream is about 25 feet wide, with a forgiving gravel bottom. Hip waders will suffice, except early in the season. In addition to a fine Trico hatch and standard eastern mayfly hatches, the Mettawee is an excellent caddis stream.

The most productive stretches of the Mettawee lie along Route 30 between the villages of North Rupert and North Pawlet. *Beware:* Much of the property along the Mettawee is posted. Several of the farmers will allow you to fish if you ask permission. *Always* inquire and *always* be sure to leave gates as you found them. Vermont Fish and Wildlife maintains a pulloff east of North Rupert.

The Mettawee has three tributaries that hold wild brookies and a few browns: Indian River, Wells Brook, and Flower Brook. These are best fished in early spring.

OTTER CREEK (BETWEEN DANBY AND WALLINGFORD)

Otter Creek, which drains Vermont's second-largest watershed, flows north from Emerald Lake (north of Manchester) 100 miles to Lake Champlain. The stream is 40 feet wide at its most productive. There are several pulloffs along Route 7, and a railroad track runs parallel to the river. Managers at the Otter Creek Campground (see below) can provide up-to-the-minute stream reports.

Otter is not a wild trout stream; it is governed by special regulations from National Forest Highway (NFH) 10 downstream 2 miles to the Vermont Railroad bridge north of the fishing access. On this stretch, the daily limit is two trout of any species, no minimum length.

BIG BRANCH

Big Branch, a scenic tributary of Otter Creek, rushes off Mount Tabor to meet Otter at Danby. It has a steep gradient, and walking or wading the upstream reaches should not be attempted by anglers with knee problems or other infirmities.

The lower end of Big Branch holds a good population of rainbows and a few browns; brookies dominate the higher reaches. The water stays cool all summer and is excellent for anglers looking for solitude and fishable water midseason.

To reach Big Branch, take National Forest Highway (NFH) 10 up Mount Tabor east of Danby. Park, and fish up- or downstream from the first bridge. Or continue along NFH 10 up the mountain to Long Trail, and walk in south on the trail to Old Job Trail (see *Vermont Atlas & Gazetteer,* listed under Resources, below). This is spectacular mountain rainbow fishing in a stream open enough for a clear cast and kind enough to let you step from rock to rock, pool to pool, catching wild rainbows as you go.

HATCHES, FLIES, AND BEST TIMES TO FISH
The best times to fish southwestern Vermont are spring and fall. Major hatches on these streams are similar to hatches on other eastern freestoners. Check with local tackle shops before you set out, but these are some of the major hatches you can anticipate and flies that imitate them:

April–May. Streamers during spring runoff; then Hendricksons, march browns, Gray Fox, and stonefly nymphs.

June. Light cahills and sulphurs (evenings), Mahogany Polywing Spinners, blue-winged olives, caddis.

July–August. Tricos (mornings), terrestrials (ants, beetles, hoppers, inchworms), blue-winged olives, caddis; female Adamses on the Mettawee.

September–October. Slate drakes, blue-winged olives (#20–#24), microcaddis.

IF YOU GO
From New York or New Jersey, take I-87 (New York Thruway) north to Albany Exit 23. Then take I-787 north to New York Route 7 east, which becomes Vermont Route 9. In Bennington, get onto U.S. Route 7 north. Get off at Exit 3, Arlington/Manchester, to Vermont Route 7A north. This will take you to Arlington, Manchester, and Danby.

From Albany, which has the closest airport to southern Vermont, take I-787 north to New York Route 7 east, and follow the directions above.

From Boston, take Route 2 west to I-91 north to Vermont Exit 2, Brattleboro. Follow signs for Route 30 north to Route 7A, Manchester.

Tackle Shops and Guides
Battenkill Anglers. Manchester. Fly-fishing school and guide service. (802) 362-3184.

Brookside Angler. Manchester. Craig Lawrence, proprietor. Fly shop and guide service. (802) 363-3538.

The Orvis Company. Manchester. The original Orvis showplace. Big tackle shop, clothing, schools, and guide service. (802) 362-3750.

Where to Stay
There is room only to scratch the surface of places to stay near Manchester. This short list includes a range of prices and favors establishments catering to anglers. Rates are seasonal.

Battenkill Inn B&B. Manchester. Overlooking river. Breakfast and evening hors d'oeuvres. Moderate. (802) 362-4213.

Brittany Inn Motel. Manchester. Very nice. Inexpensive. (802) 362-1033.

Keelan House B&B. Arlington. On the Battenkill. Moderate. (802) 375-9029.

Willows Inn B&B. Arlington. On the Battenkill. Fishing access. Inexpensive. (802) 375-9773.

Shenandoah Farm B&B. West Arlington. On the Battenkill. Special rates for fly fishers. Inexpensive. (802) 375-6372.

Quail's Nest B&B. Danby. Near Otter Creek. Inexpensive. (802) 293-5099.

Where to Eat
Restaurants abound. Options in Manchester, Dorset, Arlington, and Danby are extensive and range from delicatessens to five-star dining establishments. There are so many good restaurants in the area that it would be unfair to make a selection here.

Camping
Camping on the Battenkill. Arlington. (802) 375-6663.
Otter Creek Campground. Danby. (802) 293-5041.

RESOURCES
Manchester Chamber of Commerce. (802) 362-2100.
Arlington Chamber of Commerce. (802) 375-2800.
Camman, Peter F. *Fishing Vermont's Streams and Lakes.* Woodstock, VT: Countryman Press, 1992.
Hickoff, Steve, and Rhey Plumley. *Flyfisher's Guide to Northern New England: Vermont, New Hampshire, Maine.* Gallatin Gateway, MT: Wilderness Adventures Press, 1999.
Ross, John. *Trout Unlimited's Guide to America's 100 Best Trout Streams.* Helena, MT: Falcon Press, 1999.
Vermont Atlas & Gazetteer. Yarmouth, ME: DeLorme Mapping Company. (207) 846-7000.
Vermont Trout Streams. Northern Cartographics, P.O. Box 133, Burlington, VT 05402.

CHAPTER FOUR

NEW YORK CITY

STREAMS OF THE CATSKILLS

Eric W. Peper

I had not fished the rivers that form the Delaware River drainage (west drainage) in New York's Catskill Mountains for a decade, until I drove 1,000 miles to do so in May 1998. My destinations were the Beaverkill, the Willowemoc, and the West Branch of the Delaware River. I had fished those waters regularly from the late 1950s well into the 1980s, but I had not seen them in many years.

The Catskills can be reached in a two- to three-hour drive from New York City and in an additional two hours from Philadelphia. "How can fishing be worth a damn on rivers that offer such easy access to more than ten million people?" I used to ask when I fished these rivers weekly. I have continued to ask the question long since and returned to rediscover the answer: the quality of the water.

The first thing that struck me when I saw the Willowemoc and, a few miles farther on, the Beaverkill was their beauty. Not just the beauty of the surroundings, but the water's beauty: its clarity, the wonderfully pleasant speed of its flow, and the near-perfect, comfortably fishable blend of pool and riffle. Seeing them anew, I realized that the Catskill rivers are my "Holy Waters," the archetypes of what a trout stream should look like.

BEAVERKILL
I approached the Beaverkill on what, to differentiate it from the four-lane divided highway Route 17 (the "Quickway"), is know locally as Old Route 17. This road parallels the Beaverkill from Roscoe, where the upper Beaverkill and the Willowemoc join at the Junction Pool to form what is known as "the Big River," to the village of East Branch—where it joins the East Branch of the Delaware. The average width of the Beaverkill below Junction Pool is 150 feet. It contains a series of lovely pools separated by quick, shallow riffles.

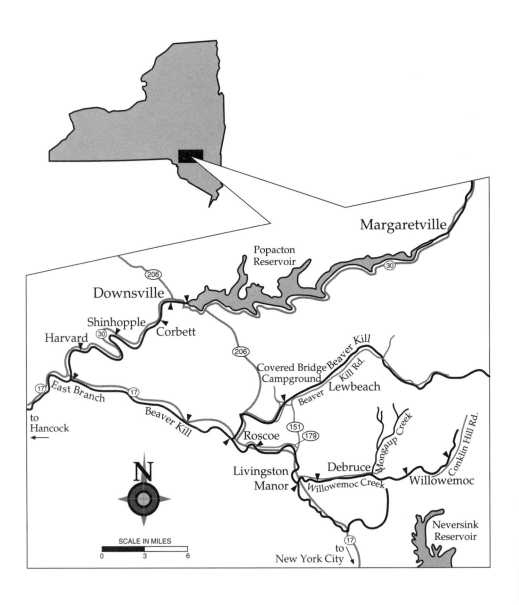

Access to the "Big River" from Roscoe to East Branch is not a problem, as the water is nearly all public, and the river runs parallel to Old Route 17. Ample pulloffs are adjacent to most of the major pools. The river is easy to wade—except following periods of heavy rain—and is a pleasure to fish.

The Beaverkill upstream of Roscoe is, with the exception of a short stretch of river near a state campground, primarily privately held by either clubs or individual landowners. Please respect No Trespassing signs.

The no-kill sections of the Beaverkill and the Willowemoc, as well as the "open" reaches, receive ample supplements of trout from the state and from independent hatcheries along the privately held sections near the headwaters. Still, each river offers excellent fishing.

I came to the Catskills early that May with hopes of meeting the Hendrickson hatch and possibly the prolific hatch of apple green Brachycentrus caddis, locally called the "shad fly" because of the coincidence of its emergence with the arrival of shad in the Delaware. The shad fly is actually two hatches of green caddis in the #14 to #16 range, one light, the other dark, which coincide with the later stage of the Hendricksons.

Spring fishing in the Catskills is a temperature-driven activity, and a water temperature of 50 degrees F is the target when one can expect both trout and insects to get active. When the water temperature is below 50 degrees, you may see some bugs, but it's doubtful that the trout will be looking up. For example, I've seen blanket hatches of *Baetis* in early April without a trout around to eat them.

Spring came late the year of my visit, and in May the Catskill water temperatures were struggling to reach 50 degrees for longer than half an hour a day, if at all. Notwithstanding these conditions, I was undeterred by either logic or low water temperatures. I was anxious to introduce a friend to the Beaverkill, so off we went. In spite of its almost perpetual crowds, one of my favorite sections of the Beaverkill is the stretch from Barnhart's Pool at the Delaware-Sullivan county line downstream about a mile and a half to Wagon Tracks Pool.

On this day, I was happy to find Wagon Tracks unoccupied, despite a subconscious knowledge that the absence of other anglers implied an absence of feeding fish. We charged across the water to an old beloved reach and spent an hour or so fruitlessly pitching nymphs into the lovely currents. Thermometers confirmed that both water and air temperatures hovered around 46 degrees, and—though there were a few caddis flitting over the water—no trout appeared.

In early afternoon we headed back to the West Branch of the Delaware to see if the Hendricksons, which had been prolific the day before, would hatch again. We were not disappointed. The mayflies emerged in a blizzard around 3 P.M. as the water temperature hit 50 degrees. Stretching my palm over the water, I covered a dozen duns and emergers, but few fish greeted them. After an hour, we had seen less than a dozen rising fish and concluded that the major hatch of the previous day had sated the fish, as their digestive processes are slower in cold water.

WILLOWEMOC

Driving up the Willowemoc from Livingston Manor about 7 miles southeast of Roscoe, I noted that more development has taken place in this valley than in other Delaware drainages. The upper Willowemoc still runs unbelievably clear and cold, however.

Above Livingston Manor, the river is—except for a few miles formerly leased by the Debruce Flyfishing Club—primarily public and clearly marked as such. Between Livingston Manor and Roscoe, the Willowemoc includes a productive stretch managed as artificials-only and no-kill.

In its upper reaches, the Willowemoc is only about 25 to 30 feet wide. Like the Beaverkill, it is pool-and-riffle water with occasional deep, inviting holes tucked behind or bordered by boulders. Except following storms, its currents run crystal clear. As the river approaches Roscoe, its flows are supplemented by several small tributaries, and the river gains strength in preparation for its meeting with the Beaverkill.

Access is easy through several state-managed areas. Access above Livingston Manor is from Debruce Road. Parking areas are marked. There are a few posted stretches in addition to the Debruce Club lease along the upper river above Livingston Manor.

The forested tributaries of the Beaverkill and Willowemoc have always been havens for trout during summer periods of high water temperatures in the more exposed lower waters. Until a few more years of survey results measuring the disastrous effects of channelization in 1996 are available, it will be difficult to judge the effects of the lost thermal refuges on the fish. Sources close to the problem guess that the greatest impact will show on wild tributaries.

Anglers should not fish the Beaverkill or the Willowemoc during hot, dry summers when the water is low and its temperatures exceed 70 degrees F. Fish are easy to spot in low, warm water, as they hold near springs and where cold water seeps into the rivers. These fish are already stressed, and hooking and playing them may force them out of their cold-water lies into water exceeding temperatures in which they can survive.

RECENT CHANNELIZATION

The winter 1997 *Trout* magazine described the major flood of 1996 and the subsequent decimation, in the interest of flood control, of most of the spawning tributaries of the rivers in the west drainage of the Catskills, the Delaware drainage. The article also described mitigation efforts by the New York City and Beamoc chapters of Trout Unlimited (TU).

Dick Smith, a thirty-year Catskill angling veteran and a guide for Beaverkill Anglers, reports that—despite the flood—he took reasonable amounts of fish in the spring of 1996, right after the flood, and saw numerous insects in the habitat. He names the 2000 season as one of the finest he and many others have had on the watershed. Clearly, in some quarters, the disastrous aspects of the flood have been reported more pessimistically than reality has proven.

Nat Gillespie, Catskills coordinator of Trout Unlimited, points out that several years prior to the 1996 flood, TU had embarked on a watershed assessment and restoration plan on the Beaverkill and Willowemoc. Soils, groundwater, hydrology, water temperatures, water chemistry, macroinvertebrate health, highway bridge scour records, and the tributary network were examined. In addition, TU completed geomorphic surveys throughout the watershed. The assessment determined that the fisheries' primary limiting factors were high water temperatures and lack of good trout habitat, in part caused by widespread alterations to the shape of the actual stream channels and increased flood flows.

The worst results of the 1996 flood were the misguided attempts at flood mitigation: bulldozing and channelizing of prime spawning streams in the Beamoc (shorthand for Beaverkill and Willowemoc) and throughout the whole Delaware River system. Since then, TU has worked to educate officials and agencies to avoid such occurrences and to provide long-term, geomorphically based protection of susceptible infrastructures. Completed habitat improvement projects include removing Darbee Brook from a 330-foot culvert and returning it to a stream channel, and reconstructing the mouth and lower reach of Horse Brook. Future projects include restoration at the mouths of three important tributaries: Horton Brook, Russell Brook, and Hazel Creek.

In an effort to reduce flash-flood runoff, the New York Department of Transportation has invested over $5 million to retrofit the stormwater drainage system on Route 17. In April 2000 the New York Department of Environmental Conservation (DEC) announced the start of a five-year research effort on the Beaverkill and the Willowemoc to measure angler use, limiting factors, and the status of fish populations. The main objective of the DEC's Beaverkill Watershed Trout Project is to develop a basin-wide management plan to optimize the drainage's potential for high-quality trout fishing.

HATCHES, FLIES, AND BEST TIMES TO FISH
The best time to fish the Catskills is whenever you can. As a rule, however, the best fishing is in spring and fall. There are exceptions to the rule, and vicious late runoffs or early hot weather can perturb fish and insects.

Recent years' hot, dry summers and unpredictable winters, from the mildest to the most severe, have taken their toll on the fish in these streams. Given the capricious Catskill weather, it's best to call a local tackle shop (listed below) for up-to-the-minute information.

The stretches of water managed as no-kill are open to fishing year-round. These can provide a nice extension to the season or a welcome escape from cabin fever on warm late-winter days.

I like to fish the Catskills from the Hendrickson hatch in late April or early May through the middle of June. I then resume fishing in late September until the first heavy frost.

Hatches begin on all rivers in the Delaware drainage around mid-April, with a #20 *Baetis* usually the first insect to appear. For years I have targeted April 28 to May 7 as the time to hit the Hendrickson hatch and the *Paraleptophlebia* (#16 Blue Quills) on the Beaverkill. Some years have long, cold springs, however, when the water temperature stays in the forties almost until Memorial Day. Even though the insects are copious, the trout do not respond, due to the colder water temperatures.

The Catskill hatch calendar has been chronicled in dozens of publications, so I'll simply say that Al Caucci and Robert Nastasi's *Hatches II*, Doug Swisher and Carl Richard's *Selective Trout,* and Art Flick's *New Streamside Guide* are as reliable as when they first appeared. For a good guide to caddis activity in the Catskills, pick up a copy of Larry Solomon and Eric Leiser's *The Caddis and the Angler.* Caddis are as important as mayflies on Catskill rivers, and at times, they are predominant. A good selection of generic pupae and adult imitations will often save the day when the mayflies don't materialize.

When I head for the Catskills, in addition to specific matches for the hatches I hope to fish, I always carry a selection of old standbys with me. My generic fly box for the Delaware drainage contains a selection of Hare's Ear and Peacock-Bodied Partridge Spiders (soft hackles) in #10 to #16 (weighted and unweighted); standard Hare's Ear Nymphs in #12 to #18 tied on both heavy and light wire hooks; several Slate Drake *(Isonychia)* Nymphs, a prolific mayfly in this drainage; light (tannish and greenish) and dark (grayish brown) Elk Hair Caddis in #12 to #20; and black ants in #16 to #20. This list isn't complete, but I'd feel I could catch fish if I had only these flies.

ALSO WORTH NOTING
Esopus River
The Beaverkill and Willowemoc emanate roughly from the west and south sides of Doubletop Mountain in the Catskill chain. Another famed Catskill trout stream has its source on the northeast side of that same mountain. The Esopus begins at Lake Winnisook, near the tiny town of Oliverea, New York, and tumbles its way some 25 or 30 miles, first north,

then east, and finally south to the Ashokan Reservoir, which ultimately drains to the Hudson River.

In its upper reaches, the Esopus flows happily through a deep hemlock and hardwood valley. As it passes through the villages of Big Indian and Shandaken, the floodplain broadens and the river gains width if not depth. In the village of Allaben, the river's flow is supplemented by a discharge of cold water from a portal built in 1923 to carry water from the Schoharie reservoir to the Esopus to supplement the New York City water supply stored in the Ashokan Reservoir. From Allaben down, the river is big water.

The Esopus's flows downstream of Allaben fluctuate depending on the level of discharge through the portal. The Esopus above Allaben is subject to warming during hot summers, and the fish find solace in the colder flows below the portal.

The water of the Esopus is very different from the gentle pools and riffles of the Beaverkill and Willowemoc. The river below the portal averages 80 to 100 feet wide and generally flows at a faster rate. Pools in the Esopus are less defined, likely to be smaller and more rocky, with greater variation in depth and flow confined to a smaller area. The water is frequently murky and discolored below the portal. This section also suffers weekend inner tubers.

Much of the river is not dry-fly friendly, since your floating fly is likely to be sucked into an eddy before it has floated 6 feet. The successful Esopus angler will cover a lot of water in a day, searching here and there with nymphs, streamers, and the occasional dry fly when a rise is spotted. The river is not easy to wade, and you'll be ready for a soft bed after a full day on the Esopus.

Hatches generally follow the standard calendar for the Catskills, although in my experience, the hatches are neither as dense nor as predictable (due to the influence of the portal) as those on the rivers in the Delaware drainage. The river provides ideal habitat for *Isonychia,* a major hatch on the river in late spring–early summer, and I would never go to this river without trying an *Isonychia* nymph.

IF YOU GO

Any of the New York airports can be used as jumping-off points for the Catskills, but the best is Newark, New Jersey, in order to avoid the New York City traffic. There is also a small airport at Newburgh, the Stewart/ Newburgh International Airport.

From any of the airports or from Manhattan, get to the New York State Thruway (I-87) and drive north to Exit 16, Harriman. Take Route 17 west to Exit 96, Livingston Manor, or Exit 94, Roscoe.

From Philadelphia, take the Northeast Extension of the Pennsylvania Turnpike (I-476) to I-81 north above Scranton, and get off at Exit 206. Get on

Route 374 east, and follow to Route 171 north. Turn east on Route 370, then take to Route 191 north across the bridge over the Delaware into Hancock, New York. In New York, take Route 17 to Roscoe or Livingston Manor.

Tackle Shops and Guides

Beaverkill Angler. Roscoe. An Orvis shop. Manager Dick Smith is a very knowledgeable resource. (607) 498-5194. www.beaverkillangler.com.

Catskill Flies. Roscoe. A "don't miss" for Catskill flies. (607) 498-4991.

Fur, Fin and Feather. Livingston Manor on DeBruce Road. Headquarters for the Willowemoc. (845) 439-4476. Mary Dette.

Where to Stay

These are my favorite motels, because of their onriver locations.

Baxter House B&B. On the Beaverkill. Inexpensive to moderate. (607) 498-5811.

Beaverkill Valley Inn. On the upper Beaverkill. Moderate to expensive. (845) 439-4844.

Debruce Country Inn. On the Willowemoc. Inexpensive to moderate. (845) 439-3900.

Red Rose Motel. Three miles west of Roscoe. Inexpensive. (607) 498-5525.

Reynolds House Inn. Inexpensive to moderate. (607) 498-4772.

Riverside Cafe and Lodging. On the lower Beaverkill. (607) 498-5305.

Roscoe Motel. Roscoe. At the Junction Pool. Inexpensive. (607) 498-5220.

Wild Rainbow Lodge and Outfitters. Starlight, Pennsylvania. (570) 635-5983 or (607) 637-4695.

Camping

Roscoe Campsites. On the river below Roscoe. (607) 498-5264.

Twin Island Campsite. On the Beaverkill near Roscoe. (607) 498-5326.

Willowemoc Campsite. On Debruce Road. (845) 439-4250.

Where to Eat

There are numerous places to eat in the Roscoe–Livingston Manor area. A few favorites are listed here.

Riverside Cafe and Lodging. On the lower Beaverkill. (607) 498-5305.

Roscoe Diner. Roscoe. Opposite Exit 94 from the Route 17 Quickway. Inexpensive. No reservations.

Rockland House. Just north of Roscoe. Along the upper Beaverkill. Moderate. (607) 498-4240.

Raimondo's. Roscoe. In the center of town. Italian fare. Inexpensive to moderate. (607) 498-4702.

RESOURCES

Caucci, Al, and Robert Nastasi. *Hatches II.* Piscataway, NJ: New Century Publishers, 1986.

Flick, Art. *New Streamside Guide.* New York: Nick Lyons Books, 1969.

Francis, Austin. *Catskill Rivers.* New York: Lyons & Burford, 1996.

Peper, Eric, and Gary LaFontaine. *Fly Fishing the Beaverkill River.* Audio tape and book. Helena, MT: Greycliff Publishing, 1999. P.O. Box 1273, Helena, MT 59624. (406) 443-1888.

Ross, John. *Trout Unlimited's Guide to America's 100 Best Trout Streams.* Helena, MT: Falcon Press, 1999.

Solomon, Larry, and Eric Leiser. *The Caddis and the Angler.* New York: Lyons & Burford, 1977.

Swisher, Doug, and Carl Richards. *Selective Trout.* New York: Nick Lyons Books, 1971.

New York Atlas & Gazetteer. Yarmouth, ME: DeLorme Mapping Company. (207) 846-7000.

UPPER DELAWARE RIVER

Ann McIntosh

The East and West Branches of the Delaware River and the Upper "Big D," or main stem, from Hancock to Long Eddy, provide what I believe is the best and most challenging wild trout fishing in the East. These are tailwaters, but unlike some popular tailwaters in the West—the Green River in Utah and the San Juan in New Mexico, for example—the Delaware gives up few fish. On a good day, you can hope for twenty fish on the Green and the San Juan, whereas hooking three or four browns or rainbows over 16 inches on the Delaware is a very good day. In this respect, the Delaware more closely resembles the Henry's Fork for delivering big, challenging fish rather than numerous gullible targets.

The Upper Delaware is a big, wide, open field of water, bordered by stands of hardwood and evergreens, overgrown meadows, and marshes. A combination of factors makes the angling exceptionally challenging, even for the most experienced fisherman. Understanding the habitat and the hatches is almost as difficult as catching the fish. Throughout the watershed are some of the wildest, wariest trout in the country.

The Delaware ranges from 50 to 100 feet wide on the East and West Branches to 600 feet wide on the main stem below Long Eddy, New York. The river nurtures an average of twelve hundred rainbow and brown

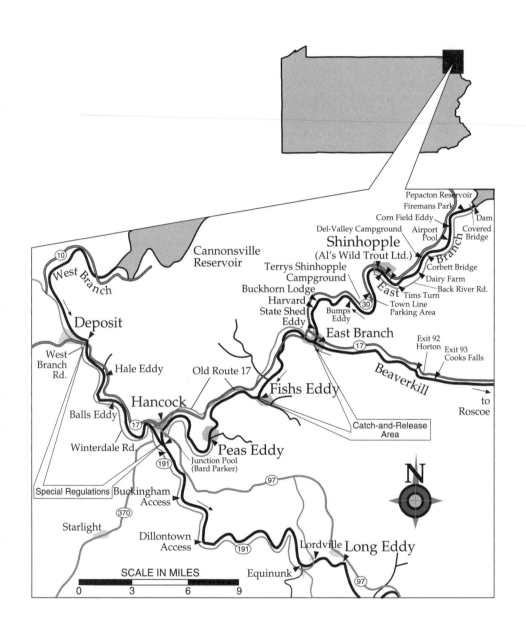

trout per mile—a healthy count, but by no means the most numerous in the East. Most of the trout are continuously on the prowl for prey.

What makes the watershed exceptional is the abundant, rich supply of trout food. The Upper Delaware boasts hatches of every mayfly, caddis, and stonefly found in the eastern United States. It has more subspecies than any other river in the region. This extensive smorgasbord influences the fish, making them very selective and difficult to fool.

On the Delaware, I've found that—most of the time—I must match the hatch or leave fishless. With so many varieties of food from which to choose, trout frequently won't give attractors a glance. Moreover, it's not unusual for Delaware trout to pass up one natural in favor of another. There are exceptions, but the best traditional attractor patterns—the Coachman, Patriot, Adams, Ausable Wulff, and so on—are often snubbed on this water. Nonetheless, a reasonable imitation of the prevailing hatch will generally produce.

UPPER "BIG D" FROM HANCOCK TO LONG EDDY

Fish roam so far and wide in the upper main stem that the primary means of locating trout is to look for riseforms. These reaches are most effectively fished from a boat. Guides row MacKenzie-style dories until they detect rising fish. They then tell their clients to work out line. Most of us mess up the initial cast and learn the Delaware lesson the hard way: There are no second chances. You must be able to place the fly precisely, accurately, and delicately in a feeding lane to fool a wild Delaware trout.

The wild rainbow of the "Big D" is considered by many to be the river's prize take. This species was accidentally introduced into the main stem more than a century ago. In the 1880s Dan Cahill, a railroad brakeman and avid angler, was transporting a strain of warm-water-tolerant rainbows from California's McCloud River to stock in the coldest part of the river—the West Branch. The train broke down at Callicoon, New York, more than 30 river miles below Cahill's destination, and he had to release the fish.

At the time, there were no reservoirs on the East and West Branches, and the Delaware was primarily a warm-water fishery. The river at Callicoon was noted for walleye and smallmouth bass fishing. The rainbows surprised Cahill and his colleagues: Once released, they were able to tolerate the warm water and took hold. The strain proved a strong one, and we hunt their descendants today. By the time the dams were built and the cold water began to flow, the 'bows thrived, becoming more numerous than ever.

Brown trout, on the other hand, were not introduced to the Delaware until after the cold-water habitat was in place, after the Cannonsville and Pepacton Reservoirs were created in the mid-1950s. According to Bruce Foster and other seasoned Delaware anglers, they did not develop a tolerance for water above 72 degrees F for very long, never having had to adapt as Cahill's rainbows did. Thus, though brown trout tolerate higher water temperatures better than rainbows on most rivers, the reverse is true on the Delaware. Many Delaware regulars view the big, wild brown as the hardest to fool.

In addition to its rich bug life and wild trout, the Delaware boasts a number of very large fish. Fry and fingerlings grow up in swift water, quickly developing into fit, muscular adults. The fish have unusual stamina. Once they get over the surprise of being hooked, they seem oblivious to opposition at the other end of the line. It's common to have a 16-inch fish take you into the backing.

Floating the "Big D" from Hancock to Long Eddy

The main stem of the Delaware starts at the confluence of the East and West Branches just below Hancock, New York (across the river from Starlight, Pennsylvania). Floating the Delaware from Hancock to Long Eddy is reminiscent of a western angling experience. On my first trip, I was guided by Bruce Foster, who also had his amiable friend, Ed Hornung, on board. We put the boat in at 11:00 A.M. at the Buckingham public-access launch and took out at 9:30 P.M. in Long Eddy, a tiny hamlet 10 miles downstream.

Although it was the Friday of Memorial Day weekend, the trip was a near-wilderness experience. Along these 10 miles, the river runs within waving distance of only three isolated hamlets in the river plain. In places, I could see up- and downstream for a mile with nothing but uncut brush, hardwoods, evergreens, and water to obstruct my view. We saw only four other boats and an occasional lone angler fishing from the bank.

I hooked my first Delaware River rainbow 2 miles upstream of Long Eddy. I was wading off reedy marshes full of big golden stonefly nymphs. The trout took one of Foster's sulphur emergers. My memory is consumed by its first long run, perhaps 50 yards, and the run after that, maybe 30 yards, and the one after that, until—after nearly half an hour—I dragged the fish to net.

That first trip was a good but not overwhelming float experience. The major disappointment was that Foster had timed the float to put us on an exceptionally active pool for the sulphur hatch at dusk. We arrived on time, tied on our emergers, and sat back to wait for the hatch. We talked and waited, cast blindly and waited some more, sighed and had a glass of wine, ever hopeful. The hatch never materialized. It had done so the preceding day, and likely it would do so the next.

My next Delaware float was earlier in the season, scheduled for the Hendrickson hatch. This time my partner was Mary Kuss, an angling instructor from Philadelphia. Foster had called a few days earlier to warn that the water was very high and cold. He suggested postponing the trip.

Then he called the day before we were to leave, reporting that the fish were "taking the ladies"—the light Hendricksons. He had turned rocks and found lots of nymphs. He was optimistic about our trip, despite the high water. While waiting to launch at Hancock, I saw a number of rising fish, apparently taking small Blue-Winged Olive patterns. It was a balmy, overcast day, and I anticipated great fishing.

The scenery was as magnificent as on the preceding trip. I relaxed into the bow, setting my rod down while Foster looked for working fish. Kuss was not as laid-back. She had never floated the Delaware and was eager to fish. After trying numerous caddis patterns, imitating the thousands of down-wings coming off the water, she tied on a brown-and-black Woolly Bugger and drifted it through deep runs and riffles. Still nothing happened. Since we launched, we'd seen one rise, and by the time we got within 60 feet of it, the fish had stopped feeding.

We were slipping down the middle of the river when Kuss spotted the second rise. She drifted a Hendrickson emerger deftly over the trout, and it took. Twenty minutes later, a 16-inch brown was in hand, posing for a picture. We thought a good time was developing.

But, no. That day the Hendricksons never took off, and the fish continued to snub our caddisflies. None of the other boats had any luck either. There is no definitive explanation for such piscatorial behavior, but I'll settle for Al Caucci's. He surmised that the water never reached 55 degrees F that day; the surface wasn't warm enough to trigger the hatch.

I remained in the area two more days, waiting for the water to drop and warm. Cruising the pulloffs along the West Branch the next day, I interviewed seven anglers, none of whom had had any luck. Soon more rain and cold weather developed, and the season Caucci dubbed "the spring from hell" marched on into summer.

The main stem and its branches will draw crowds on the weekend at the easy-access points. This, while annoying enough, has the added effect of driving the rising fish into deep water. A common phenomenon on this water is to have lots of risers that hang about 3 feet outside the best controllable cast you can make while wading in water about 6 inches above your waist. If the strongest rod you have is a 5-weight, you'll believe you needed a 6-weight to reach the fish. Of course, with a 6-weight, the fish would have slid another 6 feet farther out. . . .

If you plan to float the river, guides advise taking along the following gear in addition to tackle: cold drinks and lunch (in a cooler), polarized sunglasses, wide-brim hat, heavy and lightweight shirts, flashlight, rain jacket, sunblock, and insect repellent.

Additional Features about the "Big D"
At Equinunk, Pennsylvania, Equinunk Creek empties into the main stem. This 25-foot-wide stream is a good alternative fishery in the spring when

the water is too high to fish elsewhere. The village of Equinunk is worth a stop. There's a historical society, a church, a general store, and a few charming, decrepit houses. Access is on SR 4007 off Route 191.

Though shad lie outside the scope of this book, I would be remiss not to mention the outstanding shad run on the Upper Delaware from mid-May through June. There are a number of hot spots on the "Big D," and also on the East and West Branches. (The tackle shops listed below can provide detailed information.)

Hatches, Flies, and Best Times to Fish
Water level and temperature are the two primary factors to consider when planning a trip to the Delaware. In the early part of the season (April), wait until the water recedes and its temperature is 50 to 55 degrees F for a few days. This will trigger good hatches and rising fish.

The timing of cold-water releases from the reservoirs is important. Both season and dam releases have major effects on the water between early May and Memorial Day. This is the transitional time between natural water temperatures and cooling releases. The bugs can get totally confused during this period. You may go to a pool during the day, expecting a particular dry-fly opportunity (caddis or late Hendricksons) only to end up fishing at dusk with sulphurs and drakes. Try to avoid periods of very high or very low water, and be mindful of summer droughts.

"Big D" Regulations
A New York or Pennsylvania license is valid in the border waters of the "Big D" and the West Branch that separate these states. No-kill, catch-and-release angling with artificials and flies only is now permitted from October 1 through opening day of the next season (mid-April) on the main stem of the Delaware, beginning at the confluence of the East and West Branches just below Hancock, New York.

From opening day (mid-April) to September 30, one trout 14 inches or longer may be kept.

"Big D" Access
On the New York side, there are a few pulloffs along Route 97 south of Hancock. On the Pennsylvania side, Route 191 runs along the river, and the Pennsylvania Fish Commission maintains several large access areas:
- At the Hancock bridge.
- Downstream of the Hancock bridge 1.8 miles.
- Buckingham, Pennsylvania, access. (The stretch downstream from the boat put-in is known as Shangri-La. It's a good place to fish from the banks and the shallows; there's a long stretch of productive water.)
- Dillontown access (Pennsylvania).

- Equinunk access. (There's access for the wading angler, but it's not as easy to reach on foot.)
  - The Lordville bridge (New York; a very popular spot).
  - Long Eddy access (New York, off Route 97).

There is private land along much of the Delaware. Do not trespass. Ask permission and obey posted signs.

Hatch Matching on the Delaware

No other river east of the Mississippi has hatches as prolific as those of the Upper Delaware River and its East and West Branches. Al Caucci gives his thoughts: "Both the East and West Branches used to be rich bass streams with a high pH alkaline content. Now that the sources are icy cold bottom releases from both reservoirs, excellent bass water has been turned into a very rich trout system, especially in the West Branch and the main stem, which benefit from heavy cold releases from the Cannonsville Reservoir. If the supply of cold water were ever to be cut back or shut down, it would endanger the whole Upper Delaware system."

The Delaware is home to well-fed, privileged trout that can afford to be picky. Their buffet is constantly replenished and always fresh. They take exactly what they want, where they want, when they want it. These trout will key on the most vulnerable aspects of each hatch—whichever offers the most meal.

There are at least forty major emergences on the Delaware between February and November. Many river anglers call insects by their Latin names for purposes of accuracy and to differentiate among genera, species, subspecies, and common names or names of imitations and patterns. This approach is not pretentious; it provides clarity and accuracy in a technically confusing environment.

In addition to mayflies, there are abundant stoneflies, caddis, and terrestrials. To fish this water successfully, an angler should be able to identify and match the stage of emergence of a particular insect closely. There may be three or four species coming off the water simultaneously, but the fish may be interested only in a particular—most vulnerable—stage of one of them. Anglers will do well to educate themselves about the different phases of emergence. When selecting flies at local shops, choose imitations of all stages of the major and minor hatches, including flies imitating each stage: nymphs, emergers, duns, and spinners.

Despite the respect I have for the Delaware, it has its drawbacks. Catching its fish requires experience, skill, and patience. The neophyte, unless significantly more knowledgeable than I was when I began, will quickly feel frustrated, helpless, and stupid. Beginning anglers should seek help. Invest in a guide, take a lesson, or find an experienced Delaware angler to take you under his or her wing. There may be a lot of room for sloppy casting on this water, but your continued flailing may put fish down. Despite its size, the river demands stealth, respectful presentation, and knowledge of the hatch activity on a given day.

Fishing the Delaware, whether casting from a boat or from shore, is notoriously unpredictable. The fish seem picky, finicky, and temperamental. What they actually are is superselective: As noted earlier, fish key onto the most vulnerable insects on the water, taking the bugs that are easiest to snatch. For instance, a particular hatch may materialize on a cool, overcast summer afternoon. Unable to dry their wings and take off as quickly as on hot days, these flies stay on top of the water longer than usual, making them most vulnerable to the fish. The Delaware constantly demands this sort of technical observation and savvy fishing.

Because the most efficient way to find fish is to hunt for rising trout, guides generally prefer dry-fly angling to nymphing or using wet flies. (All regulars admit that some very fine specimens have been taken on these as well.) Because there is a huge expanse of holding water and many lies, the fish do not congregate in any one place for very long. Rainbows cruise and are difficult to locate from one day to the next. Browns hold, but their lies can change daily. Nymphs and streamers can be cast for hours without ever being seen by a trout. By presenting an emerger or a dry to a riseform, on the other hand, you can be certain of a target. Anglers very familiar with the river know good places to cast subsurface, but they do this only when nothing is showing on top.

I once took a trout drifting a nymph through a fishy-looking riffle. I was using a tandem system with a beadhead Pheasant Tail Nymph on the bottom and a Patriot as the top fly. Bruce Foster was at the oars, explaining in full voice the folly of nymphing on the Delaware. "You just can't tell if the fish are there, so why drift a nymph through the water? There's too much of it," Foster said. "You've got to wait till they show themselves and then go after them." A bump returned my attention to my rod, and I reeled in a 12-inch rainbow. Foster never missed a beat. "See that," he said. "Nice little fish. Another thing: Don't get cocky and make rules about this river—it'll prove you wrong every time!"

Careful presentation is important on the Delaware. Although the top of the water is textured, it is very clear and the fish are extremely wary—particularly about coming up for an imitation. The Compara-dun pattern was developed to duplicate the naturals in the surface film rather than on top of it. The Compara-dun, Compara-emerger, and Compara-spinner look vulnerable, like the natural.

When the first major flush of cold-water release occurs in June, the trout and the bugs are subdued by the change. It takes several days for both to acclimate and return to normal hatching and feeding activity. By the time summer arrives, they are more used to frequent temperature changes and feed with greater regularity.

To avoid the disappointment and frustration of ending a Delaware River trip empty-handed, I recommend a three-day minimum stay, with one day devoted to a float. You shouldn't go to the Delaware for one day only (if you have far to drive). You have to spend a lot of time waiting for the magnificent moments. Don't approach this water anticipating lots of hookups. A day that brings three or four fish between 16 and 20 inches is something to be proud of here. Unless there is uncommonly bad weather or a severe drought, three days will provide sufficient chances for a number of major fish.

Which hatch or hatches you should select is largely a matter of personal preference. The green and brown drakes are phenomenal, and despite the hatch's popularity, there's plenty of water to absorb angling pressure. Bruce Foster says that if forced to choose his personal preference, it would probably be the early-season Hendricksons and the brown drakes later on. Al Caucci lists the light cahills in July and August, and the *Pseudocloeons* in summer and fall among his favorites.

Though I cannot resist a spring weekend on the Delaware, my wiser self prefers the fall fishing, in September and October. The weather is more reliable, and the water temperatures are stable. Moreover, there are fewer anglers. Cold-water releases keep the West Branch and the main stem fishing well throughout most summers. Insect activity continues unabated.

Equipment for the Delaware
It's a good idea to carry an 8½- or 9-foot rod rigged with a weight-forward 5/6-weight floating line and an extra reel spooled with a 6- or 7-weight sinking tip or a 150 or 200 grain sinking line. In summer at midday, when there are few hatches or rising trout, the sinking tip will make it easier to get streamers, stoneflies, and big nymphs down to trout on the bottom.

WEST BRANCH
The West Branch has not been stocked since 1994. The record trout taken on a fly is a 33-inch brown caught in 1996. It probably fattened up in the Cannonsville Reservoir and slipped into the river.

The most fun I've had on the West Branch was fishing Jimmy Charron's Alewife Streamer on the special-regulations water near Deposit, New York. It was early on a drizzly September morning, and my friend Diane Wondisford and I were fishing together. We saw fish smashing something big, near but not on top of the water. We couldn't figure out what it was. It certainly wasn't any of the bugs we saw hatching. But the fish kept on devouring it. We were puzzled and frustrated, because these were big fish and not at all cautious.

As it began to rain hard, we left the water to seek advice. At the Delaware River Club, Jerry Wolland, one of the owners, listened to our tale. "Stop! Stop!" Jerry said, holding up a silencing finger. "I've got just what you need. I've got it right here." He handed us Charron's Alewife pattern. "Do you know what that is? No, of course you don't. It's an alewife; there are hundreds of them washing out of the bottom of the dam, floating dead on top. The trout just love 'em. Fish it on top now."

The next morning, we went back to Deposit and tied on our alewives. After we figured out how to present them in a drag-free drift, we took three nice (14-inch or longer) trout each. It was one of those rare and wonderful moments on the Delaware, in touch with the fish and landing the big ones! Since that time, I always take alewives in my arsenal when going to unfamiliar tailwaters.

When to Fish the West Branch
The prime season on the West Branch is from April 15 through August, although September and October can be the best months of all, especially in years when releases from the Cannonsville Reservoir are consistent and there has been no major drought. There are frequent pulloffs along the East and West Branches, and the unguided angler will find the fishing opportunities spectacular.

In addition to the special-regulations section at Deposit, I enjoy fishing along the road that follows the river from Balls Eddy, Pennsylvania, to Hale Eddy, New York. Except where pulloffs are near the roads, I haven't experienced much fishing pressure—even on holiday weekends—and I find it easy enough to walk fifteen minutes and be alone on the water. This is a very scenic area, and there is no stretch of unproductive water.

The West Branch and Upper Delaware can be very difficult to fish in the rare years when there has been little snowfall or spring rain. Dick Jogodnick, an experienced Delaware angler, reported one May that the Upper Delaware was very hard to fish. He found the water very low, the fish in hiding, and few bugs on the water. Under these conditions, he suggests fishing near Hale Eddy. Park at the restored bridge access, where there is an official fishermen's parking area.

West Branch Regulations
From the Pennsylvania–New York border downstream to its confluence with the East Branch, artificial lures or flies only are permitted on the West Branch from October 1 to opening day of trout season. All trout hooked must be released immediately. From opening day (mid-April) through September 30, two trout 12 inches or longer may be kept per day.

West Branch Access
Most of the land along the West Branch from Balls Eddy to Hale Eddy is public. There are pulloffs and parking areas along the road. Take Pennsylvania Route 191 west of the Hancock Bridge and travel upriver along

Winterdale Road (the first road north on the west side of the bridge). The road runs along the west side of the West Branch to Balls Eddy. Then continue on West Branch Road, a dirt road that follows the river beyond Hale Eddy. There are numerous pulloffs along the way.

The Delaware River Club owns 2 miles of streambank along the Delaware, beginning 2 miles upstream of the junction of the East and West Branches. Guests and school attendees have access to the river here.

Private access is also possible for guests at the West Branch Angler. The log cabins on the banks of the river afford easy access to fish off the front porch, although the angling is better 200 yards downstream.

To access the river from the Deposit side, take a right after the bridge near the paper mill, drive along the river a few hundred yards, and park in the lot designated for anglers. Fish upstream or down.

A New York or Pennsylvania license is valid in the border waters of the West Branch that separate these states. A New York license is required to fish the upper section.

EAST BRANCH

It is 15 miles from Downsville Dam (the outflow of Pepacton Reservoir) downstream to the village of East Branch, New York, where the Beaverkill meets the East Branch of the Delaware. Brown and rainbow trout are stocked in the East Branch. There are numerous brook trout in the upper reaches (from Shinhopple to Downsville), and wild and holdover browns coexist with their stocked brethren.

The East Branch looks and is more fishy above Shinhopple, as one drives up the river along Old Route 17. Above the town of East Branch, it changes from flat, open water to smaller reaches overhung with hardwoods and hemlocks. Do not be deceived. Despite the close cover and precipitous access, this is excellent, productive trout water. Park your car along the edge of the road, and slide down the banks to the water downstream of Al's Wild Trout shop.

Water quality in the East Branch is very good. There is a healthy pH level, and although there are long stretches without cover, there is enough shade to keep water temperatures down. Nonetheless, the East Branch is not at its best in midsummer.

Al Carpenter, Sr., owner of Al's Wild Trout Ltd. at Shinhopple, imparts a wealth of information about the Upper East Branch. He emphasizes the numbers of wild brook trout in the river, advising anglers to fish for them from the village of Corbett upstream to the Pepacton Dam. The record East Branch brook trout was 20 inches long, taken above Shinhopple in 1996. In April 1992 a 10-pound, 29-inch brown was taken in the same area.

One of the challenges of fishing the East Branch is finding good access points, as there are many stretches of slow, silted, and less-than-productive water. I spent a day early in the fall touring the river with Sara Crewes, Al Carpenter's granddaughter. Crewes is not only very knowledgeable about the East Branch, having fished it for more than twenty years, but she is also a consummate fly tier. Tutored by Larry Duckwall, Crewes creates masterful Catskill-style mayfly imitations.

Crewes, having put in an exceptional amount of time on the water, can vouch for some astounding catches. She has landed a 3½-pound brown trout from the pool at the fly shop at Shinhopple, and she caught an 18¾-inch brookie at Upper Tim's Turn (a spot on the river) a decade ago, when the river was productive in this area. It was the largest brookie Crewes has ever seen—by several inches.

Hatches, Flies, and Best Times to Fish
The East Branch fishes best from early April through mid-June and again from mid-September through late October. (It also provides excellent sport for shad from mid-May to mid-June.) The releases from the Pepacton Reservoir are not regulated, but the water comes out of the bottom at an average temperature of 42 degrees F and stays cold for about eight miles downstream in the summer. The lower East Branch (below the village of East Branch) usually gets too warm for trout by mid-June.

Like the rest of the Upper Delaware River watershed, the East Branch has rich hatches. All the standard early-season mayflies come off here. Larry Duckwall, a consummate Catskill fly tier, says his personal preference is the Hendrickson *(Ephemerella subvaria)* emergence in spring, closely followed by hatches of insects imitated by Quill Gordons, March Browns, and little Blue Dun patterns. Before the early-season hatches commence, hatches of little black and little brown stoneflies appear on sunny days as early as February, but they are more prolific in early March and April.

Crewes and other East Branch regulars assure me that the number of insects on the East Branch is equal to and very similar to those on the West Branch and throughout the western Catskill drainage. Hatches on the East Branch are also dependent on temperature-driven emergences in spring and fall.

Early effective patterns include Hendricksons and March Browns. Later spring emergences include sulphurs, *Isonychia, Baetis,* and green drakes. Summer brings on the terrestrials, with sulphurs, *Baetis,* and caddis still working. In late September and October, *Isonychia* are very important, and September and October are the months to rely on streamers and nymphs.

Crewes's fly box is wonderful. Beautifully tied Catskill patterns are neatly organized in closely stocked rows. When full, the box includes Elk Hair Caddis (#14), sulphurs (#16), Blue-Winged Olives (#18), Adamses

(#14), Dun Variants (#10), Cream Variants (#10–#14), and, during the summer, large ants (#10–#12).

East Branch Regulations

Anglers are required to have a New York license to fish the East Branch. Catch-and-release regulations apply, and only artificial lures, flies, and single barbless hooks may be used from the bridge at the town of East Branch downstream to the Fishs Eddy Bridge (below the mouth of the Beaverkill) from October 1 to the end of November. The stretch from Corbett bridge upstream to the Pepacton Dam is closed September 30 to protect spawning activity. From April 1 to September 30 one trout 12 to 14 inches may be kept.

East Branch Access

• The long, deep pool along the road downstream of Shinhopple, which is very deep and always cool.

• A half mile above Al's Wild Trout fly shop at Shinhopple. Take the first turnoff to the right above the store. Park and cross a narrow stream, then an island, then fish the far channel. (Look for hidden channels like this throughout the stream above Shinhopple.)

• Upper East Branch at Tim's Turn. This used to be more productive than it has been of late. But look for big brookies here.

• Corbett bridge. Park on the road, not in the campground. Walk across the campground to the mouth of Campbell Brook. Fish upstream. This section remains cool throughout the summer, as the water comes out of the dam at 38 to 40 degrees F year-round.

• At the hamlet of Harvard.

• At the village of East Branch. Wade the river or put a boat over the bank.

• Near the junction of Old Route 17 and new Route 17 (the "Quickway"), just northeast of Hancock. (Watch out for very strong currents here in the early part of the season.) The East Branch runs parallel to the road. You can cross land to the water anywhere that is not posted.

CONSERVATION AND WATER FLOW
IN THE DELAWARE RIVER DRAINAGE

Achieving the optimum conditions and habitat for trout from the dams that govern the Delaware River is no simple matter. An unusual number of political entities and stakeholders are involved.

The laws governing the flow in the Delaware and its branches were originally set by a U.S. Supreme Court decree in 1954. They are controlled by the state of New York, the New York Department of Environmental Conservation (DEC), and the Delaware River Basin Commission (DRBC).

While the DRBC has authority to modify the operating rules to improve fish habitat, it cannot do so without the unanimous consent of the states of Delaware, New Jersey, New York, and Pennsylvania, as well as New York City—all of which receive water supplies from the Delaware drainage.

The DEC has the authority to request additional releases to reduce thermal stress on trout if certain temperature criteria are not met. The operating rules are constantly evaluated by the DEC, which has made successful recommendations on behalf of fish habitat and acknowledges that more improvements are needed. This process is tedious, because the objectives of fishing and water supply are often at odds. Dave Langan, chair of the Delaware River Committee of Trout Unlimited's New York Council, argues that more water is needed for both the East and West Branches.

In the summer of 2000, Al Caucci met with Charles Gauvin, Executive Director of National Trout Unlimited, and they helped establish the Delaware River Coalition, which then formed the Delaware River Foundation. The Delaware River Foundation has established goals that include identifying a consistent flow rate that will meet the needs of anglers, other recreational river users, and the New York City water supply. It is now positioned to work as a diplomatic and philanthropic nonprofit organization specifically focused on the problems of the Delware River drainage. If you fish this water with any regularity, please become a member of this foundation.

IF YOU GO
From New York City, take Route 17 west toward Binghamton to Hancock, New York. Take Exit 87A or 87 to Hancock. This is a two-and-a-half-hour trip.

From Philadelphia, take the Northeast Extension of the Pennsylvania Turnpike (I-476) to I-81 north above Scranton, and get off at Exit 206. Get on Route 374 east, and follow to Route 171 north. Turn east on Route 370, then take Route 19 north across the bridge over the Delaware into Hancock, New York. It is about a three-hour drive to Hancock.

From the Baltimore-Washington area, take I-83 north to Harrisburg, Pennsylvania, then I-81 past Wilkes-Barre and Scranton. Continue north on I-81 to Exit 206, and Route 374. From here, follow the directions above. An alternative route is to take I-95 north to I-476 north in Pennsylvania, then get on the Northeast Extension of the Pennsylvania Turnpike (also part of I-476). Then follow the directions above. The trip takes four and a half to five and a half hours, depending on your exact starting point.

From Pittsburgh and points west, take I-80 east to I-81 north, and follow the above directions from Scranton.

Tackle Shops and Guides

Al Caucci's Delaware River Club Fly Shop. Starlight, Pennsylvania. Fly shop, fly-fishing schools, guides, private campground. (800) 6-MAYFLY. www.mayfly.com. E-mail: drc@hancock.net.

Al's Wild Trout Ltd. Shinhopple, New York. On the East Branch. Tackle and flies. Al Carpenter, Sr., and his granddaughter, Sara Crewes, know the East Branch better than most. Stop here for reliable advice. (607) 363-7135.

Jim "Cos" Costolnick. Hancock, New York. (877) 4FLYGUY. flyguy @hancock.net.

EastWest Outfitters. Hancock, New York. Bob Wills, guide. (860) 485-9435. eastwestoutfit1@cs.com.

Gray Ghost Guides. Hancock, New York. Jim Serio, proprietor. Float and wade trips in the Upper Delaware system. (607) 637-3444 or (800) 836-4040.

Indian Springs Camp. Lordville, New York. Lee Hartman, proprietor and guide. This establishment is several miles downstream from Hancock, near the Lordville bridge and some of the best fishing on the "Big D." Hartman is a respected Upper Delaware angler. One-on-one lessons, guide service (floating or wading). (215) 679-5022.

Mr. Moose. Hancock, New York. (570) 635-5935.

River Essentials. On Route 191, in Pennsylvania, 1 mile south of Hancock. An Orvis shop. (570) 635-5825.

West Branch Angler. Deposit, New York. Full-service tackle shop and guide service. Trips on the Beaverkill and Willowemoc, as well as the Delaware. Complete fly selection. (607) 467-5525 or (607) 467-2215.

Wild Rainbow Outfitters. Hancock, Pennsylvania. Shop on the Pennsylvania side of the Hancock bridge on Route 191. (570) 635-5983. www.rainbowoutfitters.com.

Where to Stay

Capra Inn. Hancock, New York. Recently renovated motel. Simple, clean, and convenient. Inexpensive. (607) 637-1600.

Al Caucci's Delaware River Club. Starlight, Pennsylvania. Lodge with single and double rooms. Motel suites with one and two rooms. Moderate. (800) 6-MAYFLY.

Downsville Motel. Downsville, New York. Below Downsville Dam of Pepacton Reservoir on the East Branch. Inexpensive. (607) 363-7575.

Indian Springs Camp. Lordville, New York. Lee Hartman, proprietor and guide. Well-equipped cabins near the Lordville bridge. Lodging rates based on fishing packages. Moderate. (215) 679-5022.

Inn at Starlight Lake. Starlight, Pennsylvania. A year-round traditional Pocono country inn serving breakfast and dinner. Fourteen rooms, ten cottages. Tennis, biking, hiking, and convenient to trout fishing. A nice place to take family or nonangling spouses, and a good place for dinner after a long day on the river. Moderately expensive. (800) 248-2519 or (570) 798-2519.

Pepacton Cabins. Downsville, New York. On the East Branch. Moderate. (607) 363-2094. E-mail: pepacton@catskills.net.

Smith Colonial Motel. Hancock, New York. Two miles south of Hancock on Route 97. Inexpensive. (607) 637-2989.

Glen Morangie Lodge. Starlight, Pennsylvania. Large log house with six attractively appointed guest rooms with private baths. Superb breakfasts. Moderate. (570) 798-2350.

Step-A-Way B&B. Long Eddy, New York. Off Route 97. Two-story Victorian farmhouse. Attractive house and cabin. Good getaway with hunting, hiking, and biking nearby. Inexpensive. (845) 887-4078.

West Branch Angler and Sportsmen's Resort. Deposit, New York. On the west bank of the West Branch between Hancock and Deposit. Lodge, cabins, breakfast, dinner served Thursday, Friday, and Saturday. Cabins have air-conditioning, cable TV. Moderate to expensive. (607) 467-5525.

Wild Rainbow Lodge. Hancock, New York. A fabulous site on the main stem of the Delaware. Cabins and rooms; cook yourself or order catered meals. Moderate to expensive. (570) 635-5983.

White Pillars Inn B&B. Deposit, New York. Convenient to the special-regulations section of the West Branch downstream from Deposit. Moderate. (607) 467-4191.

Camping

Delaware River Club Campground. Starlight, Pennsylvania. On the West Branch, upstream from the Delaware River Club fly shop. Water hookups and other facilities. (800) 6-MAYFLY.

Oxbow Campsites. East Branch, New York. On the East Branch. (607) 363-7141.

Terry's Campsites. East Branch, New York. (607) 363-2536.

West Branch Anglers. Deposit, New York. (607) 467-5525.

Where to Eat

Circle E Diner. East Front Street, Hancock, New York. The best breakfast in town. Open 6 A.M. to 10 P.M. daily.

Delaware Inn. Hancock, New York. Bar and restaurant. Good place for late supper—serves until 10 P.M. Inexpensive to moderate. (607) 637-2749.

Inn at Starlight Lake. Starlight, Pennsylvania. A refined dining experience in a casual and cozy atmosphere. Moderate to expensive. Reservations advised. (717) 798-2519.

Crosstown Inn. Hancock, New York. At junction of Routes 191 and 370, just south of the 191 bridge from Hancock. Anglers' hours—open late for light fare. This is where the guides hang out late to tell lies and a few secrets. Great burgers. No reservations.

La Salette. Hancock, New York. Italian-American. Moderate. (607) 637-2505.

Delaware River Delicacies. Northeast of Hancock, New York. On Green Flats Road off Old Route 17. Smokehouse delicacies, including trout, turkey, eel, grouse, and chicken. Don't miss this unusual attraction. Ask locally for exact directions. (607) 637-4443.

RESOURCES

West Branch-Delaware River Hotline (flow information). (845) 295-1006.

Pennsylvania Fish Commission. 3532 Walnut St., Harrisburg, PA 17106-7000. (717) 657-4518.

Pennsylvania Fish and Boat Commission, Publications Section. P.O. Box 67000, Harrisburg, PA 17106-7000. (717) 657-4518.

Pennsylvania State Parks. 1 (800) 63-PARKS.

Pennsylvania Department of Environmental Resources. (814) 349-8778.

Pennsylvania Atlas & Gazetteer. Yarmouth, ME: DeLorme Mapping Company. (207) 846-7000.

Armstrong, A. Joseph. *Trout Unlimited's Guide to Pennsylvania Limestone Streams.* Harrisburg, PA: Stackpole Books, 1992.

Landis, Dwight. *Trout Streams of Pennsylvania: An Angler's Guide.* Revised ed. Bellefonte, PA: Hempstead-Lyndell, 1991.

Meck, Charles A. *Pennsylvania Trout Streams and Their Hatches.* Revised ed. Woodstock, VT: Backcountry Publications, 1993.

Ross, John. *Trout Unlimited's Guide to America's 100 Best Trout Streams.* Helena, MT: Falcon Press: 1999.

Sajna, Michael. *Pennsylvania Trout & Salmon Fishing Guide.* Portland, OR: Frank Amato Publications, 1988.

Shenk, Ed. *Ed Shenk's Fly Rod Trouting.* Harrisburg, PA: Stackpole Books, 1989.

Swisher, Doug, and Carl Richards. *Selective Trout.* New York: Nick Lyons Books, 1971.

PART TWO

The Mid-Atlantic

CHAPTER FIVE

PHILADELPHIA

SOUTH-CENTRAL PENNSYLVANIA'S LIMESTONE CREEKS

Ann McIntosh

Within two and a half hours of Baltimore and Washington—and about the same time from Philadelphia—an angler can fish for wild trout on three of Pennsylvania's best limestone spring creeks: Letort Spring Run, Falling Spring Branch, and Yellow Breeches Creek. You can leave the city after work, fish the Letort or the Yellow Breeches in the evening, and finish the day with a good meal at the Boiling Springs Tavern or the Allenberry Resort. Early the next morning, get on the Letort before other anglers spook the fish. Approach cautiously, and fish the hatch or standard Letort patterns such as cress bugs and shrimp. Once the sun is high and the action slows, drive down I-81 to Falling Spring Branch. Fish through the day, and return to the Yellow Breeches for the evening hatch and late spinner fall. The Breeches will repair any injury to your ego incurred by uncooperative fish on the first two wild trout streams.

LETORT SPRING RUN

The Letort is a historic limestone creek originating at a spring south of Carlisle and flowing northeast to the Conodoguinet. The Letort was home waters to Charles Fox and Vincent Marinaro, two of America's most renowned trout fishers. Both observed the feeding patterns of wild brown trout in the Letort and authored books that resulted in lasting innovations in modern fly fishing.

The Letort is the most difficult stream I've ever fished. I've spent hours on my knees on its soggy banks trying to set down a dry fly or nymph delicately 2 feet in front of a Letort trout. When I don't line them or spook them, they usually ignore my offerings. My angling friend,

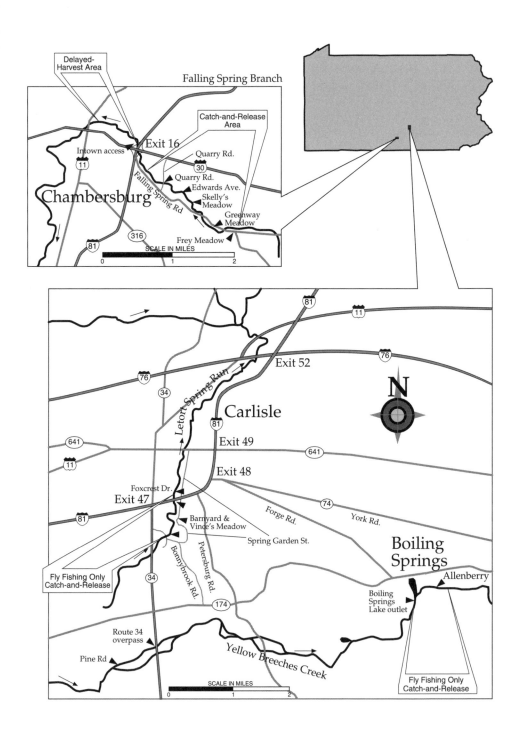

photographer Douglas Lees, spends many days on his knees, targeting as few as three fish a day. His success exceeds mine, as does his patience.

I first went to the Letort in midsummer during a hot, dry spell when other streams were not fishing well. Because it is spring fed, the Letort runs cool all year long. I attempted to fish the Trico hatch, my first experience with these minuscule flies. That was like taking a class in advanced calculus without having learned math. I was hopeless and clueless and came away fishless. Later that day I tried terrestrials—crickets and beetles—with little luck.

Over the years, my angling skills and knowledge grew, and I returned to the stream annually, usually in the summer, but I still could not catch fish. Then one year I went in March. I fished streamers and caught three fish downstream from Charles Fox's meadow. I was using a #12 Clouser Red Foxee Minnow. I drove home thinking I'd finally broken the spell. But when I returned in July, I was skunked again. That's when I promised myself I had to take action to beat the jinx.

Tom Gamper, an angling friend, and I teamed up and booked Ed Shenk as our guide for a day on the stream late in June. Shenk, an internationally recognized angler and author who has fished since he was two years old, is one of the few remaining Letort angling legends. His best fish on the Letort is a 27½-inch brown. He puts in thirty or forty hours on the stream every week. I figured if I couldn't catch fish, I could at least watch him do so.

At 8 A.M. we were approaching the water cautiously near the I-81 overpass when Shenk spotted a family of mink—a mama and five little ones—on the far bank. He cupped a forefinger and thumb around his mouth and imitated the chirping sound of an injured rabbit or field mouse. All the mink turned around, slipped into the water, and swam single file across the current to within a few feet of Shenk. The mama mink stopped cautiously at the water's edge, but two of the young came up and sniffed Shenk's boots, looked up into his puckish face, then scurried under a nearby bush. The mink must be a good omen, we all felt.

We started the day with crickets cast to fish lying across several of the braided currents that constitute the flow of the Letort. Tom and I both overshot casts and lined fish. Shenk then had us lengthen 6X tippets to 30 inches. When the crickets didn't work, we switched to Pheasant Tail Nymphs. There were fish showing, apparently feeding, but they weren't accepting our offerings. After an hour or so, we had both refined our casts, but for some reason the trout still wouldn't take. How fortunate to be with an expert, I thought. This is just the kind of experience I was used to on the Letort, and now I could discover how to change my luck.

We hiked up the meadow, taking turns casting to dimpling trout that ignored our flies. Shenk remained patient, telling us that one of these feeding fish was bound to take what we offered. He told us anecdotes about the pools we fished. He showed us where Charles Fox built his spawning beds and where, twenty-five years ago, he himself planted small willow switches that are now big shade trees. He showed us the rosebush near the lie of a legendary trout.

The feeding trout continued to elude us, and soon Shenk's stories couldn't disguise his frustration. He began to swear at the fish and mumble about anglers who walk too close to the water. Just before lunch, we picked out a sandy-colored Letort brown feeding more actively than others. "If this one doesn't take, we'll throw rocks at him!" Shenk hissed. In order, I offered a cricket, a beetle, Al's Rat, Ed's Hopper, a Patriot Emerger (to Shenk's horror), an olive caddis pupa, an inchworm, and a cress bug—Shenk's sure-thing fly. No takers. Tom cast more of the same, adding to the series a #24 black midge that had turned an earlier fish's head. Still no takers. Shenk said the day was not going well.

I suggested we try a smaller tippet—7X or 8X. But Shenk explained that he prefers to avoid these ultralight options, feeling there is a high likelihood of a large Letort trout breaking off. His seine revealed bugs too small to imitate. The fish should prefer our larger offerings, he said, because it takes less energy to get much more food. By this time, Tom and I were casting with sufficient care and delicacy not to put fish down, so we couldn't entirely blame ourselves.

We invited Shenk to try his skills. He fetched his favorite, short, 6-foot Letort rod. His technique is to cast large sculpin to fish hiding in pockets cut in under the streambanks. He puts out very little line and flips 3 feet of leader into the water right next to the streambank. Punched hard, the big imitation gets through the vegetation and plunks down on the water where the fish can hear and see it. Often a big brown comes out to grab the Shenk sculpin, and the fight is on. But not on this day.

None of us landed a fish in eight hours. I missed two, as did Tom. On the drive home, Tom and I figured Shenk would have taken a couple if he'd used his short rod earlier in the day. Nonetheless, I've seldom had a better time not catching fish. Shenk is an excellent teacher with a great sense of humor. I'd missed a nice fish after getting a take on a cricket sent out on a 60-foot drag-free drift. The expletives spewed from my lips. Lack of line control was the problem, we agreed, but knowing the reason didn't make me feel any better. When I apologized for my language, Shenk said, "Oh you're entitled to that and much, much more—anything else you can think of to call him, say it!"

Going upstream from the quarry bridge on the right-hand branch, brown trout can be found as far as the stone arch bridge. Above the bridge, wild brook trout dominate the water. There are not many large brookies, but there are dozens of them up to 8 or 10 inches. This section is very narrow and full of vegetation, and the banks are overgrown with weeds, briers, and trees. A short, 5½- to 7-foot rod is about the longest you can use. Cress bugs, shrimp, and terrestrials are the most effective patterns on this stretch.

I asked Shenk how the Letort of today compares with earlier times. He says that there is no question that the stream has deteriorated. Between development, runoff, and toxic spill from cress farms, he doesn't believe the water will ever again be the pristine stream of the 1950s. Moreover, the angling pressure increases annually.

I had wondered about this, because the trout are so difficult to catch. Shenk believes the stream is so famous that people feel they must come here to fish. Novice anglers don't understand the need to walk *well back* from the water and tread lightly to minimize vibrations through the ground. Shenk likes to be the first on the water, as once the fish are put down, it takes hours for Letort trout to feed on the surface again.

Nine out of ten fish landed on the Letort are hooked on the first cast. These fish spook so easily that you must put a drag-free fly 2 feet in front of them. Birds, primarily herons, are a big threat to Letort fish, as are anglers. Always walk as far from the banks as possible. As you approach the water, stoop or crawl till you spot fish. False casting will put them down instantly, so you have to get line out over land or pull it out by hand. Any way you can, make the first cast count.

Threats to the Letort
The Letort, a beleaguered stream for many years, is now under serious threats from commercial developers. Home Depot and Wal-Mart are planning to build facilities close enough to the water to significantly increase the stormwater runoff, which already greatly impairs the habitat. At this writing the Cumberland Valley chapter of Trout Unlimited and the Letort Regional Authority are leading the effort to preserve and protect this historic fishery. The irony is, these organizations have recently received funding for stream assessment and habitat improvement. One can only hope that the Letort can withstand this latest threat.

Hatches, Flies, and Best Times to Fish
Because it runs cool throughout the year, the Letort can be fished at any time. The Letort has few mayfly hatches, but in April and May blue-winged olives *(Baetis)* emerge. Herb and Cathy Weigel of Cold Spring Anglers like the sulphur hatch, when Letort trout are slightly less wary and will take drys more readily than at other times. I go when I'm up to the challenge; some years, although I live nearby, I don't go at all. Fish very early in the morning and again at dusk, when you are less visible. Winter fishing is the toughest.

In spring or in high-water conditions, large black or white sculpins and Clouser Red Foxee Minnows are highly effective. Tricos in July through September provide the classic Letort experience. Standard spring creek patterns such as scuds, shrimp, and cress bugs are old reliables. Terrestrials—ants, grasshoppers, beetles, inchworms, and jassids—work well from spring to early fall. Small olives and a number of midges are very dependable. The Pheasant Tail is probably the all-around most effective underwater nymph pattern.

Letort Regulations
Catch-and-release, fly-fishing-only regulations apply for 1½ miles, from 300 yards above the bridge on Township Route 481 downstream to the Reading Railroad bridge at the southern edge of Letort Spring Park.

Letort Access
To reach the catch-and-release renowned barnyard and meadow reaches, take Exit 236 on the Pennsylvania Turnpike onto I-81 south. Take I-81 south to Exit 49. Bear right onto Route 641 west, and continue to the second traffic light. Turn left onto Spring Garden Street. From there, you have several options:

- Take Foxcrest Drive off Spring Garden Street (the fifth right turn) to the dead end. Park at the pumping station.
- Park near the I-81 overpass and walk down to the water.
- Continue south on Spring Garden Street until you see a gate on the right and a picnic pavilion at the bottom of a field. This is Vince Marinaro's meadow, complete with a monument.
- Continue on Spring Garden Street several more miles to Bonny Brook Road, turn right, cross the stream, and park at the pulloff next to a wooden bridge or in the parking lot at the next bridge (at the quarry).

Lower Letort
The lower Letort, from the Colonial Peddlers about a mile downstream to where it converges with the Conodoguinet, is the best water for first-timers. You can walk the banks all the way. This section has been stocked with fingerlings for the past fifteen years. The kill that hit the upper section years ago was pretty well diluted by the time it reached the last mile or so of the stream.

If you're good at sneaking up the streambanks, you'll see a lot of fish. You'll see browns from 8 inches to 20 inches. Be prepared to start with 8X tippets and work down to 9X and 10X. Ed Koch, author of *Fishing the Midge* and a Letort legend, uses 10X with great success.

Four roads in Carlisle lead to the stocked sections of the lower Letort. Take Exit 47 off I-81, and turn onto Route 34 north (Hanover Street), heading toward Carlisle. Go north through town, and continue on Hanover Street past the Harvon Motel and the U.S. Army War College. To reach the stream, turn right from Hanover Street (now Route 11) onto any of the following roads: Post Road (just past the War College), Harmony Hall Road, Shady Lane, or South Middlesex Drive. There's good Trico fishing at a bridge just beyond the shops at Colonial Peddlers on Shady Lane.

FALLING SPRING BRANCH

This stream is currently experiencing a hard-earned comeback after many years of deterioration. The Falling Spring Greenway has completed major stream restoration projects and has purchased two meadows through which the stream runs. As a result of habitat improvement, the waters promise to resume their once-legendary status in the annals of wild trout fisheries.

The Falling Spring Greenway is a nonprofit volunteer organization dedicated to the conservation of Falling Spring Branch. In addition to stream habitat improvement, the organization has purchased land along Falling Spring that otherwise would have been developed and placed it in the public domain to be conserved in perpetuity by the Pennsylvania Fish and Boat Commission.

Falling Spring is a wild trout stream that is as challenging during surface-feeding activity as the Letort, although its surroundings are much more pleasing. The water runs through pastures and swampy meadows fed by springs throughout its length. The best approach is to make long downstream casts, especially on very smooth water.

The fish are spooky, but wading is unnecessary, as you can walk the banks along most of the regulated water. Casting is easy, as there are few bushes to hang up your backcast—just keep it high over the streamside grasses. The novice can have a good time here, but because of lack of cover, it is easy to line your target.

Hatches, Flies, and Best Times to Fish

Falling Spring Branch can be fished year-round. I like it on warm days in late winter or early spring when there is snow on the ground. In winter or early in the season, the trout are more forgiving, and the careful beginner can take trout and be proud to have done so. Stealth and accurate casting remain mandatory, however. Woolly Buggers, sculpins, cress bugs, and scud patterns are always effective.

Sulphurs start mid-May and peak around Memorial Day, finishing by July 4. The blue-winged olives emerge in April, and a second-generation hatch appears in October and November. Midday during the summer months, try terrestrials, as well as Pheasant Tail Nymphs, cress bugs, shrimp, and scud patterns. The once famous Tricos are coming back slowly, beginning in mid-July and continuing into the fall.

Falling Spring Regulations
Catch-and-release, fly-fishing-only regulations apply for 2.4 miles, from
T544 downstream to a wire fence crossing the Geisel Funeral Home property near I-81. Delayed harvest regulations apply in town for 1.1 miles
from Walker Road downstream to Fifth Avenue.

Falling Spring Access
Take Falling Spring Road right at Shoney's past the I-81 underpass. There
are five places to park along the stream off Falling Spring Road. To reach
the delayed harvest stretch in downtown Chambersburg, go west on U.S.
Route 30 into town and access by turning right on any street between
Walker Road and Fifth Avenue.

• Quarry Road. Park across the bridge in the lot with farm machinery.
• Edwards Avenue.
• Skelly's meadow. After the elementary school, turn left into a farm,
proceeding very slowly over the cattle grates, and park near the fallen
sycamore tree.
• Greenway meadow. Pass Skelly's Lane, cross the bridge over the
stream, and park in the designated parking area at Spring View Drive
and Falling Spring Road. The upper section of this meadow can also be
accessed off Garman Road, to the left off Falling Spring Road.
• Frey meadow. Access the upper stretch by Briar Lane, to the left off
Falling Spring Road after Spring View Drive. The Briar Lane bridge marks
the end of the special-regulations heritage trout water.

YELLOW BREECHES CREEK
The moderately experienced angler who leaves the Letort or Falling
Spring frustrated can fish the Yellow Breeches Creek and take nice, big
brown trout. Although these fish are not as challenging as the wild trout
on the two limestoners, they are fun to catch. The Yellow Breeches is about
30 to 40 feet wide at the Boiling Springs–Allenberry Resort stretch. It's
very easy to wade, and casting is not a problem—unless you hook a bat,
which I did late one evening during a spinner fall. The Yellow Breeches
muddies quickly after a thunderstorm; however, as it begins to clear, I've
caught big trout on Black Woolly Buggers.

The Yellow Breeches is one of the most popular trout streams in the
Mid-Atlantic region. I've never been able to figure exactly why so many
anglers like to fish here. Perhaps it's the convenience of the Allenberry
Resort, an affordable place to stay and eat located on the creek. Or perhaps it's the accessibility of the water and its proximity to northern Virginia, Baltimore, Washington, and Harrisburg. Whatever the reason,
you'll have plenty of company on the Breeches. I've found most of the
anglers friendly and pleased to let you know what patterns are working
for them—if and when yours are not.

The whitefly hatch that appears on the Yellow Breeches at dusk in mid-August must be seen to be believed. The water is blanketed with duns and then spinners, and there seem to be as many anglers as flies. This hatch is an excuse for partying with local and visiting anglers. Don't go to the Breeches for the whitefly hatch unless you like even more company than usual on the stream.

Hatches, Flies, and Best Times to Fish
The Yellow Breeches can be fished twelve months of the year. During the winter, large streamers (Woolly Buggers, Matukas, and so on) will work. Little black stoneflies appear in March, and caddis emerge by April. March browns and Quill Gordons emerge in early May, and there is an excellent sulphur hatch later in the month.

Tricos and terrestrials can be counted on throughout the summer. The famous whitefly appears in mid-August. Blue-winged olives hatch in the fall, and Tricos continue until the first heavy frost. Slate drakes and caddisflies will also produce fish.

Yellow Breeches Regulations
Catch-and-release, artificial lures or flies only are permitted from the outflow of Boiling Springs Lake downstream through the Allenberry Resort property.

Yellow Breeches Access
 • To reach Boiling Springs, take I-81 north to Exit 48; turn right onto Route 74 south and follow for about 4 miles to Route 174 west; take 174 west a few miles to Bucher Hill Road at Boiling Springs village, about half a mile beyond Allenberry. Just past Highland House B&B, turn left into the parking lot next to the stream.
 • Go into the Allenberry Resort just east of Boiling Springs, and follow the signs for the Fisherman's Parking Lot.

ALSO WORTH NOTING
There are three other streams closer to Philadelphia whose water quality is not as fine, but it's worth wetting a line there if you don't have time to go farther afield. A good source of up-to-date information on these three streams is the Sporting Gentleman shop in Media (see below).

French Creek
Located in western Chester County near Phoenixville, French Creek is a modest freestone stream that meanders through farms and horse country. The stream is well stocked, often fished, and very pretty.

Ridley Creek
Ridley is the closest trout water to Philadelphia. It's a 20- to 30-foot-wide stream in Ridley Creek State Park off Baltimore Pike (Route 1) just west of Media. This is pleasant water, a nice place for an afternoon's fishing, but you won't be alone.

Valley Creek
Valley Creek is a limestone spring creek near Valley Forge filled with challenging, PCB-ridden trout. The best fishing is upstream from the iron bridge to the Pennsylvania Turnpike overpass.

IF YOU GO
From Philadelphia to the Letort or the Yellow Breeches, take the Pennsylvania Turnpike west to Carlisle. It is about 140 miles from Philadelphia to Carlisle.

From Philadelphia to Falling Spring Run, take the Pennsylvania Turnpike (I-76) west to Carlisle, then take I-81 to Chambersburg (40 more miles). Refer to map in this chapter for access points.

Tackle Shops and Guides
In or Near Philadelphia

Chip's Bait and Tackle. West Chester. (610) 696-FISH.

Eyler's Fly 'n Tackle. Bryn Mawr. (610) 527-3388.

The Sporting Gentleman. Media. Barry Staats, proprietor. (610) 565-6140. www.sportinggentleman.com.

Local Shops

Cold Spring Anglers. Carlisle. Complete fly shop and guide service. (717) 245-2646. www.coldspringanglers.com.

Thomas E. Baltz. Boiling Springs. Guide. Baltz knows the area well. Also guides for bass on the Susquehanna and Juniata. (717) 486-7438.

Ed Koch. Boiling Springs. Master guide. Contact through Yellow Breeches Outfitters. (717) 258-6752.

Ed Shenk. Carlisle. Master guide. (717) 243-2679. Or contact through Yellow Breeches Outfitters. (717) 258-6752.

Yellow Breeches Outfitters. Boiling Springs. Complete tackle shop. (717) 258-6752. www.yellowbreeches.com.

Where to Stay
Allenberry Resort on the Yellow Breeches. Route 174 at Boiling Springs. Monday through Thursday, show a Trout Unlimited membership card for special rates. Moderate. (717) 258-3211. www.yellowbreeches.com

Pheasant Field B&B. Carlisle. Expensive. (717) 258-0717. www.pheasantfield.com

Ragged Edge B&B. Near Falling Spring. Moderate. (717) 261-1195.

Falling Spring Inn B&B. Chambersburg. Limestone farmhouse 200 feet from the stream. Moderate. (717) 767-3654.

Chain Motels. Nearly every major motel chain has a facility at the intersection of I-81 and the Pennsylvania Turnpike (I-76) in Carlisle. There are also many chain motels at the Chambersburg exit off I-81.

Where to Eat

In addition to those listed here, there are other standard eateries in Chambersburg, and fast-food establishments abound in Carlisle.

Allenberry Resort. Boiling Springs. Large dining room and cozy, casual bar. Moderate. (717) 258-3211.

Boiling Springs Tavern. Boiling Springs. Fine chef, excellent food. Moderate to expensive. (717) 258-3614.

RESOURCES

Chambersburg Chamber of Commerce. (717) 264-7101.

Armstrong, A. Joseph. *Guide to Pennsylvania Limestone Streams.* Mechanicsburg, PA: Stackpole Books, 1992.

Koch, Ed. *Fishing the Midge.* 2nd ed. Harrisburg, PA: Stackpole Books, 1988.

Landis, Dwight. *Trout Streams of Pennsylvania.* Bellefonte, PA: Hempstead-Lyndell, 1991.

Marinaro, Vincent. *In the Ring of the Rise.* New York: Lyons & Burford, 1976. (Out of print.)

McIntosh, Ann. *Mid-Atlantic Budget Angler.* Mechanicsburg, PA: Stackpole Books, 1998.

Meck, Charles. *Trout Streams and Hatches of Pennsylvania.* Woodstock, VT: Countryman Press, 1999.

Pennsylvania Atlas & Gazetteer. Yarmouth, ME: Delorme Mapping Company. (207) 846-7000.

Ross, John. *Trout Unlimited's Guide to America's 100 Best Trout Streams.* Helena, MT: Falcon Publishing, 1999.

Shenk, Ed. *Fly Rod Trouting.* Harrisburg, PA: Stackpole Books, 1989.

Wolf, Dave. *Flyfisher's Guide to Pennsylvania.* Belgrade, MT: Wilderness Adventures Press, 1999.

CHAPTER SIX

PITTSBURGH

LITTLE JUNIATA, FRANKSTOWN BRANCH, AND SPRUCE CREEK

Ann McIntosh

Only two and a half hours from Pittsburgh and less than four hours from Philadelphia, Washington, and Baltimore, the Little Juniata River and its Frankstown Branch, as well as Spruce Creek, hold some of the finest trout water in the Mid-Atlantic region. There are many other trout streams closer to Pittsburgh, but few if any have the quality water found in the upper Juniata watershed. The "Little J," the Frankstown Branch, and Spruce Creek flow through alkaline aquifers; springs and limestone tributaries contribute to the quality of the rivers throughout their flow, from their headwaters to their confluence near Petersburg. Insect and young-of-the-year trout recruitment on both rivers has been excellent for the last several years.

I've left Baltimore after work on many a balmy Friday in June and been on the Little J in Spruce Creek village in time to cast sulphurs until dark. That's only the beginning of sweeter angling. The next morning, over breakfast at a B&B or coffee at Spruce Creek Outfitters (the fly shop at the bridge), I receive knowledgeable, honest answers to my questions about hatches and effective flies for streams in the area. A weekend fishing these two rivers, with side trips to streams near State College—Spring Creek, Little Bald Eagle Creek, and Penns Creek—can provide one of the most satisfying excursions for wild trout in the East.

LITTLE JUNIATA
Flowing through sparsely populated farms and woods, this is a pretty river, one where there is always a hawk, heron, or muskrat to occupy an angler's attention. One of the nice things about the Little Juniata is that it

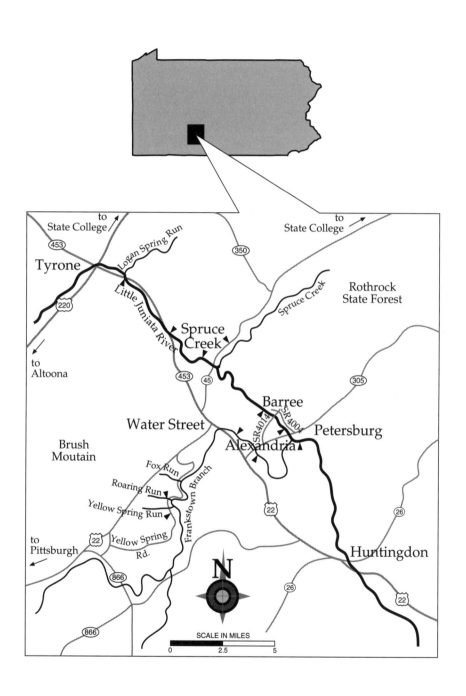

is easy to wade and wide enough (60 to 80 feet) to accommodate errant backcasts. That said, in spring the water runs high and strong, and anglers should proceed with caution. Carefully wade out a few yards and cast back to the bank, upstream and down. Dangle soft-hackled flies subsurface; twitch streamer patterns (Muddlers, Picket Pins, Woolly Buggers) in the fast water.

After spring runoff, the river subsides to a healthy flow that is seldom more than waist-high—except through the gorge section above Barree, where the water is more than 12 feet deep in some pools. I've never found the footing treacherous, but as a caution, I wear felt-soled boots and carry a wading staff.

There are lots of productive riffles, fast cuts and runs, and long, deep green pools that slice through ledge rock. One of the best ways to fish the Little J, especially above the Spruce Creek bridge and in the cornfield section above Alexandria, is to wade to the middle of the river and cast to back eddies and pools near both banks.

Little Juniata Watershed Reclamation

The story was not always so sunny. During the 1940s and 1950s, when housekeeping around industrial plants was minimal, the Little J was polluted by poorly treated sewage, railroad shops, and a paper mill. In the 1970s new regulations resulted in mitigation, and pollution was on the wane.

By 1980 water quality was deemed suitable for trout, and fingerlings were stocked in the Little Juniata from Tyrone to Petersburg. Population tallies by fisheries managers soon showed that brown trout grew very quickly in the river, reaching 5 and 6 pounds within a few years.

The river underwent a brief downturn in 1996, when an unidentified toxic agent washed into the water during one of the nasty floods of that winter. Many insect species prevailed, but mayflies declined during the first half of the year. Members of the Blair County chapter of Trout Unlimited conducted an insect-monitoring program, collecting data and demonstrating the bug recovery as it occurred. By fall trout were again feeding on mayflies.

Some anglers and conservationists feel that the Pennsylvania Boat and Fish Commission (PB&FC) should now stop stocking and let instream reproduction govern the trout population, managing the fishery according to catch-and-release regulations. There has been resistance. The commission believes that a number of anglers will use the resource only if they can keep fish. While this may not be a serious drain on the fish population, letting the wild trout dominate would seem to be the logical way to manage.

Despite my preference to fish for wild trout, I concede that the Little J holdovers that have succumbed to my flies have been deeply colored and very strong. They behaved as logically and wily as streamborns; I think Little J trout must wise up as fast as they grow.

Hatches, Flies, and Best Times to Fish
The alkaline water is rich with food: midges, caddis, mayflies, and aquatic creatures such as dace, sculpin, and crayfish. The following emergence schedule was provided by Spruce Creek Outfitters. With minor adjustments, it can be used for all streams in central Pennsylvania.

March. Black midge, gray midge, little black stonefly.

April–May. Blue Quill, blue dun, blue-winged olive, Hendrickson, Red Quill, Grannom caddis, black caddis, green caddis.

May–June. March brown, Gray Fox, sulphur, green drake, slate drake, blue-winged olive, Ginger Quill, light cahill, green caddis, yellow cranefly.

June–July. Yellow drake, slate drake, blue-winged olive, blue dun, sulphur, cream cahill, tan and cream caddis.

July–August. Trico, little white mayfly, blue dun, slate drake, cream caddis.

August–September. Trico, little white mayfly, whitefly *(Ephoron leukon)*, slate drake, winged ant, gray caddis.

September–October. Slate drake, blue-winged olive, blue dun, bronze cranefly, tan caddis.

Terrestrial patterns are effective from late May through October.

Little Juniata Regulations
All-tackle, trophy trout regulations: Between opening day (mid-April) and Labor Day, two trout 14 inches or longer may be kept. No-kill regulations prevail the rest of the year.

Little Juniata Access
The Little J is accessible from Tyrone downstream to Petersburg. South of Tyrone, Route 453 follows the river for 6 miles. There are several parking pulloffs along this route. You can also access the river from the county road that runs along the east side of the river, upstream of Spruce Creek Outfitters fly shop.

To reach the gorge stretch near Barree, take SR 4014 off U.S. Route 22 toward Alexandria. In Alexandria, make a left on SR 4004, following signs to Barree. Make a sharp left past the railroad tracks in Barree, and park at the dead end. Hike up the trail along the river at least half a mile before dropping down to fish.

To fish the water between the gorge and the mouth of the Frankstown Branch, take SR 4014 through Alexandria, then take Route 305 out of Alexandria toward Petersburg. Just before Route 305 crosses the river, turn left on a small road along the water. Pull off and park near the trestle bridge, about a mile upstream. Walk under the trestle and along the field (often planted in corn). Fishing is good from the trestle upstream as far as you can see.

There is also parking, easy access, and good fishing at the junction pool below the Route 305 bridge.

FRANKSTOWN BRANCH OF THE JUNIATA

Harry Redline, a noted conservationist, outdoor writer, and retired PB&FC waterways conservation officer, asked me to fish the Frankstown Branch several years ago. For an out-of-stater, I thought I knew the central Pennsylvania streams around Spruce Creek village pretty well. But I'd never heard the Frankstown Branch mentioned until Redline extended his invitation. It must be (or have been) the last well-kept secret in central Pennsylvania. I divulge it here only because the Frankstown is a major expanse of water with 11½ miles of public access. It can withstand considerable pressure and has much to offer the itinerant angler. Moreover, it needs help from organizations such as Trout Unlimited chapters and other conservation groups. In the words of savvy conservationists, "A river can't have too many friends! Friends develop a stake in the resource and are there to help save it when disaster threatens."

I was impressed when Redline told me that a late-1990s trout survey showed a number of 15-inch browns. "And we didn't even net any of the big boys!" he said. On average, the trout in the Frankstown Branch are larger than those in the Little Juniata, with the average fish 14 to 15 inches long and an 18-inch fish not unusual. I've found they are also very strong. The browns I've hooked were muscular and took line as effortlessly as my better fish on the Delaware.

The Frankstown Branch is a bit wider than the Little Juniata, with a similar gradient. It is about 125 feet across at its widest point, and there are long, flat, shallow stretches that do not hold trout—especially during the summer. Small stones and boulders make up the bottom, and riffles and deep pools interrupt long runs.

The only time it is difficult to wade is early in the season. When the water is high, it has considerable velocity and you must watch out for unexpected holes. A hint: *Never* set toe into this river without looking before you step. Many trout hold in the very shallow water near the bank. Redline and I spooked a number the first time we went—fish big enough to make me approach cautiously thereafter.

According to Redline, I have yet to experience the Frankstown Branch at its best. He has fished the river all his life. Growing up near Fox Run, one of the limestone tributaries of the Frankstown Branch, he remembers many twenty-five-brookie days. During the 1991 season he landed more than a hundred wild browns. In the late 1990s, during the sulphur hatch, he recorded twenty-three fish over 12 inches in a single evening without moving more than 20 feet!

The longest fish recorded from the Frankstown Branch was 28 inches—about 10 pounds. The record does not surprise Redline, who has seen many 6- to 10-pound fish hanging over redds in the fall.

All the trout in the Frankstown Branch are wild. The only stocking takes place 20 miles upstream, between Claysburg and East Freedom, near the headwaters.

The river's alkaline water is as favorable to trout as the water in the Little J. However, there is much less cover, and the water temperatures rise faster and higher in summer. During the hot weeks, the trout bunch up near the mouths of tributaries. In a drought, it's best not to target them, and *never* fish if the water temperature exceeds 68 degrees F.

Redline would like to see a conservation group undertake a project to improve the amount of shade on the river. Now that environmental policies have negated industrial pollution, he is eager for the river to achieve its full potential. He envisions willow posts planted along the banks to give the fish summer cover, as well as structural improvements in the water to create protected lies in the flat, shallow stretches.

Hatches, Flies, and Best Times to Fish

The hatches are similar to those on the Little Juniata. Flies that represent extraordinary hatches on this water include Grannom Caddis in early April, then Hendricksons; March Browns and other caddis through May; sulphurs, Light Cahills, Yellow and Brown Drakes in late spring; and Blue-Winged Olives in the fall.

Frankstown Branch Regulations

Regular put-and-take regulations prevail. From opening day until the end of trout season, eight fish per day, 7 or more inches long may be kept. The limit during the rest of the year is three fish per angler, per day.

The quality of the Frankstown Branch fishery indicates that it deserves far more restricted regulations. Perhaps if local conservation groups get involved in habitat improvement, catch-and-release or trophy trout provisions will be instituted.

Frankstown Branch Access

Take U.S. Route 22 west from Water Street, and make a left at the first road you see. Take this road down to the bridge at the mouth of Fox Run.

There is also access via Polecat Hollow Road, which runs along Roaring Run, and Yellow Spring Road, which follows Yellow Spring Run to the river.

SPRUCE CREEK

Much of the water on Spruce Creek is private, including the stretch through Wayne Harpster's dairy farm, where former president Jimmy

Carter likes to fish. Except for the Colerain Club water, the private stretches are stocked with large brown and rainbow trout. Allan Bright of Spruce Creek Outfitters has exclusive rights to a section of private water on Spruce Creek owned by the Colerain Club. These reaches hold impressive numbers of big wild trout. This is the finest piece of private wild trout water I've fished in the East. It can be reserved during the week for a reasonable fee.

The public stretch of wild trout water maintained by Penn State University is less than a mile from Spruce Creek village. Take Route 45 west, and look for the memorial sign to George Harvey on the right. Don't be deceived by the small size of this stream; there are some fine, well-educated 14-inch browns lurking here. I have a particular affinity for fishing the Observation Pool, where fish biologist Robert Bachman conducted his celebrated study of the behavior of brown trout. I find the public water a good alternative to the Little J. In fact, often when the river isn't fishing well, the creek is, and vice versa.

ALSO WORTH NOTING
Little Bald Eagle Creek
The mouth of this tributary of the Little J is near Tyrone. This stocked stream provides excellent angling and is an alternative to Spruce Creek and the Juniata River.

Penns Creek
This is the most famous water in central Pennsylvania. Its renown comes, at least in part, from its stupendous green drake hatch. It's worth the trip if only to see and listen to the bevy of anglers that gather annually in early June. Penns warms quickly; don't count on fishing it much beyond the end of June.

Spring Creek
This acclaimed limestoner runs through Bellefonte, Pennsylvania. Recent purchases of private property along the stream by the PB&FC have greatly enhanced its habitat. It's one of my favorite Pennsylvania streams; I only wish it weren't quite so popular.

Fishing Creek
About an hour and a half from Spruce Creek, and forty-five minutes from State College, this hemlock-lined limestone water is as pretty as any in the East. The fish are wild and wily and fight to the end, often running downstream over the splash dams separating pools. Unfortunately, the stream has become so popular that access to it across private property has become a problem. However, there are a few public access points, and if you ask, some cabin owners will let you cross their property.

Neshannock Creek

Heading north from Pittsburgh, a traveling angler can find good fish. Neshannock Creek is an hour and twenty minutes from the city. This freestone stream is popular with local anglers. For more information, contact Bob Shewey at the Outdoor Shop, (413) 533-3212.

Oil Creek

Oil Creek deserves to be called a river. It is one of the biggest, most beautiful rivers in Pennsylvania, with 33 miles of stocked, easily wadable water ranging from 60 to 100 feet wide. Many trout are holdovers, and this river is scenic, challenging, and provides ample casting room. Contact Mike Laskowski at Oil Creek Outfitters, (814) 677-4684.

IF YOU GO

From Pittsburgh, take U.S. Route 22 east to the town of Water Street, and turn left on Route 453/45. Make a right on Route 45 where it leaves Route 453, and follow it down a steep incline to the village of Spruce Creek. Spruce Creek has a fine fly shop and several excellent B&Bs and is about two and a half hours from Pittsburgh.

Tackle Shops and Guides
In Pittsburgh

International Angler. Pittsburgh. Tom Ference, proprietor. (412) 782-2222.

South Hills Rod & Reel. Pittsburgh. (412) 344-8888.

Local Shops

Feathered Hook. Coburn. Jonas Price, owner. (814) 349-8757. E-mail: feathrhk@vicon.net.

Spruce Creek Outfitters. Spruce Creek. Allan Bright, owner. Wonderful selection of locally effective patterns. Controls access to the private water of the Colerain Club—magnificent private water with large fish. It can be leased by the day through Spruce Creek Outfitters. (814) 632-3071.

Six Springs Fly Shop. Spruce Creek. An Orvis shop. (814) 632-3393.

Fly Fisherman's Paradise. State College. (814) 234-4189.

Trout & About. Arlington, Virginia. Phil Gay, guide and outfitter. (703) 536-7494.

Where to Stay

Cedar Hill Farms B&B. Spruce Creek. Moderate to expensive. (814) 632-8319.

Hearthwood House. Alexandria. Inexpensive. (814) 669-4386.

John Carper's Bed & Beer. Spruce Creek. Next to the Spruce Creek Tavern. Inexpensive. (814) 632-3287.

River's Edge Lodge. Spruce Creek. John and Marie Little, proprietors. This is a very special farmhouse located on the banks of the Little J about a quarter mile upstream from the bridge at Spruce Creek. Three bedrooms, one bath, extensive living and dining spaces. Breakfast included. Inexpensive. (814) 696-0530.

Spruce Creek B&B. Spruce Creek. Dean Nelson, proprietor. Moderate to expensive. (814) 632-3777.

Camping

Green Hills Campground. On the Little J below Barree. (814) 669-4212.

Jenny Springs Cabin. Sleeps eight. On the Little J at the gorge. (814) 627-5311.

Where to Eat

Old Oak Tavern. Pine Grove Mills. Lots of oak furniture and good food. Inexpensive. (814) 238-5898.

Sports Bar. Alexandria. TVs, college kids, and good eats. No reservations. Inexpensive.

Spruce Creek Tavern. Spruce Creek. Local bar with sandwiches, burgers, and cafeteria-size trays loaded with french fries. Inexpensive.

RESOURCES

Harry Redline would be pleased to give up-to-date angling information to any Trout Unlimited member planning a visit to the area. He can be reached through Spruce Creek Outfitters. (814) 632-3071.

Landis, Dwight. *Trout Streams of Pennsylvania.* Bellefonte, PA: Hempstead-Lyndell, 1991.

McIntosh, Ann. *Mid-Atlantic Budget Angler.* Mechanicsburg, PA: Stackpole Books, 1998.

Meck, Charles. *Trout Streams and Hatches of Pennsylvania.* Woodstock, VT: Countryman Press,1999.

Ross, John. *Trout Unlimited's Guide to America's 100 Best Trout Streams.* Helena, MT: Falcon Publishing, 1999.

Wolf, Dave. *Flyfisher's Guide to Pennsylvania.* Belgrade, MT: Wilderness Adventures Press, 1999.

Pennsylvania Atlas & Gazetteer. Yarmouth, ME: Delorme Mapping Company. (207) 846-7000.

CHAPTER SEVEN

BALTIMORE

BIG GUNPOWDER FALLS

Ann McIntosh

The Big Gunpowder Falls is one of the finest wild trout tailwaters in the East. It is very challenging and exceptionally scenic, bordered by hemlocks and hardwoods, lilies, wildflowers, and ferns. I am very lucky to live closeby.

The river originates as a small freestone stream above Prettyboy Reservoir; the tailwater begins at the plunge pool below the dam. The water runs through a deep, boulder-strewn canyon before settling into a series of long runs, riffles, and pools, the turn of each bend revealing a vista lovelier than the last. If you care as much about your surroundings as the number of fish you catch, the Gunpowder will delight you. There are plenty of trout, but they can play very hard to get.

From an angler's point of view, the Gunpowder is a different fishery from the new one widely heralded in the early 1990s. While the number of trout per mile has increased, the average fish caught these days is 7 to 11 inches, smaller than the former 12- to 14-inch average length. When the wild fishery was first developed, I caught a lot of fish over 15 inches, but many of these fish had been stocked as fingerlings by the state and by the Maryland chapter of Trout Unlimited (MDTU) in the course of seeding the wild trout fishery.

Now that the fish are all streambred, you may have to be the first angler to put a fly over a fish to take a trout over 14 inches. Wally Vait, an experienced Gunpowder guide, stresses the need for long, knotted leaders and tippets from 12 to 20 inches overall to fool a large fish. Keeping your profile low and crouching to cast can also improve your chances.

Vait explains that with the increased numbers of fish, anglers average a larger percentage of the smaller, more aggressive trout, which lie in the more accessible spots. The big fish dominate hard-to-reach places in streambank eddies and logjams. Over the past decade, the trout have

71

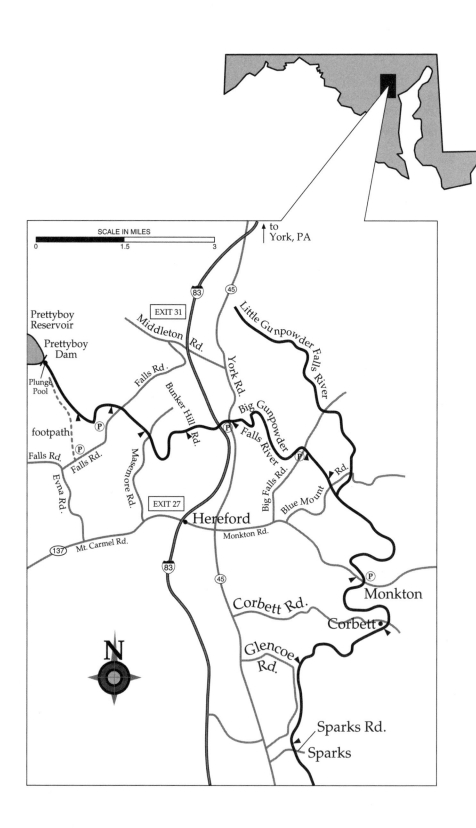

SCALE IN MILES
0   1.5   3

to
York, PA

Prettyboy
Reservoir

Prettyboy
Dam

Plunge
Pool

footpath

Falls Rd.

Evna Rd.

EXIT 31

Middleton Rd.

Falls Rd.

Bunker Hill Rd.

Masemore Rd.

York Rd.

Big Gunpowder Falls River

Little Gunpowder Falls River

Big Falls Rd.

Blue Mount

Rd.

EXIT 27

Hereford

Monkton Rd.

137   Mt. Carmel Rd.

83

45

Corbett Rd.

Glencoe
Rd.

Monkton

Corbett

Sparks Rd.

Sparks

N

grown savvy, learning quickly to be wary of the many anglers who stalk the water.

Robert Lunsford, director of freshwater fisheries for the state, puts forth the plausible theory that most of the fish over 12 inches have become nocturnal feeders, feeding after 10 P.M., when the park through which the river flows closes. "In the electroshocking surveys, we see a lot of fish over 12 inches with multiple hooking injuries. There are still plenty of big fish, but I think they learn pretty quickly it's only safe to eat at night."

Trout have not been stocked in the first 8 miles below Prettyboy Dam since 1990, and stocking ceased on the adjacent two downstream miles in 1998. Brown trout constitute 96 percent of the population; rainbows and brookies account for the rest. There are days when the most experienced anglers would conclude there are no trout at all in the river, and other times, such as at the peak of the sulphur hatch or during prolific caddis emergences, when the surface activity is startling.

The success of the fishery is the result of a statewide policy to make the protection and restoration of wild trout streams a priority. An agreement was drafted by James W. Gracie, then president of MDTU (and a former president of national Trout Unlimited); Trout Unlimited's Mid-Atlantic Council; and the Maryland Department of Natural Resources. The policy states that streams that can support a self-sustaining population of wild trout will no longer be stocked. Thus, in Maryland, there is no stocking of hatchery-bred fish over wild, streambred fish.

This policy was substantiated by Dr. Robert A. Bachman's study on Spruce Creek, Pennsylvania, which demonstrated that introducing hatchery-raised trout into a population of wild trout interferes with the feeding patterns of the latter. Bachman, who became Maryland's director of freshwater fisheries, ensured the policy was enforced. From 1986 until his 1999 retirement, he made Maryland a national model for wild trout management.

Shortly after the state policy was put in place, the city of Baltimore, which draws much of its water from Prettyboy Reservoir, agreed to a minimum release from the bottom of the reservoir of the cold water the trout need. The average year-round temperature is 52 degrees F, but the water may range from 50 to 60 degrees F, depending on air temperature, how much water is being released, and whether most of it comes from the top or the bottom of the impoundment.

At this writing, there are plans to conduct an instream flow survey that will reveal whether the current minimum flow rate from Prettyboy Dam is sufficient to protect trout in periods of low flow (current minimum flow is 11 cubic feet per second).

The river averages a width of 30 to 50 feet throughout the 17 miles from Prettyboy Dam to Loch Raven. Wading is relatively easy, although felt soles are advised. Designated access points provide easy entry.

I use an 8½-foot 5/6-weight whenever I am not using my Lyndi Cattenach 7-foot, 6-inch bamboo rod. Many anglers gear up lighter, using 4-, 3-, or even 2-weight rods, usually no shorter than 7½ feet.

HATCHES, FLIES, AND BEST TIMES TO FISH

This tailwater is a year-round fishery. Activity slows from November until the little black stoneflies appear in February, but good anglers can always fool a fish or two on the Gunpowder any day weather permits.

If there ever was a river to please the seasoned angler who doesn't care about whether he or she catches fish, the Gunpowder is ideal. Its water quality and scenery are hard to beat in the East, and you can be sure there are lots of trout and you'll have a shot at some very big ones.

The river seldom fishes well before 9 A.M., as the water is coldest in the early morning. The only reason to get on the water early is to be the first angler through it. With the exception of evening hatch times, such as the sulphur spinner fall, I've had my best luck between 10 A.M. and 5 P.M.

If you want to fish the Gunpowder and not see another angler, you'd best go during a blizzard, a tornado, or during the week, when—on a hit-or-miss basis—you may find yourself alone. The river is less than an hour's drive from Baltimore and a little over an hour from Washington, with Harrisburg, Wilmington, and Philadelphia not far distant. It's a wonder there's not *more* pressure!

The pressure is a mixed blessing. Were the fish not so well educated, the number of anglers would increase to intolerable numbers. With the situation as it is, many fishermen get discouraged and don't return. Dawn Stevens, cofounder of the Delaware Valley Women's Fly Fishing Association, drives from Wilmington to fish the river from late March through fall, regardless of angling pressure. And sometimes the pressure seems not to bother the fish. During the first good day of the sulphur hatch two years ago, I had difficulty finding a parking spot at the catch-and-release access points. So I fished between Corbett and Monkton and saw only one other angler—but caught very few fish. Meanwhile, Stevens put on a green caddis emerger and had a thirty-fish day at one of the river's most popular beats!

Gunpowder regulars are beginning to frequent the water outside the catch-and-release area, fishing between Bluemount Road and Sparks. Phil Gay, who guides on the river, often fishes between Glencoe and Corbett. His clients catch as many fish in that area as in other spots and seldom encounter another angler. Gay reports lots of wild fish and holdovers, and the scenery is every bit as pretty as it is on the upper reaches. The fish are more spread out, but their numbers are increasing annually. One remarkable day in February 1999, Gay netted sixty trout on a little green caddis pupa.

If you fish below Monkton during the summer, Gay warns about the numerous canoers and tubers in the water. Parking is difficult at Corbett and Glencoe but ample at Monkton and Sparks. To help out the landowners, carry a small bag and pick up trash if you park along the road outside designated parking areas.

Only seriously threatening winter weather makes angling impossible on the Gunpowder. Try to fish during the off-season and during the lesser hatches. September can be superb. You'll avoid the people and be rewarded. The fish are there, and with fewer people targeting them, your chances of fooling a good one improve.

The Gunpowder has nearly every major eastern mayfly hatch. However, high spring water often washes out the early emergences. Several seasons ago, when the water was low, there were extraordinary hatches of little black stoneflies and Hendricksons. But this good fortune was the result of a mild winter and can't be counted on.

There are many, many caddisflies. When and where they appear and what size they may be are somewhat unpredictable. However, caddis nymphs and emergers are always worth trying subsurface.

The river is generally too low and too cold for good streamer fishing. However, according to Stacey Smith, an experienced Gunpowder guide, there is good streamer fishing when the water is up and a little off-color. Another reliable period is when trout fry show up in the spring. A small (#8–#10) Clouser or other streamer pattern can be deadly.

Smith advocates using small Clousers such as the Foxee Minnow and chartreuse-and-white patterns during periods of high water. Other effective patterns include Mickey Finns (#8–#12), Black-Nose Dace (Picket Pin #10–#12), and that old Gunpowder standby the Woolly Bugger (as large as #4). Sculpins of the same size are also effective, especially near logjams. The following lists some of the major hatches and best patterns.

January–March. Little black or brown stoneflies (#12–#18), midges, blue-winged olives, little black stonefly (#20).

March. Black stonefly, Black Quill (#10–#12), Quill Gordon, tan caddis (#16–#18).

April. Hendricksons, olive caddis, brown and black stoneflies.

May. March brown, Gray Fox, sulphurs (#14–#20), blue-winged olives, tan or olive caddis.

June. Sulphurs continue, getting smaller (#18–#20), light cahills begin, slate drakes *(Isonychia)* begin.

July–early September. Sulphurs (#20–#22), light cahills, blue-winged olives, yellow sallies, terrestrials, especially beetles, hoppers, crickets, and Tricos. (Ask at Backwater Angler for the best Trico spots.)

September–October. Tan and dusty olive caddis, blue-winged olives, terrestrials, including ants (red and black #12–#20).

November–December. Midges (#16–#24), blue-winged olives, little blackfly.

Some year-round favorites include Olive or Black Woolly Buggers, off-white San Juan Worms, Green Weenies, Pheasant Tail Nymphs, Patriots, Trudes, and small Clousers. The Gunpowder has its share of conscientious spin fishermen. Most use small Panther Martins and spoons.

GUNPOWDER REGULATIONS

From the outflow of Prettyboy Dam to Bluemount Road, catch-and-release regulations apply. From Bluemount Road to Corbett Road, two fish per day may be kept. In the stocked water below Corbett, the creel limit is five fish per day.

IF YOU GO

From Baltimore, take I-83 out of the city to I-695 (the Baltimore Beltway), bear right (east) to I-83 north. Take Exit 27, Mount Carmel Road. The Gunpowder is one and a half hours from downtown Washington and forty-five minutes from Baltimore.

From Washington, take the Beltway (I-495) to I-95 north. From I-95, take I-695 (the Baltimore Beltway) west (toward Towson) to I-83 north. Take Exit 27, Mount Carmel Road.

To access the river at Masemore Road or Falls Road, take a left at the Mount Carmel exit.

To reach Backwater Angler, the destination fly shop, take a right at the exit, turn right onto York Road (Route 45), then left on Monkton Road (Route 138). (The shop is half a mile in from Route 45 on Monkton Road.)

To access the river at Bunker Hill Road or York Road, take a right at the exit and turn left (north) on York Road. You will come to Bunker Hill Road on the left; York Road continues straight ahead.

Tackle Shops and Guides

Fisherman's Edge. Catonsville. Joe Bruce, proprietor. Off I-95 between Washington and Baltimore. Complete tackle shop. (410) 719-7999 or (800) 338-0053.

Great Feathers. Sparks. Michael Watriss, proprietor. An Orvis dealer on York Road, 5 miles south of Hereford Road. (410) 472-6799. www.great feathers.com

Backwater Angler. Monkton, Maryland. Theaux LeGardeur and Sarah Hoffman, proprietors. This shop, formerly On the Fly, is on Monkton Road .25 mile east of York Road. Tackle, clothing, and guide service—*the* destination shop for the Gunpowder. (410) 329-6821. www.backwater anglers.com. E-mail: bckwtrfly@aol.com.

Maryland Fishing Guides Cooperative. Monkton. Several of Baltimore's best anglers have formed a cooperative guide business. I know most of them and can vouch for their abilities. (410) 472-1099.

Stacey Smith. Baltimore. Full-time guide with years of experience on the Gunpowder. (410) 668-0912.

Tochterman's. Baltimore. (888) 327-7744.

Trout & About. Arlington, Virginia. Phil Gay, guide and outfitter. (703) 536-7494.

Throughout the Stream. Nick Yowell, master guide and fine fly tier. (410) 499-2443.

Where to Stay

Gunpowder B&B. Ann McIntosh, proprietor. Restored farmhouse near Monkton. Twenty minutes from the Gunpowder. Moderate. (410) 557-7594.

Hampton Inn. Cockeysville/Hunt Valley. Off I-83 about 10 miles south of Monkton. Moderate. (410) 527-1500.

Hill House Manor B&B. Parkton. Near Exit 31 off I-83. Moderate. (410) 357-8179.

Marriott Hunt Valley. Hunt Valley. A typical Marriott. Expensive. (410) 785-8000.

Wiley Mill Inn B&B. Monkton. Just north of Hereford Road. Nice farmhouse convenient to the river. Moderate. (410) 329-6310.

Camping

Morris Meadows. Near Freeland. Private campground. (There is no public campground near the Gunpowder.) (410) 329-6636 or (410) 357-4088.

Where to Eat

Manor Tavern. Near Monkton. About 5 miles east of the river. Very popular. Reservations advised on weekends. Moderate. (410) 771-4366.

Milton Inn. Sparks. Five miles south of Hereford. Very cozy four-star restaurant in an old limestone farmhouse. Reservations advised. Expensive. (410) 771-4366.

Pioneer Pub. North of Hereford. On York Road. Part biker bar, part local bistro. Inexpensive to moderate. (410) 357-4231.

Wagon Wheel. Hereford. Just north of Mount Carmel Road on York Road. Good place for breakfast or lunch. No reservations. Inexpensive.

RESOURCES

Feeser, Tim, and Patapsco Chapter of Trout Unlimited. *The Trout Fishing Guide to Maryland and South Central Pennsylvania.* Manchester, MD. To order, send $10 check made out to Patapsco Chapter of Trout Unlmited, c/o Tim Feeser, 3407 View Ridge Circle, Manchester, MD 21102.

Gelso, Charlie, and Larry Coburn. *A Guide to Maryland Trout Fishing.* Woodbine, MD: K&D Limited, 2000.

Maryland Atlas & Gazetteer. Yarmouth, ME: DeLorme Mapping Company. (207) 846-7000.

McIntosh, Ann. *Mid-Atlantic Budget Angler.* Mechanicsburg, PA: Stackpole Books, 1998.

Ross, John. *Trout Unlimited's Guide to America's 100 Best Trout Streams.* Helena, MT: Falcon Publishing, 1999.

CHAPTER EIGHT

WASHINGTON, D.C.

Ann McIntosh

Western Maryland, one of the state's primary recreational areas, is within a three-hour drive of Washington, D.C. In addition to angling opportunities, the area offers boating on Deep Creek Lake, canoeing and rafting on the Savage and Youghiogheny Rivers, and skiing at the Wisp resort near Oakland.

There are more than 320 miles of water in Garrett and Allegheny Counties, the state's two westernmost counties. The region offers an incredible variety of water, from small mountain brooks to big rivers like those in the West, and everything in between. The area is experiencing a resurgence of interest in fly fishing, spurred by stream restoration projects on the North Branch of the Potomac and the Youghiogheny River. The combined efforts of anglers living in small western Maryland towns and the Department of Natural Resources (DNR) have resulted in the reclamation of abandoned mines and investment in sewer treatment plants.

SAVAGE RIVER
The Savage is the premier wild trout fishery in western Maryland. It's a rough-and-tumble tailwater with lots of rocky runs and rapids. The river lives up to its name. Its bottom is lined with big boulders that shrug off boiling water into swirling pockets and deep pools. A slick, pasty vegetation covers the rocks and makes wading tricky. I wade here carefully, always with a staff and cleated, felt-soled boots.

The Savage has been managed as a trophy trout stream since 1987. It was the Maryland DNR's first experiment in wild trout management. The river's predominant fish is the brown trout, although brook trout held sway at one time. It is not stocked and contains a tremendous population of native brookies, averaging 9 inches, and 14-inch browns. DNR

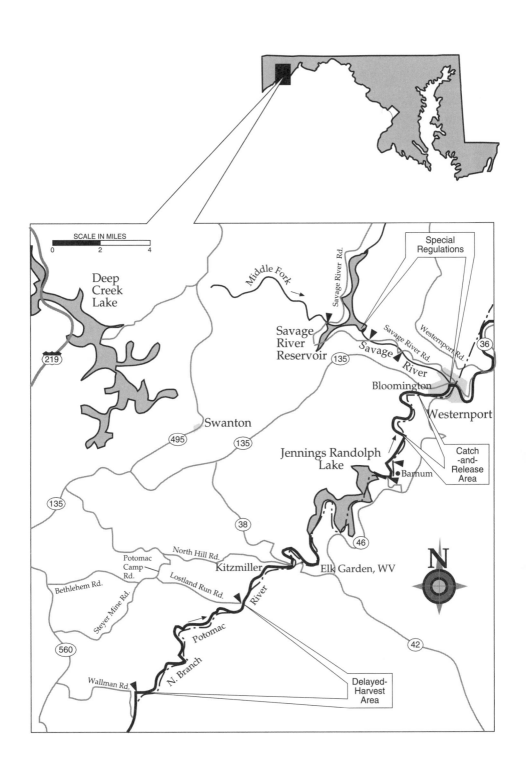

surveys show an average fish stock of 80 pounds per acre, with a maximum of 100 pounds per acre at one station.

The river receives water running between 50 and 150 cubic feet per second from the bottom of Savage River Reservoir. Stream temperatures seldom exceed 65 degrees F, and the river never freezes, making it an excellent year-round fishery. The Savage gets murky only after a tremendous amount of rain, enough to muddy the reservoir, which in turn releases off-color water into the Savage. When this happens, it takes some time for the river to clear.

Middle Fork

The Savage River State Forest contains numerous small tributaries that run into the Savage River above the reservoir, and they all hold wild brook trout. The Middle Fork is the best. Maryland Trout Unlimited members Jim Gracie and Richard Schaad took their sons camping on the Middle Fork every spring for a number of years. There are about twenty-four hundred trout per mile in the water, making it a great place for kids to fish. Gracie cautions that you have to hike in forty-five minutes down a long, steep incline, but the quality and quantity of wild fish cannot be exaggerated or surpassed in Maryland. You can also approach the stream from its lower end, but to reach the best fishing, you have to walk in at least 2 miles.

Hatches, Flies, and Best Times to Fish

The Savage can be fished year-round but is most productive from February through September. Since the bottom is treacherous, felt soles and chest waders are musts, and a wading staff and cleats will provide additional security. The telephone number for dam releases on the Savage River is (410) 962-7687. Always call before making the trip.

Joe Metz, a member of the Nemacolin chapter of Trout Unlimited, recommends visiting western Maryland in the fall, on warm days in October and November. Some of the best hatches on the Savage are *Baetis* species. Metz gets on the stream by 1 P.M. for the hatch, which lasts until about 4 P.M. Sometimes he uses two flies, a #16 or #18 Royal Coachman or another attractor pattern as the top fly, and a Hare's Ear or Pheasant Tail Nymph on a 2-foot dropper.

Wally Vait, another western Maryland devotee, likes to go to the Savage in the late spring, when the slate drakes appear. He claims that fishing this fly will boost the ego of any fisherman, because there is no wrong way to fish it. The shallower the water and the greater the drag, the more fish you will catch. The following lists some of the major hatches and best patterns.

February–March. Little black stoneflies (#16–#18).

April. Blue Quills (#16–#18), Hendricksons (#12), Quill Gordons (#14–#16), blue-winged olives (#18), midges (#20–#24), streamers (#10).

May–June. Caddis (#14–#18), blue-winged olives (#18–#20), sulphurs (#16–#18), slate drake *(Isonychia)* nymphs and drys (#14–#16).

July–September. Green and brown caddis (#14–#18), midges (#24–#26), terrestrials (ants and beetles), Pheasant Tail Nymphs, Bird's Nests, various beadheads, Hare's Ears (#14–#18).

October–November. Little blue-winged olives (#18–#22), midges, Hare's Ear or Pheasant Tail Nymphs (#18–#20), attractor patterns.

Savage Regulations
There are two trophy trout sections contiguous to one another on the Savage below the reservoir. From the river's mouth near Luke, 2.7 miles upstream to the lower suspension bridge (Allegheny bridge), artificial lures and flies may be used. Two fish may be taken daily; brookies must be 12 inches or more, and browns must be 18 inches.

The artificial fly-fishing only, trophy trout section begins at the base of the dam and continues downstream 1½ miles to the Allegheny bridge. Numbers and sizes of fish that may be taken are the same as for the lower section.

Savage Access
To reach the special-regulations sections of the Savage River from the north or east, take Lower New Germany Road (Exit 24) off Route 40 south to Westernport Road. Bear left on Westernport Road. Turn right on Savage River Road, and drive along the upper Savage (put-and-take section), past the Savage River Reservoir into the lower section. There are several pulloffs along the road.

From the southeast, take Route 135 through Westernport and look for Savage River Road on the right. Then follow the directions above.

NORTH BRANCH OF THE POTOMAC RIVER
The North Branch of the Potomac River originates from a spring near the Fairfax Stone (a historic rock from colonial times) in West Virginia, in the upper reaches of the Allegheny plateau. From there it flows 27 miles to the man-made Jennings Randolph Lake, an impoundment designed for flood control. Below the dam, the North Branch cuts a serpentine path through the eastern Allegheny Mountains. First it flows northeast through Bloomington, Luke, and Westernport, Maryland, then on through Keyser, West Virginia, to Cumberland, Maryland. At Cumberland, the water turns southeast. It is joined by the South Branch at South Branch, West Virginia, from whence it flows past Hancock, Maryland, and turns southeast once more on its way toward Washington, D.C., and the Chesapeake Bay.

The 8 miles of trout water downstream of Jennings Randolph Lake is becoming one of the outstanding tailwater fisheries in the East. It is an impressive reclamation project, given that the North Branch was completely lifeless from the 1930s until the mid-1980s, when Jennings

Randolph Lake came into being. The lake mitigated the acidic water that entered it from the North Branch, resulting in an outflow of quality water with a pH of 6.0.

The river was first stocked below the dam by the Maryland DNR at Barnum, West Virginia, in 1987 on an experimental basis to see whether trout could live in the water. When Robert Bachman, then director of resources management of the Fisheries Division of the DNR, realized that the experiment had worked and trout could live in the North Branch below the dam, he began to focus on a major reclamation project. Maryland's Conservation Fund bought 6,000 acres of land in West Virginia that otherwise would have been developed, as well as a narrow strip in Maryland between the railroad tracks and the river, to ensure that the new resource would remain intact.

The state has continued to raise trout in net pens below the dam. "This is the only place in the country where trout are being raised in the effluent of an Army Corps of Engineers dam, and an acidic one at that!" Bachman says.

The upper catch-and-release area above Barnum was opened in 1997 with great fanfare. It's probably the best area in the watershed to catch a big fish in the fall. Sull McCartney, a local angler, caught two huge rainbows, both in the 27-inch class, on streamers on successive Sundays in November 1999. The dam prevents these big fish from moving upstream to spawn, and they sometimes swim into the put-and-take area and are taken home.

Meanwhile, the DNR has continued to improve the water quality of the North Branch. Once they began to realize the potential, Bachman and his colleagues persuaded others to let them treat the major sources of acid above Jennings Randolph Lake with limestone, which improved the pH level from 6.0 to 7.0. The limestone not only purifies the water, but it also fosters parasites, which in turn nourish the mayflies, stoneflies, and caddis that trout like to eat.

The DNR has also entered into a cooperative agreement with the Army Corps of Engineers to try to fix the nitrogen supersaturation problem that occurs at the outflow of the dam. Ken Pavol of the Maryland DNR says that solid progress will be made in the next year or two. However long it takes, this should result in a significant improvement in the entire aquatic ecosystem below the dam.

The North Branch is stocked annually with brown, rainbow, and cutthroat trout in catchable sizes in the put-and-take reaches, and fingerlings in the catch-and-release sections. Brook trout are *not* stocked and reproduce naturally in the river. The presence of brook trout confirms that the water quality is acceptable.

In the 8 miles below Jennings Randolph Lake and the 5 miles on the North Branch below the mouth of the Savage, anglers have the rare chance to land a grand slam: brook, brown, rainbow, and cutthroat trout all in the same day. There are few, if any, other places in the East that offer this opportunity.

There is evidence that browns and rainbows are reproducing in the main stem, but it is not the intent of the DNR that the cutthroat trout do so. The cutts are there for recreational purposes, to bite when nothing else will. It will take a few more years until sufficient bugs and grasses develop to nourish the huge numbers of trout that could live and reproduce in this water. In the past two years, however, aquatic insect life has improved substantially, and DNR observers credit the absence of heavy flows from the dam in recent years. The North Branch is so breathtaking, the water so dramatic, that it is worth the wait for a totally streambred trout fishery. Meanwhile, I'll settle for fingerlings growing up in the wild and the occasional lunker from the put-and-take fishery.

Floating the North Branch

I floated the North Branch with my brother Dick McIntosh late one June. Harold Harsh of Spring Creek Outfitters in Oakland was our guide. We got to Barnum at 9:30 in the morning. The air and water temperatures were ideal. The thermometer read 75 degrees F, and the water was 62 degrees F. The flow from the bottom of the Jennings Randolph Dam was 250 cubic feet per second, a good flow resulting in a depth of 3 to 4 feet of water.

As soon as we rounded the first bend, I understood why floating the river is superior to wading. There are not a lot of flies—or grown fish— for this sizable expanse of water, and you need to cover a lot of territory to find fish to target.

Harsh soon had us casting large drys, such as Stimulators and Sofa Pillows. Perfect drift and precise timing were critical. As I cast a Stimulator to cutthroat under the rock ledges, I recalled the best float trip I've ever had, on the South Fork of the Snake River in Idaho. I hold high hopes for an equally magnificent fishery close to home.

The river flows through a near-wilderness area, and the vegetation is lovely. Wild azaleas and mountain laurel cover the banks. Shrubs sporting yellow, red, and white flowers jut out from ledge rock. Throughout the day, Dick and I alternated casting to the riverbanks, looking for shady spots.

I have never seen a guide work harder than Harold Harsh. He spent more time out of the raft than in it. He got through tough, boulder-strewn runs by dangling his legs off the back of the raft, kicking, pushing, and pulling us off and over boulders and shoals. It was often a roller coaster of a ride through steep drops and turbid whitewater. It was fun, but I have no idea how Harsh stayed with the raft.

The river was not generous the day Dick and I floated it. But we caught enough fish to be satisfied, and I missed enough others to realize that the fish are there and are challenging to catch.

Proximity to the nation's capital has resulted in much well-deserved publicity and angling pressure on the North Branch. The river is more than 100 feet wide below the dam, filled with boulders and rough riffles, as well as very deep pools, and there's plenty of room for a number of anglers to fish. Wading is not for the fainthearted and in many places is impossible. I'll go by raft or johnboat whenever I can.

Hatches, Flies, and Best Times to Fish

There is a 200-cubic-feet-per-second minimum release of cold water from the reservoir year-round. The best time to fish the North Branch above Jennings Randolph Lake is in the spring and fall. In the summer, look for the best sport in the catch-and-release area below the dam.

Notable hatches remain sparse, although the water quality is improving. The following lists some of the major hatches and best patterns.

April–June. March browns, sulphurs, stonefly nymphs (#8 Perlidae imitation), especially in delayed harvest area. The big (#8) black-and-yellow stonefly nymph with an orange thorax *(Stenacron)*, which local fly shop owners Harold Harsh and Allen Nolan call the "No Value" fly because Art Flick writes that it is of little value in the East, has found great value around dark on the North Branch of the Potomac.

July–September. Beetles, crickets, sulphurs, slate drakes, Dun Variants, caddis, caddis emergers.

October–November. Blue-winged olives (#22–#24), caddis, caddis emergers.

North Branch Regulations

Maryland and West Virginia have reciprocal agreements on the North Branch, so a valid license from either state will suffice.

Whitewater releases for recreational rafting are made four weekends in April and May, and fishing below Jennings Randolph Lake is almost impossible at these times. To get the schedule of releases, call (301) 962-7687.

The catch-and-release area is managed as a put-and-grow fishery: Fingerling brown, cutthroat, and rainbow trout are released to mature in the wild. The downstream regulated stretch begins at a red post and cable with a catch-and-release sign, located 1.2 miles downstream of the parking lot at Barnum (just below the Blue Hole pool), and continues downstream about 4 miles to the confluence with Piney Swamp Run.

The state stocks catchable-size trout in the put-and-take sections above and below the catch-and-release area; rainbows, browns, and cutthroat trout may be taken there.

Above Jennings Randolph Lake, the trout water is managed as a put-and-take, delayed harvest fishery. This section runs from the lower boundary of Potomac State Forest near Lostland Run upstream to the upper park boundary at Wallman. From October 1 to June 15 only artificial lures and flies may be used, and all fish must be returned to the water. From June 16 to September 30 two trout may be taken each day, with no minimum size. This area is stocked several times during the spring and early summer, and again in the fall.

North Branch Access
Managed trout water consists of 21 miles above and 8 miles below Jennings Randolph Lake.
 • Barnum, West Virginia, access. Access to the North Branch below the dam is through Elk Garden, West Virginia, from the west or via Westernport, Maryland, from the east. From Elk Garden, take West Virginia Route 46 to Barnum Road. Turn left at the two churches.

From Westernport, take Maryland Route 135 west to Luke. Turn left on West Virginia Route 46 and drive about 5 miles, bearing right at all intersections. At the second of two white churches at the top of a hill, turn right onto Barnum Road. Follow Barnum Road through the hamlet of Barnum to a large parking area.

To access the upper catch-and-release area, upstream of Barnum, park at the parking area and walk upriver about 200 feet. A cable across the river marks the downstream boundary of the catch-and-release area. You can take the trail through the aluminum gate from the parking area to reach areas even farther upstream. If you do so, fish from the Maryland side, as the West Virginia side tends to be steep and difficult to fish. The river can be crossed when the flow is less than 250 cubic feet per second, depending on your skill. A staff and studded boots are highly recommended.

To reach the lower catch-and-release area, drive on the dirt road from Barnum to a locked gate. Park and walk downstream along an old railroad bed. The best downstream fishing begins in the big riffle below the concrete bank. It's not possible to wade across the river along most of this section.

Above Jennings Randolph Lake, there are two access points in Maryland: Lostland Run area and the Wallman area.
 • To get to Lostland Run, take Maryland Route 495 south from Exit 19 of I-68, approximately 20 miles to Swanton. Make a right at the stop sign, staying on Route 495 to Loch Lynn Heights. Turn left on Maryland Route 560 south, and after 2 miles, take a left on Bethlehem Road, then follow signs to Potomac State Forest. Go 2 miles, and make a right on Steyer Mine Road. Go about 1 mile to Combination Road, and turn left. Go another 0.5 mile or so, and turn left on Potomac Camp Road. Pass the park headquarters and follow signs to Lostland. The road ends at a parking lot next to the river.

To reach Lostland from the west (Deep Creek Lake, Oakland, Mountain Lake Park), take Maryland Route 135 east from Mountain Lake Park to Maryland Route 560, then proceed as above.

• To get to the Wallman area, continue on Maryland Route 560 south 3 miles past Bethlehem Road, and turn left on White Church–Steyer Road. Go 1 mile, until the road turns abruptly right. Go straight on Audley Riley Road, bear right at fork, and follow signs to Wallman.

On the West Virginia side, railroad tracks run parallel to the entire river. The river is too strong to cross, but there is a trestle to the Maryland side near Wallman. Fishermen can use it as a trail to reach areas up- or downriver, especially when the river is too high to wade across. This is a really beautiful area that receives little pressure. Felt soles with cleats, chest waders, and a staff are advised.

YOUGHIOGHENY RIVER

This river, fondly referred to as the "Yough" (pronounced "Yock"), is a favorite with whitewater sportsmen and anglers. Youghiogheny is an Indian name meaning "river that flows in a contrary direction," because the Yough runs north in an area where most rivers flow south.

In 1996, after twenty-eight years of classification as Maryland's only wild and scenic river, Garrett County adopted a formal plan to protect the watershed. More than 4,700 acres and 28 miles of water may not be developed, and habitat supporting wildlife is guaranteed intact in perpetuity.

Ken Pavol has taken the lead in converting the Yough to a trout fishery. He played a key role in establishing the catch-and-release fishery between the Deep Creek Lake Power Plant and the Sang Run bridge. He and the Youghiogheny chapter of Trout Unlimited negotiated an agreement with the Reliant Corporation, the company that owns the power plant. The contract stipulates a minimum flow (40 cubic feet per second at the tailrace) of cold water, and the water temperature at Sang Run must be maintained below 72 degrees F so that trout can live in the river through periods of low flow and high temperatures.

Pavol and I drove to the river one hot July morning several years ago. As we left Oakland, he explained the state's plan: to stock fingerling browns and an experimental strain of warm-water rainbows in the Yough between the power plant and the Sang Run bridge—where catch-and-release regulations would be enforced. The Department of Natural Resources (DNR) wanted to create a challenging catch-and-release fishery on one of the state's most productive waters.

Despite the low flow that summer, we saw rising trout, and the water was clear. We didn't fish, not wanting to stress the trout during the hottest part of the day. I've since caught 12-inch trout on the Yough during the summer, and many angling friends have caught more and larger trout in the last two years. I recommend fishing early in the morning or in the evening, when trees on one side or the other shade the water.

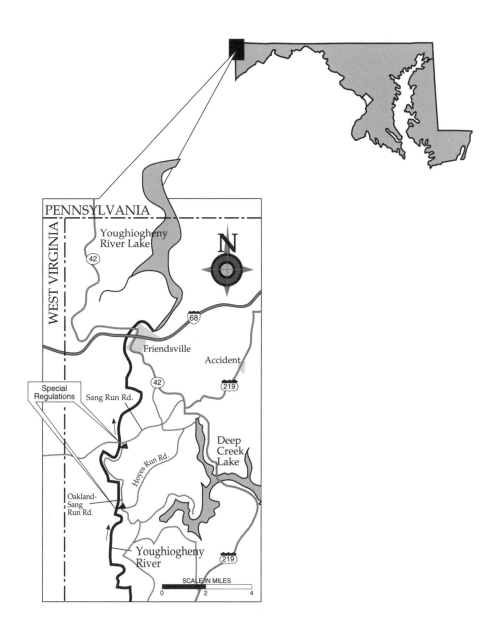

Allen Nolan, co-owner of Spring Creek Outfitters, has caught rainbows up to 20 inches in the stretch between Hoyes and Sang Run. Pavol and Gary Yoder, a DNR colleague, have had fall evenings where each caught and released more than 20 foot-long trout. Green drakes, which have always shown up in respectable numbers on the river, are now profuse. Look for them in late May and June.

The strain of warm-water-tolerant rainbows is flourishing in the Yough. Fourteen-inch fish have weighed in at 2 pounds, and Spring Creek Outfitters reported an 18-inch brown weighing 4 pounds. Apparently, these rainbows expand their girth even as they grow longer, for these are unusually heavy fish for their length.

Pavol explained that sediment (topsoil) prevents the Yough from sustaining trout reproduction. The DNR has documented spawning fish but currently has no plan to mitigate the huge load of runoff that enters the Yough from agricultural and developed property. The sediment smothers roe that would otherwise hatch in the river and help establish wild trout. Though the growth rate of fingerlings illustrates that there is enough food and sufficient cold water to support streambred trout, fish will not be able to reproduce until this runoff is greatly reduced.

Standing crops of trout have almost tripled since 1995, when temperature control and minimum flow maintenance were established. This is a super fishery now, offering more chances to target larger trout than ever before. Pavol says it's the best place he knows to try to fool individual rising trout. During midsummer, trout rise almost every morning and evening, usually to small bugs such as cream-colored midges. The evening activity lasts into deep dusk. The Yough is becoming Maryland's newest quality put-and-grow trout fishery, in no small part due to the beauty of the surroundings and the water itself.

Unlike the North Branch of the Potomac and the Savage, the Yough is easy to wade *when there is no water being released from the power plant.* The river is about 80 feet wide, with a moderate gradient and a bed of cobble and occasional boulders. The release schedule varies widely, and there are no warning alerts. The released water takes one and a half to two hours to travel from Hoyes to Sang Run. *Beware:* The water is swift, and wading can be dangerous during release periods. Suddenly this wide, friendly water becomes a rushing torrent with unseen pitfalls: invisible holes and trenches, slimy boulders and rocks. For stability, take a wading staff and wear studs if you can. Before fishing, call (814) 533-8911 for the water release schedule.

Hatches, Flies, and Best Times to Fish
The best time to fish the Yough is between mid-April and the end of October. Pavol stresses the importance of caddis hatches on the Yough. He takes eight out of ten fish with caddis. Use nymphs, emergers, soft-hackle wet flies, and drys. Gary LaFontaine's Tan Emerger pattern—fished dry

on top of the water—is particularly effective. Fish pursue midges on the Yough year-round. Gnat clusters, such as the Griffith's Gnat in sizes #20–#22, work well. The following lists some of the major hatches and best patterns.

Mid-April–May. Blue Quills (#16–#18), Quill Gordons (#14–#16), Hendricksons, march browns, blue-winged olives (#18), caddis, streamers (#10), Woolly Buggers, alewife patterns, minnow imitations. Green drakes usually appear between Memorial Day and the end of the first week in June and continue for two weeks. It's the best green drake opportunity in the state.

May–June. Caddis (#14–#18), blue-winged olives (#18–#20), sulphurs (#16–#18), slate drake nymphs and drys (#14–#16), Cream or Dun Variants (#14–#16).

July–September. Caddis, midges, terrestrials.

Youghiogheny Regulations
The regulated catch-and-release water begins at a red post about 100 yards upstream of the Deep Creek Lake tailrace and extends downstream 4 miles to the Sang Run bridge.

Youghiogheny Access
• To reach the 4-mile catch-and-release stretch of the Yough, take Route 219 south from I-68. Just before Deep Creek Lake, turn right on Sang Run Road, which leads to the river. There is ample parking.

• The section from Hoyes Run to Sang Run provides the most consistent fishing. Park at Sang Run parking lot and walk north through the field, cross Sang Run, and continue another twenty minutes on an unimproved trail next to the river. This short hike will put you on one of the most productive, little-fished reaches of the river.

• At Hoyes Run, parking is more limited, but this area has more fish. The stretch between the power plant and Hoyes Run tends to be swift. It's filled with pocket water, and the best fishing is right at the edges of the water.

The Yough is stocked with catchable-size fish for 15 miles in the put-and-take fishery. After the first blush of the season, these fish are often ignored by anglers. Search for them anytime after Memorial Day.

• The Yough can also be fished downstream in southwestern Pennsylvania. Good access is available at Ohiopyle State Park. A bike path runs from Ohiopyle to the take-out above Connellsville.

ALSO WORTH NOTING
Casselman River
The Casselman and the Youghiogheny are the only rivers in Maryland that flow into the Ohio River basin. Located near Grantsville, the Casselman River is the easternmost stream in the Mississippi–Ohio River drainage.

Stocked by the state, the river originates between Frostburg and Grants-ville west of the Eastern Continental Divide and joins the Youghiogheny at Confluence, Pennsylvania. I like to go to the Casselman as soon as the water become fishable in the spring. The river is regulated as a delayed harvest stream. Prior to June 15, all fish must be released. As on the Sav-age, some of the best hatches are *Baetis* species.

IF YOU GO

Frostburg, the nearest large town to the Savage and the North Branch of the Potomac, is about 150 miles from Washington, Baltimore, or Pitts-burgh. Take I-70 (from Baltimore) or I-270 (from Washington) to I-68 west to Cumberland, Frostburg, and points west. From Pittsburgh, take I-79 south to I-68 east.

To reach Oakland and Deep Creek Lake (near the Youghiogheny River) from Baltimore or Washington, take I-70 or I-270 to I-68 west to U.S. Route 219 south. From Pittsburgh, take I-79 south to I-68 and east to U.S. Route 219 south. The trip is three to three and a half hours from Baltimore or Washington and about two and a half hours from Pittsburgh.

There is plenty for the nonangler to do in western Maryland. Cum-berland has many Revolutionary War sites, including George Washing-ton's Headquarters, and antiquing is good throughout the area. Parks and other recreational areas abound, where you can hike, bike, ski, canoe, kayak, or ride horses.

Tackle Shops and Guides

The Angler's Lie. Arlington, Virginia. Large tackle shop. Fine flies. (703) 527-2524. www.anglerslie.com.

The Gentleman Hunter, Inc. Bethesda, Maryland. (301) 907-1668.

Hudson Trail Outfitters, Ltd. Don't count on this chain for custom-tied local patterns, but they have a good supply of basic tackle and cloth-ing. Rockville, Maryland, (301) 881-4955; Gaithersburg, Maryland, (301) 948-2474; Fairfax, Virginia, (703) 591-2950.

Maryland Fishing Guides Cooperative. Monkton, Maryland. Nine of the Baltimore area's best guides have formed a cooperative guide busi-ness. I know most of them and can vouch for their abilities. (410) 472-1099.

Orvis. Tyson's Corner. A complete Orvis dealer. (703) 556-8634.

Spring Creek Outfitters. McHenry, Maryland. Harold Harsh and Allen Nolan, proprietors. Full-service fly shop. Provides guide service on the Savage, Casselman, and Yough, as well as pack and float trips on the North Branch and floats on the Yough. (301) 387-2034. www.springcreek outfitter.com.

Where to Stay

Brookside Inn. Near Aurora, West Virginia. Only twenty minutes from Oakland, Maryland, via U.S. Routes 50 and 219. Charming B&B in

Victorian summer resort house. Fabulous breakfast. Dinners cooked to order. Moderate. (304) 735-6344 or (800) 588-6344.

Casselman Inn. Grantsville. Amish-run and very convenient. Inexpensive. (301) 895-5266.

Comfort Inn. Deep Creek Lake. Moderate to expensive. (310) 387-4200.

Comfort Inn. Frostburg. Moderate to expensive. (301) 689-2050.

Holiday Inn. Grantsville. Exit 22 off I-68. Moderate to expensive. (301) 895-5993.

Point View Inn. Deep Creek Lake. Moderate to expensive. (800) 244-1598.

Red Run Lodge B&B. Deep Creek Lake. A private location on the woody banks of Deep Creek Lake. Also a good restaurant. Moderate to expensive. (800) 898-7786.

Savage River Inn B&B. Deep Creek Lake. Moderate. (310) 245-4440. E-mail: sri@iceweb.net. www.savageriverinn.com.

Starlite Motel. Oakland. Next to Denny's restaurant. Inexpensive. (301) 8686.

Streams & Dreams. Don and Karen Hershfeld, owners. Deep Creek Lake. Located on Hoys Run a stone's throw from the Youghiogeny River. A good fishing B&B. Rooms expensive. Weekend apartments moderate. (310) 387-6881. E-mail: fishing4u2@juno.com. www.streams-and-dreams.net.

Town Motel. Oakland. An old standby. Inexpensive. (301) 334-3955.

Walnut Ridge B&B. Grantsville. Restored 1860s farmhouse. Moderate. (301) 895-4248.

Camping

Statewide camping information. (301) 461-0052.

Big Run, Casselman, New Germany, and Savage River State Parks. New Germany (301) 895-5453 and Herrington Manor (301) 334-9180. The state parks have cabins.

Little Meadows Campground. Grantsville. (301) 895-5675.

Deep Creek Lake State Park. Swanton. Near the Yough and the North Branch. (301) 387-5563.

Potomac State Forest. Oakland. On the North Branch. (301) 334-2038.

Where to Eat

Au Petit Paris. Frostburg. Dinner only, Tuesday through Saturday. Chef Louis Philip St. Marie is a rare find. Expensive and worth it. (301) 689-8946.

Canoe on the Run. Deep Creek Lake. Moderate. (301) 387-5933.

Casselman Inn. Grantsville. Good, hearty food. No cocktails. (301) 895-5266.

Cornish Manor. Oakland. Very attractive restaurant in Victorian house with wraparound porch. Moderately expensive but worth getting off the stream for. (301) 334-3551.

McClive's Restaurant and Lounge. Oakland. On Deep Creek Lake. No reservations. Moderate. (301) 387-6172.

Penn Alps. Grantsville. Home cooking. Moderate. (301) 895-5985.

Larry's Blues Bar. Deep Creek Lake. Larry's is a blues bar and seafood restaurant. Moderately priced. (301) 387-4040.

Red Run Lodge Restaurant. Deep Creek Lake. Good food. Moderrate to expensive. (800) 898-7786.

Savage River Lodge. Grantsville. Very good food. Moderate to expensive. (301) 684-3200. www.savageriverlodge.com.

Twila's Old Mill. Friendsville. Home-style cooking. Good place for a lunch break while fishing the Yough. No reservations. Inexpensive.

Uno's Pizzeria. Deep Creek Lake. No reservations. Inexpensive.

RESOURCES

Allegany County Visitors' Bureau. (800) 872-4650.

Garrett County Promotion Council. (301) 334-1948.

Western Maryland Department of Freshwater Fisheries. (301) 334-8218.

Feeser, Tim, and Patapsco Chapter of Trout Unlimited. *The Trout Fishing Guide to Maryland and South Central Pennsylvania.* Manchester, MD. To order, send $10 check made out to Patapsco Chapter of Trout Unlimited, c/o Tim Feeser, 3407 View Ridge Circle, Manchester, MD 21102.

Gelso, Charlie, and Larry Coburn. *A Guide to Maryland Trout Fishing.* Woodbine, MD: K&D Limited, 2000.

Maryland Atlas & Gazetteer. Yarmouth, ME: DeLorme Mapping Company. (207) 846-7000.

McIntosh, Ann. *Mid-Atlantic Budget Angler.* Mechanicsburg, PA: Stackpole Books, 1998.

Ross, John. *Trout Unlimited's Guide to America's 100 Best Trout Streams.* Helena, MT: Falcon Publishing, 1999.

STREAMS OF THE SHENANDOAH NATIONAL PARK

Ann McIntosh

Virginia's native brook trout population is the state's most valuable coldwater asset. There are hundreds of mountain streams where the adventurous angler can find these little fish. They are so fragile and so brilliantly colored that it makes you smile to hook one and sad to see any sign of hook damage.

These bright brookies account for 80 percent of Virginia's trout on 1,800 miles of wild trout streams. Virginia has more miles of native brook trout streams than all other southeastern states combined. Many of them

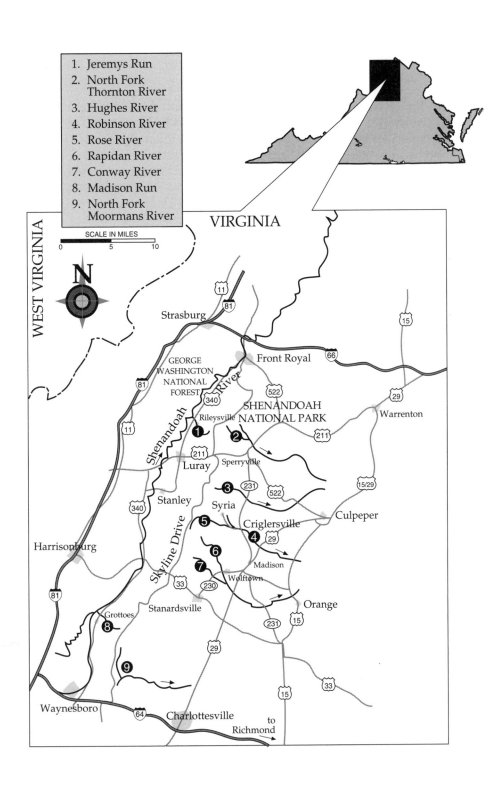

1. Jeremys Run
2. North Fork Thornton River
3. Hughes River
4. Robinson River
5. Rose River
6. Rapidan River
7. Conway River
8. Madison Run
9. North Fork Moormans River

VIRGINIA

WEST VIRGINIA

SCALE IN MILES
0   5   10

N

Strasburg

GEORGE WASHINGTON NATIONAL FOREST

Front Royal

Shenandoah River

SHENANDOAH NATIONAL PARK

Rileysville

Warrenton

Luray

Sperryville

Stanley

Syria

Criglersville

Culpeper

Skyline Drive

Madison

Wolftown

Harrisonburg

Stanardsville

Orange

Grottoes

Waynesboro

Charlottesville

to Richmond

are in the Shenandoah National Park. They are gems and are worth the trek up the mountains.

According to Larry Mohn, regional manager with the Virginia Department of Game and Inland Fisheries (VDGIF), most of the state's trout are found in its western region, in the Blue Ridge and Allegheny Mountains, where the elevation is high enough that the streams stay cool through the summer. Also between these two ranges are limestone subsurface formations from which water feeds productive spring creeks. Virginia no longer permits stocking fish in wild brook trout water and has greatly reduced all stocking where natural reproduction can take place.

The state has implemented more effective wild trout management policies, as the efforts of the Shenandoah National Park indicate. In the last few years, most park streams have been opened to year-round fishing under catch-and-release regulations. Virginia trout fishing has also been boosted by a year-round season, which eschews opening day in favor of letting put-and-take as well as catch-and-release anglers catch fish year-round. Fisheries biologists say the continuous season also improves trout management by clearing fish tanks before diseases develop.

The biggest threat to wild trout in Virginia is siltation and warm water temperatures in summer. The VDGIF's Mohn points out that as little as ¼ inch of silt over trout roe can result in 100 percent mortality. In the last twenty years, habitat degradation, as a result of poor logging techniques, lack of riparian buffers on agricultural land, and stream channelization, has slowed, and the VDGIF has become more effective at protecting the trout environment.

In the spring, the mountain streams of Virginia's Shenandoah National Park cascade down the steep slopes of the Blue Ridge Mountains, running through Catoctin gray-green stone, hemlocks, and hardwoods. In March, the water tumbles through the pools and overflows the boulders. By April, wildflowers appear in the moss, their blooms reflected in the morning dew. Beginning in late April and early May, if the water conditions are conducive, the fishing is very good. By May and June, the water recedes; boulders are bone dry and riffles very shallow.

Like the streams, which range from 7 to 20 feet wide, the trout are small and very beautiful. All brook trout in the park are a wild native strain, their colors as bright as the water they inhabit. As adults, they average 6 to 10 inches and seldom exceed 11. (The browns grow to 14 inches.)

Angling for brook trout in these mountains is an experience to be treasured. The brookies are a native American strain that has been in these streams for centuries. An angler accustomed to western rivers will have to hone his or her skills to a finer point here. The streams require exact delicate casts, often while kneeling behind a boulder. Food is scarce in the park, so trout are hungry. They eagerly take drys, shooting up from deep pools to snatch their prey.

Most park streams fish best in their upper reaches. The nicest way to fish them is to hike in and, if possible, camp overnight. If you park at the lower end of a stream, the farther upstream you walk, the more productive the fishing will be. There will be fewer anglers, and the trout are less susceptible to drought and low water. You can also approach nearly all the streams listed here by hiking down from Skyline Drive. Ask the local tackle shop owners for the best approach and stream conditions when you go. Tactics for fishing these mountain streams are described simply and clearly by Harry Murray in the "Reading the Water" chapter of his book *Trout Fishing in the Shenandoah National Park.* Murray describes where fish lie in the pools and riffles and how to approach them to get the most out of each pool. Begin by fishing the tail and edges of one pool from the pool below, maintaining a low profile and casting where the fish can't see you. Then bend over and move stealthily to the banks near the tail of the pool, and fish upstream carefully.

Murray, a park superintendent, points out that park managers are charged with protecting all the natural resources in the park, but game fish are the only species of wildlife in the park that visitors are allowed to take out. A fine is imposed on anyone who so much as picks a wildflower or shoots a squirrel, although there is no penalty for taking home six 9-inch wild brookies from many streams.

HATCHES, FLIES, AND BEST TIMES TO FISH

I wish I could count on fishing the park in March, because—when weather permits—fishing the park is a glorious way to begin the angling year. But you have to wait until late April or early May for predictable weather.

April–May. The key to finding good spring fishing is water temperature. Because it snows and freezes in the park on spring nights when temperatures in the valley may be balmy, it's not easy to predict stream conditions more than a few days in advance. One way to do so is to watch the television weather map. When a system passes over the Blue Ridge Mountains with three or four days of sunny skies and temperatures in the high forties to low fifties, the water temperature in park streams will reach 40 to 45 degrees F. Once the water is 40 degrees F, hatches begin and trout will feed on the surface, regardless of water level. When the water is high, anglers should hike to headwaters above feeder streams, where the water temperature is a little warmer.

The following patterns should work, all in sizes #12–#16: Quill Gordons, Hendricksons, Blue Quills, Yellow Humpies, Adamses, March Browns, Mr. Rapidans, Ladyslippers, Patriots, Royal Wulffs, Royal Coachmen. Also recommended are Woolly Buggers, squirrel-hair nymphs, Gold-

Ribbed Hare's Ears, Elk Hair and Grannom Caddis. Try small minnows and crayfish patterns during periods of high or off-color water.

May–June. Try Yellow Sallies, big black stoneflies, Gray Fox, March Browns, sulphurs, Light Cahills, Green Drakes (if you can find the naturals), crickets, beetles, ants.

June 15–September 30. If you've never fished the park in low water, you may find it a little sad. Pools are clear and shallow. Cover is sparse. Fish are very spooky, and only the little ones are likely to get caught. Sections of many streams dry up completely (the water runs underground). Under extreme conditions, you should refrain from fishing to avoid stressing the trout.

If the water is fishable, try a big black stonefly, Disco Cricket, Letort or Dave's Hopper, inchworm, beetle, or ant (black or cinnamon).

September–October. Park fishing in fall is magnificent. Falling leaves add moisture to the streams. Insect life increases. The fish grow bolder. If you're on a park stream in October, you may see a female brookie making her redd. This is a moment to remember—witnessing the reproduction of an indigenous American strain that has survived for millennia.

Fish from the banks in October. The redds disappear quickly, but the roe remains invisible in the gravel. If you step on it, you will kill the eggs. Continue to use terrestrials, but also try Blue-Winged Olives, caddis patterns, or small nymphs, such as Pheasant Tail Nymphs or Gold-Ribbed Hare's Ears.

PARK REGULATIONS
Regulations in the park are important and byzantine. To fish the Shenandoah National Park, *you need a Virginia state fishing license,* although you *do not need* a Virginia trout license or a national forest stamp.

To obtain a license in advance, contact the Virginia Department of Game and Inland Fisheries, 4010 W. Broad Street, P.O. Box 11104, Richmond, VA 23230-1104, telephone (804) 367-1000. Licenses may also be purchased at Kmarts and Wal-Marts in the state, as well as at the Panorama, Big Meadows, and Loft Mountain waysides.

In 1996 most of the park streams were opened to fishing, but only a portion of them permit harvesting fish. Ask for a list of closed streams, streams designated for harvest, and catch-and-release regulated streams when you get your license. All fishing is with single hooks, flies, or artificial lures.

Nearly a decade ago, park managers conducted an extensive regulatory review, with input from several Trout Unlimited chapters and the Virginia Council of Trout Unlimited. Under the resulting revisions, park authorities have opened streams designated as open for harvest or catch-and-release to fishing year-round, using single hooks and artificial lures or flies only. It is hoped that the Rapidan and the North Fork of the Moormans, upon their recovery, will be regulated as catch-and-release-only streams. On streams allowing harvest, the daily limit will be six trout of 9 inches minimum length. For more information, call the park office at (540) 999-2243.

PARK ACCESS

Because the scale of this chapter's map is large, I could not include every road or stream named in the text. In most instances, I have referred to DeLorme's *Virginia Atlas & Gazetteer (VAG)*. Harry Murray's book *Trout Fishing in the Shenandoah National Park* provides detailed stream descriptions and directions to all the park streams, both from Skyline Drive and from roads outside the park. The maps listed in the Resources section, below, are also excellent aids for fishing the park. The streams discussed below, listed north to south, are my favorites, but there are many others, and with the advent of 1996 regulations permitting catch-and-release fishing on nearly all open park streams, anglers can explore smaller streams and discover new treasures.

Jeremys Run

An early-season stream, Jeremys Run receives a lot of pressure because it's easily accessed from Skyline Drive. It tends to dry up in summer. Jeremys Run Trail runs along the stream. For access, follow Skyline Drive to the Elkwallow picnic grounds, about 7 miles north of Panorama. Follow the trail to the stream. (*VAG*, page 74, B-1.)

North Fork of the Thornton River

This is another early-season fishery. My diary indicates that one year I caught six brook trout ranging from 8 to 11 inches using Black Woolly Buggers in high, off-color water. That was a good morning, but many anglers boast twenty-five- and thirty-fish days. Access from Route 612 just north of Sperryville. Follow Route 612 to the end of the road at the park boundary. Limited parking available. (*VAG*, page 74, B-2.)

Hughes River

This is a good dry-fly stream. Lower access: Take U.S. Route 211 west to Sperryville, turn left onto U.S. Route 522 south, then right onto Route 231. Continue 8.5 miles to a right turn onto Route 602, after crossing the lower Hughes River (stocked trout water). Stay on this route approximately 3 miles; the route numbers will change from 602 to 601 to 707 to 600 in that stretch. Follow Route 600 to the first parking area on the left. Obtain a permit for a fee, and hike less than a mile to Nicholson Hollow Trail. The best fishing is upstream to Corbin Cabin. (*VAG*, page 74, D-2.)

Robinson River (White Oak Canyon Run)

Don't be alarmed by the number of parked cars at the lower end. This is an exceptionally pretty stream, popular with hikers. It suffered some flood damage in September 1996, but it should offer lovely early-season fishing soon. Make a cautious approach; use fine tippets and small flies. Access from Skyline Drive or off Route 600. (*VAG*, page 74, D-2.)

Hogcamp Branch of the Rose River

This is accessible from Skyline Drive, approximately 20 miles south of Panorama. Hike down the Dark Hollow Falls Trail or the Rose River Fire Road to the stream. Or, for a less heavily hiked alternative that offers an easy walk, start at Fishers Gap; cross the drive and follow the Fire Road to Hogcamp Branch, or take an immediate left off the trail (onto a horse trail) to Rose River Falls.

This stream is a favorite of angler-photographer Douglas Lees of Warrenton, Virginia. Lees feels that fishing the Hogcamp/Upper Rose is what Shenandoah fishing is all about: small stream fishing at its best, with a hike in from Skyline Drive past lovely deep pools and lots of fish. (*VAG*, page 74, D-1.)

To fish the Dark Hollow Falls area, pass the Fishers Gap Overlook on the right, past Mile Marker 50 to the Dark Hollow Falls parking area and trail on the left.

Rose River

To fish the upper section, walk about 1.5 miles from the lower parking area, past the fire road gate, until the road bears left, away from the stream. Drop down there, and fish up- or downstream. The lower section can be accessed from Route 231 to Route 670 until it ends at a parking lot. The Rose is heavily fished, because many anglers look for holdover browns from the lower (stocked) water. (*VAG*, page 74, D-1, and page 68, A-1.)

Ivy Creek

This little stream (not shown on map) should be attempted only with a compass and a Shenandoah National Park or Potomac Appalachian Trail Conference map. Off Skyline Drive, the gradient is steep and the trails are poor. It's a tough walk in and out, but it's worth it when you get there. There's a good trout population the length of the stream. (*VAG*, page 67, B-5.)

Rapidan River

Catch-and-release regulations apply from Hoover Camp downstream through the Rapidan Wildlife Management Area. This is a fabled stream, but it was damaged by floods in 1995 and 1996. The upper and middle sections were not seriously harmed, and the stream had recovered by 2001.

From Criglersville, take Route 670 to a left turn onto Route 649 to reach the middle and upper sections. Access the downstream sections via Route 662. (*VAG,* page 68, A-1.)

Conway River

Take U.S. Route 33 to Stanardsville, then turn left on Route 230. Go 3 miles, and turn left on Route 667, which parallels the stream. Drive as far as you can, then walk in to the second ford. Fish upstream. (*VAG,* page 68, A-1.)

Madison Run

Madison Run is on the western slope of the park. I fished it with Jim Finn on a dank April day just before a cold front settled in. We caught only a few brookies before the rain lowered the water temperature and the fish ceased to feed. This is a stream to which I will return regularly. It is 15 feet wide with enticing long pools, short riffles, and an easy gradient. For the best fishing, walk in for at least fifteen minutes. The water gets bigger, prettier, and more productive as you walk upstream.

To get to Madison Run, take Exit 245 off I-81 onto Route 659 east (Port Republic Road). Make a left on Route 663 to the parking lot and stream. Or take Route 663 off U.S. Route 340 in the town of Grottoes. (*VAG,* page 67, B-5.)

North Fork of Moormans River

Before a flood devastated this river in 1995, it was an extraordinary example of what catch-and-release regulations can do to improve a fishery. My first fish on a good morning was a 14-inch brown trout. I thought I was caught around some of the deadfall under which the trout lay. But no, and luckily it was a big trout for a small mountain stream. Needless to say, I was very proud of myself, and I didn't encounter a snake throughout the entire morning.

Moormans was closed after a flood in 1995 and had a second major slug of water in 1996; it still suffers from the damage. I understand a number of trout over 12 inches were taken there in 1999 and 2000, but I believe these might be exceptions until the stream can nourish a larger number of trout.

It's worth calling a local fly shop for a status report about the conditions on this stream, although I believe it will take until 2003 to see marked improvement. This stream is very special, with wonderful trout and a lovely, easy walk up the mountain for a fine day's fishing.

To reach the catch-and-release section, take U.S. Route 29 south to U.S. Route 250 west to Route 240 west to Route 810 north to Route 614. Park at the locked gate. Special regulations begin at the gate and continue upstream to the headwaters. (*VAG,* page 67, C-6.)

IF YOU GO

From Washington, the northern entrance to Shenandoah National Park is on Skyline Drive, about 70 miles west of Washington via I-66. To access secondary roads to eastern slope streams, take U.S. Route 522 south off I-66. An alternative route south is U.S. Route 340 to Front Royal, Luray, and points south.

From Richmond, take I-64 west through Charlottesville to Exit 107, Crozet, or Exit 99, Afton, at the south entrance of the park.

Tackle Shops and Guides

The Angler's Lie. Arlington. Large tackle shop. (703) 527-2524. www.anglerslie.com.

Blue Ridge Angler. Harrisonburg. William Kingsley, proprietor. Tackle, guide service, schools. (540) 547-3474.

Murray's Fly Shop. Edinburg. Harry Murray, proprietor. Flies, tackle, schools, guides. Murray wrote the book on Shenandoah Park streams and also specializes in bass on the Shenandoah River. (540) 984-4212. www.murraysflyshop.com.

Orvis. Tyson's Corner. (703) 556-8634.

The Outdoorsman. The Plains. Henry R. (Hank) Woolman, guide. Experienced guide and former president of the Rapidan chapter of Trout Unlimited. (540) 253-5545.

Rhodes Fly Shop. Warrenton. Orvis dealer. Flies, tackle, schools. (540) 347-4161.

Shenandoah Lodge & Outfitters. Near Luray. Alec Burnett, proprietor. Orvis fly-fishing outfitter. Emphasis on native spring creek trout and smallmouth bass. Lodging available (see below). (800) 866-9958.

Thornton River Fly Shop. Sperryville. Paul Kearney, proprietor. A fine fly shop that can also get you access to private streams in northern Virginia. Highly recommended. (540) 987-9400. www.thorntonfly.com.

Trout & About. Arlington. Phil Gay, guide. Gay fishes park streams, the Jackson River, and many others. (703) 525-7127.

The Tackle Shop. Charlottesville. Flies, tackle, guides. Also carries spin-fishing and hunting equipment. (804) 978-7112.

Where to Stay

Graves Mountain Lodge. Syria. Route 670. Near the Rapidan and the Conway. Rooms, cabins, restaurant. Moderate. (540) 923-4231.

The Hatch. Edinburg. Nice inn in the valley near the Shenandoah River and Murray's Fly Shop. Breakfast, dinner available. Moderate. (540) 984-4212.

Holiday Inn. Afton. At the junction of I-64 and U.S. Route 250. Convenient to southern park streams. Restaurant on premises. Moderate. (540) 942-5201.

Mimslyn Inn. Luray. Large, old-fashioned hotel overlooking Luray. Bar, restaurant. Inexpensive to moderate. (540) 743-5105.

The Inn at Sugar Hollow Farm. Thirteen miles west of Charlottesville. Private baths. Expensive. (804) 823-7086.

Shenandoah Lodge & Outfitters. Near Luray. Alec Burnett, proprietor. Orvis-endorsed tackle shop and guide service. The lodge has one-day and multiday packages including lodging and meals. A hospitable, quality establishment. Reasonably priced, nice place to spend a weekend. (800) 866-9958.

Skyland and Big Meadows Lodge. Two big family-oriented lodges on Skyline Drive. Moderate. (800) 999-4714.

Camping

Camping in Shenandoah National Park. (540) 999-2282.

Bud-Lea Campground. Madison. (540) 948-4186.

Endless Caverns Campground. New Market. (540) 740-3993.

Where to Eat

The Shenandoah Valley is a rural area with few noteworthy restaurants. In addition to those listed below, some of the lodgings listed above include dining.

Dan's Steakhouse. West of Luray. On U.S. Route 211. A local tradition. Great steaks and seafood. Moderate. (540) 743-6285.

A Moment to Remember. Luray. Restaurant, espresso, and juice bar. Tasty sandwiches, baked goods, exotic beer. (540) 743-1121.

Parkhurst Restaurant. Two miles west of Luray. On U.S. Route 211. Moderate to expensive. (540) 743-6009.

RESOURCES

Park information. Shenandoah National Park, Route 4, Box 348, Luray, VA 22835. (540) 999-2243.

Licenses. Virginia Department of Game and Inland Fisheries. (804) 367-1000.

Virginia Department of Game and Inland Fisheries. P.O. Box 996, Verona, VA 24482. Larry Mohn, regional fisheries biologist. (540) 248-9360.

Virginia Atlas & Gazetteer. Yarmouth, ME: DeLorme Mapping Company. (207) 846-7000.

The Potomac Appalachian Trail Club (PATC). 118 Park Street SE, Vienna, VA 22180. (703) 242-0693. Offers very good maps that are clear, published in color, and show all streams, tributaries, trails, and roads in the park.

Camuto, Christopher. *A Fly Fisherman's Blue Ridge.* New York: Henry Holt and Company, 1990.

Murray, Harry. *Trout Fishing in the Shenandoah National Park.* Edinburg, VA: Shenandoah Publishing Company, 1989. To order a copy, call (540) 984-4212.

Murray, Harry. *Virginia Blue Ribbon Trout Streams: A Fly Fishing Guide.* Portland, OR: Frank Amato Publications, 2000.

Ross, John. *Trout Unlimited's Guide to America's 100 Best Trout Streams.* Helena, MT: Falcon Publishing, 1999.

Slone, Harry. *Virginia Trout Streams: A Guide to Fishing the Blue Ridge Watershed.* 3d edition. Woodstock, VT: Backcountry Publications, 1999.

USGS Survey Maps, Box 25286, Federal Center, Denver, CO 80225. (303) 236-7477.

PART THREE

The Southeast

CHAPTER NINE

CHARLOTTE, NORTH CAROLINA

DAVIDSON RIVER, NORTH AND SOUTH MILLS RIVERS, JACOB FORK

Ann McIntosh

Anglers with business in Charlotte, the Research Triangle, or Winston-Salem can find excellent trout fishing within a few hours' drive. To the west, between Asheville, the jumping-off point for the waters described here, and the Great Smoky Mountains, 4,000 miles of trout streams descend from the Blue Ridge mountains in the Pisgah and Nantahala National Forests. There are wild trout streams regulated for catch-and-release, as well as stocked delayed harvest and hatchery-supported put-and-take fisheries. There are tiny, tightly covered streams and water that presents no casting challenges. The fisheries described here barely scratch the surface of the water in the Tarheel State.

Asheville is 122 miles from Charlotte, 146 from Winston-Salem, and 230 from Raleigh. Asheville itself is a tourist destination, featuring the Biltmore Estate, a 250-room French Renaissance chateau built as a "summer cottage" by George Vanderbilt in 1895. The area offers numerous indoor and outdoor activities, as well as fine restaurants and accommodations.

Brook, brown, and rainbow trout all are available in western North Carolina, but the little wild brookies are my favorite. The streams of the Blue Ridge mountains don't grow monster trout, but they offer the beauty of colorful wild fish and feisty browns in shallow waters. The brookies range from 6 to 9 inches long, a trophy 'bow is a foot long, and the biggest brown you're likely to encounter could be 16 inches. If you want big trout, you can catch these on the big tailwaters—the Nantahala, Watauga, and Hiwassee. These streams are very pretty, accessible, and uncomplicated to fish, but the more accessible the water, the more company you'll have. To have a solitary experience, ask at the fly shops, and be willing to walk some distance to water off the beaten track.

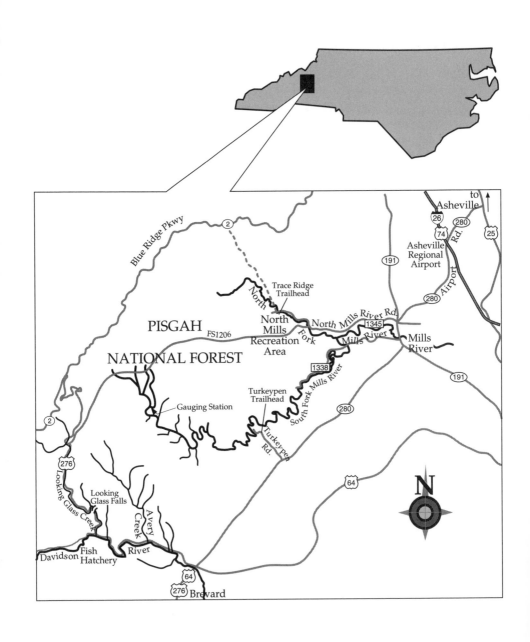

DAVIDSON RIVER

The Davidson is an evergreen- and hardwood-lined sparkling river ranging from 20 to 30 feet wide. The wading is easy and the fishing is tough. This river is one of the most popular in the state, and the fish have had an excellent education. I fished in late May, between the Hendrickson and the sulphur hatches. Very few bugs appeared on the water that day, and though I did get a couple fish to look at an Elk Hair Caddis, the rainbows and browns I caught were taken with a beadhead Green Weenie. I wonder if perhaps these fish had never before seen the chartreuse wonder fly. I had to leave the water before the green drake emergence at dusk, but anglers told me the following day that it turned into a fine evening.

Despite my serendipitous experience with the Green Weenie, the Davidson River is a notoriously difficult stream. The water is often skinnier than its cover. Any wake, any water pushed ahead of yourself upstream, will result in fish scattering into hidden hidey-holes before you realize you've spooked them. I observed this by walking upstream as much like a Native American as I could, no rod in hand, then getting off and away from the water to circle upstream and see how far the fish had run. They had run six pools upstream! Many Davidson regulars like to fish with a dry fly and a dropper, giving the fish the benefit of selecting a morsel from the deepest part of pocket water and pools.

Hatches, Flies, and Best Times to Fish

The prettiest and best seasons to fish western North Carolina are spring and fall. It's not hard to imagine the beauty of flowering mountain laurel and rhododendron in the spring and the luster of fall colors in October. All wild trout streams are open throughout the year; those that are hatchery supported are closed for stocking in March. Winter provides good fishing, since North Carolina gets very little snow. Effective patterns include Pheasant Tail Nymphs, midges as small as #28s, little olives, and #18 black stoneflies.

Western North Carolina trout streams have most of the standard East Coast hatches. The streams are not rich with aquatic creatures or insects, however, so the trout eat eagerly and opportunistically. According to Michael R. ("Squeak") Smith, Trout Unlimited's national resource director for the Southeast Region, these mountain trout are not selective. He suggests that you use your own favorite attractor patterns, saying that presentation is more important than fly selection, with choice of color and size a close second.

Smith fishes a #16 Elk Hair Caddis every month of the year. He also likes to fish it with a dropper, a beadhead nymph such as a Pheasant Tail. Stealth is very important, as the water is shallow and clear.

The spring emergences begin with *Paraleptophlebia* (#18 Blue Quill), followed by Quill Gordons, Hendricksons, and march browns. May brings light cahills, Gray Foxes, sulphurs, and green drakes. There is a great variety of midges on the Davidson. Ants, inchworms, and beetles take fish in summertime. Caddis appear throughout the year.

Davidson River Access

The Davidson River is about forty minutes southwest of Asheville. To get there, take I-26 south to Route 280 (Airport Road). Head west on Route 280 to U.S. Route 276 west, which runs along the river. There are numerous pulloffs for angler parking. The best fishing is in the fly-fishing only, catch-and-release section, from the mouth of Avery Creek upstream to the fish hatchery. Bear left at the fork to get to the hatchery parking lot. If you stay right, on Route 276, you will come to Looking Glass Falls and the Slippery Rock Recreation Area. The recreation area above Looking Glass Falls offers excellent rainbow habitat, albeit reserved for experienced casters used to dealing with heavy cover.

NORTH MILLS RIVER

The North Mills River is a small mountain stream regulated as a delayed harvest fishery. This narrow 20- to 25-foot-wide stream is stocked with brookies, browns, and 'bows. Under delayed harvest regulations, fish may not be kept from October 1 to the first Saturday in June, after which time seven fish may be creeled.

This is a pretty stream with hardwood canopy and rhododendron cover. Keeping your backcast high and out of the bushes is easier than it would first appear. I caught five brookies and a 'bow the morning I fished there. The fish took either a #16 Patriot or the beadhead Green Weenie fished in tandem.

This stream can get crowded on weekends, particularly in the spring, and the fish quickly learn to lie in tight to the banks under rhododendron roots. Casting straight up the middle of the water is not a problem, but under most circumstances, that's not where the trout are. They hold in lies close to the banks, and you'll have to use some kind of sidearm or curve cast to reach them.

North Mills Access

To reach the North Mills River, take I-26 south from Asheville to Exit 9. Turn right on Route 280 (Airport Road), then turn right on North Mills River Road and follow to the North Mills River Recreation Area Campground. Then turn right on FS 5000 (not on map). Bear left at the fork onto FS 142 (not on map). The road will end at the parking lot for the campground. From the parking lot, go to the Trace Ridge Trailhead (see map), and walk fifteen to twenty minutes down to the stream. You can access the upper reaches at the gauging station off FS 1206. I prefer to cast upstream on small mountain streams, but if you find you have company, fish downstream. You'll need long leaders and drag-free drifts, whichever way you go.

SOUTH MILLS RIVER

This is one of the most popular wild mountain trout streams in the state. Although it requires a steep, twenty- to thirty-minute walk in, you won't be alone on the water. I walked down the steep path imagining the first pool, then picturing myself working upstream to another lovely pool. My fantasy included no other anglers. As I approached the water, I saw a fisherman standing ankle-deep in the nicest pool. I could tell he had approached carefully and looked forward to taking one of the fish rising under the rhododendron. I turned downstream.

The South Mills is another small stream, with bright water running over caramel-colored rocks. On the banks are shade trees and shorter, tippet-snatching bushes. The South Mills is slightly wider than the North Mills, and the gradient is more gradual. It too requires stealth and very careful wading. If you're fishing downstream, long, drag-free drifts are a must, and the lighter the tippet, the greater your chances of a strike.

I found the fishing on the South Mills the most difficult of the waters I explored on my brief foray into North Carolina. The fish are all wild and are fished over daily. I took only two, one on the reliable Green Weenie, another on a Patriot dry.

The North Carolina Council of Trout Unlimited and the U.S. Forestry Service are working on the trail that goes down a very steep incline to the water. Runoff is being deflected and dispersed from the dirt trail to reduce sediment loading in the stream.

Hatches, Flies, and Best Times to Fish

Hatches follow the same schedule as on the Davidson River. Since it's not stocked, the South Mills River can be fished year-round. Either the North or South Mills River will take a good six- to seven-hour day to fish thoroughly. The earlier you arrive on the water, the less likely you are to find another angler in the nicest pools.

South Mills Access

- Turkey Pen Road, off Route 280 at the Turkey Pen Trailhead. Walk down the trail marked by a U.S. Forest Service sign barring motorized vehicles. When you get to the stream, walk up at least 100 yards before you begin to fish. There are 15.5 miles of water from the Turkey Pen Trailhead to the gauging station. It's also a 15.5-mile trail, so if you want to make the trek, it will require camping overnight.
- Take U.S. Route 276 north, then turn onto FS 1206. Go about 2.5 miles to a "Y," and bear right onto FS 476, which dead-ends at the gauging station. A path to the river begins here.

JACOB FORK

"Squeak" Smith is a very knowledgeable North Carolina angler and conservationist, and I was fortunate to have him as my guide on the Jacob Fork, a productive trout stream near Morganton, 40 miles east of Asheville. This small stream runs through South Mountains State Park and is readily accessible along most of its length. It's less than a two-hour drive from Charlotte's Douglas International Airport. The park has more than 20 miles of wild trout water for those willing to walk into the 16,000 acres of backcountry. Designated and primitive campsites are available on a first-come, first-served basis.

The Jacob Fork is 15 to 20 feet wide, with moderate overhead and streamside foliage to test your casting skills. Ample delayed harvest regulations and stocking have made this an angler's mecca. March, April, October, and November are the prime times to fish. Twenty-fish days are the norm. Dry flies in #14–#18, combined with nymphs dropped 12 to 18 inches below the dry, are consistent producers. There are some very large brown trout—16 inches and up—in this water. Compared with the North and South Mills, Smith says the Jacob Fork is easier than the South Mills and more challenging than the North Mills.

The Jacob Fork is stocked and regulated as delayed harvest water for 2½ miles from the lower South Mountains State Park boundary to the confluence with Shinny Creek. The Jacob Fork above the mouth of Shinny Creek offers 2½ miles of wild trout water. Brown, brook, and rainbow trout can all be found in this stream. Though the stream is narrow, Smith and I were almost able to fish side by side, taking turns in deep pools, runs, and pocket water.

Jacob Fork Access

To reach South Mountains State Park and the Jacob Fork from Charlotte, take I-77 north to I-40 west. Get off at Exit 105 (Morganton), and head south on Route 18. Follow signs to South Mountains State Park—about 18 miles, with good signage. Park only at the lower, middle, or upper parking lot in the park. Do not park in the pulloffs running past the lower part of the delayed harvest area, or you'll have a ticket when you return.

ALSO WORTH NOTING
Shinny Creek

A wild trout tributary of the Jacob Fork, Shinny Creek can be fished upstream for 200 yards to Shinny Falls; above the falls, the water is very overgrown and bushy, but it holds excellent populations of wild rainbows.

East Fork of the Pigeon River

Fourteen-inch fish are stocked and fed by local Trout Unlimited members. Access is at Camp Hope at Cruso, on U.S. Route 276. Sign in and fish if you're looking for larger trout.

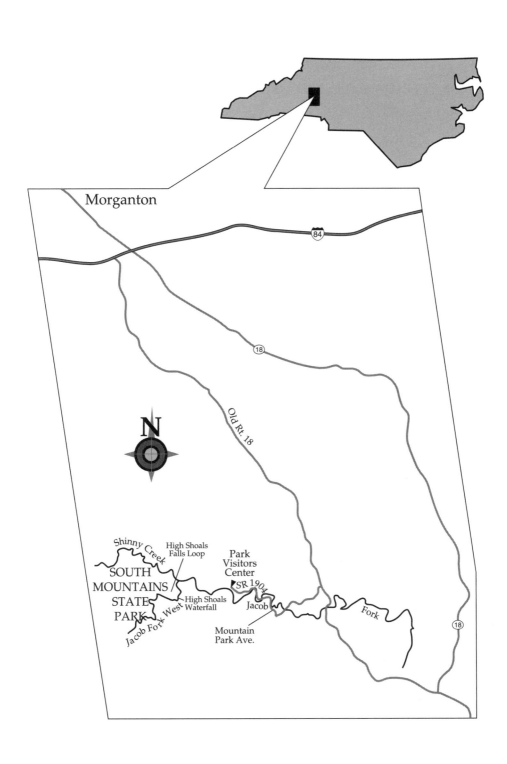

Morganton

SOUTH
MOUNTAINS
STATE
PARK

Shinny Creek
High Shoals
Falls Loop
Park
Visitors
Center
SR 1904
Jacob
High Shoals
Waterfall
Jacob Fork West
Mountain
Park Ave.
Fork

Old Rt. 18

Looking Glass Creek
This is a major tributary of the Davidson that is teeming with not-so-small rainbows—up to 15 inches. There are pulloffs along U.S. Route 276.

Other Streams
There are probably four or five times the number of worthy trout streams in the Pisgah National Forest area than those described here. Ask at local and urban fly shops. You'll find far fewer people on streams requiring a mile or so walk in. Nevertheless, don't overlook the water along major highways, which often gets little pressure.

Northeast of Asheville, near the town of Boone, there are numerous quality trout streams as good as those noted here. For more information, contact Theo or Hayden Copeland at the Appalachian Angler near Boone, (828) 963-5050.

Nantahala River
The Nantahala is one of the jewels in the North Carolina trout river crown. It is located about four and a half hours west of Charlotte. The nearest fly shop is Highland Hiker, in Highlands.

From Charlotte, take I-85 south to Gaffney, South Carolina, and then turn right on South Carolina Route 11, a beautiful, scenic, two-lane highway along the foothills. Turn right on South Carolina Route 130, left on South Carolina Route 413, then right on Route 107 north to Cashiers, North Carolina.

To get to Highlands from Cashiers, make a left on U.S. Route 64 west. Take this 10 miles to Highlands and the Highland Hiker shop.

To get directly to the Nantahala, stay on North Carolina Route 107 north to U.S. Route 441. Take Route 441 north to U.S. Route 19/74. Continue on Route 19/74 through the beautiful Nantahala Gorge, and the delayed harvest section is left on Road #1310 (Ball Road), which winds along the delayed harvest section.

At its widest above the dam, the Nantahala is about 30 feet; this is a narrow stream, with a high gradient, boulders, and pocket water in the most productive trout fishing reaches. The catch-and-release season is from October 1 to the first Saturday in June. Streamers will produce on the river year-round.

For more information, call Highland Hiker, David Wilkes, proprietor, in Highlands, North Carolina, (828) 526-5298. This is a full-service tackle shop for the Nantahala, providing guides and selling the best local patterns.

IF YOU GO
From Raleigh and Durham, as well as Greensboro and Winston-Salem, take I-40 west to Asheville. To continue on to Brevard, take I-26 south. Get off at Exit 9, and take Airport Road (Route 280) south.

Tackle Shops and Guides

Davidson River Outfitters. Brevard. Kevin Howell, proprietor. On the edge of the Pisgah Forest at the junction of Routes 280 and 276. (828) 877-4181. E-mail: davidsonrivr@infoave.com.

Bruce Harang. Ashville. Guide. (828) 281-1618.

Hunter Banks Outfitters. Asheville. Frank Smith, proprietor. A full-service fly shop with good guides and excellent schools. (800) 227-6732. www.hunterbanks.com/stream.htm.

Table Rock Angler. Morganton. Robert Cash, proprietor. By appointment. (828) 433-RODS.

Where to Stay

In Brevard, Near the Davidson River

Hampton Inn. Moderate. (828) 883-4800.

Days Inn. Close to Brevard. Moderate. (800) 329-7466.

Super-8 Motel. Inexpensive. (800) 800-8000.

In Asheville

Beaufort Inn. One of the best B&Bs in western North Carolina. Expensive. (800) 261-2221.

Econolodge. Inexpensive. (800) 424-4777.

Grove Park Inn Resort. One of the region's oldest and most famous grand hotels, overlooking Asheville from the Blue Ridge mountains. Expensive. (800) 438-8000. www.groveparkinn.com.

Holiday Inn. Moderate to expensive. (800) HOLIDAY or (828) 298-5611.

Quality Inn. Moderate. (800) 228-5151.

The Lion and the Rose B&B. Elegant Georgian house in the historic Montford district. Expensive. (800) 546-6988.

Sleep Inn. Inexpensive. (704) 277-1800.

Wright Inn. A Victorian B&B in the historic Montford district of Asheville. Moderate to expensive. (828) 251-0789. www.wrightinn.com.

Asheville B&B Association. (877) 262-6867.

Where to Eat

Cafe on the Square. Asheville. Very good food. Moderate. (828) 251-5565.

Clock of Brevard. Brevard. Good burgers and basic fare. Inexpensive. (828) 844-5010.

El Chapala. Brevard. Mexican food. Inexpensive. (828) 877-5250.

Falls Landing. Brevard. Moderate. (828) 884-2835.

Golden Horn Restaurant. Asheville. Good Mediterranean and American food. Moderate to expensive. (828) 281-4676.

Grovewood Cafe. Asheville. One of the best restaurants in town. Expensive. (828) 258-2798.

La Paz. Asheville. In Biltmore Village. Moderate to expensive. (828) 277-1558.

Magnolia's Raw Bar and Seafood Grille. Asheville. Seafood, low country, and continental cuisine. Moderate. (828) 251-5211.

Richmond Hill Inn. Asheville. World-renowned restaurant. Expensive. (828) 252-7313.

RESOURCES

Camuto, Phil. *A Fly Fishermans' Blue Ridge.* New York: Henry Holt and Company, 1990.

DeHart, Allen. *North Carolina Hiking Trails.* Boston, MA: Appalachian Mountain Club Books, 1996.

Howell, Don, and Kevin Howell. *Tying and Fishing Southern Appalachian Trout Flies.* Clayton, GA: Fern Creek Press, 1999.

North Carolina Atlas & Gazetteer. Yarmouth, ME: DeLorme Mapping Company. (207) 846-7000.

Ross, John. *Trout Unlimited's Guide to America's 100 Best Trout Streams.* Helena, MT: Falcon Publishing, 1999.

CHAPTER TEN

ATLANTA

CHATTAHOOCHEE RIVER, DUKES CREEK, WATERS CREEK, AND SOQUE RIVER

Eric W. Peper and Leroy Powell

Atlanta is arguably *the* major southeastern business hub in the nation, and its Hartsfield International Airport, in addition to being the home base of Delta, is, at various times of year, the busiest airport in the world. Atlanta's location in the foothills of the north Georgia mountains also puts it close to some high-quality trout fishing, much of which is available to the visiting angler twelve months of the year.

The north Georgia mountains form part of the southern Appalachian spine. From its outward appearance, this part of the state could be transplanted visually to New York's Catskills, Pennsylvania's Poconos, or rural New England. The valleys are deep, and the streams run fast and clear through forests populated with hemlocks, cedars, rhododendrons, laurel, and hardwoods.

The streams are the extreme southern end of the range of the native brook trout of North America. Once you drive 60 miles north of Atlanta, you'll find many streams with brown, rainbow, and a few brook trout. The brookies have been decimated by extensive stocking of the other two species and by poor logging practices. Many people find it remarkable that there are any brook trout in the South, believing that the beautiful little fish exist only in the Northeast and upper Midwest.

Whether you want a challenge or a sure thing, Waters Creek and Dukes Creek, in addition to metropolitan Atlanta's Chattahoochee River, are tailored to your wishes. These streams have their origins in the Chattahoochee National Forest. Dukes Creek was stocked in 2000, a measure needed to increase the numbers of fish after many were killed by a severe drought. Waters Creek can also support trout reproduction. Though both Waters and Dukes hold sizable trout, these creeks are small, surrounded with vegetation. The Chattahoochee, locally called the "Hooch," is a

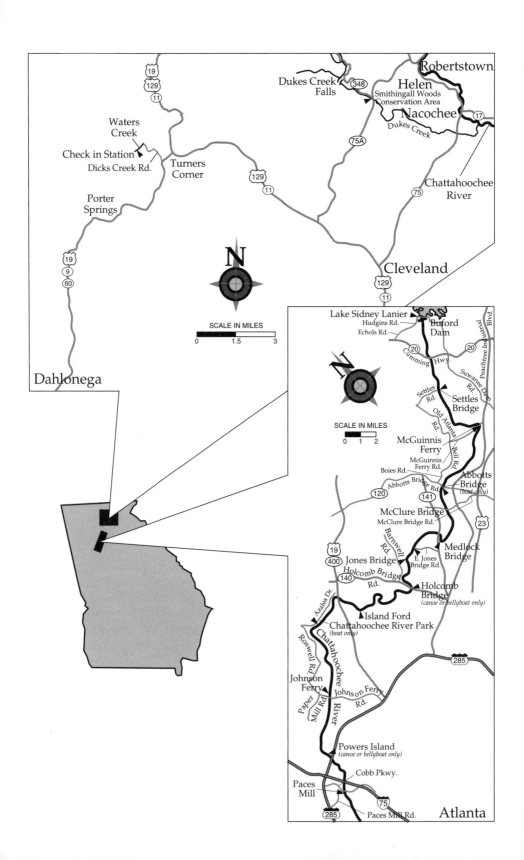

full-blown river, wide, varied, and with plenty of casting room. By the time it reaches the Atlanta area, the Hooch is man-made trout water.

CHATTAHOOCHEE RIVER

The Chattahoochee is set in fast-growing metropolitan Atlanta, beautiful and tree-shaded in the midst of shopping centers and subdivisions. In the Hooch, fish are relatively easy to catch.

In 1956 the Buford Dam was completed, forming Lake Lanier. Its purpose was flood control and hydropower generation on the Chattahoochee, but an unintended side benefit was the creation of a trout tailwater extending 46 miles downstream into the city of Atlanta.

Water for the Buford Dam generators is drawn from the bottom of Lake Lanier, 30 degrees colder than the surface water. The discharge (at about 50 degrees F), and what was a warm-water stream before the dam was built, became a cold-water trout fishery. There is no closed season for trout on the Chattahoochee below the dam, so the river provides a winter escape when cabin fever sets in.

Each year the Department of Natural Resources (DNR) stocks thousands of rainbows, browns, and brookies in the river. This is necessary because fluctuating water levels, siltation, and lack of gravel spawning beds make for limited natural reproduction. The stockings of brown trout have resulted in a significant increase in reproduction. Anglers who come to the Chattahoochee, however, don't seem to mind the artificial situation, and many leave satisfied with their eight-fish limit. Night crawlers and corn account for a large part of the catch, but for some 15 miles, between the Route 20 bridge and Route 141 at Medlock bridge, only flies and artificial lures are allowed. There is a delayed harvest stretch between Soap Creek and Route 41, in the vicinity of Cochran Shoals.

Most of your catch will be rainbows or browns in the 8- to 14-inch range. But there's always the chance for a hefty carryover from previous years.

The river bottom consists of sandbars with occasional shoals and old fish weirs. If the water is low enough, wade to the middle of the river and cast a fly to the logs and brushpiles along the banks. Watch your line, and if it hesitates, lift the rod. Once the fly begins to swing across the current, you don't even have to watch it; eager trout will slam it with enthusiasm.

As you work your fly in the blowdowns and brushpiles along the bank, or through the boulders in the shoals, you'll see industrial plants as well as near-wilderness areas. There is a sand-dredging operation at McGinnis Ferry, while just above, posh residences are springing up. Heavy traffic rumbles across Abbotts bridge, but not far downstream, you'll be fishing alongside the fairways of a golf course.

The areas between the bridges are calm and quiet, the banks shaded by poplars and sycamores. You'll see squirrels, an occasional otter, numbers of great blue herons, and mallard ducks. This is pleasant water, cool and shady, with plenty of fish eager to take your lure, and you don't even have to leave greater Atlanta to get there.

The headwaters of the Chattahoochee flow right through the center of Helen. The river is small here and is stocked annually. The upper Hooch is open year-round and provides reasonably good fishing for stocked fish until its waters are taken over by recreational tubers during the summer. As an example, on a post–Labor Day visit, the river produced several hatchery-bred rainbows up to 12 inches, despite the angler's having to dodge tubers several times in a couple of hours.

Hatches, Flies, and Best Times to Fish

The enormous surge of water released from the dam scours the river bottom in the special-regulations section, so there is little aquatic vegetation and few predictable hatches. With few insects, the fish are in the market for just about anything that drifts by. Most fly fishers use nymphs or streamers fished across and down. Caddis are a mainstay. You can check with the people at the fly shops as to what's working, but if you go equipped with #14–#16 Gold-Ribbed Hare's Ears, #14–#16 Beadhead Prince Nymphs, Pheasant Tail Nymphs (#16–#18), a few #8 Golden Stoneflies, and a selection of Olive and Black Woolly Buggers, you can count on success. Good numbers of olives start in late February and continue into autumn. If you spot rising fish, try a #14–#16 Adams or a Royal Wulff in the same size.

Chattahoochee Regulations

Everyone on the water must wear a life vest and have a Georgia fishing license and trout stamp. Trout fishing is permitted year-round, so the Hooch provides a convenient cure for cabin fever.

Chattahoochee Access

Much of the public access to the river is on land in the Chattahoochee River National Recreation Area, administered by the U.S. Park Service. There are sixteen park sections along 48 miles of the river. A delayed harvest section runs from Soap Creek to U.S. Route 141. In the artificial lures and flies only section, there are boat ramps at Abbotts bridge and Medlock bridge parks. There is access to the delayed harvest section from Soap Creek to U.S. Route 141.

It's difficult to wade much of the river, so fishing from a canoe, a johnboat, or a float tube is the most effective way to avoid the more heavily fished areas. Many fishermen launch and motor upstream, then drift back to the put-in. Float tubers take two vehicles, leaving one at the takeout point and driving back to put in.

For the release schedule at Buford Dam, call (770) 945-1466. For the Morgan Falls Dam release schedule, telephone (404) 329-1455. Call before you go. When the generators turn on, the river can rise 5 feet in fifteen minutes. Don't ignore the discharge schedule; it's not worth risking your life.

DUKES CREEK

Dukes Creek is a major tributary of the Chattahoochee in its upper reaches. In 1994 the state of Georgia purchased a little over 5,000 acres along Dukes Creek, which runs between Helen and Cleveland, Georgia, about an hour and fifteen minutes north of the junction of I-285 and Route 400. The property, called Smithgall Woods, was the private preserve of an Atlanta family who used it as their weekend and vacation hunting and fishing retreat. Since the purchase, the state has managed the property as a quality hunting and fishing preserve and has succeeded remarkably well. The property abounds with deer and small game, and the stretch of Dukes Creek the state manages is a jewel of a trout stream. Except for a narrow, paved, two-lane private road that runs parallel to the stream through hardwoods, rhododendron, hemlock, and cedar, there is little evidence of human trespass. You're just as likely to find a doe watching you fish as another human.

The Smithgall Woods section of Dukes Creek has not been stocked with anything but fingerlings in many years, and it supports healthy populations of wild brook, brown, and rainbow trout. The careful angler stands an excellent chance of sight-casting to trout of 18 and 20 inches.

Smithgall Woods is open to trout fishing year-round. During the off-season, from November through February, reservations may be made for a full day (8 A.M. until 4:30 P.M.) on Wednesdays, Saturdays, and Sundays. During the regular trout season (March 1 through October 31), the state accepts reservations for up to fourteen anglers for half-day sessions (sun-up to noon and 2 P.M. until sunset) on the stream on Wednesdays, Saturdays, and Sundays.

Hatches, Flies, and Best Times to Fish

Hatches on Dukes can begin as early as late February, with a variety of small caddisflies. By mid-March, Hendricksons and olives appear, followed by sulphurs and more caddis. Dense mayfly hatches are seldom seen, which is not to say they don't occur. There are frequent large caddis hatches during the day, and the fish key on them. Hare's Ear Nymphs and caddis larvae and pupae are excellent subsurface prospecting patterns, and if fish are rising, a #18 brown-gray Elk Hair Caddis will often produce.

Dukes Creek Regulations

Only barbless hooks on artificial lures or flies may be used while fishing, and all trout caught must be released. You park at the check-in station and are either shuttled by van or may walk to your selected section of stream. Beats are not assigned, and you may fish anywhere you wish along the several miles of this pool-and-riffle stream, which averages about 20 to 25 feet across. The only fee associated with the angling at any time is a $2 parking charge. Make reservations well in advance, as much as thirty days, if possible, although last-minute cancellations are a possibility. Call (706) 878-3087.

Dukes Creek Access
The Smithgall Woods section of Dukes Creek may be reached from Route 75A just west of the town of Helen.

WATERS CREEK
Anglers come to Lumpkin County's Waters Creek prospecting for bragging-size trout. Waters Creek is isolated, completely surrounded by the Blue Ridge mountains of the Chestatee Wildlife Management Area. This water, in contrast to the Chattahoochee, gives up its fish reluctantly.

In a cooperative effort, the Georgia Department of Natural Resources, U.S. Forest Service (USFS), and Georgia Council of Trout Unlimited established and maintain Waters Creek as a trophy trout venue. It is a classic north Georgia stream. There are only 2½ miles of fishable water, and the creek is no more than 10 feet at its widest. Much of the stream is overhung with mountain laurel, rhododendron, and dog-hobble.

Rainbow trout reproduce naturally here, and for diversity, the DNR occasionally stocks browns and brookies. Three times a week, wildlife technicians feed commercial trout rations to the fish to supplement the natural food and promote rapid growth. Combined with stringent angling regulations, this program results in specimens of mind-boggling proportions for any water, much less a tiny mountain stream. In past years, anglers have recorded catches as large as 5-pound brook trout, 9-pound browns, and 12-pound rainbows.

But the big fish are exceedingly wary, and even the smaller ones spook easily. This is especially true during the summer months, when the creek runs low and clear. Many experienced anglers don't even attempt to go between June and September.

Hatches, Flies, and Best Times to Fish
Waters Creek is a typical Georgia mountain stream, with scarce food and unpredictable emergences. Hatches of caddis and mayflies are irregular, so it's wise to observe and be prepared.

Effective flies include midges, Elk Hair Caddis, Adamses, Woolly Buggers, and Gold-Ribbed Hare's Ears. One fly tied specifically for Waters is a bit of cork half the size of a pencil eraser glued to a hook. The size, shape, and color are similar to trout feed pellets used to supplement the food supply. This fly is dead-drifted through pools at leisurely intervals to keep the fish from getting too used to it.

No matter what your choice of fly, no matter how careful and quiet your approach, chances are the fish will get the better of you. Serious anglers wear full forest green camouflage and approach the water slowly and carefully. Very good anglers have spent hours emptying their fly wallets on Waters Creek and come away with little to show for their efforts. Experts say that if you catch anything at all during the summer months, you can count yourself as lucky, and during the spring and fall, an average of one fish per hour is considered a good day.

When you fish Waters Creek, remember that this small stream holds its secrets tight to its bosom and does not release them willingly. There is a cadre of dedicated anglers who are willing to make regular pilgrimages and give the stream the study it requires. These anglers are rewarded with regular catches of quality fish. For the occasional visitor, any fish caught, no matter its size, can be considered a trophy.

Waters Creek Regulations

The area is open from 6:30 A.M. to 6:30 P.M. (7:30 P.M. EDT) Wednesday, Saturday, and Sunday, from the last weekend in March through the end of October. Check in and out at the check station on FS 144. Anglers must have a Georgia fishing license, trout stamp, and wildlife management area (WMA) stamp.

A nonresident seven-day fishing license with trout stamp costs a reasonable $20, but the nonresident fee for a WMA stamp is another $73. Licenses are not available at the check station but can be bought by telephone at (888) 748-6887, on the Internet at www.georgia.org/dnr/wild, or at local convenience stores and tackle shops.

Only single-hook, barbless flies and artificial lures are allowed, no larger than #6. You can't even have flies that don't fit the regulations on your person while you're in the area. Only one fly may be used at a time. Landing nets must be no longer than 2 feet. You may keep one fish a day. The minimum size for keepers is 22 inches for browns and rainbows, and 18 inches for brook trout.

Waters Creek Access

Access to the water is limited, as noted above. The stream runs parallel to FS 144, which intersects Waters Creek Road at the junction of Waters and Dicks Creeks. The check station is on FS 144 before the parking lot and stream access.

SOQUE RIVER

Travelers to the area around Clarkesville, Georgia, will often drive along Route 197 past the Soque (pronounced either "SO-kwee" or "SO-kee"), a river that looks like it could be excellent trout water. The Soque is almost entirely private water, but visiting anglers may satisfy their curiosity about the river through a handful of private, pay-to-fish facilities located there. At $150 or more per day, this fishing is not for the budget angler, but it is worth mentioning.

The fishing on the Soque may be well worth the money to some readers, because the fish maintained by the owners of these river sections may be the largest trout you'll ever land or even target *anywhere*. Trout in the 8- to 10-pound class are quite common. The river is 20 to 25 feet wide, pool and riffle in character, with occasional long, flat stretches that flow through tunnels of trees. The fishing is primarily with nymphs and is, if the truth be told, a fish-catching experience rather than a technical challenge, as the fish feed eagerly to big Hare's Ears and Woolly Buggers. At the same time, I don't believe any of us would find anything wrong with occasionally landing a dozen or so healthy 20-inch-plus fish in a day's angling!

The private facilities are accessible by reservation only and allow fly fishing and catch-and-release in order to maintain the quality of the fishery. They are open only on selected days in order to rest the fish and the water to provide consistent high-quality fishing experiences. Guide services are available, if desired, but the water is certainly fishable solo.

For additional information on the Soque facilities, contact the Fish Hawk in Atlanta, (404) 237-3473. The people at the Fish Hawk can put you in touch with Blackhawk, one of the private facilities on the Soque. If you go, be sure to take your camera or camcorder, because your buddies will never believe you when you come home and tell 'em you took an 8-pound trout on the fly in Georgia.

Brigadoon Lodge is another angler-oriented facility on the Soque. Rod fees through the lodge range from $150 a day (winter) to $250 a day in prime time (March 1 to June 15). Guides are available for an additional fee. (706) 754-1558. E-mail: brigadoo@alltel.net. Website: www.brigadoon lodge.com.

Within two hours of Atlanta are Noontootla Creek and the Toccoa, northeast of Ellijay, Georgia, off I-575, and the Chattooga, the filming location and subject river in *Deliverance,* in extreme northeastern Georgia, accessible via I-85 to I-985 south of Clarkesville.

IF YOU GO

If you plan to include trout fishing in a visit to Atlanta, it's wise to stay on the north side of town for convenient access to streams. Hartsfield Airport is located south of the city.

To reach the Chattahoochee, take Atlanta's perimeter highway, I-285, to Route 141 north. After 7.5 miles, you'll pass the Medlock bridge public-use area on the left. Continue north on Route 141 for 4 more miles to Route 120, and turn left. After a mile, you'll come to Abbotts bridge. Continue .75 mile farther on Route 120, and take a left on Peachtree Industrial Boulevard. Either turn left at the 5-mile point to get to McGinnis Ferry, or turn left at 6.2 miles onto Suwannee Dam Road, then turn left on Route 20 to reach the river bridge.

To reach Dukes Creek, take Route 400, a multilane divided highway, north from Atlanta, and continue straight on the road after it narrows to two lanes. At the first stop sign after you're on the two-lane, take a right and follow signs to White County High School on U.S. Route 129. After passing the high school on your right, continue about a mile to Alternate Route 75 (75A) on your right. Take 75A for 5 or 6 miles to the Smithgall Woods turn on your right.

You can also take Route 75 out of Cleveland directly to Helen. From Helen, drive west on Route 75 along the upper Chattahoochee, turn left onto Route 75A, and follow to the Smithgall Woods entrance on your left.

From the Atlanta area, you can approach Waters Creek through either Cleveland or Dahlonega. From Cleveland, take U.S. Route 129 north about 10 miles to Turners Corner (the junction of U.S. Routes 19 and 129). Turn left on U.S. Route 19, and go .5 mile to Dicks Creek Road (FS 34). From Dahlonega, take U.S. Route 19 north 13 miles to Dicks Creek Road. Follow Dicks Creek Road north 2.7 miles, and turn left onto FS 144. Access to Waters Creek is through a check station located on FS 144, a couple hundred yards from its intersection with Dicks Creek Road.

Tackle Shops, Guides, and Licenses
In or Near Atlanta

Bass Pro Shops/Sportsman's Warehouse. Shackleford Road. A huge selection of tackle and a large fly-fishing section. (770) 931-5050.

The Classic Angler. (404) 233-5110.

The Fish Hawk. Features a full range of fly- and spin-fishing gear and is a good source for information and guides. (404) 237-3473. www.thefishhawk.com.

Atlanta Fly Fishing Outfitters. Dunwoody. (770) 689-0707.

Orvis Atlanta. (404) 841-0093.

River Through Atlanta. Roswell. Chris Scalley, guide. (770) 650-8630. E-mail: Troutguy@mindspring.com. www.riverthroughatlanta.com.

In Cleveland and Dahlonega

Waters Creek. A number of hardware and convenience stores sell fishing licenses and limited tackle and bait near Waters Creek.

River Through Atlanta. Roswell. Chris Scalley, primary guide. (770) 650-8630. E-mail: chris.scalley@mindspring.com. www.riverthroughatlanta.com.

Unicoi Outfitters. Helen. A full-service fly-fishing shop and a good source of up-to-date information on Waters Creek and other local streams. (706) 878-3083.

Mountain Sports. Just north of Cleveland on Route 75. Bait, tackle, selection of locally tied flies. (706) 865-5917.

Where to Stay
Alpenhof Motel. Helen. Moderate. (706) 878-2268.
Alpine Village Inn. Helen. Moderate. (800) 844-8466 or (706) 878-2296.
Chattahoochee Riverfront Motel. Helen. (800) 476-8331 or (706) 878-3144.
Helendorf River Inn. Helen. Moderate. (706) 878-2271.
Dutch Cottage. Helen. B&B. Moderate. (706) 878-3135.
Glen-Kenimer-Tucker House. Sautee. Just south and east of Helen. B&B on National Register of Historic Places. Moderate. (706) 878-2364.
Hilltop Haus. Helen. B&B. Moderate. (706) 878-2388.
Cabins on the Creek. Between Cleveland and Helen. On Route 75. Moderate. (706) 865-5917.
Dukes Creek Cabins. Helen. (706) 878-2625.

In Cleveland and Dahlonega
Days Inn. Dahlonega. Moderate. (706) 864-1338.
Econo Lodge. Dahlonega. Inexpensive. (706) 864-6191.
Worley Homestead. Dahlonega. A pleasant B&B. (706) 864-7002.
Gateway Inn. Cleveland. Inexpensive. (706) 878-3121.

In Duluth and Norcross
Near the Chattahoochee, in the Duluth and Norcross area, there are a number of reasonably priced hotels and motels convenient to the river.
Motel 6. Norcross. Inexpensive. (770) 446-2311.

In Helen
The town of Helen provides a good base for fishing north Georgia streams—Dukes Creek and Waters Creek, and the upper Chattahoochee. Helen has been fashioned after a Bavarian village, with a quaintness that competes with kitsch for the visitor's attention. Many national motel chains, other accommodations, and restaurants, including Comfort Inn, Ramada Inn, Best Western, several B&Bs, and cabins, can be found here. There also are other motels, in addition to chains, all in the $60 to $80 range. Rates may vary with season. For complete information packages for Helen and the surrounding area, contact the Alpine Helen/White County Convention and Visitor's Bureau, P.O. Box 730, Helen, GA 30545, telephone (706) 878-2181.

Camping
The forest service's Waters Creek Campground is on Dicks Creek Road. It offers campsites, drinking water, and sanitary facilities. Dicks Creek,

which borders the campground, is heavily stocked during trout season. A fishing license and trout stamp are required to fish there, but no WMA stamp.

Primitive camping is available at sites in the national forest on Dicks Creek Road beyond Waters Creek. Unicoi State Park & Lodge, east of Robertstown on Route 356, offers RV and tent sites, as well as cottages and a lodge.

Where to Eat
In Helen
Helen offers numerous eateries, many featuring German-style food. Almost everything in Helen is within a mile's walking distance from anything else. Most restaurants are moderately priced.

Alt Heidelberg Restaurant & Lounge. (706) 878-2986.

Cafe International. (706) 878-3102.

Paul's Restaurant and Lounge. Steakhouse overlooking the Chattahoochee in downtown Helen. A longtime favorite. Moderate. (706) 878-2468.

Troll Tavern. Moderate. (706) 878-3117.

In Cleveland and Dahlonega
There are a number of fast-food establishments in Cleveland near Waters Creek.

Ma Gooches. In front of the Gateway Motel. A local favorite.

Smith House. Dahlonega. Famous for huge meals served family-style.

Holt Brothers Barbeque. On Jimmy Carter Boulevard.

Mick's Gwinnett. Near Gwinnett Mall.

Chinese or Thai food. Drive south on Buford Highway to Chamblee's Asian enclave.

RESOURCES
A USFS map of access points for the Chattahoochee tailwater may be purchased at local fly and tackle shops.

Georgia Atlas & Gazetteer. Yarmouth, ME: DeLorme Mapping Company. (207) 846-7000.

Jacobs, Jimmy. *Trout Fishing in North Georgia.* Atlanta: Peachtree Publications, 1996.

Jacobs, Jimmy. *Trout Streams of Southern Appalachia.* Woodstock, VT: Backcountry Publications, 1994.

Ross, John. *Trout Unlimited's Guide to America's 100 Best Trout Streams.* Helena, MT: Falcon Press, 1999.

CHAPTER ELEVEN

NASHVILLE AND KNOXVILLE

CLINCH RIVER

John Thurman

Many experienced anglers who have fished the premier trout waters of the United States consider the Clinch River tailwater to be one of the finest in the country. It is a challenging river. The clear, shallow, slow-moving Clinch demands a stealthy approach, delicate presentation, small flies, and drag-free drifts. It's very much like fishing a spring creek, but this "spring creek" is over 75 yards wide! To catch its wild, wary rainbow and brown trout requires concentration, careful execution, and patience.

The Clinch tailwater is 13 miles long and flows from Norris Dam, at river mile 80, to the Route 61 bridge near Clinton at river mile 67. The upper reaches of Melton Hill Reservoir extend to the Route 61 bridge, where the Clinch changes from riverine character to slack water.

Fly fishers will find their experience on the Clinch to be extremely rewarding. The valley through which the river flows is a beautiful, pastoral setting of wooded ridges, limestone escarpments, and pastures. The banks are lined with huge sycamores and silver maples. Spring and late-summer wildflower blooms are spectacular. The river valley supports a rich mix of birds and mammals.

The Clinch is unlike large western tailwaters such as the Bighorn and Missouri in that it has a minimum flow of only a little over 200 cubic feet per second. The river at low flow with the turbines turned is a series of long pools (¼ to ½ mile in length) separated by intermittent ledges and occasional shoals. The character of the river is similar to the Arkansas tailwaters—the Little Red, White, and Norfork. At first glance, the pools appear to be very shallow and have no flow. Upon closer inspection, you'll find that the pools have extensive areas where depths reach 8 feet and there is visible current. The seemingly flat, smooth surface is riddled with almost imperceptible surface currents that can make drag-free drifts difficult. Often, the inexperienced angler will not be able to detect that he or she is getting a bad drift.

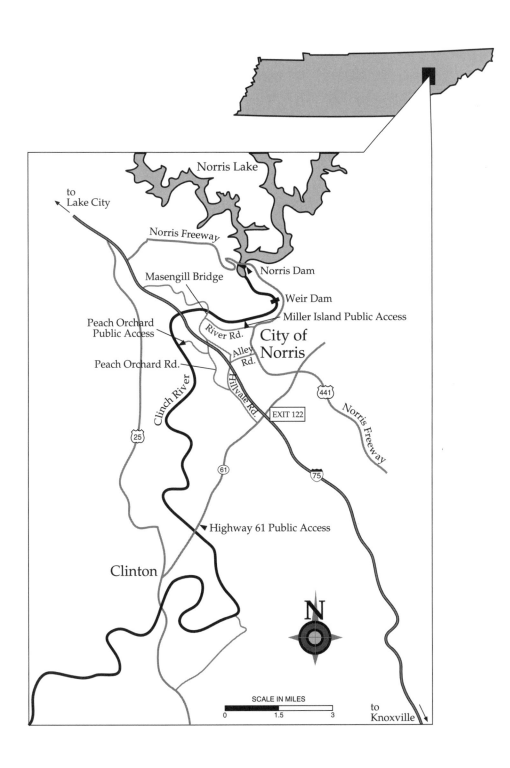

Norris Lake

to Lake City

Norris Freeway

Masengill Bridge

Norris Dam

Weir Dam

Miller Island Public Access

Peach Orchard Public Access

River Rd.

City of Norris

Peach Orchard Rd.

Alley Rd.

Hillvale Rd.

441

EXIT 122

Norris Freeway

Clinch River

25

61

75

Highway 61 Public Access

Clinton

N

SCALE IN MILES
0   1.5   3

to Knoxville

Rainbows constitute 80 to 90 percent of the catch. Almost all of the fish caught will be robust, wild, quality fish. Trout will average 11½ inches. Fish in the 14- to 16-inch range are common, and on most days an experienced angler has an excellent chance to hook one or two fish of over 18 inches. It is not uncommon for a skilled angler to land several big fish during the spring sulphur emergence.

The Tennessee state-record brown, weighing 28 pounds, 12 ounces, was taken from the Clinch in the late 1980s. Browns over 30 pounds have turned up in electroshocking surveys. Spin fishermen float the river in boats during one- and two-generator flows in pursuit of these big trophy browns. Rainbows exceeding 10 pounds have been caught.

It's best to fly-fish the Clinch when both turbines are off. The river is not suited for wade fishing with one- or two-generator flows. You can fly-fish from a boat when one generator is in operation, and this can be an effective way to fish the river in spring and summer during the sulphur hatch.

The river averages 75 yards wide at minimum flow. Typically, you'll be wading in water that is 2 to 4 feet deep, but some of the channels and pockets in the pools are 8 to 10 feet deep. The Clinch is a wader-friendly stream, but felt soles are needed. The bottom is largely composed of medium to large stones and broken ledge material.

Most experienced Clinch fly fishers prefer a 9-foot, 3-, 4-, or 5-weight rod. Because of low flows, smooth water, and water clarity, it's important to use long leaders. Twelve- to 16-foot leaders and 6X tippets are best for these wild, wary fish; some anglers occasionally go to 7X, but it generally is not necessary. Subtle surface currents that are difficult to read make line and leader management very important.

HATCHES, FLIES, AND BEST TIMES TO FISH

The prime time of the year to fish the Clinch is April through July. The water is very cold, dissolved oxygen (DO) levels are optimal, and the fish are hungry and very active. This is also the time of year when the major sulphur emergence occurs. Water temperatures in spring will typically be in the mid-forties and warm to the mid-fifties by late summer.

Fishing slows in September as the water temperature rises into the low sixties and DO levels drop. Fishing in the fall is slow, but the patient angler can catch fish in solitude. By December, DO levels have risen and the water temperature has dropped, and the fish become more active.

Throughout the year, early-morning fishing can be productive, but on most days, there is no need to be on the water before 9 A.M. As the sun gets on the water, the aquatic invertebrates become more active, and the fish begin to feed more actively. During the spring and summer sulphur emergence, the nymphs will be active throughout the morning well into the afternoon. Emergers and duns normally begin showing up in late morning, and the hatch is well under way by midafternoon. Spinner falls can be spectacular in late evening. During the rest of the year, late morning through early afternoon is generally the best time to fish.

The Clinch receives a fair amount of fishing pressure during spring and early summer, but it's very easy for the angler who wants to be alone to walk up or down the river and get away from other fishermen. During the remainder of the year, the angler will be able to fish alone.

The Clinch is primarily a midge fishery but does have an excellent sulphur hatch (primarily *Ephemerella invaria* and *E. dorothea*) that begins in early April and runs well into June. Midge pupae and blackfly larvae make up the highest percent composition of the annual diet. Sowbugs, scuds, and snails are important to a lesser extent, and sulphurs and caddis (primarily a little black caddis, *Micrasema*) are of importance in spring and summer. Throughout the year, a #18 or #20 black or olive midge pupa fished under a strike indicator is a favorite pattern. Sowbugs and scuds (#16–#18) fished under a strike indicator work year-round.

During the mayfly emergence, Pheasant Tails work well in the morning before the emergence. Thorax and Compara-dun patterns are the favorite to match the sulphur duns. Various emerger patterns, including soft hackles and trailing shuck patterns, are popular. You'll also need sulphur spinners.

During June and July, the small (#20) black caddis emerge in fair numbers. Most Clinch anglers carry a few adult and pupal patterns to imitate this caddis. Shad and sculpin patterns and Woolly Buggers also will take fish, but few use them.

The following are the important patterns and when to use them:

January–March. Dark olive, dark brown, or black midge pupae (#18–#20), light gray sowbugs (#16), light olive-gray scuds (#16).

April–May. Large sulphur emergers, duns, spinners, and nymphs (Pheasant Tail) (#16), in addition to flies listed for January through March.

Late May–June. Small sulphur emergers, duns, spinners, and nymphs (Pheasant Tail) (#18–#20), in addition to patterns listed for January through March.

June–July. Small sulphurs, little black caddis pupae and adults (#20), and patterns listed for January through March.

August–January. Same patterns as January through March.

CLINCH REGULATIONS

There are no special regulations on the Clinch, which is open for year-round fishing. Seven trout may be creeled, and there is no size limit. Non-residents must buy a $12 trout permit, as well as an annual ($26), ten-day ($15.50), or three-day ($10.50) permit. A ten-day all-fish permit is also available for $30.50, or an annual all-fish permit for $51.

CLINCH ACCESS

- River Road. At the Miller Island public boat/canoe access and parking lot. Take U.S. Route 441 about 2 miles from its junction with Route 61. You'll see the Miller Island access on your right. This is a good place to start fishing and meet other anglers.
- The dam. Stay on U.S. Route 441, pass River Road, and the highway will abut the river. Drive for about a mile, and pass the weir dam near the mouth of Clear Creek. About .5 mile beyond this point on your left, you'll come to the access road that will take you to the dam. The Tennessee Valley Authority (TVA) owns the shoreline from Miller Island to the dam, so all of this water is open to the public; the fishing is good above and below the weir.
- Peach Orchard. About 2 miles downstream from Miller Island. All of the shoreline from Miller Island to the Route 61 public launch area is privately owned, and much of it is posted. Some landowners will allow access if asked.

ALSO WORTH NOTING

Hiwassee

For fans of big-water angling and beautiful locations, the Hiwassee River tailwater below the TVA's Appalachia Powerhouse is an excellent destination. The Hiwassee is located in southeastern Tennessee near Benton, not far from Chattanooga. Travel about 6 miles north of Benton on U.S. Route 411, and turn right onto Route 30. Follow Route 30 along the river east about 8 miles to Reliance. There is a bridge over the Hiwassee at Reliance, which marks the central access point to the river's trout fishery.

The TVA's Appalachia Dam is actually located in southwestern North Carolina and impounds Appalachia Lake. Cold water from this lake is piped about 10 miles to the powerhouse, which is in Tennessee. Release of this cold water through the turbines creates about 10 to 12 miles of excellent trout fishing, extending to well below the Route 411 bridge. This is truly big water, averaging 150 yards or so in width throughout most of its length, and there is a fair amount of whitewater. The fishery is dependent on stocking, but there are plenty of holdover fish.

Fifteen- to 20-inch fish are not uncommon, and many fish longer than 20 inches are taken each year. Excellent hatches of mayflies, caddis, and stoneflies occur from late February until early November. The hatching season begins with cream, green, and black caddis in #16–#18 in early March; followed by Hendricksons, olives in a variety of sizes, sulphurs, *Isonychia* (*sadleri* early and *bicolor* later) and more caddis throughout the season.

Most of the trout-producing stretch of the river flows through the Cherokee National Forest, and the river here is at least as strong an attraction for canoeists and kayakers as it is for anglers. Recreational boating creates its share of distractions for anglers, but it also ensures the presence of campgrounds and associated facilities. Many local anglers fish the Hiwassee from float tubes. While this does give one considerably more fishing range when the TVA is generating power, I don't recommend it. This is big, rock-strewn, fast water. A number of fatal accidents involving float tubers have occurred on the river. For up-to-date information on the generator schedule, call the TVA, at (800) 238-2264, or Hiwassee Outfitters, at (423) 338-8115.

On the Hiwassee and all southern tailwaters, flows change quickly and without warning. Be alert to changing water conditions, and always keep your escape path in mind when wading. *Power generation information obtained from the TVA is always subject to change,* even when obtained on the day you are fishing. When no generators are running, most of the Hiwassee is wadable. When one generator is running, some sections of the river may be waded. If two generators are in use, fishing is pretty much restricted to boats.

Unquestionably, the best way to see the Hiwassee and to have the best chance to catch a big fish is to hire a guide with a drift boat. Several services float the river, but the best, in my opinion, is Outdoor Guide Services, telephone (770) 386-0413. Owner and guide Ronnie Hall and guide Scott Murdoch know the river intimately. They are enjoyable people to spend a day with and provide a superb experience. They schedule your trip to match the hatching activity on the river, and because they enjoy seeing you catch big fish, they will stay as late into the hatch as you want to fish.

IF YOU GO
The Clinch is located about thirty minutes north of downtown Knoxville. The Knoxville McGhee/Tyson Airport is located about 15 miles south of Knoxville on U.S. Route 129 (Alcoa Highway). From Knoxville, take I-75 north to Exit 122 (Clinton/Norris). Take a right onto Route 61, and then travel about 2 miles to the U.S. Route 441 junction.

Tackle Shops and Guides
The Creel. Knoxville. On Kingston Pike, between the Paper Mill and West Hills exits of I-40. Scott Rogers, proprietor. Complete fly shop with guides. (865) 588-6159.

Clinch River Outfitters. Andersonville. Mike Bone, proprietor. (865) 494-0972.

Where to Stay
Holiday Inn Express. At Exit 122 (Clinton/Norris) of I-75, 17 miles north of Knoxville. Moderate. (865) 457-2233.

Super 8 Motel. At Exit 122 (Clinton/Norris) of I-75, 17 miles north of Knoxville. Moderate. (865) 457-0565.

Days Inn Interstate. At Exit 129 (Lake City) of I-75, 5 miles north of Clinton/Norris exit. Moderate. (865) 426-2816.

Camping
Norris Dam State Park. Located on the Norris Dam Reservation near Norris. Cabins, trailer space, and tent camping. (865) 426-7461.

Fox Inn Campground. Near Norris. About .25 mile east of I-75 Exit 122 on Route 61. Tent and trailer sites. (865) 494-9386.

Where to Eat
Cracker Barrel. At Exit 129 (Lake City) of I-75, 5 miles north of the Clinton/Norris exit. Inexpensive. (865) 426-6429.

Golden Girl's Restaurant. At Exit 122 (Clinton/Norris) of I-75, 17 miles north of Knoxville. Inexpensive. (865) 457-3302.

Lamb's Inn Restaurant. At Exit 128 (Lake City) of I-75, 5 miles north of the Clinton/Norris exit. Inexpensive. (865) 426-6899.

China Inn. Clinton. On Route 61, 5 miles west of I-75 Exit 122 (Clinton/ Norris). Inexpensive. (865) 457-5301.

RESOURCES
Information on releases at Norris Dam. (800) 238-2264 or (865) 632-2264. www.tva.gov.

Jacobs, Jimmy. *Tailwater Trout in the South.* Woodstock, VT: Countryman Press, 1996.

Trout Unlimited Clinch River chapter. www.coalcreekaml.com/ Clinch_River_Chapter_TU.htm

USGS 1:24,000 topographic map, Lake City and Norris, Tennessee.

Tennessee Atlas & Gazetteer. Yarmouth, ME: DeLorme Mapping Company. (207) 846-7000.

SOUTH HOLSTON AND WATAUGA RIVERS

George Grant

I suppose you could think of it as a "two-fer." Be the first on your block to have your very own two-fer fishing trip to the South Holston and Watauga Rivers. Have your credit card ready and call now. The trout are standing by.

The South Holston and the Watauga are not second-class imitation tailwaters filled with constantly stocked hatchery trout. Each is a superb tailwater that will challenge and reward anglers of all skill levels. Both rivers have varied and prolific insect life and forage fish populations that

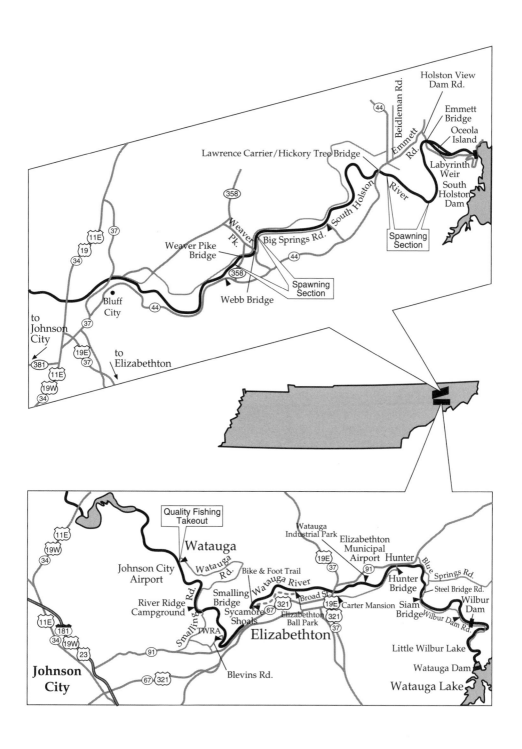

sustain naturally reproducing strains of brown trout and excellent numbers of carryover rainbows. Both rivers fish well during minimum flow and generation. A trip to either one is well worth the time and trouble. They are only a few miles apart, and their combined lengths make up 30 miles of the finest trout fishing in the Southeast. If you headquarter in Johnson City, Tennessee, a ninety-minute drive from Knoxville, you can fish them both on the same weekend, even the same day, with only a few moments spent in transit.

Both rivers are part of the Tennessee Valley Authority's system of dams and reservoirs. Created by President Roosevelt in the 1930s, the Tennessee Valley Authority (TVA) was charged with controlling flooding in the Tennessee River Valley, providing cheap electricity for the Southeast, and maintaining navigation on the Tennessee River. The TVA certainly didn't intend to create trout steams when it dammed the Watauga in the 1940s and the South Holston in the 1950s. However, the lakes created turned out to be the deepest, cleanest, and coldest in the TVA system. The water released from them changed two very good smallmouth rivers into trout water.

For a very long time, the management of the rivers was "accidental." The TVA didn't care about water quality downstream of its dams and ignored important environmental aspects, such as the oxygen content of the water it released. The Tennessee Wildlife Resources Agency (TWRA) regarded the tailwaters as put-and-take holding tanks for the distribution of hatchery fish to citizens with a trout stamp and a frying pan. That began to change in the late 1980s, when John Waters became TVA chairman. He initiated programs to monitor and improve water quality on the TVA's tailwaters and established cooperative liaisons with the TWRA and Trout Unlimited. With everyone working together, the fisheries below Holston and Watauga Dams improved from "pretty darn good" to "fantastic!" The TWRA responded to the improved conditions by creating a quality fishing section on the Watauga, placing slot limits on the Holston, and closing portions of the Holston during spawning season.

SOUTH HOLSTON RIVER

The South Holston flows through farm country on the north flank of Holston Mountain. In most places, it is 75 to 100 feet wide. There are no majestic wilderness vistas here, just vignettes of classic country landscape. Little things make it sweet: an old barn knocked out of plumb by wind, a battalion of cornstalks in ordered ranks and files waiting for the combine to charge, a horse in the pasture on the far bank watching as you stalk a rise. Osprey, herons, and river otters often share the river with you.

During minimum flow, the tailwater has many attributes of a spring creek: a mild gradient, a limestone bedrock channel, a stable flow and temperature range, and extensive vegetation that supports a prolific insect population. The food base is so good that growth rates for trout as high as an inch per month have been recorded. It also has a native population of brown trout and a high survival rate for overwintering stocked rainbows. This applies to all 14 miles of the river between the dam and Boone Lake. There aren't any dead spots or unproductive sections of the river. Wherever you fish, the fishing will be as good.

Sound like heaven? Well there are one or two flies (pun intended) in the ointment. The first is the limestone bedrock. In most places it's covered with a layer of algae, a species known as *Dumpya onyerbuttus,* that makes felt soles with cleats or spikes a must. That bedrock also means that there are very few classic riffles and runs where turbulence and noise can cover up careless wading and sloppy casting. In fact, the surface currents produced by the streambed are subtly complex and place a premium on accurate casting and line control during the drift.

All those bugs mean plenty of dry-fly opportunities for you and plenty of opportunities for the trout to develop standards for what they will eat. It's rumored that one old Holston brown had a jeweler's loupe and an entomological key in his pocket when he was caught. The stable temperature is in the forties and fifties Fahrenheit, even in July. You'll need lightweight neoprene or breathable waders over warm clothing to stay comfortable.

Holston's flow goes from 130 to 3,300 cubic feet per second when the TVA decides to make electricity. If you're wading when that happens, you'll have a few moments to get to shore. Stay alert to changes in water temperature, sticks and leaves appearing in the drift, and increased noise from the river. You don't have to panic, but you can't dawdle.

During generation, the hatches still come off and the trout still rise. The river is easily floated with a drift boat, canoe, or raft. Finding places to launch and take out is more of a challenge than any rapids on the river. Most guides have made private arrangements with landowners and are reluctant to share their facilities. Drifting from the launch site at the dam to the take-out in Bluff City is almost impossible due to time considerations. The TWRA is trying to develop more public launch sites on the Holston. Until it does, your best choice for a float trip is to book a guide.

WATAUGA RIVER

The Watauga (pronounced "wah-TAW-guh") is on the south side of Holston Mountain. Even though they are only a few miles apart, roughly the same size and length, and have many of the same hatches, there are some important differences between the Holston and the Watauga. Above Elizabethton, the Watauga flows through a more developed area than does the Holston. This means less scenery but more access. The riparian zone along the river screens out some of the less attractive elements of its location, even when you're fishing in town.

The Watauga's gradient is steeper than the Holston's, and the river has a classic freestone configuration of riffle-run-pool. In addition, Watauga's minimum flow is higher due to several large tributaries. That makes it easier to read the water and stalk closer to your fish. Wading here can be just as tricky as on the Holston. The rocks are just as slick, and extensive patches of underwater weeds, anchored only in soft muck, will mire you to your knees if you step into them.

The Watauga's flow also increases substantially during full generation. The Holston is either "off" or "on," but the flow on the Watauga has a few more variables. Here, the TVA pulses the generators in order to maintain oxygen levels in the river. Every three hours, they run one generator for an hour if they aren't already generating. During a pulse, the river will rise but remain wadable in most areas. Quite often the change in temperature and oxygen levels turns the fish on. During most of the summer months, the TVA has a sustained recreational release for the benefit of rafting outfitters that makes a self-guided float trip on the Watauga practical if you have some whitewater experience. Often one river is "on" when the other is "off." Drive time between them is less than half an hour.

HATCHES, FLIES, AND BEST TIMES TO FISH

Tailwaters can have some very interesting quirks. Their stable temperatures can be just perfect for some bugs and completely exclude others. That's the case on both of these rivers. There is a limited number of species, but they are there in large numbers and often multibrooded.

The first major hatch of the season is the Hendrickson *(Ephemerella subvaria)* in April. They are more prominent on the Watauga but do appear in limited numbers on the Holston.

The sulphur hatch *(Ephemerella dorothea)* is the premier hatch on both rivers. It begins in May and lasts into late August, even September. On the Holston, it can run later. In the first mile below Holston Dam, I've even seen hatches in midwinter. On most good days, you can fish the hatch midday and the spinner fall at dusk.

Caddisflies are prominent throughout the summer on both rivers. They range from the tiny black sedge *(Chimarra)* to large *Rhyacophila* and *Brachycentrus*. Terrestrial patterns, especially Japanese beetles, are also effective summer flies for searching the water.

During the fall and through most of the winter, blue-winged olives *(Baetis)* can be depended on for dry-fly action. Midges are irritatingly numerous and frustratingly small. If you're capable of fishing a #22 or smaller fly effectively, you can try landing large trout on 7X tippet any time you'd like near the dam on the Holston.

If you're floating the river and no hatch is coming off, streamer and attractor patterns can be fished effectively. Both rivers have excellent populations of sculpin and other forage fish. The really big browns and rainbows make them a regular part of their diet.

SOUTH HOLSTON AND WATAUGA REGULATIONS

For many years, the TWRA's approach to trout management on the Holston and Watauga was limited to routing and scheduling stocking trucks. Through the efforts of many local anglers and Trout Unlimited, that attitude has changed in the past decade.

The first change was the establishment of a quality fishing section (everyone calls it the trophy section) on the lower part of the Watauga. It begins at Smalling bridge and extends downstream to the bridge at the town of Watauga. Tackle is restricted to artificial lures, and the creel limit is two fish over 14 inches per day.

There are no tackle restrictions on the Holston, but a slot limit prohibits the harvest of trout between 16 and 22 inches. Only one trout over 22 inches can be harvested. Two sections of the Holston are closed to all fishing during the spawning season, from November 1 through January 31. One section extends from Hickory Tree bridge upstream to Bottom Creek about 1½ miles below the dam. The other is midway on the river from just upstream of Webb bridge to the tip of Boy's Island. These sections are marked with buoys in the river and signage on the bank.

SOUTH HOLSTON ACCESS

Take Route 381 in Johnson City to U.S. Route 11E north toward Bristol. Just beyond the community of Piney Flats, take Exit 11E to the right onto U.S. Route 19E, then take Route 44 north through Bluff City. Route 44 will go by different names. In Bluff City, it's Main Street. Outside the city limits, it becomes Dry Branch Road until it intersects with Chinquapin Grove Road at a Y intersection. Bear left. At that point, it becomes Hickory Tree Road. The name changes, but the number stays the same.

• This stretch of Route 44 provides some access to the river. However, it veers away from the water just past Rock Hold Methodist Church. Watch on your left for the intersection with Big Springs Road, which loops away from Route 44 and runs parallel to the river for a couple miles, providing more pullover parking and access.

• Just past Hickory Tree bridge on Route 44 is a four-way-stop intersection. Be sure to stop, because none of the locals do. Continue straight through this intersection, and make a right onto Emmett Road. Follow Emmett Road to another Y intersection with Holston View Dam Road. Bear right, and you're at Holston Dam. The area around the dam is TVA Reservation property and has paved parking, picnic areas, fishing trails, and public restrooms.

WATAUGA ACCESS

Head south through Johnson City on I-181/U.S. 23 to the junction with Route 67 and U.S. Route 321. Take 67/321 east to Elizabethton.

- To access the quality fishing section of the Watauga, turn back toward Johnson City at the junction with Route 91. Take an immediate right onto Blevins Road to reach the TWRA access.
- If you follow Route 91 toward Johnson City, it will intersect with Smalling Road in Midway. Turn right there and follow Smalling Road. The quality fishing section begins at Smalling bridge.
- Public access is almost nonexistent in the portion of the river around River Ridge Campground, but this commercial campground located just beyond the bridge has trails that provide wading access, as well as a launch ramp and RV and tent camping facilities.
- Sycamore Shoals State Park provides paved parking and trails that follow the river upstream for several miles.
- If you continue on into Elizabethton on Route 67/321 (Elk Avenue), you can access the middle and upper sections of the river. (If you follow 67/321 through town, by turning left onto Broad Street, it intersects with U.S. Route 19E and Route 37, a four-lane highway that allows you to reach the Holston from the Watauga.) There is a paved foot and bike trail that terminates at Elizabethton Ball Park. There is limited parking.
- If you continue through the intersection with U.S. Route 19E and Route 37, you'll reach a state historic site known as Carter Mansion, with public parking and trail access to the river.
- Several miles beyond Carter Mansion is a TWRA access point at Hunter bridge.
- If you cross the river on 19E/37 and make a right onto Route 91, you can access the river at Watauga Industrial Park on the right. Despite the fact that it is an industrial park, it provides access to some of the best fishing on the river. The North and South Bank routes rejoin at Hunter bridge. From that point, follow Route 91 through the community of Hunter, and make a right onto Blue Springs Road.
- Steel Bridge Road intersects with Blue Springs Road in a sharp curve. Follow Steel Bridge Road to Siam bridge. Access along Steel Bridge Road is in the form of pullover parking near the bridge.
- Cross the bridge and follow Wilbur Dam Road to the access point at Wilbur Dam. A private utility company built Wilbur Dam in 1912. It impounds a small lake less than a mile in length below the outlet of the Watauga Dam Powerhouse. The lake is very scenic and has picnic facilities, camping, and public restrooms.

IF YOU GO

Getting to Johnson City is relatively straightforward. From Knoxville, take I-40 east to I-81 north to I-181 south, which will take you into Johnson City.

Tackle Shops and Guides

Mike's Little River Fly Fishing. Adams. Mike lives on the Holston River just outside Bluff City. He's one of the best guides for the Watauga or the Holston. (423) 538-0121. www.adamsflyfishing.com.

Mahoney's Sportsman's Paradise. Johnson City. Well-stocked fly-fishing department. (423) 282-5413.

Mountain Sports Limited. Bristol, Virginia. An Orvis store. Tim Landis runs the fishing department and is the acknowledged expert on the Holston and Watauga. (540) 466-8988.

Virginia Creeper Fly Fishing. Abingdon, Virginia. Bruce Wankl, proprietor. An excellent guide service and well-stocked shop. (540) 628-3826.

Where to Stay

Days Inn. Johnson City. Moderate. (423) 282-2211.

Hampton Inn. Johnson City. Moderate. (423) 929-8000.

The Garden Plaza Hotel. Johnson City. Expensive. (423) 929-2000.

The Carnegie Hotel. Johnson City. Expensive. (423) 979-6400.

Camping

River Ridge Campground. On Smalling Road in Watauga. Located at the start of the quality fishing section on the Watauga. Facilities for RV and tent camping, a launch ramp, and foot trails. (423) 542-6187.

Where to Eat

Peerless Restaurant. Johnson City. Superb steaks are the specialty. Reservations necessary. Be prepared to pay for their top cuts. Moderate to expensive. (423) 282-2351.

Pardner's Bar-B-Que. Piney Flats. On Route 11E. A great place to grab a sandwich on your way to the Holston. No reservations.

Dino's on Elk Avenue. Elizabethton. Good food cheap. Try the lasagna on your way to the Watauga. No reservations.

Other. Johnson City. Moderately priced chain restaurants all along North Roan Street, just off I-181, including the Olive Garden, Grady's, Bennigan's, and Applebee's.

RESOURCES

TVA Lake Information Line. (800) 238-2264. Information on generating schedules for the Holston and Watauga. An automated service. When you connect, press 4. Then press 1 for Holston or 2 for Watauga. Skip the information on the past discharges by pressing the pound key. Listen carefully and take notes, unless you enjoy Russian roulette. Keep in mind that the TVA can change this schedule at any time. The TVA also maintains a website at www.lakeinfo.tva.gov/, where generation data is available. TWRA license and regulation information may be found at www.state.tn.us/twra/fish005b.html.

Jacobs, Jimmy. *Tailwater Trout in the South.* Woodstock, VT: Countryman Press, 1996.

Tennessee Atlas & Gazetteer. Yarmouth, ME: DeLorme Mapping Company. (207) 846-7000.

PART FOUR

The Midwest

CHAPTER TWELVE

DETROIT

Ann McIntosh

My lasting impression of my trip to the trout country near Grayling, Michigan, is of wood—good and bad uses of wood. The good wood: the shellacked hull of an antique Au Sable riverboat, the warm gleam of a custom-made bamboo fly rod, cedar branches sweeping the upper Manistee, deadfalls making lies for fish. And the bad wood: the logs that clogged the rivers, the dams that warmed the water, the timber that took the shade, the lumber that destroyed streams. As Ernest Schweibert has pointed out, these were waters once so full of grayling that anglers would catch three at a time—one on each of three flies on every cast.

The Au Sable and Manistee originate from springs that bubble up in marl bogs and forests north of Grayling, in the north center of Michigan's Lower Peninsula. These forests mark the lowest reach of a glacier before it receded thousands of years ago. It left behind the ground-up rock, including limestone, and porous, sandy soil that constitute the riverbeds today. Rainwater percolates into the land surface, penetrating the limestone and returning to the streams enriched. The result is water-bearing sand or, as one old-timer put it, "hundreds of miles of extensive, shaking marsh." The Au Sable and the Manistee have two of the most stable streamflows on the continent. In fact, according to Steve Southard, owner of the Fly Factory, they are two of the most stable watersheds in the world.

Whether floating in a classic Au Sable riverboat or wading, fishing these rivers is a rarefied experience: peaceful woods, pine-scented air, clear water, deer, birds, and the comforting sound of a paddle in gentle water. The trout here are all streambred, if not native. A handful of rainbows were introduced to the Au Sable, and until recently, a few browns were stocked in the Manistee. Brown, rainbow, and brook trout were first introduced in 1889–90 and began to be stocked in earnest by 1900, once the demise of the grayling was assured.

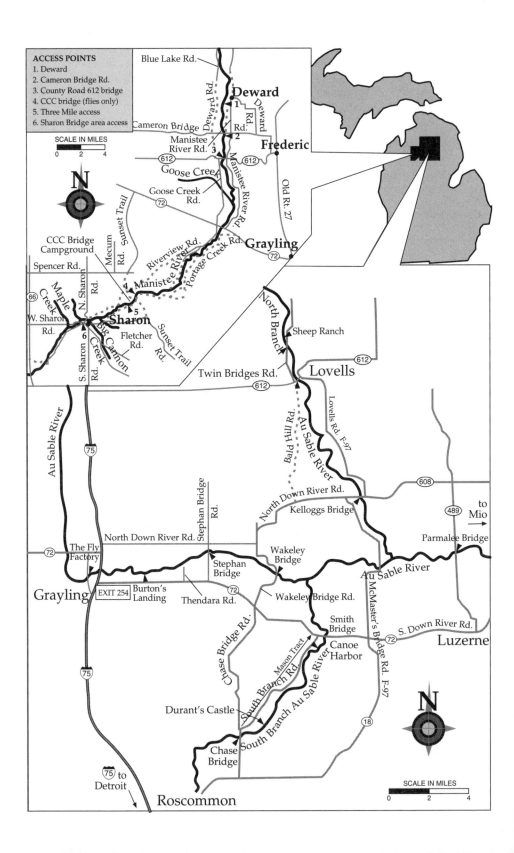

I journeyed to Grayling late in June 1996 to meet a group of Trout Bum Bar-B-Q members gathering for a three-day party to fish the famous Hex *(Hexagenia limbata)* hatch. (The Trout Bum Bar-B-Q is now a non-profit organization and has raised more than $60,000 for stream conservation and youth education projects.) The Hex is a huge Michigan mayfly that burrows in silt and marl. Since the hatch was late in 1996, I never saw a single Hex. But that made no difference. The scenery and the delight I took in hooking eager little wild trout in isolated wetlands and forests more than compensated for the lack of nocturnal browns sipping Hex spinners in the dark.

Whether fishing the Au Sable or the Manistee, or venturing north to the Pigeon, Black, or Sturgeon River, the visiting angler will have no trouble accessing north-central Michigan rivers and discovering how to fish them. The Challenge chapter of Trout Unlimited has published seven spiral-bound books that map the major rivers. These maps number all access points and roads, and include main highways and towns. When combined with Robert Linsenman and Steve Nevala's *Michigan Trout Streams,* a book that discusses hatches and tactics, the angling picture of the area is complete.

Local fly shops update hatch charts and fly lists daily. One of the advantages of engaging a guide is that he or she will get you quickly to the best water for the day you go—in an area where there is much to choose from.

Generally, the wading is some of the nicest I've experienced. The riverbed is sand and gravel, with some very silty areas and few large rocks or slippery places. Look out for deep holes at the river bends and swift pulls where the water narrows. If you're wading, be cautious of downed trees, logjams, and underwater snags, which provide good cover for brown trout.

The casting is not difficult, except in narrow streams where brushy banks provide cover for the fish and impair your backcast. The trout are selective, and long tippets and drag-free drifts make a difference. Be prepared to match the hatch closely and to try different flies to determine which of the simultaneous emergences the trout prefer.

AU SABLE RIVER
Main Stream of the Au Sable
This is the "in-town" stretch of the river. According to Victor Edwards, who lives on the stream, it is mostly fished out. The fish that are left are extremely small. I caught an 11-inch brown, but I think this was a fluke. I don't recommend this stretch to visiting anglers.

Floating the section of the main stream from Stephan bridge to Wakeley bridge is another story. This stretch is all inside the "Holy Water" (the fly-fishing only, catch-and-release stretch from Burton's Landing to

Wakeley bridge). Some big browns lurk under cover here and in the bigger water below Wakeley bridge, waiting for nightfall and the whiff of a big spinner. My first experience on the Au Sable was here. Steve Southard, owner of the Fly Factory, piloted cane-rod builder Wayne Cattanach and me in his Au Sable riverboat. Victor Edwards and Ti Piper, the noted New Mexico angler and instructor, floated in a second riverboat. All of us wanted to investigate the status of the *Hexagenia* hatch before the Trout Bums arrived.

I caught three small, wild browns on our drift downstream. I was a little disappointed, for I had imagined foot-long fish in addition to the nocturnal lunkers and youngsters. Later in my stay, I learned that there is much controversy about reasons for the decrease in 11- to 13-inch Au Sable trout. Trout Unlimited cofounder Art Neumann summed up the situation by saying that no one knows what the problem is. Bob Linsenman, who has written frequently about the river, believes that canoe traffic with aluminum hulls continually banging against the wood downfalls stresses the trout.

Since my last visit, the Au Sable system has fished far more productively. Credit has gone to relatively mild winters and increased cover resulting from restoration projects. Many more 10- to 16-inch fish have been taken throughout the season from the "Holy Water." During the last two years' Hex hatches, there have been more big browns hooked than in the previous ten to fifteen years. Southard attributes this to the cyclical nature of the Au Sable fishery, noting that it has gone through a cycle or two during the forty to fifty years it has been studied by fish biologists.

The closest I came to experiencing the Hex hatch happened that first night. We were approaching the take-out, and as I slowly lifted my rod from the water to punch out the huge Muddler one last time, we heard an enormous splash. Southard yelled, "Ann just rolled a big one!" I heard a lot of congratulatory noises and wishes for better luck next time. I hadn't felt a thing.

North Michigan browns are noted for being extremely wary and for feeding during low-light periods. They are also noted carnivores, so if you fish streamers on overcast or rainy days, or at dawn or after dark during warm weather, you'll be rewarded with the real brutes.

North Branch of the Au Sable

The upper reaches of the Au Sable consist mostly of flat, shallow water 40 to 50 feet wide. Lots of instream vegetation provides food and cover for the trout. I liked the look of the area around Twin Bridges north of Lovells, and anglers who fish there have had good experiences. Wading is over sand, gravel, and bottom vegetation. The water is manageable and friendly.

The largest fish are generally below Kelloggs bridge. There are two walk-in access points and it's a relatively easy wade from Twin Bridges to Lovells. Below Lovells, there is also good access and cover at Dam Four and at the Jackson Hole.

By the time the North Branch reaches Kelloggs bridge south of Lovells on North Down River Road, the water has widened to 70 feet. There is easy access at the bridge, making for one of the most pressured reaches of the North Branch. In *Michigan Trout Streams,* Linsenman suggests fishing sculpin or crayfish patterns early or late in the day.

A 21-mile stretch of fly-fishing only water begins at the Sheep Ranch (.5 mile north of Twin Bridges) and continues to the main stream. I stopped and looked at almost every access point along the North Branch above and below Lovells, and never saw water I didn't thirst to fish.

South Branch of the Au Sable

The South Branch is noted for the Mason tract, a stretch of fly-fishing only water (with 4 miles designated catch-and-release), much of which was donated to the state by the generous conservationist George W. Mason. Mason was an early proponent of founding an organization to protect trout. "Why don't we have a Trout Unlimited like we have a Ducks Unlimited?" he asked. And in 1959, five years after his death, Trout Unlimited was born. Art Neumann and George Griffith are credited as cofounders, but many others did their share. In a continuing tradition, Griffith, now deceased, donated his home on the main stream, the Barbless Hook, to the Michigan Council of Trout Unlimited.

The Mason tract includes both sides of the river, and the land has been allowed to return to its natural state. There is no development, and the full-day float from Chase bridge to Smith bridge, a flies-only, catch-and-release stretch, is magnificent. Grouse, deer, woodcock, and many other birds are present. The South Branch, which originates from Lake St. Helen south of Roscommon, is more subject to flow fluctuations than the other branches of the Au Sable and is noted for holding more large browns than the "Holy Water" section of the main stream.

The river ranges from 40 to 60 feet wide within the Mason tract and has deep holes and swift runs in places. Be careful wading, and take a staff to balance yourself and test the depth of the water.

The east and west sides of the river offer twenty-two access points. The fly-fishing only, catch-and-release stretch is the 4 miles between Chase bridge and lower High Banks. The book *Trout Angler's Guide for the Au Sable* clearly maps the river and numbers the parking and access points. However, the signs on the stream are not numbered as they are in the book, so to find a particular spot, pay attention to the mileage. The South Branch can be accessed from the U.S. Forest Service (USFS) roads on the north and south banks.

Au Sable below Mio

During the 1990s relicensing process, a new flow regime was put in place, and the section of the river from just below Mio Dam to the upper reaches of the Alcona Dam impoundment gradually became a top-notch big brown fishery. The Federal Energy Regulatory Commission mandated "run of the river" (no peaking flows) regulations at the hydroelectric dam in Mio.

The water below Mio is much bigger than the upper reaches above Grayling. There are wide riffles and very big, deep holes, and the river is as much as 100 yards wide. While some hatches will bring browns to the surface, fishing deep with large streamers and full-sinking lines is often the most successful approach.

There are a number of access points along this stretch of the river. Parking permits are required at some of the USFS locations. There are three productive float trips: from Mio to Comin's Flats, from Comin's Flats to McKinley, and from McKinley to FS 4001. Each provides solitude with only occasional cabins along the way.

MANISTEE RIVER

The Manistee originates a few miles west of the headwaters of the Au Sable. It soon turns west toward Lake Michigan, while the Au Sable empties into Lake Huron to the east. During my trip, I grew very fond of the Manistee, particularly its upper reaches near Deward. The stream is not as heavily fished or as developed as the Au Sable. Many Manistee fans see it as a more natural experience.

The Manistee has benefited from a lot of stream improvement. Several sand traps have been installed to diminish the sand load in the river, and instream structures have greatly improved the holding water. The river has outstanding hatches—as good as those on the Au Sable—including *Hexagenia limbata* and the brown drake from mid-June into early July.

I floated the Manistee twice: once from Cameron bridge to Whispering Pines Campground (County Route 612 access), and once from Whispering Pines to Long's Canoe Livery.

Wayne Cattanach launched with his daughter Lyndi and me on the trip from Whispering Pines. His restored cedar riverboat showed its mettle on the trip, sliding through narrow passages between logs and gliding over deadfalls in shallow water.

Ranging from 20 to 25 feet long and 24 to 28 inches wide, the Au Sable boats were designed in the late nineteenth century to minimize the problems of floating cargo down log-filled streams. They are long enough to carry a big load and narrow enough to slip between obstructions. Their design is unique, suited to the stable flows of northern Michigan streams. They are only 12 inches deep from the gunwale to the waterline and draft only a few inches of water. Both bow and stern sweep up, causing the boats to glide silently through the alternating riffles and deep pools.

We floated through deserted acres of wetlands, with evergreens and hardwoods giving cover to the fish, and logjams and stream deflectors creating holding water. Cattanach is a virtuoso with a pole, handling the boat so that the angler gets the maximum drift from every cast. Since the boat glides along the water at the same speed as the fly, long, drag-free drifts are the goal. Cattanach helps his passengers by positioning the boat so the angler can make the surest cast without disturbing the fish.

Several times we pulled the riverboat onto a sandy shoal and got out to cast into back eddies. All the fish I hooked took a Robert's Drake and a #14 mahogany dry, but I found that my reliable Patriot moved fish when the other patterns did not. All the wild brook and brown trout I hooked and landed were small (6 to 9 inches), spry, and feisty.

I was very sad when my trip came to an end, and I tried to figure out what made me feel so sentimental. I think it had something to do with feeling like I was fishing through history, looking at streams that have been through the worst and still struggle to remain alive. I realized that casting bamboo from a cedar riverboat drifting through scenery that looks as if Winslow Homer painted it is as good as it's likely to get in the Lower Forty-eight. There are some places with more big fish, but there certainly are not a lot with more big, natural resident fish. Few can claim the history and the challenges embodied in the old Au Sable and Manistee.

ENVIRONMENTAL CONCERNS

Brian Benjamin, Au Sable and Manistee watershed coordinator for Huron Pines Resource Conservation and Development, explains the problems with the Au Sable and Manistee systems: "While the sandy soil allows these great watersheds to recharge after rain, the tradeoff is the fragility of their sandy banks. This leads to easily eroded soils, silt clogging stream channels, and insufficient cover." The Anglers of the Au Sable, the Federation of Fly Fishers (FFF), several Trout Unlimited (TU) chapters—notably, the Challenge, George Mason, Paul Young, Mershon, and Lansing chapters—and the Trout Bum Bar-B-Q have raised funds and contributed hundreds of man-hours to improve habitat for bugs and fish on the two rivers. In excess of $1 million has been spent on sand traps, bridge replacement, bank stabilization, and instream deflectors and structure, with $500,000 spent on the Au Sable in 1996 alone.

HATCHES, FLIES, AND BEST TIMES TO FISH

Late April–early June. This is an excellent time for Hendrickson and March Brown patterns, as well as black and olive caddis, and Mahogany Drakes. Sulphurs and light cahills usually appear from late May to early June, so these are also very productive patterns.

Mid-June–early July. This is the time to anticipate the brown drake and *Hexagenia limbata* emergences. Much like the salmon fly of western rivers, these flies are lots of fun to fish, since they are big flies and attract big fish. Most of the hatching activity occurs at or after dusk; take the time during the day to become familiar and comfortable with the sections of the river you will be wading after dark.

From late May to early July, be sure to have on hand a supply of the Robert's Drake in several sizes. This is a very effective local deer hair parachute pattern that is used to imitate a wide variety of creamy and yellowish bodied mayflies, from a #16 sulphur to a #4–#6 Hex. Other hatches to match include little yellow stoneflies, giant amber stoneflies, and *Isonychia* (slate drakes and White-Gloved Howdies).

July 4–September. From the Fourth of July on, the main stream and South Branch are popular with canoeists. Inquire about peak canoeing hours.

Steve Southard likes to fish the leading edge of a warm rain. He says the streamer fishing on the Au Sable and the Manistee can be awesome as the water begins to rise and discolor.

On hot, sunny days when the air temperature is in the high seventies, the Au Sable springs come in at 53 to 55 degrees F. This makes for good fishing throughout the summer.

In July and August, after the Hex hatch has come to an end, grasshoppers, ants, and other terrestrial patterns are effective. Tricos begin to appear in the mornings, and later, the white mayflies (*Ephoron leukon* and *E. album*) hatch in the evening, particularly on the big water below Mio.

September–October. Midges (try Trout Unlimited founder George Griffith's Gnat), slate drakes, small blue-winged olives, terrestrials.

ALSO WORTH NOTING

It would be a shame to go to Grayling and fish the Au Sable and the Manistee without seeing some of the more isolated streams only an hour north. Near Gaylord and Vanderbilt, the Pigeon, Sturgeon, and Black Rivers run through near-wilderness areas and receive far less angling pressure than the streams near Grayling. To the west are the Boardman and the Jordan. Within an hour to an hour and a half drive from Grayling, there are hundreds of miles of wadable trout streams.

I spent a wonderful day with Steve Southard and his son Lucas exploring the Pigeon River Country State Forest and fishing that river. We spent more than an hour stalking a pair of very cautious elk, and finished the day with each of us catching several brown trout in the 10- to 12-inch range.

IF YOU GO

Grayling is about 200 miles (three and a half hours) from Detroit and its airport. Take I-75 north from Detroit to Exit 254, Grayling. Make a left off the interstate, and the Fly Factory tackle shop will be on the right as Business I-75 crosses at the bridge over the Au Sable.

The nearest commercial airport is in Traverse City, but private planes can land at the Grayling Air Field. Visit the website www.birdseyeavia tion.com for more information.

Tackle Shops and Guides
In or Near Detroit
The Flymart. Royal Oak. (248) 584-2848. Southfield. (248) 350-8484. www.flymartflyshop.com.
West Bank Anglers. Detroit. (248) 538-3474.

Destination Shops
Dave's Guide Service. Grayling. David Wyss is an excellent guide who also rents cabins on the Au Sable at Wakeley Bridge Road. Float and wade trips. (989) 348-3203.
The Fly Factory. Grayling. I-75 Business Loop at the Au Sable River bridge. Steve Southard, proprietor. This is the Au Sable River's original fly shop and guide service. Stream condition reports, emergence schedules, enormous selection of flies, tackle, and clothing. Also conducts schools, provides guide service, rents canoes, and has a livery service. (989) 348-5844 or toll-free 88-troutbum. www.Troutbums.com.
Gates Au Sable Lodge. Grayling. At Stephan bridge. Rusty Gates, proprietor. Orvis dealer with twenty-five years of experience on the Au Sable. Flies, tackle, schools, and guide service. (989) 348-8462.
Hartman's Fly Shop. Lovells. (989) 348-9679.
Skip's Sport Shop. West of Grayling. On Route 72. (989) 348-7111.

Where to Stay
Borcher's B&B. Grayling. Near the Fly Factory. Also offers canoe rental and livery service. Inexpensive. (989) 348-4921 or (800) 762-8756.
Gates Au Sable Lodge. Located on the fly-fishing "Holy Water" of the Au Sable. Three meals a day. Inexpensive to moderate. (989) 348-8462.
Penrod's Au Sable River Resort Cottages. Grayling. On the Au Sable. Inexpensive. (989) 348-2910.
Chamber of Commerce/Grayling Area Visitor's Council. Call or check the website for listings of the many additional accommodations in Grayling. (800) 937-8837. www.grayling-mi.com.

Camping
State Park campgrounds. (800) 543-2YES.
DNR camping information. (989) 348-6371.
Hartwick Pines State Park. (989) 348-7068.
River Park Campground. (989) 348-9092.

Where to Eat

Crawford Station. Grayling. At the Holiday Inn. Inexpensive to moderate. (989) 348-7611.

Grayling Restaurant. Grayling. A great breakfast spot. Inexpensive. (989) 348-2141.

Larry & Joan's Place. Grayling. The "I Forgot Store" on Route 72 at Wakeley Bridge Road. Conveniently located with sandwiches, sundries, and some terminal tackle.

Spike's Keg o' Nails. Grayling. Across from the Fly Factory. The most congenial place to eat and drink after a river float. Serves late to accommodate anglers. Inexpensive. (989) 348-7113.

RESOURCES

Michigan Department of Natural Resources. (989) 348-6371.

Hendrickson, Gerth E. *Twelve Classic Trout Streams in Michigan.* Ann Arbor, MI: University of Michigan Press, 1994.

Linsenman, Robert, and Steve Nevala. *Michigan Trout Streams.* Woodstock, VT: Backcountry Publications, 1993.

Ross, John. *Trout Unlimited's Guide to America's 100 Best Trout Streams.* Helena, MT: Falcon Publishing, 1999.

Trout Angler's Guides. Detailed, easy-to-read, spiral-bound books with good maps and access points to most Michigan rivers. Write to Challenge Chapter, P.O. Box 63, Bloomfield Hills, MI 48303, or purchase at destination fly shops.

Michigan Atlas & Gazetteer. Yarmouth, ME: DeLorme Mapping Company. (207) 846-7000

PERE MARQUETTE RIVER

Jerry Warrington

It is a paradox of sorts, but the Pere Marquette serves as both a destroyer of the long rod and a maker of angling legends. Generous to a fault one day and stingy in the extreme (with bugs and fish) the next, this water is proof positive of the ever-present feast or famine situation that exists on any good trout river. While you sometimes can get by with less than a precise presentation, it's far more effective to match the hatch. There are places on the river that do need a little extra power stroke on your cast to work a series of runs and riffles with a pool down below or to showcase your mastery of a delicate touch around a logjam. Together, along with the Au Sable and the Manistee Rivers, the three are some of the best the state has to offer an angler.

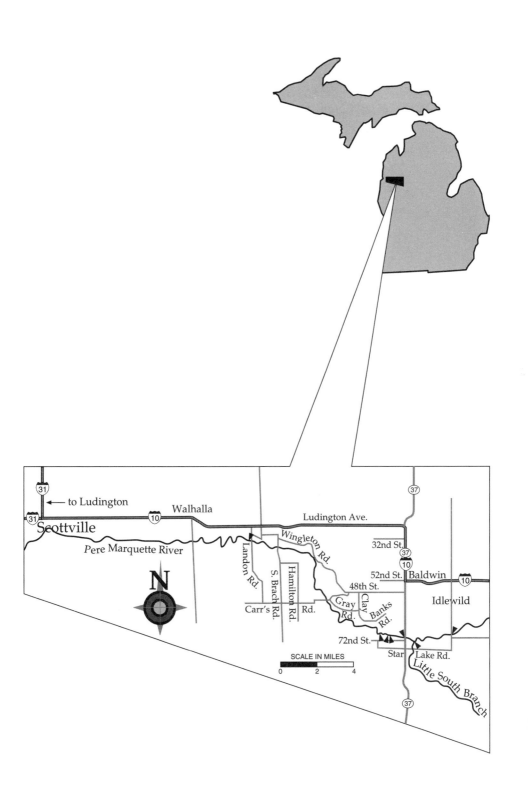

The P.M., as midwestern anglers like to call the Pere Marquette, is a collection of almost every type of trout stream there is, making it a teaching river from which you can learn a fair share of lessons. Sections range from areas that run so hard that the turbulence acts like a scrubber for the gravel spawning beds, to placid, almost pasturelike runs, each demanding a vastly different style of fishing.

To a small minority, the P.M. is considered a salmon and steelheading river with a few trout, but most see it as it really is: pure vintage trout water, with the occasional lake fish taken. It all depends on your methodology and your point of view. Most days, it's enough just to call the P.M. home.

The Pere Marquette was named in honor of Father Jacques Marquette, a Jesuit priest who was held in high regard by the Indian tribes of the rivers. Father Marquette died at the mouth of the river while trying to hold on long enough to see his mission built in Sault Ste. Marie. The Indians decided to bestow the name Pere Marquette on the river. Loosely translated, it means "River of the Black Robe," a tribute to both the man and his Jesuit attire.

Within years, the river tribes were run out of the areas near the P.M., and, with Michigan ceded to the United States in the late 1700s, the all-out wholesale plundering of the area's natural resources began. First, beaver pelts were sent off in quantities so vast it was only a matter of time before the pressure proved too much. Attention was then turned to trees.

As the populations grew in the East, demand for building materials, especially pines and other hardwoods, was at an all-time high. The P.M. was in the right place at the wrong time. Its currents were perfect for carrying logs downriver, so the massive cutting of trees nearby began in earnest, continuing for years. As the amount of sediment and logjams grew, the river warmed, and Michigan grayling began to die off in quantity. Unable to reproduce, let alone survive, the fish were soon gone, officially extinct by 1905. It's a history lesson not unlike that of the Au Sable.

During this time, however, after the lumber barons had vacated the shoreline, anglers were breaking their backs to revitalize the P.M. The river was honored to receive the first stocking of German brown trout in the United States. The trees needed little help to reforest the area and reduce the water temperature to more trout-tolerant levels. In spite of man's sins against the P.M., she came back stronger than ever. Gradually, and with occasional assistance, the healing process took care of itself. As the waters cleared, trout, steelhead, and salmon were soon found in increasing numbers. It began to live up to its reputation as a destination river, one you could spend an entire lifetime exploring—plying its pools, riffles, and numerous collections of bends and undercut banks.

The P.M. has continued to take its rightful place among the Midwest's best rivers, living up to its reputation as a triple-play proposition. The steelheading is excellent, as can be the salmon fishing. The bread-and-butter trout remain the river's mainstay, however. And thanks to regulations setting aside flies-only stretches and protecting the water by enrolling the P.M. into the National Wild and Scenic River program, it should continue to enjoy its status as a truly great river, one capable of going head-to-head with other rivers of legend.

Above all else, treat the P.M. and its residents with kid gloves. The river has seen enough destruction in its time, and by gently releasing your fish, you ensure the future of the river for years to come.

Don't trespass to get to the river. Michigan has some strict laws regarding illegal trespassing, and riverside residents are entitled to respect for their privacy and their property. Besides, most of the good spots have sufficient access trails scattered along the river system.

Wade gently and enjoy your trip. And don't be surprised if the P.M. calls you back from time to time. . . . It'll do that.

HATCHES, FLIES, AND BEST TIMES TO FISH

The right fly selection can often spell the difference between a brown trout snubbing you time and again and having a real heavyweight take you far into the backing. There are some "must haves" for every Pere Marquette River fly box, most of which are either imitations or attractors. Much of it depends on where and when you're going to be fishing the P.M.

You can't go wrong with a selection of little black caddis, sulphurs, and Gray Drake patterns early on. Parachute flies are good for both visibility and profile. Adamses, Cahills, Blue-Winged Olives, Hendricksons, and even *Hexagenia* imitations such as Dun Parachutes are reliable patterns. Also, Elk Hair Caddis, Royal Wulff, Rusty's Spinner, Griffith's Gnat, and Marabou Muddlers are good additions.

By early May, you'll want to stock up on big Hex and Gray Drake patterns in order to be ready to converge on the stream when the large flies come off the water. The Hex hatch is thrilling enough. But when you add the gray drake hatch to the combination, it can be some of the most exciting fishing you'll ever have at dusk and throughout the night.

PERE MARQUETTE ACCESS

• An excellent stretch of about 7 to 8 miles of fly-fishing only waters, with numerous access points for the angler, runs from the Route 37 bridge down to Gleason's Landing. To reach Gleason's Landing, take Carr's Road west out of Baldwin for just over 2 miles to 62nd Street, then follow Shortcut Avenue to Gray Road and onto Gleason's Landing. Here the river demands respect; it's over 75 feet wide and as challenging as any stretch you'll fish.

This area of the river is renowned for its brown trout fishing, as it offers an angler reliable and strong hatches, and water that can only be described as classic holding water for trout. There also seems to be no end to the variation in the size of the resident trout.

• Just south of the river and running to the west is 72nd Street, which provides good access points to fine trout waters.

• The Lumber Jack access and the Green Cottage access at the end of Peacock Road off 72nd Street are also good places to enter the water. Whichever direction you take, once you're at the river, it will be wide—50 feet in most places and up to 80 feet in others. The Route 37 bridge water gives you a good chance for a steelhead.

• The Clay Banks are easy to reach and tough to fish. To reach them, take 56th Street west to Astor, then head south on Astor, and within minutes, you'll be looking at Jigger Trail (sometimes called Clay Banks Road), which ends as the Clay Banks.

The best part of these fly-fishing only areas is that they're all just minutes away from downtown Baldwin. Exercise great caution in wading the Clay Banks stretches. The surface below the water is clay in some spots as well as sand, making your waders feel like a pair of ice skates.

• Farther north on Route 37, the highway intersects with westbound U.S. Route 10. This roadway runs parallel to and just north of the P.M., ending near the mouth of the river at Ludington. It only takes a slight detour south off U.S. Route 10 to enjoy more of the river's excellent fishing possibilities.

• It's been said that some of the best Hex water on the P.M. lies just southwest of the village of Branch, off Landon Road near the High Banks access. There must be some validity to that statement, as every year the gathering of anglers there seems to grow. The *Hexagenia limbata* hatch brings out some of the best and biggest fish, all of which are involved in a nocturnal feeding frenzy. Despite the hatch's popularity with fish and anglers alike, there is always room for one more rod wielding a barbless #6 or #8 hook. Barbed hooks are too difficult to remove easily from your neck or ear when you're attempting to do microsurgery in the dark!

• I'm partial to the waters below Barothy's Lodge. Once the turbulent snowpack finishes feeding the river, the blizzards of *Hexagenia* hatches start coming on from late May to early June. Just standing there among the bugs while the lunker browns and steelhead go into a feeding frenzy is something to behold. A smooth casting stroke is difficult at best, as the Hex hatches descend on you with a thickness that nearly suffocates, bugs banging into your rod as well as your eyes. For a chance to hook up with one of the P.M.'s best, however, it's worth facing the Hex storm.

These are some of the best areas in which to cast a fly, but there are others. As you fish the river and hang around the area fly shops, you'll discover more of its secrets. There are holes such as Bawana's Bend, Bass

Wood Run, Alligator Alley, and others that often aren't included on maps of the areas. Some are known by a scattered few, while others wade past them without acknowledging that they exist.

In due course, if you choose to include the Pere Marquette on your list of frequently fished rivers, keep a meticulous journal. You'll find it acts as a great reference manual when you've been away too long.

IF YOU GO
From Detroit take I-96 west toward Lansing. Continue on I-96 from Lansing to Grand Rapids, where you pick up U.S. Route 131 north to Reed City. Here, get on U.S. Route 10 west to Baldwin. The drive should take about three and one-half hours.

Tackle Shops and Guides
Ed's Sport Shop. Baldwin. Good fly and tackle shop. (231) 745-4974.

Pere Marquette Lodge. Baldwin. An Orvis-endorsed outfitter and lodge. (231) 745-3972.

Where to Stay
Baldwin Creek Motel. Baldwin. Owner is an experienced P.M. fisherman. Clean and comfortable. Inexpensive. (231) 745-4401.

Pere Marquette Lodge. Baldwin. An Orvis-endorsed lodge. Nice accommodations. Moderate. (231) 745-3972.

Camping
Ivan's Campground. Baldwin. Tent sites and efficiency cabins. (231) 745-9345.

Where to Eat
All Seasons. Baldwin. Very good food. Inexpensive. (231) 745-7731.

Government Lodge. Just north of Baldwin. On Route 37. Fabulous food. Moderate. (231) 745-3000.

Main Stream Restaurant. Baldwin. Good food. Inexpensive. (231) 745-3377.

RESOURCES
Michigan Department of Natural Resources. (989) 348-6371.

Bedford, Jim. *Flyfisher's Guide to Michigan.* Gallatin Gateway, MT: Wilderness Adventures Press, 2000.

Hendrickson, Gerth. *Twelve Classic Trout Streams in Michigan.* Ann Arbor, MI: University of Michigan Press, 1994.

Linsenman, Robert, and Steve Nevala. *Michigan Trout Streams.* Woodstock, VT: Backcountry Publications, 1993.

Ross, John. *Trout Unlimited's Guide to America's 100 Best Trout Streams.* Helena, MT: Falcon Publishing, 1999.

Trout Angler's Guides. Spiral-bound books with detailed maps and access points to Michigan rivers. Write to Challenge Chapter, P.O. Box 63, Bloomfield Hills, MI 48303, or inquire at fly shops.

Michigan Atlas & Gazetteer. Yarmouth, ME: DeLorme Mapping Company. (207) 846-7000.

CHAPTER THIRTEEN

CHICAGO

Stephen M. Born

Locked in traffic in downtown Chicago or bustling through busy O'Hare Airport northwest of the city, it might seem unimaginable to an avid trout angler that one of the largest concentrations of spring creeks on the North American continent is less than four hours away. Southwest Wisconsin's Driftless Area—that region of the state that escaped the southerly and westerly advance of the continental glaciers a scant ten thousand years ago—is largely rural, characterized by steep, verdant hills and picturesque valleys dotted by the occasional village, small dairy farm operations, and increasingly, recreational homes.

Wisconsin has almost 10,000 miles of trout streams. Some 1,000 miles of these waters are classic spring creeks; most are located in the southwest—an easy drive from Chicago.

The region's bedrock geology and climate team up to produce abundant groundwater flows to streams. Gushing springs and seeps, often covered with watercress, are landscape expressions of the cold, constant flow of fertile groundwater—the lifeblood of trout streams. The alkaline, nutrient-rich inflows resulting from the groundwater's passage through the flat-lying carbonate bedrock lead to the luxuriant growths of aquatic plants and the enormous insect and other fish food populations found in these spring creeks. The creeks are small, rarely longer than 15 miles or wider than 30 feet. But don't let the small size fool you—these highly productive waters have native trout populations measured in thousands of trout per mile.

Brook trout are the only native inland trout (they are actually char), and they once flourished in our spring creeks. Native populations can still be found in the headwaters of some spring creek drainages, and in the past few years, the state has launched a brook trout restoration program

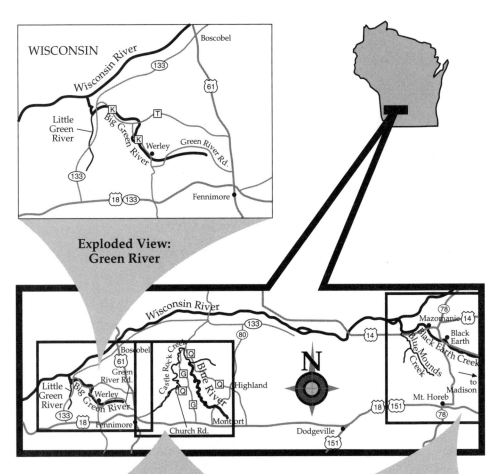

WISCONSIN

Boscobel

Wisconsin River

133

61

Little Green River

Big Green River

K

T

K Werley

Green River Rd.

133

18 133

Fennimore

**Exploded View:
Green River**

Wisconsin River

133

80

14

Mazomanie 78 14

Black Earth

Boscobel

61

Green River Rd.

Castle Rock Creek

Q

Blue River

Q

Q

Highland

Black Earth Creek

Blue Mounds Creek

to Madison

Little Green River

Big Green River

Werley

133 18

Fennimore

G

G

Church Rd.

Montfort

N

Dodgeville

151

18 151

Mt. Horeb

78

**Exploded View:
Castle Rock Creek and Blue River**

**Exploded View:
Black Earth Creek**

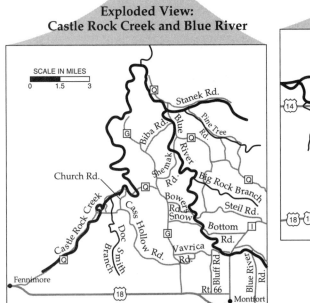

SCALE IN MILES
0   1.5   3

Q Stanek Rd.

G Biba Rd.

Blue River

Pine Tree Rd.

Church Rd.

Q

Shemak Rd.

Big Rock Branch

Q

Castle Rock Creek

Cass Hollow Rd.

Bower Rd.

Snow

Steil Rd.

Bottom Rd.

Doc Smith Branch

Vavrica Rd.

Bluff Rd.

Blue River Rd.

Q

Fennimore

18

Rt. 66

Montfort

78 14

Mazomanie

14

14

Black Earth

Blue Mounds Creek

Black Earth Creek

KP

Cross Plains

P

14

P to Beltline, Madison

Mt. Horeb

18 151

78

in specified watersheds. Brown trout, introduced in 1887, are now the dominant trout in Wisconsin spring creeks. In the late 1960s and 1970s fishery managers discovered that stocking hatchery brown trout over wild browns tended to suppress the growth of wild populations.

Led by Dave Vetrano, southwest regional fishery manager of the Department of Natural Resources (DNR), experimentation began with wild trout stocking. Wild brood stock are taken from their home waters, stripped of eggs and sperm, and released back to the stream. The eggs are fertilized, and the young trout are raised in hatcheries to be released in streams with attributes favoring the establishment of a naturally sustaining trout population. The results have been spectacular, and angling for wild and wily browns is the norm in these spring creeks.

In a 1999 study of state fish propagation programs and policies, Trout Unlimited (TU) identified Wisconsin's program of using hatcheries in support of expanding its wild trout program as a model for the nation. Fishery managers on occasion decide to stock rainbow trout in some streams to increase the catchable numbers of trout, including some large brood stock. The spring creek angler may be surprised from time to time to find a 20-plus-inch rainbow testing his skills.

Wisconsin spring creeks are user-friendly. The bountiful trout waters of the Badger State are highly accessible. If you've encountered problems getting on rivers and streams in other states, you'll find Wisconsin stream access laws almost too good to be true.

The state's strong public trust doctrine (the waters of the state are held in trust for the public) allows anglers to enter a stream at a bridge crossing or public access point and fish up- or downstream as long as they stay in the stream—in other words, keep your feet wet.

An array of governmental land acquisition and resource protection programs provides widespread public-access points, often with stiles to facilitate entry, and most landowners and farmers, if asked politely, will give anglers permission to access streams through their property. You may not, however, cross private lands without permission. When in doubt, ask the landowner, because Wisconsin's trespass laws do not require landowners to post their lands, and the fines can be onerous.

Please remember to close gates, and treat lands as if they were yours; the next angler to seek the landowner's permission will be thankful for your good manners. The spring creeks are not only accessible, they're relatively shallow and easy to wade. Anglers in less than stellar physical condition and seniors can readily enjoy these wonderful small streams.

You'll appreciate your days astream on the waters described here even more if you're aware of the many conservation efforts that have gone into restoring and protecting Wisconsin trout streams, especially these highly vulnerable spring creeks. These streams are threatened by loss of habitat, polluted runoff from agriculture and other sources, and consequent impaired water quality, road construction, and the threat of urbanization.

Fortunately, the state DNR has a progressive, science-based reputation. Their work, along with the efforts and support of many TU chapters, Federation of Fly Fishers clubs, and other sports and conservation groups, has resulted in habitat improvements, dam removals, pollution control programs, stream restorations, public land acquisitions, and fishery management innovations. Wisconsin has pioneered many of the stream improvement measures that anglers see and fish during a day afield on other waters: bank cover structures, wing deflectors, submerged shelters, and lunker structures—erosion-controlling fish condominiums that provide cover for trout and a great place to lose flies.

When you buy your license and required inland trout stamp, remember that this TU–supported surcharge generates revenue exclusively for habitat improvements on inland trout streams—more than $11 million to improve almost 600 miles of Wisconsin trout streams since 1977.

I'll focus on three relatively well-known spring creeks: the Big Green River and Castle Rock Creek in Grant County, near the community of Fennimore, and Black Earth Creek in Dane County, in the shadow of metropolitan Madison, the state capital. Consider these as a good introduction to our spring creeks, but there are other streams to explore, including many tributaries and lesser-fished waters. Without question, the coulee country of southwestern Wisconsin can provide a lifetime of trout fishing for anglers of every skill level.

CASTLE ROCK CREEK

Castle Rock Creek is northeast of Fennimore. It flows northerly and provides more than 7 miles of quality spring creek fishing. It joins another trout stream, the Blue River, before entering the Wisconsin River. Championed by the area fish manager Gene Van Dyck, Castle Rock became one of the state's first fish-for-fun no-kill streams in 1977. Accessible from many points along County Route Q (watch for public fishing signs and access stiles), the stream flows through pastoral agricultural land with many riffles, runs, and pools. Major groundwater inflow comes from Swenson Springs, easily seen from an overlook on Route Q, where thousands of gallons per minute discharge into Castle Rock.

BIG GREEN RIVER

The Big Green River heads a few miles northwesterly of Fennimore, flowing through one of the prettiest valleys in the state. The stream has great access from Green River Road and County Route K. Anglers have access to meadows and cow pastures, but you should also hike through some of the scenic wooded sections away from the roads for challenging and secluded angling experiences. Although the stream has some good-size pools, it is never intimidating to wade. Though uncommon, the occasional rattlesnake may be seen on rock outcrops along both the Big Green and Castle Rock once the weather warms. You should keep your eyes open, but cows—especially bulls—pose a more noteworthy risk.

BLACK EARTH CREEK

Black Earth flows west from the outskirts of the burgeoning Madison metropolitan area through rapidly suburbanizing farm country. From its spring-fed headwaters to the community of Black Earth, there are 12 miles of designated trout water, although habitat improvements and improving water quality allow trout to exist almost to Mazomanie during some seasons. Busy State Route 14 parallels the stream, affording excellent access from above the village of Cross Plains (there's superb fishing right in town!) to below Black Earth.

The creek is the home waters of the largest Wisconsin TU chapter. Heavily pressured and nobody's secret, the stream offers some of the most challenging spring creek fishing anywhere. You would be well advised to try to fish during the middle of the week. Black Earth Creek is never very wide, averaging about 20 to 30 cubic feet per second in flow; however, big runoffs can produce peak flows exceeding 1,700 cubic feet per second, so you should consult local fly shops before making the two-and-a-half-hour drive from O'Hare Airport.

Black Earth is the only stream among the three that has a major *Hexagenia* hatch, cause of the nighttime fishing mania that grips fly fishers in Wisconsin in June and July. If you've never experienced it (admittedly, it's an acquired taste) and can handle crowds, mosquitoes, bats, night vision problems, and attacking muskrats and beavers, put Black Earth on your agenda for mid to late June.

These spring creeks are not the big waters of the West. Come with reasonable expectations about small stream fisheries. An experienced angler might catch ten to twenty trout in the 9- to 14-inch range on a good day. Several fish over 20 inches are caught from all these spring creeks every season, particularly during evening angling, and some anglers report fifty-fish days, but a 14-inch, resplendently colored wild brown from a crystal-clear spring creek is the angler's goal here.

Be prepared to approach the stream cautiously, stalk and wade with care, dress to blend with the natural surroundings, and in general, try to emulate the stream behavior of a heron. Traditional upstream nymphing, streamer fishing, and dry-fly tactics will work fine as long as you're reading the water, fishing good lies, and haven't disturbed or scared the trout.

HATCHES, FLIES, AND BEST TIMES TO FISH

One of southern Wisconsin's great angling characters, Tom Wendelberg, an acknowledged trout-fishing bum and spring creek guru, frequently cites a refrain from one of his many articles: "There's always something happening on a spring creek." Translated for the visiting angler, unless streams are blown out from rainstorms or intense spring snowmelt, or the season is closed, it's always a good time to fish Wisconsin spring creeks.

The season is open in the southwest from early March until the end of September, except for a five-day period prior to the general opening date on the first Saturday in May. Given the pent-up desires of anglers throughout the winter months, angling pressure can be heavy on, and subsequent to, opening day. You can enjoy less competition and crowding by fishing midweek rather than weekends. But whenever you can get to these streams, there's plenty of water, and crowding is localized at worst. Expect to find snow-covered streambanks in March.

The timing of angling opportunities and the hatches are very similar on all three spring creeks. Upstream dead-drift nymph fishing is always a deadly technique here during nonhatch periods, although nymphing can be difficult and frustrating during summer months, when aquatic vegetation is dense and casting must be accurate. Rods of 7 to 9 feet in 4- to 6-weights are good tools for nymphing. Leaders of 9 to 12 feet with 4X to 5X tippets and a strike indicator are the norm.

I like a tandem or two-fly nymph rig, with a weighted #10–#12 scud, caddis larva imitation, Girdle Bug, or Hare's Ear Nymph at the point, with a smaller trailer nymph tied 12 to 15 inches back from the curve of the lead nymph hook. A #16–#18 scud, Serendipity, Pheasant Tail Nymph, or Brassie is a good choice for the trailer. An Olive, Black, or Brown Woolly Bugger (#6–#14) or other leech imitation is always a deadly offering, especially when worked back under logjams, trees, and other difficult lies.

Like spring creeks everywhere, these streams have numerous hatches and the associated dry-fly fishing opportunities. Starting in March, midge and *Baetis* hatches prompt surface feeding by trout. Being multibrooded, these hatches will be prevalent on and off throughout the season. A #20–#24 Griffith's Gnat is a standard for imitating the midges. A variety of #16–#18 Blue-Winged Olive emerger and dry patterns will work for the *Baetis*.

Hendricksons *(Ephemerella subvaria)* in late April and May and the smaller sulphurs *(Ephemerella sp.)* in late May and June are next in the succession of primary mayfly hatches. Standard imitations work well. I'm partial to trying a #14 floating nymph or greased Hare's Ear for simulating the Hendrickson emergence and #16 Sparkle Duns, parachutes, and Compara-duns for the sulphurs.

If you wish to try fishing the nighttime Hex hatch, consult a local fly shop for a selection of #6–#8 dry-fly imitations, many of local origin. For this outlandishly sized mayfly, I've always found a #8 White Wulff to be an effective representation and have caught many fine browns in June and July on that pattern.

As the season moves on, tiny blue-winged olives offer challenging thin-water casting and angling during late August and September. Though nobody I know has the perfect imitation, small (#20–#26) Parachute Adamses and no-hackle drys are good selections. This is a good time for your 2- to 3-weight rod.

Caddisfly hatches can be very prolific and provide excellent and dependable spring creek fishing for much of the trout season. The little black caddis *(Chimarra)* can provide good fishing in April and early May, especially in upstream areas. A size #16–#18 Black Elk Hair Caddis or Hemingway Caddis will normally do the trick. The Grannom *(Brachycentrus)* can offer phenomenal fishing throughout May. Be prepared to fish #16 pupa imitations or soft-hackles prehatch and a #16 LaFontaine Emergent Sparkle Pupa or Elk Hair Caddis during the hatch.

Tan and green-bodied caddis are active throughout the summer, especially in the evenings, and can be imitated with a range of appropriate-size caddis patterns. Don't hesitate to jerk the dry flies underwater to mimic the diving behavior of many egg-laying caddis, or to pull them underwater at the end of a dry presentation.

Terrestrial imitations offer some of the most exciting fishing on these creeks, especially in meadow sections or reaches where land-based insects can be dislodged on windy days. Ants, beetles, crickets, and hoppers in a variety of sizes and colors are worth trying.

Angling here is often sight fishing, and fly fishers will be surprised at the size of trout lurking in shallow water seams and edges awaiting a terrestrial treat. This is far and fine angling for wary trout, with long leaders and 6X to 7X tippets required. Even hopper fishing may require finer tippets and longer leaders than you're used to; try to condition yourself to react with care, no matter how vicious the strike.

ALSO WORTH NOTING
Blue River
The Blue River, east of and tributary to Castle Rock Creek, offers 14 miles of trout angling. For access, head west from Madison on U.S. Route 18, turn north on County Route G, then go east on either Bowers Road or Snowbottom Road to intersect the scenic valley of the Blue.

Mt. Vernon Creek
This is an angling gem about a half hour west of Madison worth investigating. To reach this small spring creek, turn south on Wisconsin Route 92 from U.S. Route 18/151 in Mt. Horeb, and proceed less than 10 miles to the small community of Mt. Vernon. The more than 8 miles of trout water flows through town and generally parallels Route 92. You can intersect the stream via several county roads, and access is excellent. This is delicate small-stream angling at its most challenging.

IF YOU GO
From Chicago's O'Hare Airport, take I-90 northwest to Madison, Wisconsin (about two and a half hours), and get on U.S. Route 12/18 west (the Beltline around Madison). To reach the Big Green and Castle Rock, take the U.S. Route 18/151 exit, and stay on U.S. Route 18 west from Dodgeville to Fennimore. County Route Q east of Fennimore leads to Castle Rock Creek. U.S. Route 61 north from Fennimore hits Green River Road a few miles north of town; turn left, and follow to County Route K.

To get to Black Earth Creek, go around Madison on the Beltline, exiting at U.S. Route 14 west to Cross Plains.

Tackle Shops and Guides
In the Chicago Metro Area
   Fly 'n Field. Glen Ellyn, Illinois. Steve Fanelli, proprietor.
   Trout 'n Grouse. Northfield, Illinois. Peter Sykes, proprietor. (847) 501-3111.

In Wisconsin
   Fontana Sports Specialties. Madison. John Hutchinson, proprietor. (608) 257-5043.
   Madison Outfitters. Madison. Todd Polacek, proprietor. A full-service Orvis shop located on the west side of town at 7475 Mineral Points Road (in High Point Center). (608) 833-1359.
   Spring Creek Specialties. Median. Jim Bartlett, guide. (608) 241-4789.
   Lunde's Fly Fishing Chalet. Mount Horeb. About 2 miles south of town on Route 92. Vern Lunde, proprietor. (608) 437-5465.
   Silver Trout Spring Creek Fly-Fishing Service. Black Earth. Tom Ehlert, guide. (608) 767-2413.
   Fly Fisherman's Lair Guide Service. Fennimore. Jim Romberg, guide. (608) 822-3575.

Where to Stay
In Madison
Madison has a wide variety of chain hotels and motels located along the west side of the Beltline, providing easy access to the spring creeks. You'll also find several B&Bs in Madison.
   Mansion Hill Inn. Expensive. (608) 255-3999. www.mansionhill inn.com.
   The Collins House. Expensive. (608) 255-4230. www.collinshouse .com.

Near Black Earth
   Bel-Aire Motel. Two miles west of Black Earth on U.S. Route 14. Moderate. (608) 795-2806.

Near Castle Rock Creek and Green River
Fennimore Hills Motel. Fennimore. Just west of town on U.S. Route 18. Moderate. (608) 822-3281.
    Napp's Motel. Fennimore. Inexpensive. (608) 822-3226.
    Silent Woman Suites. Fennimore. Expensive. (608) 822-3783.

Camping
    Blue Mounds State Park. (608) 437-5711.
    Governor Dodge State Park. North of Dodgeville. (608) 935-2315.
    Wisconsin Department of Natural Resources, Bureau of Parks and Recreation. (608) 266-2181.
    Castle Creek. Jerome Kohout runs a small private campground on Castle Creek. (608) 822-3226.

Where to Eat
In Madison
In Madison, the eating and entertainment options are endless. I list just a few here.
    Avenue Bar. 1128 East Washington Avenue. Try it for a look at real Badger hospitality. Moderate. (608) 257-6877.
    Stamm House. In a historic building in Middleton, just west of Madison. Moderate. (608) 831-5835.
    L'Etoile. One of the best restaurants in the Midwest. Expensive. (608) 251-0500.

Near Black Earth
    Monk's Retreat. Cross Plains. Tavern. No reservations.

In Fennimore
    Castle Rock Inn. Just off County Route G on Shemak Road. No reservations.
    Cottonwood Supper Club. North of town at Green River Road. Moderate.
    Silent Woman Restaurant. Expensive. (608) 822-3783.

RESOURCES
    Madison Convention and Visitors Center. (608) 255-2537.
    Wisconsin Department of Natural Resources (WDNR). (608) 266-2131. www.dnr.state.wi.us.
    Essential fishing information and maps are found in the WDNR Trout Fishing Regulations and Guide.
    Wisconsin State Council of Trout Unlimited and local chapters can be accessed through the Trout Unlimited website. www.tu.org.
    Wisconsin Fly Fishing website. www.wisflyfishing.com/.

Wisconsin Travel Information. www.wistravel.com.

Born, Steven M., Jeff Mayers, Andy Morton, and Bill Shogren. *Exploring Wisconsin Trout Streams: The Angler's Guide.* Madison, WI: University of Wisconsin Press, 1997.

Mueller, Ross A. *Fly Fishing Midwestern Spring Creeks.* R. Mueller Publications, 1999.

Wisconsin Atlas & Gazetteer. Yarmouth, ME: DeLorme Mapping Company. (207) 846-7000.

CHAPTER FOURTEEN

MILWAUKEE

MENOMONEE, MILWAUKEE, AND SHEBOYGAN RIVERS

Jeff Mayers

It may come as a surprise to Milwaukee visitors that, because of years of stocking, midwestern anglers often are rewarded with not only world-class steelhead, but also brown trout and salmon. You can fish the Milwaukee Harbor or in the Lake Michigan tributaries, where anglers hook into big, tackle-testing fish (the biggest weigh as much as 30 pounds), or you can go farther afield to the Sheboygan, Pigeon, or Root.

MENOMONEE AND MILWAUKEE RIVERS

Anglers new to this trout-steelhead-salmon venue may find themselves in the shadow of Miller Park, the new stadium of the Milwaukee Brewers, hip-deep in the Menomonee River. The fish they're after aren't able to reproduce because of a variety of temperature and environmental factors. However, because of successful planting techniques, these fish are going through the motions anyway, programmed to head upstream to spawn in the river's gravel beds. This industrial corridor is slowly giving way to green space, allowing anglers to find a little respite from the freeway. There are so many trees shielding sight and sound, you can easily forget where you are.

Bill Schreiber, manager of Laacke & Joys, a venerable Milwaukee outfitter, notes that twenty years ago, most midwestern fly anglers would have laughed at the prospect of fishing for trophy-size fish in waters like the Menomonee and the Milwaukee. Now they're streaming here to taste a little bit of Alaska without the travel time and cost. If flooding and severe winter weather don't interfere, anglers can fish from September through May.

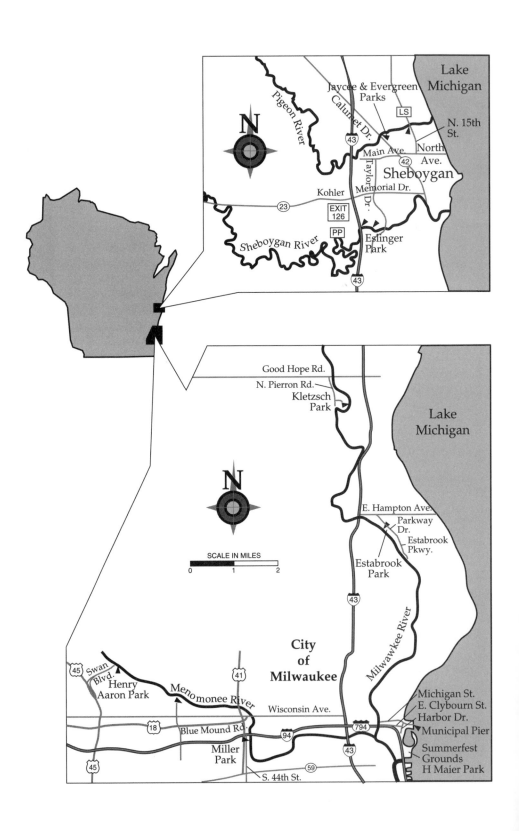

The heavy stocking up and down the Lake Michigan coast, first stocked on the Wisconsin side in the early 1960s, results in more frequent catches. Some people catch four, five, or six steelhead a day. But the word is getting around, and to avoid other anglers, you should try to sneak out to the Milwaukee Harbor early on weekdays before other anglers appear. Once there, you can target 30-pound chinook, king salmon, coho salmon, brook trout, brown trout, and the mighty steelhead—the migratory lake-run rainbow. You can approach from the shore or the breakwater, within eyeshot of the spectacular, shiplike design of Milwaukee Art Museum.

The harbor's clean water is a product of responsible environmental stewardship and the proliferation of the accidentally imported zebra mussel. The mussel, which is rushing up the Great Lakes chain, is cause for concern in many areas. However, one of its effects is cleaner water filtered through the mass of shells.

You can blind-cast along the breakwater or from shoreline rocks. The breakwater seems to collect fish. Other times, there's extraordinary sight fishing. The water is clear as an aquarium. Sometimes you see great pods of fish. Use a 7- to 9-weight outfit with sinking tip or full-sinking line. Tie on big white Zonkers or green Lefty's Deceivers in #4–#6, and strip line in short bursts, letting the lure sink to the level of the fish between strips.

The Skamania steelhead run occurs during the summer, and fish remain in the river through the winter. Skamania have lengthened the angling season, augmenting the spring steelhead run. Anglers should not target Skamania during the summer months; the water warms and fish can be stressed. In a mild winter, the trout-steelhead-salmon season fills the gap in the inland trout season, which usually runs from the first weekend in May to the end of September, with a special catch-and-release early season starting in early March.

On the inland tributaries, use a floating line unless you're plying the deep, dark pools of the Milwaukee, searching for fish when runs aren't in progress. Normally on the Milwaukee, use an 8- or 9-weight to fight a fish in the heavy current. On the Menomonee and other smaller waters, use a 9-foot, 7-weight.

Hatches, Flies, and Best Times to Fish

Inland, try an egg fly in chartreuse or fluorescent orange, egg-sucking leech, or big weighted nymphs such as Green Caddis Larvae and stonefly nymphs. These flies are tied with weight or driven down with split shot. Use a bright yarn strike indicator so you can detect the soft strike.

For a greater challenge, avoid sight-fishing for quarry on the spawning beds. If you want to take a fresh fish that hasn't shown itself, you need to go deep. You won't catch as many fish, but their bright color and fighting stamina make up for fewer numbers. Getting the fly down to the bottom is critical.

Fish can be taken at all times of the day. Low-light periods in early morning and late afternoon are most productive. On very cold days, fish feed more readily in the middle of the day when the water warms a little.

The biggest factor in catching a trophy fish, next to proper presentation, is the condition of the water. Veteran anglers prefer steady, light rains that trigger runs in moderately cloudy to clear water. When water is plentiful, smaller watersheds such as the Menomonee and Oak Creek, in Milwaukee County south of downtown, fish well. Big rains, on the other hand, can blow out the rivers, muddying them so much as to make them unfishable. The best fishing occurs when the rivers are clearing up after the torrents that turned waters chocolate brown.

Milwaukee Access

Though pressure can be a problem (less so during mild winters), the good news is that access and stream miles are increasing every year along the Lake Michigan coast. Dams are being breached, and fish are moving farther and farther upstream, where anglers have good access from parklands.

On the Milwaukee, trout and salmon used to be blocked at the North Avenue Dam on Milwaukee's north side. Now that dam is breached, and fish are moving as far up as Mequon, a well-to-do northwest suburb.

Popular Milwaukee River access spots include the following:

• The harbor, from the Municipal Pier at the end of East Clybourn Street, just north of the Summerfest Grounds.

• Estabrook Park, located between Capitol Drive and Hampton Avenue. Take I-43 north from downtown, then take the East Hampton Avenue exit. Go east, cross the river, and make a right (south) on North Pierron Road to the park.

• Kletzsch Park. Take I-43 north from downtown. Exit on Good Hope Avenue west. Cross the river and take a left on North Pierron Road south to the park.

Menomonee Access

Salmonids migrate in the Menomonee all the way to Menomonee Falls, traveling through parks such as the Little Menomonee River Parkway.

• Miller Park. From I-94 west, take U.S. Route 41 south to the Miller Park stadium's eastern parking lot.

• Honey Creek Parkway. This reach stretches along the river north and west of the stadium. There is good access at North 68th Street and State Street. From downtown, take Wisconsin Avenue until it becomes U.S. Route 18, which is called Bluemound Road after crossing the bridge over the Menomonee. Take a right on North 68th Street to the river.

• James Currie Park. Take I-94 west from downtown, then take U.S. Route 45 north. Exit on Capitol Drive and proceed a little bit east to the water.

SHEBOYGAN RIVER

In years when there is little or no rain, local veteran anglers head to big water, such as the upper Milwaukee and the Sheboygan (in the city of Sheboygan), about an hour north of Milwaukee on I-43.

Fish in the water above Lake Michigan often hold in deep pools; later they move into the riffles or tails of pools. Heavy rains can make these rivers unfishable for days. But fish *can* be caught even when water conditions are marginal. Look for fish in stillwater—a no-current holding area where fish rest.

Lou Jirikowic has been fishing for trout, steelhead, and salmon in the rivers around Sheboygan since the Department of Natural Resources opened the fishery. Once, after a flood spooked other anglers, Jirikowic spied four big steelhead at his feet. He ended up catching fish on a day when most people wouldn't have bothered fishing. He suggests that you fish if you can see at least a foot into the water. And he says fishing in low-light conditions—especially early in the day, before sloppy waders and heavy fishing pressure have made fish wary—can increase the odds of your success.

Jirikowic must be doing something right. He caught a giant, lake-run brown in the fall of 1998. It measured 39 inches and had a 22-inch girth. The fly was a White Woolly Bugger. That magnificent fish was released. Imagine how big that brown might be now!

Hatches, Flies, and Best Times to Fish

Jirikowic remembers when he and his father-in-law were a curiosity to spin- and bait-casting anglers, who chuckled when they saw flies thrown at fish. Jirikowic went from using his inland trout stream tackle, usually a 5-weight rod, to heavier tackle in the 6- to 8-weight range. For years, he's been tying his own special flies to attract the migrating fish.

With floating line and a 7- to 9-weight rod, Jirikowic often casts a couple of dependable patterns sent at the fish with split shot on a 6-foot leader. He uses a sinking tip if the water is unusually high. Two of his favorite attractors for a tandem rig are a White Woolly Bugger (#6) tied upside down on a curved hook (pink head and Krystal Flash) and a chartreuse egg-trailing fly. Upside down, the fly reduces chances of foulhooking and provides a better drift.

Jirikowic also likes to cast big stonefly nymphs. When water is high, he uses an indicator and casts upstream with a short line. When it's low, he lengthens the leader, lightens up on the split shot, and casts down and across so the rig swings to holding fish.

Don't leave your smaller trout nymphs at home. Include patterns such as Prince Nymphs and Hare's Ears in #14–#16. When the water is very low and clear, try micro eggs in pink or orange. Use tiny split shot on a light leader, and drift the fly to spooky fish.

Sheboygan Access
- Eslinger Park. Take Exit 126 off I-43. Go east on Route 23, then south on Taylor Drive, then right on County Route PP back toward I-43. The park parallels the river upstream to and under the I-43 bridge.
- There is also a pulloff as you head farther east on Route PP from Taylor Drive.
- A new urban bike trail parallels the river from Deland Lakefront Park, 715 Broughton Drive, upsteam to Kiwanis Park at North 17th Street and Ontario Avenue.
- Kohler Company property. The property includes the company where plumbing fixtures are made, as well as the American Club, a resort that includes four golf courses. The river runs through the golf courses to a dam downriver of the community of Kohler. Unless you wade upstream from Eslinger Park—staying in the river the entire time—the Kohler riverbank is available only to the guests of the American Club or the Inn on Woodlake, which purchases daily guest passes, or to those who have an annual membership in the Kohler Company's River Wildlife. Call (920) 457-0143 for more information.

ALSO WORTH NOTING
Pigeon River
Access is easy on the nearby Pigeon River, which is protected by a ribbon of green space on both sides. But the Pigeon is smaller and doesn't fish well in low-water conditions; the mouth clogs with silt that blocks fish entry.

Access to the Pigeon can be found north of Sheboygan off I-43. Take Exit 128 and then Route 42 south toward Sheboygan. There is a good access point at Route 42 (Calumet Drive) as it crosses the river at Jaycee and Evergreen Parks.

To access the river farther downstream, continue southeast on Route 42. Turn left on North Avenue and travel east toward Lake Michigan. Then turn north (left) on County Route LS until you get to the Pigeon River. Park there. Fish up- or downstream.

Root River
The Root, with water characteristics much like those of the Pigeon, lies an hour south of Milwaukee in Racine. It is a very well-known fishery and gets a lot of angler traffic because of its proximity to Chicago and Milwaukee. The Root is one of the rivers where the Department of Natural Resources strips eggs and milt from fish on their way upstream. The eggs are fertilized under controlled conditions and grow into young salmonids. Steelhead are stocked as yearlings; chinook are entered at six months.

Tributaries are assigned priorities for stocking depending on depth, flow, mouth opening, and pollution levels. These young fish are released in the stream, allowing them to taste their home water before venturing into the big lake for years of feeding and growth. In several years, they return to their spawning waters. Though most of the migrating salmonids are native to the Pacific coast, they have come to be a great complement to the Wisconsin fishery.

The best access to the Root is upstream of the Root River Steelhead Facility. Take I-94 south from Milwaukee. Exit at Route 20 and go east toward Lake Michigan. Turn left on Route 31 and go north until you intersect County Route C. Go east on Route C until you see the Root River egg-stripping station on the left. Fish upriver through the Racine CC campgrounds.

Downstream, the river goes through the Washington Park Golf Course, just off Route 20 at West Boulevard.

IF YOU GO

The Milwaukee and Menomonee Rivers flow through the city of Milwaukee. Fish migrate to the first dams.

To reach the Sheboygan and Pigeon Rivers, take I-43 north to Route 23. To reach the Root River in Racine, take I-94 south from Milwaukee, then head east on Route 20.

Tackle Shops and Guides

Laacke & Joys. Milwaukee. 1433 North Water Street. Specialists in steelhead flies and tackle. (414) 271-7878. www.LaackeandJoys.com.

Lou Jirikowic. Milwaukee. Guide. (920) 457-7060.

Where to Stay

Milwaukee has numerous economical motel chains close to General Mitchell International Airport south of the city. Additional motels are located west of the city on the way to Madison and north on the way to Sheboygan.

In Milwaukee

The American Club. Luxury resort accommodations. Expensive. (800) 344-2838.

Astor Hotel. East side of Milwaukee, within walking distance of lakeshore. Moderate to expensive. (800) 558-0200.

Milwaukee Hilton. Downtown Milwaukee, close to the interstates and across the street from the Midwest Express Convention Center. Moderate to expensive. (414) 271-7250.

The Pfister. Downtown Milwaukee. An elegant, century-old hotel midway between interstates and lakeshore. Expensive. (414) 273-8222.

In Kohler

Inn on Woodlake. Located on a lake near a shopping plaza. Moderate to expensive. (800) 919-3600.

In Sheboygan

There are numerous economical motels near I-43 in Sheboygan.

Where to Eat

Karl Ratzsch's. Downtown Milwaukee. A fine German eatery with Old World atmosphere. Within walking distance of the Milwaukee River and its Riverwalk. Expensive. (414) 276-2720.

The King & I. Downtown Milwaukee. Curried food of the Orient. Moderate. (414) 276-4181.

Luke's Sports Spectacular. Milwaukee. Near Laacke & Joys tackle shop. A sports bar with good food. (414) 223-3210.

George Webb. Milwaukee. A chain with locations around the city. Breakfast and lunch. Inexpensive. No reservations.

In Sheboygan

Sheboygan is the self-appointed bratwurst capital of the world.

Charcoal Inn. Two locations. 1637 Geele Avenue. (920) 458-1147. 1312 8th Street South. (920) 458-6988.

RESOURCES

Fishing regulations, conditions, license information, and maps. Laacke & Joys. (414) 271-7885.

Department of Natural Resources, Southeast Regional Headquarters. (414) 263-8500.

Wisconsin Innkeepers Association. Lodging information. www.lodging-wi.com.

The Greater Milwaukee Convention and Visitors Bureau. 510 W. Kilbourn Avenue, Milwaukee, WI 53203-1402. (800) 554-1448. www.milwaukee.org/visit.htm.

Wisconsin Department of Tourism. (800) 432-TRIP. www.travelwisconsin.com.

Born, Stephen, and Jeff Mayers. *Exploring Wisconsin Trout Streams.* Madison, WI: University of Wisconsin Press, 1997. (800) 621-2736.

Wisconsin Trails magazine. www.wistrails.com.

Wisconsin Atlas & Gazetteer. Yarmouth, ME: DeLorme Mapping Company. (207) 846-7000.

Milwaukee Map Service, 959 N. Mayfair Road, Milwaukee, WI 53226. A set of four regional Wisconsin maps.

CHAPTER FIFTEEN

MINNEAPOLIS AND ST. PAUL

KINNICKINNIC RIVER, HAY CREEK, TROUT RUN, AND WHITEWATER RIVER

Bill Shogren

The Twin Cities of Minneapolis and St. Paul have long been an important business destination because of several major financial, agribusiness, and high-tech companies either headquartered or with significant branch offices there. The Twin Cities are also an attractive destination because of their cleanliness, physical beauty, and wide range of sports, entertainment, and cultural offerings.

What is not so widely known is that Minneapolis and St. Paul are also the "jumping-off spot" to some good trout fishing. Many of the western Wisconsin and eastern Minnesota tributaries to the St. Croix and Mississippi Rivers are trout streams in their upper reaches. Flowing through a combination of forest and farmland, they are within one to two and a half hours from either the Minneapolis–St. Paul Airport or hotels in the Twin Cities.

The variety of streams is remarkable. Some streams rush through channels carved in stone; some meander through groves of sighing trees. Many empty into green meadows where the air is pure and the wildflowers exude intoxicating bouquets. This is the land of family farms, picturesque valleys, gentle hills, idyllic rivers and creeks. Jim Humphrey and I named this area "A Green and Gentle Land" in our book, *Wisconsin & Minnesota Trout Streams*.

KINNICKINNIC RIVER

The Kinnie, as it is known locally, is the closest premier stream to the Twin Cities. The Kinnie has profuse natural reproduction of brown and brook trout. The river has improved over the last few decades, thanks to better farming practices, habitat work by the Kiap-TU-Wish chapter of

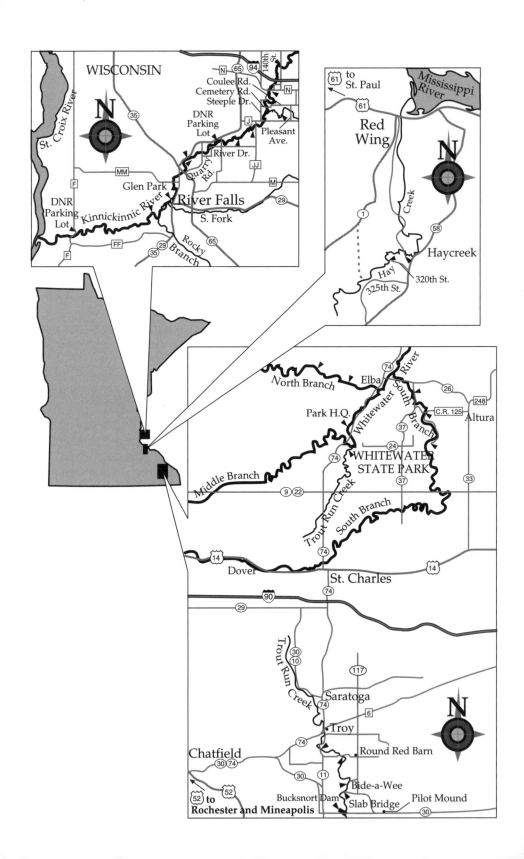

Trout Unlimited (headquartered in Hudson, Wisconsin), and the Wisconsin Department of Natural Resources (DNR). Some reports indicate as many as eight thousand trout per mile. This gem of a trout stream is considered one of the best brown trout streams in the state of Wisconsin. All 20 miles are productive, from the spring holes above I-94 in St. Croix County to County Route F, near the St. Croix River in Pierce County.

Upper River

The Kinnickinnic is really two rivers. Upstream from River Falls for about 10 miles, the river is a spring creek. Chest-high waders are in order for some of the cold, deep spots. You'll experience a variety of water—deep, smooth slicks, shallow riffles, and deep, pristine pools. The river averages approximately 20 feet across in most places. There are at least seventeen access points, including a DNR parking lot on Wisconsin Route 65, and more than 75 percent of the streambank is either owned by or under easement to the Wisconsin DNR.

Hatches, Flies, and Best Times to Fish

An older entomological survey of this part of the river records the presence of *Dannella simplex*, five species of *Baetis*, *Pseudocloeon*, and four species of *Stenonema*. There is still a small *Hexagenia limbata* hatch—maybe you'll be lucky some evening in late June. Trophy-size trout are rare in the upper Kinnie; they make their living feeding continuously on small mayflies. The usual Hare's Ear and Pheasant Tail Nymph patterns work well, as well as Adamses, Blue-Winged Olives, and Hendricksons.

Lower River

Downstream through River Falls, you can gain access below the last dam, at Glen Park. Park by the tennis courts and follow the path down to the river. Here you enter the gorge. I suggest walking down for forty-five minutes, then fishing back upstream. Good access also can be attained on the lower reaches by going upstream from County Route F. Below the dam, the lower river takes on the characteristics of a western stream. The scenery is sensational, with small coulees, flat little valleys, and woodlands, giving you ample space for solitude. These lower stretches are generally wider and shallower than those on the upper river. There are plenty of riffles, sweeping bends, pools, and flats—all with plenty of trout.

The lower Kinnie is a little warmer and has fewer trout, but a larger percentage of them are big ones. There are more forage fish for the trout, such as minnows and crayfish. Hip boots usually suffice here.

Hatches, Flies, and Best Times to Fish

Because of the forage food present, streamers such as Pass Lake, Muddlers, Woolly Buggers, and Black and Gray Ghosts all work well. Besides streamers, my favorite flies are regular and beadhead Hare's Ears, Pheasant Tails, and Prince Nymphs, #16–#18. The early season (March 1 through the last day of April) gets exciting with black stonefly imitations, such as Prince Nymphs and Black Hare's Ears. Scud patterns are always a good bet throughout the early and regular season.

Just below the dam by Glen Park, the river gets incredible *Ephemerella* hatches in late May and early June. Light and Dark Hendricksons and sulphurs work well at this time of year. Have an assortment of emerger patterns and soft-hackles, because there are times when these are the only things they are gulping.

Caddis hatches are a constant this time of year, and they can be coming off in midafternoon and evening. For these caddis, most fly fishers use Elk Hair Caddis and Henryville Specials.

All patterns in this stretch are usually in the #16–#18 range. I love to fish fast riffles with an Elk Hair Caddis even when there is no hatch, because the trout have to make a quick decision and they will most often suck it in.

From July 15 to the end of September, be ready for the Tricos in #18–#22, starting around 7 A.M. and lasting for about two hours.

Twenty miles of superb trout water awaits the itinerant angler who is willing to tread lightly the narrow track of the upper river, matching the hatch with a tiny fly at the end of a spiderweb tippet, or who is willing to walk into the lonely reaches of the lower Kinnickinnic. These Kinnie trout are wild and love to show you their aerial acrobatics.

HAY CREEK

The southeastern section of Minnesota is called the Driftless Area. It's the only part of the state that was not flattened by glaciers. When entering this country, the traveler will be impressed by the scenic coulees, bluffs, pleasant valleys, and crystal-clear creeks. These ancient watercourses wend their way through limestone cliffs down to the Mississippi River.

Less than 60 miles from the Twin Cities is Hay Creek, the first stream you encounter in the Driftless Area. Hay Creek is near Red Wing, Minnesota, in Goodhue County. This little gem of a stream meanders through woods, pasture, and cropland. It is loaded with wild brown trout. Above the slab bridge on 320th Street Way are about 4 miles of stream improvement: rip-rap, crib shelters, and plunge pools. This special-regulations area requires releasing the trout and the use of barbless hooks; crimped or filed is acceptable. The entire stretch is open to winter angling.

Hay Creek is very cold (low fifties Fahrenheit in August), and waders are your best choice. In order to have good fly fishing after June—when the bank weeds are high—you'll need to get off the banks and into the water. I use a 9-foot, 4-weight rod to get my backcasts above the bank weeds.

The trout population from 320th Street Way to Germann's pasture on 325th Street is approximately thirteen hundred per mile. In the water on Germann's property the count has been as high as thirty-five hundred browns per mile. You will know you are at Germann's when you see the sign "Do not cross the pasture unless you can do it in 3.7, the bull can do it in 3.8." This is just local humor; don't worry, there has never been an encounter.

Germann's is a real challenge. The water is so inviting, consisting of enticing little pockets, crystal-clear pools, nice runs and riffles, and you always see fish and vice versa. The trout are sophisticated, so you will have to sneak up on the pools. Often it's best to wait for a breeze on the water to disguise your presentation. One August day, out of one pool, I caught several browns on hoppers and Pass Lake streamers by staying low and using the breeze to ruffle the clear pool.

Hatches, Flies, and Best Times to Fish

In May and September, there can be some great *Baetis* (blue-winged olive) hatches in the faster stretches. The sulphurs and pale morning duns are significant in the meadow areas. Scuds produce all season long fished in the seams between weed patches. Tan and brown caddis (#16–#18) occur all spring.

The lucky fly angler who gets to Hay Creek in August and September is in for a blast. Hoppers are best, but foam beetles and ants also work. Don't let the weedy water discourage you; the trout lie ready to strike under and between the weed patches. You should get in the water and cast at 45- to 90-degree angles so you don't line the fish. The strikes are startling at such close quarters.

TROUT RUN

Just two and a half hours from the Twin Cities is the exquisite trout stream named Trout Run, in southwestern Winona County and northern Filmore County. This spring creek is in a class of its own. Some people refer to Trout Run as the Letort of the Midwest. The entire 12 ½ miles teem with wild brown trout, from the springs near Saratoga to where the creek empties into the Root River.

Starting south of the town of Troy at the first bridge on Minnesota Route 43, upstream and down is great riffle and pool fishing in pastureland. This area will make you think you're fishing the Emerald Isle in spring. Work all the usual patterns: Hare's Ear and Pheasant Tail Nymphs and scuds, in #14–#18.

Moving south on Route 43, take the first left and find the bridge by the famous round, red barn. Upstream is inviting but tough. The water is slow and shallow, but there are a couple of 18-inchers lurking about that have seen it all—I can never resist a try.

Down from the red barn, if you take the path on the west side of the stream, you'll eventually arrive at a long, slow stretch of emerald-colored water. You can sit on the bank and watch huge browns sipping midges or minuscule mayfly emergers. I've caught only a few big trout here, and I usually need help from a breeze or a drizzle. Try a Griffith's Gnat. Don't get discouraged if you don't fool the bigger trout. The entire course of Trout Run is not difficult, only certain stretches. Actually, this spring-fed creek, with its nearly six thousand trout per mile, is usually very coopera-tive for the fly angler. You will always see trout and their rises. You will catch trout. You will be turned on the entire time.

The next bridge down is Bide-a-Wee. Upstream and down to the slab bridge both offer superb fishing, with a great variety of water. Moving south, the next road takes you to Bucksnort Dam, on Route 30. Below Bucksnort, there has been extensive habitat improvement by Trout Unlimited (TU) and the Minnesota DNR. Even before the streamwork, a friend, Dick Frantes, raised thirty browns on a hopper one August afternoon.

Trout Run alone is worth the trip to southeastern Minnesota. It's clearly one of the premier spring creeks in the United States. This veiled treasure can be difficult or easy. Usually you can solve the riddle. I've had days when I could do no wrong. The trout are beautifully colored and vividly marked. These natural browns love to jump; I've had as many as six jumps out of a fish.

WHITEWATER RIVER

Before the 1851 treaty with the Dakota Indians, the Whitewater River val-ley was pristine with black soil and beautiful forests. The streams were teeming with native brook trout. Then came the Europeans to make their fortune off the land, mostly by farming. Soon the land was cleared and the streams flooded, resulting in muddy waters. What errant farming practices and nature didn't do to thwart the spirit, the Great Depression did. Eventually a good percentage of the settlers moved on to greener pastures. As early as 1919, the state of Minnesota purchased its first parcel of exhausted land to be included in the projected Whitewater State Park. Fifteen miles of the Whitewater and many miles of tributaries are now included in the park. In 1938 Richard J. Dorer joined the Minnesota Department of Conservation, now the Department of Natural Resources, and began the visionary and painstaking work of rebuilding the battered valleys of the Whitewater.

Today most of the Whitewater River and its tributaries have a healthy population of naturally reproducing brown trout and some brook trout. The fly hatches are varied and prolific. You can never visit the Whitewater system without seeing trout dimpling the surface while taking emergers or duns.

Your first stop should be the Whitewater management area headquarters, just 2 miles south of Elba. Here you can get a park sticker for one day or the season, gather information from the park personnel about camping facilities, and access the good fishing. Browse and learn about this great success story. Don't miss the live trout and stream display, funded in part by local TU chapters.

Middle Branch of the Whitewater

Six miles of the Middle Branch snake through Whitewater State Park. This is great trout water. Browns are wild, and a few rainbows are stocked to satisfy the campers. Four- and 5-pound browns are taken every year, and their weights are posted at the local tavern.

About 3 miles from the confluence with Trout Run (a different Trout Run from the one previously mentioned), near the south picnic grounds, downstream to the Route 74 bridge in section 9, the stream is open January 1 through March 31. This section is regulated as catch-and-release with barbless hooks. Midges will be on the wing most winter days. *Baetis* (blue-winged olives in #18) may show as early as late February. Tiny black stoneflies are present, so #18 Little Black Stonefly imitations work well. Weighted orange scuds are a killer any time of year.

Upstream, outside the park boundaries, the Hiawatha chapter of TU (Rochester, Minnesota) has devoted years of hard work to improving the stream. The results are extraordinary. This project proves that little water can support good numbers of big trout if there is proper water movement and shelter.

South Branch of the Whitewater

For 10 miles, the South Branch is a favorite haunt of fly fishers, offering a great mix of habitat: a few deep jade-colored pools, swift runs over gravel, beckoning flats over limestone rubble, and some grass verges where grasshoppers are short-lived during breezy dog days. During the summer months, try the upper pastures of the South Branch. Take County Route 112 (a dirt road going west out of Altura), which is east of the river, to find the abandoned bridge, then go south along the east bank. Determined anglers can spend hours casting to scores of visible rising browns. All branches of the river have the usual midwestern hatches: midges, *Baetis*, Hendricksons, sulphurs, caddis, march browns, stoneflies, and Tricos.

All southeastern Minnesota streams are user-friendly, with native trout, good hatches, and easements for public usage. Stiles are numerous, and most landowners are agreeable, if asked first. There are no real dangers; you'll always find something to mark your way back to the car, like a silo or fencerow.

HATCHES, FLIES, AND BEST TIMES TO FISH
Here is an abbreviated hatch chart and suggested flies for Wisconsin and Minnesota:

March. Black midges, black stoneflies.

April–May. Baetis, blue-winged olives, dark Hendricksons, tan and gray caddis.

May–June. March browns, light Hendricksons, light cahills, tan caddis, sulphurs.

June–July. Sulphurs, light cahills, craneflies.

July–August. Tricos, blue duns.

August–September. Tricos, tiny white-winged blackflies, blue-winged olives.

IF YOU GO
Kinnickinnic River
To fish west-central Wisconsin, it's convenient to stay on the east side of St. Paul, Minnesota. From the Twin Cities, it's only a forty-five-minute drive to the Kinnickinnic. Go east on I-94 past Hudson, and exit south on Wisconsin Route 35 to the college town of River Falls, which is situated in the middle of the Kinnickinnic River.

Tackle Shops and Guides
Gander Mountain. The four Gander Mountain stores in the Twin Cities area are good sources of up-to-date local information on western Wisconsin and southeastern Minnesota streams. These are incredibly well-stocked outdoors stores, staffed with well-informed and helpful people. Another Gander Mountain store is located in Rochester, Minnesota. Telephone numbers are as follows:

Bloomington. (612) 884-8842.

Roseville. (612) 633-7343.

Minnetonka. (612) 474-4133.

Woodbury. (612) 735-6101.

Rochester. (507) 289-4224.

Bentley's Outfitters. Eden Prairie. (952) 828-9554.

The Fly Angler. Minneapolis. (952) 572-0717.

Lund's Hardware. River Falls, Wisconsin. (715) 425-2415.

Bob Mitchell's Fly Shop. Lake Elmo, Minnesota. (651) 770-5854.

Summit Fly Fishing. St. Paul. (651) 225-1200.

Where to Stay

The following motels are inexpensive and the B&Bs are expensive but include amenities:

The Baker Brewster B&B. Hudson. (715) 381-2895.

Grapevine Inn B&B. Hudson. (715) 386-1989.

Hudson House Motel. Hudson. (715) 386-2394.

Knollwood House B&B. River Falls. (715) 425-1040.

The Phipps Inn B&B. Hudson. (715) 386-0800.

River Falls Motel. River Falls. (715) 425-8181.

Super 8 Motel. River Falls. (715) 425-8388.

Camping

Hoffman Park Campgrounds. River Falls. (715) 425-0924.

Where to Eat

River Falls. The main drag of town has all the usual eateries, fast food and slow food.

JR Ranch. Northwest corner of I-94 and U.S. Route 12. Take Wisconsin Exit 3 off I-94 east. This excellent supper club features Black Angus steaks, priced from $15. (715) 386-6190.

Trout Run

Take U.S. Route 52 south out of the Twin Cities. Travel past Rochester to Chatfield, about a two-and-a-half-hour drive. Go east on Minnesota Route 30, which merges with Minnesota Route 74. Continue to the town of Troy. Take a right at Troy, and drive to the first bridge.

Where to Stay

Headquartering in the picturesque town of Lanesboro is a good choice. The town is located south of Trout Run, at the junction of Minnesota Routes 16 and 250. Lanesboro is scenic, surrounded by big hills, and has several antique shops and many charming B&Bs. The following are all located in Lanesboro and are moderate to expensive, depending on the amenities.

Berwood Hill Inn B&B. (800) 803-6748.

Mrs. B's Historic Lanesboro Inn and Restaurant B&B. (507) 467-2154 or (800) 657-4710.

Cady Hayes House B&B. (507) 467-2621.

Carrolton County Inn B&B. (507) 467-2257.

Cottage House. (800) 944-4225.

Green Gables. (800) 818-4225.

Habberstad House B&B. (507) 467-3560.

Highland Country Inn B&B. (507) 875-2815.

Historic Lodge Inn B&B. (507) 467-2257.

Historic Scanlan House B&B. (507) 467-2158 or (800) 944-2158.
The Sleepy Nisse B&B. (507) 467-2268.
The Victorian B&B. (888) 345-2167.

Camping
Eagle Cliff Campground and Lodging. (507) 467-2598.

Where to Eat
Lanesboro has a few cafes on the main drag with standard fare of good quality. For a special treat, the B&Bs have sumptuous evening meals, some five-course gourmet-style.

Hay Creek

Travel southeast out of the Twin Cities on U.S. Route 61 through Hastings to Minnesota Route 50. Take a left here and proceed east on a continuation of U.S. Route 61, to Red Wing, Minnesota. From Red Wing, go south on Minnesota Route 58. Go to the burg of Haycreek (tavern, store, and campground). To find the creek, go south on Route 58 about 1 mile, then take a right on the gravel road 320th Street Way. Drive about 2 miles to the slab bridge and park. Fish down- or upstream. There are additional access points upstream.

Where to Stay
Best Western Quiet House and Suites. Red Wing. Moderate. (651) 388-1577.
Candlelight Inn B&B. Red Wing. Expensive. (651) 388-8034.
Golden Lantern Inn B&B. Red Wing. Expensive. (651) 388-3315.
Pruitt Taber Inn. Red Wing. Victorian B&B. Moderate to expensive. (651) 388-5945.
Red Wing Blackbird B&B. Red Wing. Moderate to expensive. (651) 388-2292.
St. James Hotel. Red Wing. Moderate to expensive. (651) 388-2846.

Camping
Hay Creek Campground and Saloon. Hay Creek. (888) 388-3998

Where to Eat
St. James Hotel. Red Wing. Historic Registry hotel. An exquisite dining experience with historical charm. Steaks and seafood. Expensive. (651) 388-2846.
Other. Red Wing also has many fast-food emporiums.

Whitewater River

Drive south on U.S. Route 52 from the Twin Cities for about one hour and fifteen minutes to the town of Oronoco, and turn left (east) on Minnesota Route 12. This road turns into Minnesota Route 247, which takes you to Plainview. Take Minnesota Route 30 south out of Plainview, and you will drop down into the Whitewater Wildlife Area. Then go south on Minnesota Route 74 to the town of Elba.

Tackle Shops and Guides

Bentley's Outfitters. Eden Prairie, Minnesota. (952) 828-9554.
Bob Mitchell's Fly Shop. Lake Elmo, Minnesota. (651) 770-5854.
The Fly Angler. Minneapolis. (952) 572-0717.
Summit Fly Fishing. Street Charles, Minnesota. (651) 225-1200.

Where to Stay

Down Town Motel. Street Charles, Minnesota. Inexpensive. (507) 932-4050.
White Valley Motel. Street Charles, Minnesota. Inexpensive. (507) 932-3142.

Camping

Whitewater State Park Campgrounds. Elba, Minnesota. (507) 932-3007.

Where to Eat

Elba House. Elba, Minnesota. (507) 932-4578.
Other. There are several good eateries in surrounding towns, such as Plainview and Street Charles.

RESOURCES

Lanesboro Visitor Center. (800) 944-2670.

Minnesota Atlas & Gazetteer. Yarmouth, ME: DeLorme Mapping Company. (207) 846-7000.

River Falls (Wisconsin) Chamber of Commerce, Monday through Thursday. (715) 425-2533.

Born, Stephen, and Jeff Mayers. *Exploring Wisconsin Trout Streams: An Angler's Guide.* Madison, WI: University of Wisconsin Press, 1997.

Humphrey, Jim, and Bill Shogren. *Wisconsin & Minnesota Trout Streams: A Fly Angler's Guide.* Woodstock, VT: Countryman Press, 1995.

Johnson, Mickey. *Flyfisher's Guide to Minnesota.* Gallatin Gateway, MT: Wilderness Adventures Press, 2001.

Ross, John. *Trout Unlimited's Guide to America's 100 Best Trout Streams.* Helena, MT: Falcon Publishing, 1999.

NAMEKAGON AND BOIS BRULE RIVERS

Michael Furtman

They are not exactly secret rivers—the Bois Brule and Namekagon—but they are rivers of secrets. Both arise in the pine and sand country of northwestern Wisconsin, a region of scraggly oak and jack pine that famed outdoor writer Gordon MacQuarrie termed the sand barrens. And although their headwaters are but a few miles apart, these sibling trout rivers part company and character soon: the Brule to course its way, often steeply, north toward glistening Lake Superior, and the Namekagon to slip gently south and west to join the St. Croix.

Both are storied rivers and, to be honest, living in part on fame gained generations ago. The nearby burg of Hayward is the home of a lumberjack festival and is a reminder that the logging that opened up this portion of the Wisconsin wilderness, with its dams, logjams, and river drives, played the main role in diminishing these streams, burying or blowing out important spawning areas and springs. Decades of catch-and-keep angling helped things not one bit.

Yet the streams persist and still provide quality trout angling, both lovely rivers admirably suited to (though not limited to) the art of fly fishing. Wide and open enough to loop a line, the Namekagon is well suited to wading at all times of the year. The wild Brule is best accessed by canoe. Special regulations now do a much better job of protecting these streams and their trout, and the future of their fisheries grows brighter by the year.

NAMEKAGON

Over 20 miles of gentle trout water await the angler visiting the 60-mile-long Namekagon River. In its dark waters, stained with the tannin of headwater bogs, native brook trout still live, joined by brown trout and rainbows. Because of the dams on the Namekagon, water temperatures rise during the summer—as warm as 80 degrees. Thankfully, it cools quickly come nightfall, and the wise angler will concentrate his or her effort during the evening or morning hours.

Since natural reproduction is somewhat limited, the river's own offspring are supplemented with hatchery fish. Wisconsin has five trout stream classifications, for which angling techniques and bag limits change. On the Namekagon, the classification changes no less than four times in the stretch discussed here, so pay attention to the regulation booklet you receive with your license.

Although brown trout can be taken—quite large ones, at that—for the first few miles below the town of Hayward, the better trout waters lie upstream. The Namekagon headwaters flow from man-made Namekagon

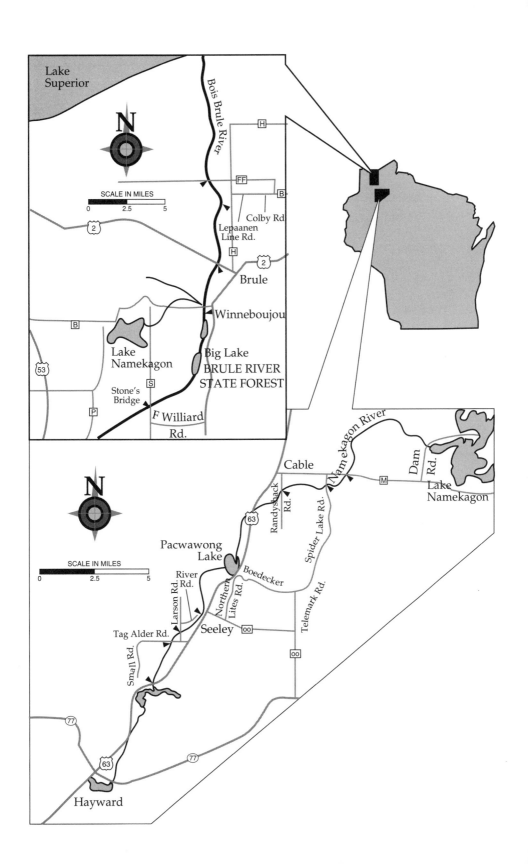

Lake. The 8-mile stretch from County Route M to the town of Cable on Route 63 is quick and narrower, inhabited by brookies, rainbows, and browns, banked by forest and alder brush, providing tight and intimate angling. Access is gained at highway bridges.

From the point where the river appears along Route 63, just below Cable and on down to Seeley, the river widens and opens up. Brown trout start to outnumber the other species in the many rips and pockets. Big Brook, an important tributary and a trout fishery in its own right, enters the river midway through this stretch, adding to the Namekagon's width and flow. Since this entire stretch of river is bounded by the highway and is under the protection of the National Park Service (the Namekagon is part of the St. Croix Wild and Scenic Waterway), you'll find numerous places to park and exceptional access on the public land.

The next section, from Seeley to the Phipps flowage, is classified as an artificial flies and lures only section. Access is excellent from Route 63 and numerous small roads that cross the river. Don't let the highway or the roads turn you off. Shoreline development is rare, thanks to federal protection, and the river is bounded by mature forest. There are sections of small rapids and riffles, with a number of large pools, and some braiding and islands. Flow here continues to increase, exceeding 135 cubic feet per second, and the river varies between 50 and 150 feet in width.

With a nod to the occasional deep spot, wading is excellent, and much of the best trout water is along the banks. Anglers can safely wade up or down the middle of the river, working shorelines, sweepers, and pockets. It's as delightful a trout water as can be found in Wisconsin. Watch for areas with watercress, which indicates springs entering the stream. These places can be especially productive when the weather and water warm.

From the Phipps flowage to Hayward Lake, the Namekagon continues to both grow in size and increase in temperature. Browns far outnumber other species now, although in places with springs, don't be surprised to catch a brook trout. The largest brook trout I've ever taken on this wonderful river came from a spring pool near Airport Road. Access continues to be good from the highway or Airport Road, but private land increases, so respect landowner rights. Long runs and deep pools make wading a bit trickier, but it's far from dangerous if you're careful.

The last section of trout water, just downstream of Hayward, is considered marginal by most, yet there are behemoth brown trout to be found here—in excess of 10 pounds—mixed in with brawling smallmouth. Indeed, good-size browns are found throughout all the sections just described, and 15- to 20-inch specimens are not uncommon.

Hatches, Flies, and Best Times to Fish

Fly anglers will delight in the Namekagon's array of aquatic insects. Hendricksons appear first in early May, followed by a two-week sulphur hatch at the end of May and into June. Large stoneflies inhabit the river, and although hatches are sporadic, nymphing with a stonefly pattern can be productive throughout the season. Late May and June also see gray drake hatches, as well as numerous caddis emergences. Although not noted as one of the best *Hexagenia limbata* rivers in the region, truly impressive Hex hatches can occur on sections with silt and marl. Watch for Hex hatches after dark in late June and early July, followed by a spinner fall that can last until morning.

As the hatches subside and the summer wears on, the ease of wading and the Namekagon's width allow for classic downstream presentation of nymphs and streamers. Soft-hackle flies, Woolly Buggers, and an array of nymphs (my personal Namekagon favorite being a #12 Beadhead Zug Bug) fished down and across can result in electrifying hits. An alluring, classic trout river, the Namekagon should rank high on anyone's visit to northwestern Wisconsin.

BOIS BRULE

In another life, and a different glacial epoch, the Bois Brule drained the ancestor of Lake Superior south into the St. Croix and eventually the Mississippi River system. In more recent geologic time, it reversed its course to flow north to the great, cold lake, but it still served as a route to the St. Croix for the canoes of the Ojibwa and the fur-trading voyageurs.

Today the Brule is as famous a trout stream as we have in the Midwest. You will likely fish this famous stream sooner or later. A half century ago, Gordon MacQuarrie noted that most serious anglers will fish this famous stream. Sooner or later, everyone does. If you have not yet, you owe yourself.

If the Namekagon is gentle and easily accessed, the Brule is swifter, wilder, and more difficult to get to know. Much of the land along its best reaches is private, limiting access, although a number of angler access points provide at least some access to every stretch. Canoes provide popular transportation for anglers on this river, and for the uninitiated, excellent guides work this river to provide both the canoe and the knowledge needed to be successful. Should you have the skill, rental canoes are available at the little burg of Brule, as are shuttles.

Once a fabulous brook trout fishery, habitat changes and overfishing have hurt this, the only native trout. But they still exist in number, if not in size, and have been joined by a few resident rainbows, numerous browns, and runs of steelhead, anadromous brown trout, and chinook and coho salmon.

Bois Brule Access

This river can be easily broken down into three stretches: the upper headwaters to Stone's bridge; the middle section down to Route 2; and the lower reaches from the highway to the big lake.

The compact, cool, and brushy headwaters upstream from Stone's bridge on County Route S is brook trout country. This upper section is relatively slow water, with much sand and thick brush. The brook trout are small but plentiful, and access is extremely limited due to private land ownership, a problem that continues to Winneboujou Landing near County Route B.

Stone's bridge is the first good access point. You can walk upstream from this point or do as many anglers do: put in a canoe here and fish downstream to Winneboujou—a float that takes about five hours and covers some 12 miles of delightfully meandering river. Brook trout still constitute the bulk of the fish in this stretch, but brown trout begin to show their spots as well.

Most of the numerous small rainbows in the Brule are the smolts of steelhead, but some are clearly residents. About halfway through this float, anglers will encounter some noteworthy landmarks: Cedar Island Estate, a wonderfully preserved, ninety-five-year-old showpiece for that era's landed gentry that once also served as a retreat for trout-fishing President Calvin Coolidge, and two broad, calm spots known as Big and Luscious Lakes—home to outsize brown trout and the silt that gives rise to both the brown drake and *Hexagenia limbata*. The entire section from Stone's bridge to Winneboujou recently received a much deserved designation as an artificial-lures-only section with larger minimum size limits in the hopes of bolstering both the size and number of trout.

From Cedar Island to U.S. Route 2 and the tiny town of Brule, the river gains speed, with more rips and rapids. Access gets better; in addition to the parking lot and canoe landing just upstream from County Route B, you can put in at the campground near the ranger station or at Route 2. This section offers anglers a delightful array of stillwater, rips, rapids, deep holes, and shady banks to fish.

The Brule is a complex river. Wading is generally good, although crossings need to take place above or below the deep holes. Except for the impressive estates, which somehow fit the Brule's noble character, most of this wonderful river is undeveloped, thanks to state ownership of those acres not part of estates. It is wild country, quiet country, full of the sounds of the river and its wildlife. MacQuarrie was right, of course. Everyone should fish this river at least once.

Within a mile or two downstream of U.S. Route 2, although it is still wild and lovely, the Brule's resident trout populations decrease. This lower section is utilized heavily by the anadromous fish that ascend both spring and fall, and indeed, if you find yourself near the Brule in April or May, or again in October, you might just want to fish this section for steelhead. Access is very good, since the river can be gained from many county roads or designated angler access points. In addition to steelhead, anadromous brown trout up to 12 pounds ascend the Brule in August and September, a difficult fishery awaiting those in search of giant browns.

Hatches, Flies, and Best Times to Fish

Fishing for the resident fish follows a pattern similar to that on the Namekagon. May and June are the best months, and the first hatch of the season is early May's Hendricksons, followed late that month by the sulphur. The most impressive hatch on the Brule, especially below Big Lake down to Winneboujou Landing, is that of the brown drake, which in a normal year will appear in mid-June. Pay special attention to the spinner fall.

A good hatch of giant Hexes follows in the last half of June and, like the brown drake, they are most numerous in areas with slow water and silted bottoms. Caddis are present everywhere, as are stoneflies. Tricos are common in the upper reaches and hatch from mid-July into August.

Blue-winged olives are present in most fishing months. Nymphs and streamers are productive all season long, but because the Brule isn't quite as wader-friendly as the Namekagon, they are a tad more difficult to fish here.

Between the ease of the Namekagon and the wilds of the enchanting Brule—a mere half hour apart by car—no visiting angler should have difficulty in finding both beautiful water to fish and handsome trout to catch. The contrast in their natures adds to the experience, challenging anglers and providing both scenic and angling diversity.

IF YOU GO

From Minneapolis/St. Paul, it's about 125 miles to Hayward. Go north on I-35 to U.S. Route 8 east, and cross over the border into Wisconsin. Take U.S. Route 63 north to the Namekagon. To get to the Bois Brule from here, take Wisconsin Route 27 from Hayward.

From Duluth/Superior, it's 40 miles to Brule. U.S. Route 53 in Duluth, Minnesota, will take you to I-535 and Superior, Wisconsin. Head south on U.S. Route 2 to Brule. To the Namekagon from the Bois Brule, take Wisconsin Route 27 south.

Tackle Shops and Guides

Duluth/Superior

The Outdoor Company. Complete fly-fishing shop in Duluth. Can arrange for guides. (218) 722-8450.

The Superior Fly Angler. A new fly shop in Superior with a complete line of tackle and tying materials. Guide service available. (715) 395-9520.

Brule

Brule River Classics. A full-service fly shop just minutes from the Brule on Route 27. A good place to book guide service for the Brule and Namekagon. Also has four comfortable cabins and RV campsites with full hookups. (715) 372-8153.

Namekagon

Pastika's Sport Shop. Tackle, licenses, and local information in Hayward. (715) 634-4466.

Brule River Canoe Rentals. (715) 372-4983. Though a canoe isn't essential to fish the Brule, it is the best way to access many parts of the river. Upstream of U.S. Route 2, there are only a couple of rapids worth worrying about. Downstream of U.S. Route 2, only experienced canoeists need apply. Brule River Canoe Rentals can provide you with a canoe and excellent maps, and shuttle you to and from the river. (715) 372-4983.

Where to Stay
In Hayward
The Hayward area has a highly developed tourism industry, with numerous accommodations ranging from a Super 8 to B&Bs. Call the Hayward Chamber of Commerce for details. (715) 634-8662.

In Brule

Brule River Motel and Campground. A new motel with campground located right on the river and U.S. Route 2. (715) 372-4815.

Brule River Classics. Cabins, RV hookups, and fly shop on Wisconsin Route 27. (715) 372-8153.

Iron River Trout Haus. A fly fisher's B&B, complete with its own private trout ponds. About 10 miles east of Brule off U.S. Route 2 near the town of Iron River. (715) 372-4219.

Camping
Namekagon

KOA Campground. Just north of Hayward on U.S. Route 63. (715) 634-2331.

Perch Lake National Forest Campground. About 12 miles north of Cable, off U.S. Route 63 on the Delta-Drummond Road (FR 223). Lovely sites.

Brule

Brule River Motel and Campground. RV sites.

Brule River Classics. RV sites.

Bois Brule Campground. Midway between Winneboujou (County Route B) and U.S. Route 2. State campground located right on the river.

Copper Range Campground. A couple miles downstream of U.S. Route 2 on County Route H. Another state campground right on the river.

These two primitive but lovely state campgrounds are best suited to tents and small campers.

Where to Eat

Visitors to the Namekagon will find numerous "supper clubs" and other eateries along U.S. Route 63 from Cable to Hayward. When in Brule, check out the Twin Gables Restaurant at the intersection of U.S. Route 2 and Wisconsin Route 27.

RESOURCES

Born, Stephen, and Jeff Mayers. *Exploring Wisconsin Trout Streams: An Angler's Guide.* Madison, WI: University of Wisconsin Press, 1997.

Humphrey, Jim, and Bill Shogren. *Wisconsin & Minnesota Trout Streams: A Fly Anglers Guide.* Woodstock, VT: Countryman Press, 1995.

Johnson, Mickey. *Flyfisher's Guide to Minnesota.* Gallatin Gateway, MT: Wilderness Adventures Press, 2001.

Minnesota Atlas & Gazetteer. Yarmouth, ME: DeLorme Mapping Company. (207) 846-7000.

Ross, John. *Trout Unlimited's Guide to America's 100 Best Trout Streams.* Helena, MT: Falcon Publishing, 1999.

PART FIVE

Texas and the
Northern Rockies

CHAPTER SIXTEEN

SAN ANTONIO AND AUSTIN

GUADALUPE RIVER

Ann McIntosh

The Guadalupe River is the southernmost trout fishery in the United States. It looks more like a river in a tropical rainforest or the Everglades than a tailwater. For most of the year, the azure water is framed by deep green Spanish moss draped over cypress trees. During the winter, skeins of gray witches' hair hang off the pecan, cedar, and sycamore trees along the banks. Along vast reaches, thousand-foot-high red-and-yellow rocky bluffs dwarf the water. In other places, cottages and canoe or raft outfitters are tucked into the banks behind the trees.

The water quality of the Guadalupe is excellent, with a pH level of as much as 10 parts per million. Except along the shallow water near the banks, there is little cover over the Guadalupe, but there are large boulders, natural and man-made weirs that give fish protection from herons, osprey, cormorants, and an occasional bald eagle. According to Scott Graham, president of the Guadalupe River chapter of Trout Unlimited (GRTU), the chapter would like to add structure to make safe harbor "fish condos" out of cedar logs and other natural material. The river bottom consists of scoured limestone, cobble, some weed growth, and algae. The wading is not difficult except when the water is flowing at a high volume.

With about four thousand members, GRTU is the largest TU chapter in the country. GRTU stocks more than fifteen thousand catchable-size (14- to 18-inch) rainbows and browns between October and March, and the Texas Parks and Wildlife Department (TPWD) stocks seventeen thousand fish in the 8- to 14-inch range. Both groups also hatch eggs and stock fingerlings. Monitoring spawning beds has revealed some evidence of trout reproduction, as has the fact that 3- and 4-inch trout were caught in the summer after seasons in which no trout were stocked in the spring.

Traveling to the Guadalupe in late February, I intended to experience and recommend a winter trout fishing trip. I can still recommend the

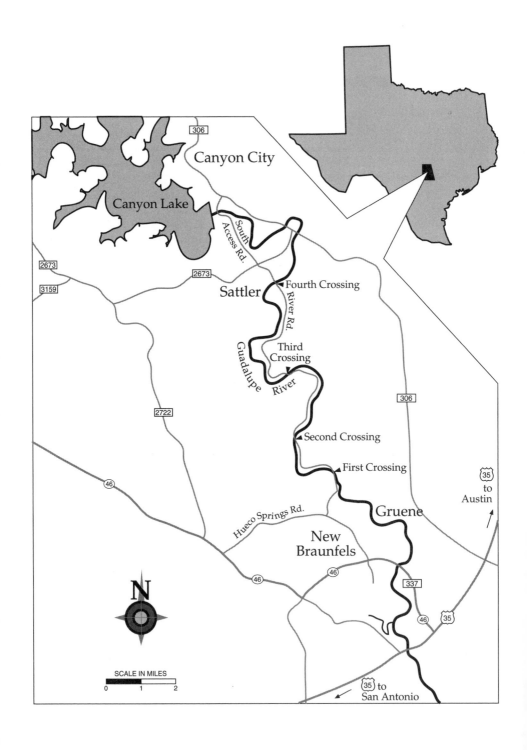

trip, but my timing was less than fortuitous. Had I been there a week earlier, I might have had several twenty- and thirty-trout days! The river ran at an angler-friendly 250 cubic feet per second from December through the third week of February.

A few days before I arrived, it began to rain, and the river rose and got cloudy but remained fishable. Steve Kaufman, owner of Guadalupe Trout Outfitters in San Antonio, reported that three clients caught and released sixty fish in the 16- to 20-inch range not quite a week before I left home. I believe they were spin-fishing.

By the time I arrived, the Army Corps of Engineers had raised the volume of flow from Canyon Lake, the source of this 15-mile tailwater, from 300 to 1,000 cubic feet per second. The water level in the lake had come up enough that a major release was required to prevent flooding.

By the time I met Scott Graham, the river was up more than a foot, and visibility was poor. Moreover, it was still raining. But my good mood and Graham's enthusiasm were not to be dimmed. We went on an extensive tour of the river and its access points, several of which I fished when the water dropped three days later.

HATCHES, FLIES, AND BEST TIMES TO FISH

The best time to fish the Guadalupe is from late November to May, or any time the flow is between 200 and 400 cubic feet per second; the optimum volume for fly anglers is about 250. A flow of more than 600 cubic feet per second is dangerous.

Beginning in March and continuing through summer and early fall, the water is covered with inner tubers, rafters, and canoeists. While some anglers fish through this "rubber hatch," most head for warm- or saltwater fishing grounds. Water temperatures have reached 80 degrees F in the summer, but as long as the flow is sufficient (200 cubic feet per second or better), the trout will survive for 10 miles.

The Guadalupe has a number of caddisflies and aquatic worms, as well as a respectable population of mayflies. (Stoneflies were decimated by a flood.) Hatches occur, as elsewhere, when the air temperature is 50 to 60 degrees and the water temperature is around 55.

The late Bud Priddy, in his book *Fly-Fishing the Texas Hill Country,* wrote that *Tricorythodes* (Tricos in #22–#24) and *Baetis* (blue-winged olives in #18) are two of the most common mayflies in the river. Priddy recommended fishing a small Quill Gordon nymph, Blue-Winged Olive (#18 emerger or dun), or Mahogany Dun (#18). He identified seven *Baetis* species.

Priddy also named the *Isonychia* (slate drake and Zug Bug nymphs) and six species of *Pseudocloeons* (#20 olive nymphs or emergers) as important. The huge yellowish brown *Hexagenia limbata venusta* mayfly occasionally appears. Priddy liked to use a large #8 or #10 Chartreuse Woolly

Worm when it emerged. He also lists hatches of *Stenonema femoratum tripunctatum* (light cahills) and *Stenomena ares* (march browns), noting that the number of march browns had decreased since the floods of the early 1990s.

All my informants told me to be prepared to select patterns according to flow and weather conditions, rather than to emergences. In other words, the variety of water levels and the weather have a much greater effect on what is going on in the water than the time of year.

Graham selects his flies according to water levels. In high water, he uses San Juan Worms, Krystal Buggers, Black and Brown Woolly Buggers, and various large streamer patterns, such as a #10 Clouser Deep Minnow, Black-Nose Dace (Picket Pins), or Black Ghost. In lower, but off-color, water, he relies on #6–#8 dragonfly or damselfly nymphs, crayfish patterns (there are five species in the Guadalupe), and large (#6–#8) Olive Woolly Buggers. Another veteran angler told me he always carries a #4 Bitch Creek Nymph in this water.

When the water level is between 200 and 400 cubic feet per second and the visibility is good, peacock herl beadhead nymphs, Gold-Ribbed Hare's Ears, Pheasant Tails, and Prince Nymphs entice fish when tied on hooks in #12–#16. Midge patterns work well on overcast or rainy days.

The Guadalupe experiences a "hatch" of fire ants almost every spring. This nasty phenomenon kills fish and makes angling very uncomfortable. The creatures (from South America) sprout wings and swarm in May. When they land on the water, the fish gorge on them, swallowing them alive. The ants sting the trouts' stomachs and intestines, and they die. TPWD reported an 8-inch brown with more than three hundred ants in its gullet. They also inflict a nasty poisonous blister on humans.

REGULATIONS

Catch-and-release regulations require anglers to release all but one trout more than 18 inches per day in the 9.6-mile trophy trout water between the easternmost bridge below the dam on Route 306 and the Second Crossing. Only flies or artificial lures may be used. Bait may be used for other species, but if a trout is hooked, it must be released immediately. Above and below the trophy trout water, five trout per day caught by any means may be taken.

You need a Texas fishing license and a trout stamp to fish the Guadalupe. A three-day out-of-state license costs $20, and the trout stamp is an additional $7.

ACCESS

Because of the recreational value of the river to canoeists, kayakers, tubers, and whitewater rafters, which brings in $300 million a year, most of the access to the water is through private land owned by outfitters, campground owners, and individuals. An angler must pay a fee to access 90 percent of the trout water. (The river itself is public, however. Anyone may wade or float through it.)

To provide entry for its members, GRTU leases twenty accesses to the Guadalupe. Some of the leases allow *anyone* to pay a fee and access the water. Other leases permit only GRTU members and their guests to use the angling access. The TPWD has leased two campgrounds for free public access to winter trout anglers.

Otherwise, to fish the water from anywhere except at the free public parking lot below the dam, you must fish from your own or a rented canoe, or pay a fee to one of the recreational areas or outfitters. If you have your own canoe, you can access the water from the parking lot and take out downstream at one of the bridge crossings. There are five other public access points, with a nominal parking fee of $3 or $4.

GRTU leases on private access to public trout water are unique among chapters nationwide. The initiative is somewhat controversial. Guides and fly shop owners would like to see more public access, but they don't want to oppose their best customers, many of whom are GRTU members. They also appreciate GRTU's stocking and educational efforts. Also, without the intensive efforts of GRTU (supported by and supporting TPWD), there likely would be no trout fishing in Texas.

Since the GRTU leases do not allow commercial activity, professional guides take their clients on float trips or walk-ins, using public and other private access. The river is about 100 feet wide for most of its length in the first 15 miles below Canyon Lake. At some places, it narrows into steep chutes that feed deep, productive pools. In others, it widens and flattens into riffles and long pools.

When the water dropped to 700 cubic feet per second and we were finally able to fish, Graham took me to the lower Rio access. There we met Ray Chapa, another angling friend. The water in front of the Rio Raft Company is a long, deep pool with lots of ledges and cuts in the limestone. It's scattered with boulders that create current braids and tongues and challenge you to make drift-free dry-fly presentations.

Graham was able to land several trout in a trough just below the access. I had better luck fishing upstream, sticking close to the bank and using a #10 olive beadhead Woolly Bugger with a peacock herl body that Chapa gave me for the occasion. There is a wide open stretch of water just above the lower Rio access that, had the water been a few inches lower, I believe would have been very productive using small nymphs or emergers. I took fish in the shallows and saw several enticing water-displacing rises in midriver.

One of GRTU's leases, about 5 miles below the dam, is magnificent. It's about 75 feet wide, lined with trees and ledge rock. At two historic irrigation weirs, the water drops 2 feet into pools that feed into deep, productive runs for half a mile. This water was the clearest and most complex that I saw. The fish were not very cooperative the day we were there, but it will be the first place to which I return. I used nymphs, standing on a ledge and swimming the fly through the deep run right below me, and casting a dry fly over the current to rising fish along the far bank.

ALSO WORTH NOTING

If you are in the Austin or San Antonio area, and fishing the Guadalupe is not an option, consider a trip to the Texas coast for redfish, drum, speckled trout, tarpon, and whatever else is running. It's a three-hour drive from San Antonio. The coastal scenery and wildlife are spectacular, reminding me of the barrier islands and wetlands on the Atlantic side of the Eastern Shore of Virginia. Guides will take you to wadable flats in small flat scooters with 6-inch sides. There are also plenty of walk-in flats along the shore.

The better-known destinations are Rockport, South Padre Island, and Corpus Christi Bay, but amenities are less expensive in the Port Aransas and Port O'Connor areas. For information, contact Gruene Outfitters in Corpus Christi at (361) 994-8361, or one of the guides or tackle shops listed below. Before you go, call (830) 964-3342 for current flow information. Less than 450 cubic feet per second means safe wading.

IF YOU GO

You can reach the Guadalupe River from either Austin (about one hour) or San Antonio (forty-five minutes) from I-35. The river is also within a four-hour drive of Dallas or Houston. Take I-35 south from Dallas to New Braunfels and follow book map. From Houston, take I-10 to San Antonio and I-35 north to New Braunfels.

Tackle Shops and Guides

Austin Angler. Austin. A superb fly shop. (512) 472-4553.

Austin Outfitters. Austin. (512) 329-6061.

Guadalupe & Beyond Flyfishing Adventures. Wimberley. Captain Scott Graham guides on the Guadalupe and other rivers, as well as on the saltwater flats near Port O'Connor. An enthusiastic and knowledgeable guide. Toll-free: (877) TXTROUT. www.fiyfishingtexas.com.

Gruene Outfitters. Gruene. Ray Box, owner. Full-service shop with tackle and clothing. (830) 625-4440. Another shop in Corpus Christi. (361) 994-8361.

Harry Lane. Lives in New Mexico, but guides on the Guadalupe in winter months. (505) 324-8149.

Hill Country Outfitters. San Antonio. (210) 491-4416.

One Shot Outdoors. San Antonio. (210) 402-5344.

Orvis Austin. (512) 261-1645.

Tackle Box Outfitters. San Antonio. Carries a full line of tackle. (210) 821-5806.

Where to Stay
Gruene Country Inn. Close to New Braunfels and Gruene. Luxurious Victorian farmhouse. Expensive. (830) 606-0216.

Gruene Mansion Inn. Gruene. Victorian cottages overlooking the Guadalupe River. Restaurant. Moderate. (830) 629-2641.

Days Inn. New Braunfels. Moderate. (830) 608-0004.

Holiday Inn. New Braunfels. Moderate to expensive. (830) 625-8017.

Maricopa Motel. Rooms a little shabby, but in a beautiful location on the river 3 miles south of Canyon Lake. Inexpensive. (830) 964-3600.

Scenic River Properties. Two miles south of Sattler on the river. I stayed in a two-bedroom cottage overlooking the river. Fishing out your door! Plan in advance, since many cottages rent by the week or month. Moderate. (830) 964-3127 or (800) 765-7077.

Where to Eat
Adobe Verde Tex-Mex. Gruene. I didn't eat out much on this trip, but when I did, it was here. The food is terrific. Moderate. (830) 629-0777.

Grist Mill. Gruene. Excellent food. Moderate. (830) 625-0684.

Bavarian Village. New Braunfels. Good German and American food. Moderate. (830) 625-0815.

Huisache Grill. New Braunfels. Good southwestern food. Moderate. (830) 625-9001.

Camping
Canyon Lake. The Army Corps of Engineers maintains several campsites on the lake. (830) 967-1168.

RESOURCES
Guadalupe River Trout Unlimited (GRTU). Contact through the website: www.GRTU.org.

Canyon Lake Chamber of Commerce. (800) 528-2104.

New Braunfels Chamber of Commerce. This is a tourist destination and has many motels, B&Bs, and restaurants. Call for a complete listing. (830) 625-4205.

Guadalupe-Blanco River Authority, 933 East Court St., Seguin, TX 78155. (830) 379-5822.

Texas Parks and Wildlife. Austin. (512) 389-4800.

Priddy, Bud L. *Fly-Fishing the Texas Hill Country.* 2nd revised ed. Barksdale, TX: W. Thomas Taylor, 1996.

CHAPTER SEVENTEEN

MISSOULA, MONTANA

CLARK FORK RIVER AND ROCK CREEK

Stephen and Kim Vletas

When we visit the middle section of western Montana, we make our headquarters in Missoula, close to some of the best trout water in the West. Driving up I-90, drift boat in tow, we pass through miles of high plains with an endless series of humpbacked hills. The Clark Fork River begins near Warm Springs at the confluence of Silver Bow Creek and Warm Springs Creek. We become aware of it just below the Anaconda Settling Pond.

CLARK FORK RIVER
The Clark Fork is one of the most troubled rivers in the West. It has been abused by the timber and mining industries and by agricultural interests. Toxic wastes, including heavy metals, have been dumped into the river by miners for more than a hundred years. During the summer months, farmers drain some stretches of the river almost dry to fulfill their irrigation needs. In spite of all this, the Clark Fork provides good fly fishing for brown and rainbow trout. There are also a few brookies, some cutthroat trout, and bull trout. Bulls are listed as endangered and if caught must be handled with extreme care and returned to the water as quickly as possible.

A number of groups are fighting to clean up the Clark Fork and prevent further mining projects from going forward, including mining projects that could destroy the popular Rock Creek fishery. Groups involved in the fight include Avista Corporation (a hydroelectric power company), Trout Unlimited, and the Clark Fork Coalition.

Avista Corporation took an unprecedented step when it invited Trout Unlimited, in addition to more than thirty other groups and agencies, to participate in two of its dam relicensing efforts with the Federal Energy Regulatory Commission. Avista has funded state and federal efforts to

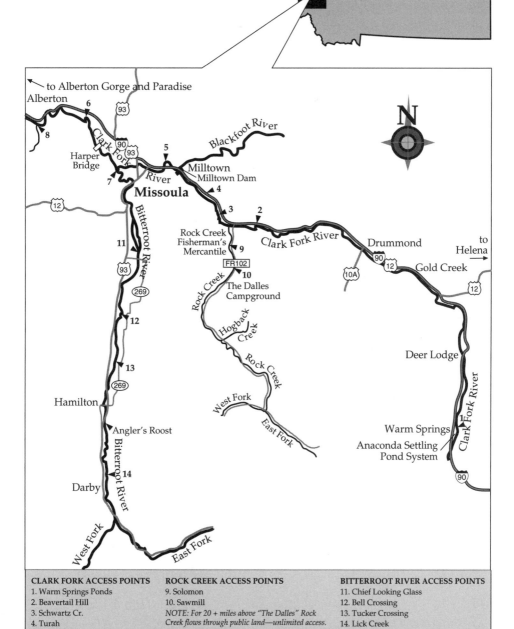

to Alberton Gorge and Paradise

Alberton

Blackfoot River

Clark Fork

Harper Bridge

Milltown
Milltown Dam

River

Missoula

Clark Fork River

Drummond

to Helena

Gold Creek

Rock Creek
Fisherman's
Mercantile

FR102

The Dalles
Campground

Bitterroot River

Rock Creek

Hogback Creek

Rock Creek

Deer Lodge

Hamilton

West Fork

East Fork

Warm Springs

Anaconda Settling
Pond System

Clark Fork River

Angler's Roost

Bitterroot River

Darby

West Fork

East Fork

N

CLARK FORK ACCESS POINTS	ROCK CREEK ACCESS POINTS	BITTERROOT RIVER ACCESS POINTS
1. Warm Springs Ponds	9. Solomon	11. Chief Looking Glass
2. Beavertail Hill	10. Sawmill	12. Bell Crossing
3. Schwartz Cr.	*NOTE: For 20 + miles above "The Dalles" Rock Creek flows through public land—unlimited access.*	13. Tucker Crossing
4. Turah		14. Lick Creek
5. Sha Ron		
6. Erskine		
7. Kelly Island		
8. Petty Cr.		

enhance the native fish populations in the river. This is a one-of-a-kind partnership among a major corporation and agencies and conservation groups to work toward a common goal.

Upper Clark Fork

For fly fishers, the Clark Fork is really two different rivers: the upper river, which is smaller and easily waded, and the lower river, which is huge and best fished from a drift boat. Most of the Clark Fork is easily accessed from I-90. Much of the upper river consists of small channels with grassy or brush-covered banks, and brown trout are the predominant species. The population of browns is especially good around Warm Springs, then drops off toward Deer Lodge. From Garrison Junction to Rock Creek, trout populations are very low. This is the section that is nearly dewatered by irrigators during the summer months. Fishing improves after Rock Creek enters the river.

Hatches, Flies, and Best Times to Fish

Caddis are the ticket in this section of river from just after runoff in late June on through the summer and into fall. Two different types of sedges— the spotted sedge and the little sister sedge—are the most common varieties. We like to match the spotted sedge with a Schroeder's Parachute Caddis (#12–#14) as the adult. We use LaFontaine's Emergent Sparkle Pupa (#12–#16) in the surface film, and a Bright Green Beadhead Serendipity (#14–#16) subsurface or as a dropper off a variety of drys such as an Elk Hair Caddis or X-Caddis (#12–#16). There are evenings during the summer when the caddis hatch is so thick you think you might suffocate.

If you fish this section of river during the early season (March and April), you could run into a *Baetis* hatch, and you'll have some luck drifting cranefly larvae along with one of our favorite new nymph patterns, the Copper John (#14–#16). Depending on when runoff starts and how heavy it is, anglers might be able to enjoy the salmon fly hatch in mid to late May. This emergence takes place below the Rock Creek confluence and runs up into Rock Creek. Big stonefly nymphs, black rubber legs, and Yuk Bugs (#2–#6) are the subsurface flies of choice; you can also take fish on top with Black and Orange Chernobyl Ants, Fluttering Stones, Stimulators, and Double Humpies (#2–#6).

By late July, the terrestrial fishing really picks up, with hoppers the major attraction. Schroeder's Parachute Hopper, the Henry's Fork Hopper, and Dave's Hopper (#6–#12) are our favorites, but you can't go wrong with a Chernobyl Ant or a Club Sandwich (#6–#10) either. We're also big fans of fishing ants and beetles everywhere in the West. A Parachute Black Ant or a foam beetle (#10–#16) will be effective along the bank edges even during the heat of the day. By September, some Tricos and *Baetis* begin to emerge again, with *Baetis* continuing into early November.

Lower Clark Fork

The lower Clark Fork starts below the Milltown Dam and runs to the confluence with the Flathead River at Paradise. Below Paradise, trout fishing is spotty at best—all the way to Idaho. This stretch of river is wide and flat, with long stretches of dead water. Anglers will have more success in this area accessing the river by drift boat, though wading anglers can catch fish during hatches, especially below the Pretty Creek bridge. The river character exception is the whitewater stretch of the Alberton Gorge. Rainbow trout are the dominant species here, with some large browns, and a few cutthroat and bull trout. You'll find the most fish in the wide riffles, long runouts, and deeper pockets.

Hatches, Flies, and Best Times to Fish

Mayflies are the aquatic insects that most frequently bring trout to the surface. *Baetis* emerge March through May and are the major prerunoff hatch. Parachute *Baetis* and Blue-Winged Olive Sparkle Duns (#16–#20) dead-drifted to pods of rising fish will produce consistent strikes, but you need to be stealthy and use a 5X or 6X tippet. Using spring creek tactics will bring the greatest rewards. We also like to nymph with Pheasant Tails and Copper Johns (#14–#18). While mayflies are fine bugs, the main reason we make the trip here in early season is to hit the *Skwala* stonefly hatch on the lower Clark Fork and, even more so, on the Bitterroot.

Though the *Skwalas* may not be obvious on the Clark Fork, they're there, and the fish are eating them. The best time for this hatch is usually the last week in March through the first week in April. Our favorite dry fly is a Natural Muddler Trude (#8–#10), and we often fish it with a Beadhead Red Squirrel or Gold Beadhead Biot Golden Stone (#6–#10) as a dropper. Nice-size rainbows, 14 to 18 inches, with some over 20 inches, congregate in the riffles, seams, and along the banks to chow on these stoneflies. These two weeks also offer a good gray drake hatch, plus *Baetis* and midges.

After runoff in late June, the summer season kicks in with good pale morning dun (PMD) and gray drake hatches that go into August. We like to fish PMD Sparkle Duns (#16–#18), Parachute Adamses (#12–#18), and Gray Paradrakes (#10–#14) for these hatches. As in the upper river, the hopper fishing turns on in August, though you'll take finicky rising trout most consistently on ant patterns.

Tricos emerge in late August and run through September, when the *Baetis* return. At times, fishing the lower Clark Fork can be extremely difficult for anglers trying to figure out which bug, or which stage of a bug, the fish are taking. When in doubt, try a small ant pattern, a #18 Hemingway Caddis, or a #18 Copper John dead-drifted on a 12-foot, 6X leader. If you get the presentation right, you'll have a good chance of success.

October is another of our favorite times on this river. The fish are podded up to feed on *Baetis*, drakes, and other odds and ends. The way to be most successful is to push downstream in your drift boat looking for these pods, then target rising trout. Just because the trout are feeding on small mayflies doesn't mean they won't eat a giant steak. We like to fish Woolly Buggers, Conehead Sculpins, and other streamers throughout the lower river. If you're looking for the larger brown trout, this is definitely the way to lure them.

The stretch from Harpers bridge to Pretty Creek is the best section we've seen for the bigger browns. For experienced rafters, the Alberton Gorge is the way to go, as this section has the highest concentration of trout in the lower river, and the streamer fishing is great. You should not attempt this stretch on your own. The serious whitewater is full of an endless string of rafters and kayakers in the summer months. Fish it at other times of the year, and hire a guide with a boat to do so.

Clark Fork Regulations
The trout season is from the third Saturday in May through November 30. An extended whitefish season, with catch-and-release for trout, runs from December 1 to the third Saturday in May. The river is open year-round under catch-and-release regulations. Refer to the complete Montana regulation booklet handed out with your license for special regulations regarding daily possession limits for trout.

ROCK CREEK
Rock Creek is one of the most popular trout streams in Montana. It runs through an idyllic small valley and has easy access and good populations of trout throughout its 50-mile length. Anglers looking for a Montana grand slam know to fish this stream, as it's possible to catch browns, rainbows, cutthroats, and brookies on this eye-pleasing water. If you should hook a bull trout—it's illegal to target them—handle it with extreme care and return it to the water as fast as you can.

Beginning in the Sapphire Mountain Range as the West Fork, the creek gains volume at the confluence of the East Fork. The upper section of the creek is a nice combination of riffles and pocket water, with some deeper pools. Most of the upper river runs through private property, though anglers can gain access to the river in several places. Rainbows and cutthroats are predominant in this part of the river that ranges from 40 to 75 feet in width. Use caution when wading, as the rocky bottom is definitely slippery, especially in the spring when flows pick up.

The middle section of the creek, which runs for about 16 miles, begins near Big Hogback Creek and zips down to The Dalles Campground area. This is a tough section to fish during high flows, as there is not a lot of holding water, and wading is difficult. During lower flows, anglers can consistently find fish in all likely lies. The Dalles area offers some wider bends and large boulders that attract bigger browns.

Downstream from The Dalles, all the way to the confluence with the Clark Fork, you find pristine classic trout water. Long runs drop into slower pools that feed riffles rich in aquatic life. Nice bends feature undercut banks that filter off into side channels here and there. Anglers who enjoy reading water will have a great time matching their wits against many rainbows and browns.

The Rock Creek story is not all good, however. Whirling disease has hurt the population of rainbows, and the creek's popularity is sometimes a detriment. There is definitely such a thing as loving a river to death, which is what occurs during the late-May to early-June salmon fly hatch.

There is also the constant threat of new mining activities in the headwaters. Fortunately, Rock Creek has many friends, and new mine development has been kept at bay for the time being. Trout populations have made a comeback the past couple years, and anglers are once again catching plenty of fish between 14 and 17 inches.

Hatches, Flies, and Best Times to Fish

Our favorite time to fish Rock Creek is in March and April. We made our first trip to Missoula to fish the *Skwala* stonefly hatch here and on the Bitterroot. We then discovered that the march brown (sometimes called the march brown drake) hatch on Rock Creek was even better than fishing the *Skwalas*. Some local anglers told us that the march brown was their favorite hatch of the year. A Wulff or Paradrake (#10) pattern will take fish consistently during the hatch. For the *Skwala* adults, we like a Natural Muddler Trude (#8–#10). For nymphing at this time of year, we like a #8 Gold Beadhead Biot Golden Stone or a Gold Beadhead Squirrel (#8–#12). Hare's Ear and Pheasant Tail Nymphs (#10–#14) are also effective, but you need to achieve a good dead drift, and you *must* get your nymph down on the bottom.

We really like to fish streamers and often throw Woolly Buggers in unusual situations. They have worked for us with a variety of fish, including finicky New Zealand brown trout, Argentine rainbows, and some very smart fish on well-known western spring creeks.

Our first time on Rock Creek was one early April morning. It was shaping up to be a frustrating beginning. There was no hatch. Our nymphs were being ignored; so out came the Beadhead Woolly Buggers. And then we were off—into one hot rainbow after another, plus a couple of nice browns!

Most anglers show up on Rock Creek around mid-May, when the salmon fly nymphs start crawling to the banks. This hatch usually lasts into mid to late June, moving upstream sporadically. We've been told that the river can be a nightmare of anglers and rafts from the beginning of this hatch through June.

Starting July 1, fishing from boats is not allowed. After the salmon flies fade, golden stones and pale morning duns are the focus of dry-fly fishing into July. As on many other rivers, the pale morning dun spinner fall on Rock Creek is a fine experience for anglers who like to cast to individual rising fish. Some of our favorite patterns include PMD Sparkle Duns and Para-Cripples (#14-#18), as well as Red Quill CDC Spinners (#16–#18). In August, hopper patterns are effective along the banks, but we prefer ants and beetles.

The crowds start to diminish in September as the *Baetis* hatches return. A *Baetis* parachute or a Blue-Winged Olive Captive Dun (#18–#20) will take dimpling or rising fish. October is a favorite month for local anglers. Fall-run brown trout move up into the lower river and, along with fat rainbows, provide great sport. Woolly Buggers and Conehead Sculpins (#2–#6) are the best way to target big browns, though a Dark or Light Spruce Fly (#2–#6) also works well.

Rock Creek Regulations

Trout season runs from the third Saturday in May to November 30. An extended whitefish season, with catch-and-release for all trout, runs from December 1 to the third Saturday in May. Only artificial lures and flies may be used. Anglers can keep three trout per day under 12 inches, or two trout under 12 inches and one trout over 20 inches. No fishing is allowed from boats between July 1 and November 30. See the complete Montana regulation booklet, available at all license-selling agencies.

ALSO WORTH NOTING

Bitterroot River

This is one of our favorite rivers in the area, and we especially like to drift it in late March and early April during the *Skwala* stonefly hatch. This is the time of year when we've caught brown trout over 20 inches on dry flies.

The town of Hamilton is growing like crazy, and even the quiet community of Darby is seeing some growth. Spring runoff usually ends by the Fourth of July weekend. Wade-fishing the upper river, along with the two forks (East and West), during the summer and fall is a pleasure, as the good population of cutthroats with some rainbows and browns provides good sport.

The best area of the river for numbers of browns and rainbows is from Darby to Angler's Roost. While it's possible to wade here, fishing from a drift boat is best. The Bitterroot Valley, wedged between the Sapphire and Bitterroot Mountains, is one of the most visually splendid angling destinations in the Rockies. The Bitterroot Valley has some of the fastest population growth rates in the nation. This asset is a potential detriment, as more and more people are attracted to the area. Access to the Bitterroot

River is via U.S. Route 93 from Missoula. There are a number of clearly marked angling accesses, boat ramps, and campgrounds.

IF YOU GO

Missoula is the focal point of five valleys and home to the University of Montana. The town has a laid-back, welcoming atmosphere, and with more than fifty thousand residents, all major services are available.

Delta, Skywest, Horizon Air, and Northwest Airlines serve the Missoula International Airport. Rental cars are available from all major rental agencies.

Travelers driving into the valley have easy access via I-90 from the east or west, and U.S. Route 93 from the south and north. As it is a college town, airlines can be booked up around school holidays, spring break, graduation time, and then again during the summer tourist season. Hotels, motels, and campgrounds also fill quickly during prime times, so you need to call ahead for reservations. Please refer to the map accompanying the chapter for precise directions to river access.

The town of Hamilton is another good option for an angling headquarters. Located on U.S. Route 93, south of Missoula, this is a pleasant community of three thousand residents in the scenic Bitterroot Valley.

Tackle Shops and Guides

Missoulian Angler. Missoula. (406) 728-7766.

Grizzly Hackle. Missoula. (406) 721-8996.

Streamside Anglers. Missoula. (406) 543-6528.

The Kingfisher. Missoula. (888) 542-4911.

Riverbend Flyfishing. Hamilton. (406) 363-4197.

Riffles and Runs. North of Hamilton. Route 93. (406) 961-4950.

Fisherman's Mercantile. Rock Creek. Rock Creek Road .5 mile up from I-90. (406) 825-6440.

Where to Stay

4B's Inn North. Missoula. Rooms, restaurant. Moderate. (406) 542-7550.

4B's Inn South. Missoula. Rooms, restaurant. Moderate. (406) 251-2665.

Days Inn Westgate. Missoula. I-90 and Route 93. Rooms, restaurant. Moderate. (406) 721-9776.

Town House Inns of Hamilton. Hamilton. Moderate. (406) 363-6600.

Sportsman Motel. Hamilton. Inexpensive to moderate. (406) 363-2411.

Camping

National Forest and Bureau of Land Management campgrounds. Campgrounds on Rock Creek include The Dalles, Sawmill, Norton, and

Bitterroot Flat. Reservations are accepted for some campgrounds, so it is advised to call ahead whenever possible.

U.S. Forest Service. 340 North Pattee, Missoula, MT 59802. (406) 329-3511.

Missoula El-Mar KOA. Reserve Street exit off I-90, then south 1.5 miles. (406) 549-0881.

Angler's Roost Campground. Three miles south of Hamilton on Route 93. Rental cabins also available. (406) 363-1268.

Where to Eat

Missoula and Hamilton offer a number of inexpensive restaurant choices, including all the national chain fast-food joints. The following are a few of our favorites after a day on the water.

Bad Bubba's BBQ. Hamilton. Inexpensive. (406) 363-7427.

The Depot. Missoula. Steaks, seafood, salad bar, and microbrews. Moderate. (406) 728-7007.

The Stage Station Restaurant. Hamilton. Next to the Fisherman's Mercantile. Moderate. (406) 677-2227.

Staver's Restaurant. Hamilton. This is a fun bar and grill. Moderate. (406) 363-4433.

RESOURCES

Missoula Chamber of Commerce. (406) 543-6623.

Bitterroot Valley Chamber of Commerce. Hamilton. (406) 363-2400.

Montana Department of Fish, Wildlife, and Parks. Missoula. (406) 542-5500.

Ross, John. *Trout Unlimited's Guide to America's 100 Best Trout Streams.* Helena, MT: Falcon Publishing, 1999.

Thomas, Greg. *Flyfisher's Guide to Montana. Wilderness Adventures Fly-fishing Guidebook.* Belgrade, MT: Wilderness Adventures Press, 1997.

Montana Atlas & Gazetteer. Yarmouth, ME: DeLorme Mapping Company. (207) 846-7000.

CHAPTER EIGHTEEN

JACKSON HOLE, WYOMING, AND IDAHO FALLS, IDAHO

SNAKE RIVER AND FLAT CREEK

Stephen and Kim Vletas

SNAKE RIVER

Visitors flying into the Jackson Hole Airport on a clear summer day are treated to dreamlike visual thrills. The dramatic peaks of the Teton Mountains, speckled with glaciers, dominate the skyline, while the Snake River serpentines through the lush green valley, its maze of channels and tributaries glistening in the sunlight.

Most summer flights approach Jackson Hole from the north, over Yellowstone and Grand Teton National Parks. As the aircraft descends, the character of the Snake River becomes clearer. It's a big river. Over time, it has sliced into the earth, creating a wide river plain with high banks, forested islands, and long, sweeping gravel bars. The braids of the Snake are each a small river, as many of the side channels are streams unto themselves.

From the airport, a visiting angler is no more than ten minutes' drive from the Snake River. The Jackson Hole Airport is unique in that it's the only commercial airport inside a national park, and landing here puts an angler within easy reach of trout fishing of the best variety in the Lower Forty-eight.

Anglers have numerous choices of fishing headquarters. The town of Jackson, loaded with motels and restaurants, is a ten-minute drive to the river. Additional accommodations are spread out across the valley, from Teton Village, on the west side of the Snake, to Moose, north of the airport, and up to Jackson Lake in Grand Teton National Park. If you like to camp, you'll not run out of options in every direction.

You could spend an entire summer in Jackson Hole and not scratch the surface of fly-fishing options. Or, like my wife, Kim, and me, you could spend twenty years here and still marvel at the waters you haven't yet fished. When we consider all the options, we always come back to the

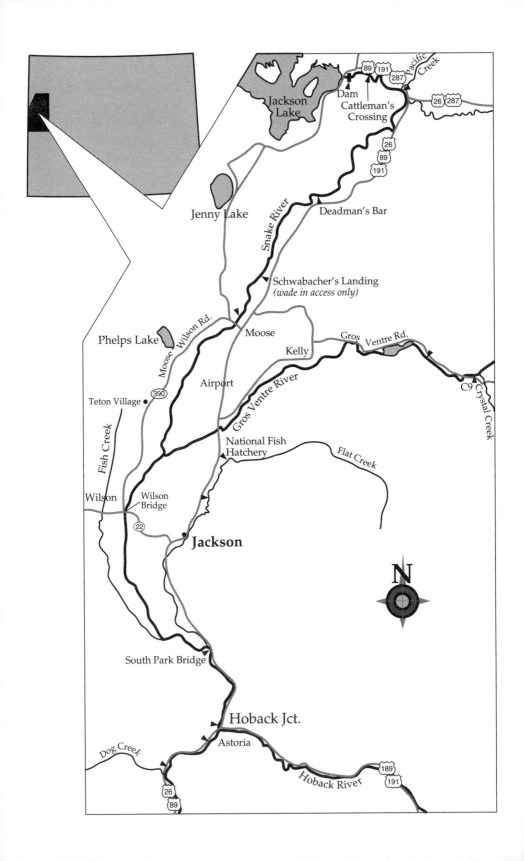

heart of our fisheries—the Snake River—and the fish that make it so special, the Snake River finespot cutthroat. These are all wild trout, beautiful natives that were here long before man set foot in the valley. The finespot cutthroat is the king of its species, the most hardy and adaptable, and the most aggressive to a dry fly.

The headwaters of the Snake River begin north of Jackson Hole in Yellowstone National Park and the Teton Wilderness. The Continental Divide at Two Ocean Pass is where the drainage splits. Atlantic Creek spills to the northeast into the Yellowstone River, which is the largest tributary of the Missouri River. Pacific Creek winds down to the southwest to meet the Snake River just above Moran Junction. The Snake is the largest tributary of the Columbia River.

The upper Snake picks up volume from a number of small creeks and from the Lewis River, before it empties into Jackson Lake. The lake was created in 1911 with the building of the Jackson Lake Dam, which forever changed the character of the river. The dam was built as an irrigation project for Idaho farmers before the existence of Grand Teton National Park. After a major flood in 1950, the Army Corps of Engineers began building a dike system, starting below Moose, to protect private property. This system, which now extends almost to South Park, has dramatically changed the character of the river over the years, as have the irrigation release policies from Jackson Lake.

The Wyoming Game and Fish Department (WGFD) and the Jackson Hole chapter of Trout Unlimited have done a good job over the last ten years improving the native fishery. One of the most important steps was establishing a winter minimum flow of 280 cubic feet per second. Other vital efforts included the rehabilitation of spawning habitat in a number of spring creeks and special regulations to protect the finespot cutthroat.

The greatest efforts of all, however, must be credited to Mother Nature. Like rivers all over the world, the Snake has undergone a number of weather-related cycles. Through the early 1980s, the Snake was an incredible fishery, producing good numbers of fish, and big ones. Then a number of low-water years, combined with a four-year project to rebuild the Jackson Lake Dam, put too much stress on the trout, and fishing quality diminished. From 1996 through 1999 higher-than-normal snow-packs provided an abundance of water, which has made the native trout fat and happy again. The Snake River is now set for great fishing for the next four to five years.

The most popular sections of the Snake flow through Grand Teton National Park, from the Jackson Lake Dam to the highway bridge at Moose. This is also one of the most spectacular sections of river in the world. Bald eagles, ospreys, herons, and hawks soar overhead, while moose, deer, elk, beavers, and muskrats inhabit the river. Mount Moran and the Teton Range fill the western skyline, and the vistas change as you float downstream.

From the dam to Cattleman's Crossing and through the Ox Bow Bend area to Pacific Creek, the river is a slow-moving tailwater fishery. There is good wading access along the river in a number of spots, though fishing from a drift boat or canoe will provide access to more water. For those looking for hatches, this section offers match-the-hatch fishing from June into October.

Access, Hatches, Flies, and Best Times to Fish

The Ox Bow Bend to Pacific Creek area is the only section of the Snake you can count on fishing in June and early July, as the remainder of the river below Pacific Creek is in runoff. Hatches of golden stones, yellow sallies, caddis, pale morning duns, mahogany duns, *Baetis,* Tricos, and midges keep the native finespot cutthroats looking up, as do midsummer terrestrials.

Yellow Stimulators (#14–#16), Hemingway Caddis (#14–#18), Sparkle Caddis (#14–#18), Pale Morning Dun Sparkle Duns (#16–#18), Trico Thorax patterns (#18–#20), and Black Parachute Ants (#14–#16) are some of our favorite flies. Anglers also need to be prepared for the pale morning dun and Trico spinner falls. When the trout key on these bugs, you'll need Rusty Hen-Wing Spinners (#14–#18) and Trico Hen-Wing Spinners (#18–#20).

Starting at the Pacific Creek access, the character of the Snake changes, becoming the rambling swift river people expect to see, with numerous braided channels and lots of deadfalls. Both Pacific Creek and the Buffalo River pump tons of silt and mud-red water into the river during June runoff. This sediment makes all the downstream sections of the river off-color. By early July, Pacific Creek clears and is a good fishery in its own right, but the Buffalo is unstable. Hard rains any time in August and September can turn the Buffalo to mud and consequently turn the Snake off-color.

July is often a difficult month for anglers to wade the Snake, with flows still relatively high. Drift boat fly fishers pound the banks with big drys and streamers, looking for seams, riffles, runout pools, and deadfalls that create good holding lies. Boat and wading access is available at Pacific Creek, Deadman's Bar, Schwabacher's Landing (boat access is not always available), and Moose. Boaters should be particularly cautious in the section of the river between Deadman's Bar and Moose.

Anglers launching rafts or drift boats at the national park access in Moose will float down to the Wilson Highway bridge (Route 22), leaving Grand Teton Park about a mile downstream from the Moose bridge. After you leave the park, most of the land on either bank is private. Wyoming law gives the landowners rights to the riparian land, so you are technically trespassing if you step out of your boat or drop your anchor on private land. Walking around on midstream gravel bars is no problem, but you should not walk on the private sections of the dikes without permission.

The river grows restless within the dikes, whipping back and forth in rebellion and creating frequent side channels. While casting big drys and streamers to the dikes will produce some nice fish, you'll find your biggest rewards in the smaller channels and in the slower sections of the main channels. Hatches of pale morning duns and golden stones occur from July into September. A Parachute Cahill or an Ausable Wulff (#12–#16) usually imitates the pale morning duns, and Stimulators (#10–#14) work well for the stoneflies. A highlight of this stretch is the confluence with the Gros Ventre River on the east bank just north of the West Gros Ventre Butte.

Downstream from the Wilson bridge, the character of the river is much the same, with side channels branching off from the main channels as they slither back and forth between the dikes. The Bureau of Land Management (BLM) has created good wading access below the bridge, but you need to be aware of private property in this stretch also. Fish Creek and other private spring creeks feed this piece of water all the way to the South Park bridge.

Hopper fishing along the dikes is especially good in August and early September. By late August, a good stonefly hatch begins working its way upstream. These are big stones, often the size of salmon flies, with golden brown bodies. Chernobyl Ants, dry Muddlers, Double Humpies, and Club Sandwiches (#6–#10) will take large trout looking for these juicy bugs.

The character of the river changes again below the South Park bridge, becoming one main channel in most places. U.S. Route 89 parallels much of the river here and crosses the river twice. Good bank structure and midriver gravel bars hold the most fish, and the average fish size increases from 12 to 14 inches. Throughout the river, you can expect most of the trout you catch to be between 10 and 14 inches, with good numbers of 15- to 18-inch fish, and some hogs up to 24 inches. The larger trout are usually caught from late August through early October, or in April during the opening weeks of the season before runoff.

Wading anglers can have good fishing in this section starting in August, but this is one of our favorite areas to float. We like to fish a dry and a dropper here, with a Muddler Trude (#10–#12) on top and a Beadhead Red Squirrel (#10–#12) or a Copper John nymph (#12–#14) below. Hopper fishing is also great in August and September, and September is the perfect time to get down deep with streamers for the big boys.

The Hoback River joins the Snake at Hoback Junction, where the river makes a hard right and enters the Snake River Canyon. This is a gorgeous float in the fall, when the water is low and the hillsides are burning with yellow, orange, and red colors. There is also good wading access between the Astoria bridge and the Elbow Campground.

U.S. Route 89 follows the river all the way downstream to the Palisades Reservoir. From East Table to Sheep Gulch, commercial whitewater dominates the river. It should be floated only by experienced boaters, especially in the spring, when high flows have reached over 30,000 cubic feet per second.

If you're planning a fishing vacation that includes the Snake River, you'll want to visit Jackson Hole between July 20 and October 10, with August and September the two best months. Though the Snake might fish well earlier in July some summers, July 20 is a good target date. More anglers fish the Snake in August, because that's a popular time for family vacations and it's the month the terrestrial fishing really turns on.

September is our favorite month for a variety of fishing. Anglers will have success fishing blind with big attractor drys, targeting rising fish, drifting nymphs, or casting streamers. After Labor Day, the summer crowds are gone, and you can enjoy the change of seasons from summer to fall. This is also the best time to consistently take the larger cutthroats on dry flies.

The Snake is primarily an attractor pattern river. The Trude family of flies—Muddler Trudes, Adamses, Royal Coachmen, and Lime Trudes (#8–#14)—was made famous on the Snake River, with the Lime Trude the winning fly in the First Annual Jackson Hole One-Fly Contest in 1986. The common denominator in these flies is the single, white, laid-back calf-tail wing. The calf tail is important, because it's easy to see and it floats well. Trude flies are best fished with some action, and on the Snake, varying a dead drift with twitching and skittering movements will produce the most consistent strikes.

Double Humpies (#6–#8) and Chernobyl Ants (#6–#10) are also popular attractors on the Jackson area streams. The newest attractor is the Club Sandwich (#6–#8), a three-layer, foam-bodied fly that can match a stonefly or hopper. We also like to use a variety of Stimulators (#8–#16), Wulffs (#10–#18), and regular Humpies (#10–#18). Even though hopper patterns are intended to imitate terrestrials, Parachute Hoppers (especially Shroeder's) are also taken for stoneflies. Other favorite hopper imitations include the Parachute Hopper (#6–#12), Dave's Hopper (#6–#12), and Henry's Fork Hopper (#6–#12).

Streamer fishing is popular on the Snake throughout the season, especially among anglers looking for larger trout. Kiwi Muddlers (#2–#6), Muddler Minnows (#2–#12), and Matuka Sculpins (#2–#6) are longtime favorites, with the locally created Double Bunny (#2–#6) the most popular pattern in recent years.

Most nymph fishing is done with an attractor dry and a dropper, though fishing stonefly patterns like a Brown Rubber-leg Stone (#2–#10) along the dikes and in deeper runs is often effective for large trout. Beadhead Prince Nymphs (#8–#14), Beadhead Squirrel Nymphs (#10–#14), and Beadhead Hare's Ears (#10–#16) are all effective, but the best new fly to come along in years is the Copper John (#10–#16). We try our best not to let any angler leave our shop without a good supply of Copper Johns.

Snake River Regulations

The Snake River upstream from Palisades Reservoir is closed to trout fishing from November 1 through March 31. An extended whitefish season, with catch-and-release for all trout, runs from November 1 through February. The Snake River is closed to all fishing throughout March. You can pick up a copy of Wyoming regulations wherever licenses are sold. Special regulations on various stretches of the Snake are as follows:

• From Yellowstone National Park boundary to Jackson Lake, three trout per day in possession, only one over 20 inches.

• From 150 feet below Jackson Lake Dam to the gauging station 1,000 feet below the dam, three trout per day in possession, only one over 20 inches. It is prohibited to use (or possess) fish, fish parts, or fish eggs for bait.

• From 1,000 feet below the dam to the Wilson bridge (Route 22), three trout per day in possession, only one over 18 inches. All trout between 12 and 18 inches (inclusive) must be released. Artificial flies and lures only.

• From the Wilson bridge to West Table boat ramp, three trout per day in possession, with only one trout over 12 inches.

FLAT CREEK

Flat Creek is an intimate, meandering meadow stream located in the National Elk Refuge north of Jackson. Flat Creek has the character and feel of a spring creek. The clear, glassy water glides from bend to bend, filling deep pools, sweeping beneath undercut banks, spilling over fine gravel bars, then pouring into long runs and back into deep pools.

Flat Creek is one of the few places anglers can sight-cast small dry flies to native finespot cutthroat trout day in and day out, with a legitimate shot at a fish over 20 inches any day during the August 1 to October 31 season. Flat Creek has fished consistently well for the twenty years we've fished it, though it's had a few downturns due to silting and other habitat problems.

Several restoration projects, sponsored by the Jackson Hole Trout Unlimited chapter, repaired eroding banks, reduced silting, and stabilized banks while providing more cover and holding water. WGFD also introduced a stocking program to augment the native finespot cutthroats.

The opening of Flat Creek, on August 1, is a major fly-fishing happening. Back in the 1980s we knew everyone on the creek on opening day. Now we hardly know anyone, and the place is a madhouse. In spite of all the people, a lot of cutthroat trout over 20 inches are caught on opening day, with some fish going up to 24 or 25 inches. After the first five or six days of the season, the character of the fishing changes dramatically, as the shell-shocked trout become superwary and hard to catch. As far as we're concerned, this is when the real fun begins.

Hatches, Flies, and Best Times to Fish
The hatches in the first part of August are amazing. Opening week anglers will see brown drakes, pale morning duns, mahogany duns, march browns, caddis, craneflies, and a variety of terrestrials. The brown drakes will have the most fish rising, from 10 A.M. to 2 P.M., but individual fish key on different bugs. If you want to trigger explosive strikes from huge fish, skitter an adult cranefly pattern across the surface of the deeper pools or along the grassy, undercut banks.

Stealth is important on Flat Creek, and as the season progresses, it becomes vital. Approach the banks slowly and quietly, and stop at least 10 feet away from the water's edge. Take some time to watch the water carefully for rising fish. Some trout barely dimple the surface when they take an emerging insect. Make your final approach to the stream on your knees. Use 5X tippet to start for small dry-fly fishing, though you'll need to go to 6X or 7X at times, later in September and October.

A drag-free drift is essential; you'll need to read the water and determine the best way to present your fly. Because the stream winds back and forth on itself so many times, it's easy to cross most places, so you can work into a position to use the currents to your advantage. Most anglers will do best working for a downstream presentation. If you're an advanced angler, up-and-across casts are most effective. Fishing a long leader, throwing a reach mend, then maintaining the mend will get even the most finicky trout to take your fly.

We consistently catch fish during the appropriate hatches on Pale Morning Duns and Mahogany Sparkle Duns (#16–#20), Brown Paradrakes (#10–#12), Ginger Quills (#12–#14), Pale Morning Dun and Blue-Winged Olive Para-Cripples (#16–#20), CDC Transitional Duns (#16–#18), Parachute *Baetis* (#18–#20), and Hemingway Caddis (#16–#18).

For really tough fish, we use a variety of emergers and nymphs in the fall, with the most consistent producers being a Copper John (#18) or a Spotlight Emerger (#16–#20). Parachute Hoppers (#6–#10), Parachute Black Ants (#12–#16), Foam Beetles (#10–#16), adult craneflies (#4–#6), and a variety of other attractors will fool fish early in the season. If all else fails, you can often catch some nice trout subsurface with Beadhead Woolly Buggers (#6–#8) or Muddler Minnows (#4–#8) cast to the undercut banks.

Flat Creek Regulations
Flat Creek on the National Elk Refuge is open to fly fishing only, August 1 through October 31, in the following areas: from Old Crawford bridge upstream to McBride bridge, and on the mouth of Nowlin Creek, up to

the closed-area signs. Above McBride bridge, the season runs from May 21 through October 31. Below Old Crawford bridge, the creek is closed to fishing all year. You may have one cutthroat trout in possession per day over 20 inches; all fish under 20 inches must be released. You can pick up a copy of Wyoming regulations wherever licenses are sold.

Flat Creek Access
The two main accesses to Flat Creek are at the U.S. Route 26/89/191 turnout and at the National Fish Hatchery. From August 1 to mid-September, the best hatches occur from 10 A.M. to 2 P.M., and again in the evening, after 7 P.M. Later in September and in October, the best dry-fly fishing is from 11 A.M. to 4 P.M. Cold fall mornings can push the hatch starting time into the afternoon.

ALSO WORTH NOTING
Gros Ventre River
The headwaters of this river are high up in the Gros Ventre Mountains, some 50 miles above its confluence with the Snake River. The upper river, above Upper Slide Lake, offers good access to small-stream fishing for native finespot cutthroats and some rainbows. Most fish range from 10 to 14 inches, with 16 to 20 inches possible.

Fish Creek, Cottonwood Creek, and Crystal Creek are tributaries of the Gros Ventre that all fish extremely well. The best time to fish the upper Gros Ventre is from mid-July through September. While there are some hatches, fishing attractor dry-fly patterns like Wulffs, Humpies, Trudes, and Stimulators, along with your favorite hopper patterns, will produce the most consistent action. The campground at Crystal Creek is popular, and it's sometimes hard to get a spot, though there is plenty of public land for all campers. The lower Gros Ventre, below Lower Slide Lake, is also a good fishery, but irrigation demands can reduce the flows to almost nothing, and private landowners don't welcome the public.

The Gros Ventre is accessed off U.S. Route 26/89/191 by turning east on the road to Kelly. Out of Kelly, take the Gros Ventre Road up to Lower Slide Lake. The paved road becomes a dirt road after you pass the lower lake.

South Fork of the Snake River
This is one of America's all-time best trout rivers. To float it is to see some of the finest scenery in the West. This float is not to be missed; nonangling partners will be glad they decided to come along. The water holds lots and lots of cuttthroat, rainbow, and brown trout. You'll do lots of blind casting with big drys to huge fish under rock ledges. For information, call West Bank Angler, at (800) 922-3474, or Bob Bressler, through the Orvis Store in Jackson, at (307) 733-5407.

Green River

The upper Green River, from the BLM public accesses above the Warren bridge down to the Daniel Junction bridge, is one of our favorite rivers anywhere. It's a 56-mile drive south from Jackson on U.S. Route 191/189 to the Warren bridge, with the scenic Wind River Mountain Range as your companion the last 15 miles. There's a public campground just south of the bridge, plus twelve public-access areas, with camping allowed, above the bridge.

This area offers good wade fishing for rainbows, browns, cutthroats, and brookies, though we prefer covering this water by drift boat. Trout average 10 to 14 inches, but there are plenty of fish in the 15- to 18-inch range, plus some hog rainbows and browns up to 28 inches.

Dry-fly fishing is excellent from early July through mid-September. The best hatches occur in July, with a gray drake hatch that brings up every fish in the river, including all the big boys. A variety of mayflies, caddis, and clouds of golden stoneflies have plenty of fish on the surface most days. August brings on great terrestrial fishing, and streamer fishing is good throughout the season, especially in the lower river.

Below the Warren bridge, most of the land is private, and landowners in this area are strict when it comes to enforcing the law. You need to fish this water by raft or drift boat, and don't get out of your boat. A professional guide trip on the Green from Warren to the hatchery or from the hatchery to Daniel Junction is well worth the money.

IF YOU GO

The town of Jackson is a major tourist destination, with three million visitors passing through Yellowstone and Grand Teton National Parks during the summer season and many thousands during the winter skiing months. There are many places to stay and to camp, but you need to call ahead for reservations if you plan to visit between mid-July and Labor Day. Delta, Skywest, United, and American Airlines offer regular service to the Jackson Hole Airport. Rental cars are available from all major rental agencies.

Driving visitors come into the valley from the south through the Hoback Canyon on U.S. Route 191 or through the Snake River Canyon from Alpine on U.S. Route 89. These highways merge at Hoback Junction, about 12 miles south of town.

You can also get to the valley from the west via Route 22 over Teton Pass. From the east, you can drive from Dubois over Togwotee Pass on U.S. Route 26/287. From Yellowstone or Grand Teton Park, drive south on U.S. Route 89/191/287. If you're driving down from Yellowstone in July or August, expect heavy RV traffic to make it slow going, so plan your day accordingly.

The weather is always an important factor, one way or another, for visiting anglers and outdoor enthusiasts. Be prepared for a dramatic change in the weather at all times. The most beautiful, warm, calm mornings often turn into windy, cold, harsh, rainy, and hailing afternoons. Always take extra layers of clothing, including good rain gear, with you on any fishing, hiking, or camping trip.

Tackle Shops and Guides
Bob Bressler and the Orvis Company Store. Jackson. (307) 733-5407.

High Country Flies. Jackson. Fine locally tied patterns. (307) 733-7210.

Snake River Angler. Moose Village, also known as Dorman's. William Dorman, proprietor. (307) 733-3699.

Jack Dennis Outdoor Shop. Jackson. One of the first fly shops in the Jackson Valley. (307) 733-3270.

Westbank Anglers. Teton Village. On Moose-Wilson Road. Stephen and Kim Vletas and Reynolds Pomeroy, proprietors. Major tackle, flies, and clothing outfitter. (800) 922-3474 or (307) 733-6483.

Where to Stay
The following are inexpensive or moderately priced options. Prices are relatively high in Jackson Hole (there's seldom a room for less than $65 a night per person). Other options include luxurious high-end hotels, condos, and houses. Contact the Jackson Hole Chamber of Commerce (under Resources, below) for additional information.

Anglers Inn. Jackson. (307) 733-3682.

Anvil Motel. Jackson. (307) 733-3668.

Elk Refuge Inn. Jackson. (307) 733-3582.

Flat Creek Motel. Jackson. (307) 733-1447.

Motel 6. Jackson. (307) 733-1620.

Wagon Wheel Village. Jackson. (307) 733-2357.

The Hostel. Teton Village. (307) 733-3415.

Camping
There are national forest, national park, and Bureau of Land Management campgrounds throughout the region. Reservations are accepted for some campgrounds, so call ahead if possible.

U.S. Forest Service Jackson Ranger District. (307) 739-5400.

U.S. Forest Service Pinehaven Ranger District. (307) 367-4326.

National Park Service, Grand Teton National Park. (307) 739-3602 or 3603.

National Park Service, Yellowstone National Park. (307) 334-7381.

Teton Village KOA Campground. 2780 N. Moose-Wilson Road, Teton Village, WY 83025. (307) 733-5354.

Astoria Mineral Hot Springs. About 2 miles south of Hoback Junction, in the Snake River Canyon. (307) 733-2659.

Snake River Park. 6705 South Route 89. Good river access. (307) 733-7078.

Where to Eat
There are many choices, including national fast-food chains and some very nice high-end options with gourmet food and superior service. The following are among the most popular, combining good food with moderate prices.

Merry Piglets Mexican Grill. Jackson. (307) 733-2966.
The Gun Barrel. Jackson. (307) 733-3287.
Mountain High Pizza Pie. Jackson. (307) 733-3646.
Jedediah's House of Sourdough. Jackson. (307) 733-5671.
Calico Italian Restaurant & Bar. Teton Village. On the Teton Village Road, between Wilson and Westbank Anglers. (307) 733-2460.
Vista Grande Mexican Restaurant & Bar. Teton Village. On the Teton Village Road, near Westbank Anglers. (307) 733-6964.
The Bunnery. Jackson. (307) 733-5474.
Bubba's Bar-B-Que Restaurant. Jackson. (307) 733-2288.
Teton Steak House Family Restaurant. Jackson. (307) 733-2639.
Mangy Moose Restaurant and Saloon. Teton Village. (307) 733-4913.
Anthony's Italian Restaurant. Jackson. (307) 733-3717.

RESOURCES
Jackson Hole Chamber of Commerce. Box E, Jackson, WY 83001. (307) 733-3316.
Wyoming Department of Game & Fish. Regional Office, 360 N. Cache Dr., Jackson, WY 83001. (307) 733-2321.
Retallic, Ken. *Flyfisher's Guide to Wyoming.* Belgrade, MT: Wilderness Adventures Press, 2000.
Wyoming Atlas & Gazetteer. Yarmouth, ME: Delorme Mapping Company. (207) 846-7000.

HENRY'S FORK OF THE SNAKE RIVER

Ann McIntosh

The Henry's Fork is my wintering-over stream. When I'm staring out the window at a blanket of snow, aching to fish, I imagine fish heads, big rainbow faces gulping spinners on the flat water of the Henry's Fork. I'm not alone. Ranked the number one trout stream in the United States by the membership of Trout Unlimited, the Henry's Fork is fished regularly by some of the best anglers in the country. It also confounds its share of novices and can stump the best of guides.

The main stem of the Henry's Fork begins at the confluence of the outlet of Henry's Lake and the spring creek formed by Big Springs, the spawning nursery. The stream then flows into Island Park Reservoir.

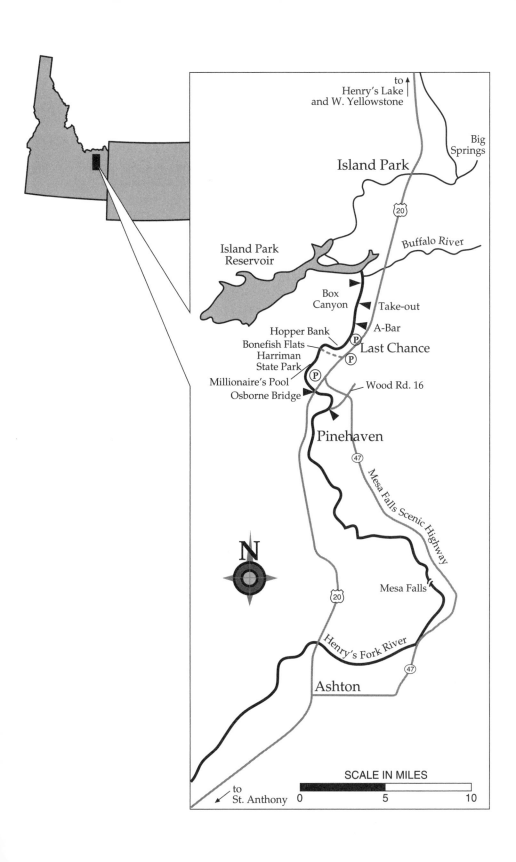

The large pools below the dam are very productive. I've done well there on July afternoons using caddis patterns. This is where guides put in to float the Box Canyon.

Below Box Canyon, the Henry's Fork enters its most popular reaches: From Pelican Rock to the take-out at Riverside, this 13-mile stretch includes the water behind the A-Bar; Harriman State Park (formerly known as the Railroad Ranch), including Bonefish Flats, Millionaire's Pool, and the Osborne bridge reaches; the secluded area accessed from Wood Road 16; the wonderful water at Pinehaven; and the faster water from below Pinehaven past Henry's Fork Lodge to the Riverside Campground.

The enormous spring creek water of Harriman State Park known for its dry-fly challenges lies largely between the upper Ranch parking lot (just south of Last Chance) through the Ranch, below Osborne bridge to Wood Road 16 and Pinehaven. It's the memories of these pools that sustain me through the winter doldrums. The river runs through rough, cobbled hummocks of meadowland populated with nesting birds. Be alert; you'll spook the birds as you unknowingly walk up on them. The area is a preserve for sandhill cranes, which serenade you with their calls throughout the day. I find the flat pools the most beautiful, challenging trout waters I've ever fished.

Wading is easy in these reaches, but hooking fish is not. Fish constantly prowl the water, seldom rising in exactly the same place twice. To approach a target, you must wade very carefully, pushing no waves, and be able to make a downstream, drag-free drift to rising trout. When you hook into one of these fish, you'd better bow when they jump and play them skillfully. You'll be fishing 5X to 7X tippets to fish often over 16 inches. The small ones don't count here. In the lexicon of the Henry's Fork, they're called "dinks." My personal definition of a dink on this river is any trout under 14 inches. You don't go to the Henry's Fork to catch large numbers of fish; you go to put your dry-fly fishing skills to the ultimate test. If you catch one or two lunkers in the 17- to 20-inch range on this mirror-clear water, you deserve congratulations at the day's end. This is a stalking game, and it presents a challenge that, when met, deserves the telling it will get at the A-Bar later that evening.

Although I prefer the dry-fly water, I can attest to having taken my share of fish on big streamers below Pinehaven and on nymphs in the Box Canyon. For a couple years, the fish in the Box were not as large as in previous years. But as Rene Harrop points out, guides who float Box Canyon today have changed their methods: Instead of slinging big, leggy nymphs and streamers as in the past, they use tiny nymphs, #18 and smaller, to get the best day-to-day results. Trouthunter guide Marty Reed took a 10-pound hog in 2000 on a #18 midge larva. The Box can be waded by crossing the water above Last Chance and working your way upstream.

The lower river flows between the confluence with Warm River and Chester Dam, north of St. Anthony. This section holds a number of large brown trout and is best fished from a boat. It is particularly popular with guides during the salmon fly hatch in May and June. Water from this section is used for irrigation from mid-July through August, lowering its productivity at that time, but otherwise the lower tailwater is a fantastic fishery. Big browns and rainbows, as well as whitefish, are in the river here, with browns dominating as you go farther downriver.

The water flows easily through a canyon with grassy, wildflower-strewn banks. A dirt road runs along the north side of the river between the put-in at Warm Springs and Route 20, and a railroad bed runs along the south bank. There are a number of spots where the river is sufficiently shallow to wade, but it is more efficient to use a boat. There is a lot of private property along this stretch of the river, and access is often restricted.

I haven't fished much of the West, and one reason is that I find it hard to pass up the Henry's Fork to try some of the other impressive western rivers. Its sirens beckon in long, seductive wails. I could easily spend two or three weeks on this water, with breaks to the Madison River below Quake Lake, Montana, and to Henry's Lake, Idaho, or Hebgen Lake, Montana, all less than an hour's drive away.

Bob Lamm, John McDaniel, and Ron Sorenson have guided me on this river—three guides many anglers, including myself, believe are the best on this water. What I've learned from these three extraordinary individuals is far too much to condense in these pages. Lamm and Sorenson work through Henry's Fork Anglers, and McDaniel through Trouthunter (see Tackle Shops and Guides, below). They each have somewhat different tactics, but I've found I can put them all together to great advantage and without contradiction. If you're new to the Henry's Fork, or to large western spring creeks in general, I recommend hiring a guide for a day or two, until you learn the tactics.

The first time I was guided by Ron Sorenson, he gave me etiquette tips for fishing this river. These have stood me in good stead ever since. Give all wading anglers *very* wide berth upstream and down, to right and to left. Don't get into the water until you spot a rising fish. No two anglers should ever target the same fish. People in the houses along the river are supposed to keep their dogs out of the water when they see anglers targeting rising fish. You may ask them to do so.

The Henry's Fork has had its share of threats to its fish and their habitat. Though it is fishing well now, this has not always been the case. Continued challenges are posed by development and the march of tourists headed toward West Yellowstone. The Henry's Fork Foundation was founded to bring together all those with vested interest in maintaining a world-class fishery. Write to the Henry's Fork Foundation, P.O. Box 61, Island Park, ID 83429, or call (208) 558-9041.

HATCHES, FLIES, AND BEST TIMES TO FISH

Hatches on the Henry's Fork are prolific and include mayflies, caddis, and terrestrials. This is a river where matching the hatch can be critical, and you'll often have to detect which stage of what emergence the fish are taking, for there are often many kinds of bugs on the water simultaneously.

Though my activities on the Henry's Fork have been confined to July, I know that it also fishes well in August, and that June, September, and October can be spectacular. To protect nesting birds, Harriman State Park does not open until June 15. The least crowded time to fish is after Labor Day.

Below, I list the major hatches on the Henry's Fork. There are many other emergences, as well as multiple effective flies to imitate each stage of each hatch. I recommend buying or tying flies once you arrive at this destination. You'll have a long way to go to beat the House of Harrop patterns.

April–May. Iron Blue Quills.

May–June. Salmon flies; golden stoneflies; black, tan, and olive caddis; western green drakes; pale morning duns; brown drakes.

July. Tiny Blue Quills, pale morning duns (most important in the first half of August), small western drakes, light cahills, speckled duns, caddis, black, red, and honey wicked ants, mid through late summer.

July–August. Terrestrials (beetles, ants, hoppers), gray drakes, speckled spinners, blue-winged olives, Tricos. There is a good August hatch, with an amazing morning spinner fall.

September–October. Iron Blue Quills, mahogany duns. October sees caddis as well as gray and black midges.

Nymphs can be very effective offerings to Henry's Fork fish. Try the nymphal stages of the caddis and mayflies listed above, and use them not only on the deeper, faster reaches, but also on the flat water, fished as carefully and drag-free as their dry counterparts.

REGULATIONS

The lower reaches of the Henry's Fork, from Vernon bridge to the South Fork of the Snake, may be fished year-round. From Ashton to St. Anthony, two fish over 14 inches may be taken. There is a six-fish creel limit below St. Anthony. Catch-and-release regulations prevail from Island Park Dam to the take-out at Riverside Campground.

ACCESS

Few rivers are more accessible than the Henry's Fork. If you want to encounter fewer anglers, pick an access spot and walk as far up- or downriver as necessary to get away from people. Access at Pinehaven is private. *Do not* attempt to reach the Henry's Fork via these riverbank houses without an invitation. The Henry's Fork Lodge does not have a public boat put-in, but lodge guests are often dropped off here after a float downstream. Public-access areas are as follows:

- The put-in for Box Canyon below Island Park Reservoir (wading possible).
- The take-out at the beginning of the flat water south of the Box.
- From the banks at Last Chance to the parking lot at the top of the Harriman State Park. There are ample pulloffs.
- On the left (south) side of Route 20, opposite the gate (Mailbox) and dirt track into Bonefish Flats and Cattle Bridge.
- At either of the two parking lots at the Railroad Ranch (in the park).
- At Osborne bridge.
- At Wood Road 16. Take this dirt track to the right (south) off Route 47, Mesa Falls Scenic Highway. If you don't bottom out, you'll arrive at the river. You'll likely see a few other people, some of whom may be camping overnight.
- Riverside Campground, a major take-out after a float from Osborne bridge.
- Lower Mesa Falls.
- The town of Warm River. (Put-in for the float from Warm River to Ashton Reservoir.)
- U.S. Route 20 bridge north of Ashton.
- Below the dam on Ashton Reservoir.
- Vernon bridge.
- Chester Dam.

IF YOU GO
From Idaho Falls take I-15 to U.S. Route 20 north. Continue through St. Anthony to Last Chance and Island Park.

Tackle Shops and Guides
Henry's Fork Anglers. Last Chance. Mark Rockefeller, owner, Mike Lawson, manager. Bob Lamm, Ron Sorenson, and other excellent guides can be booked through this extensive tackle and fly shop. (800) 788-4479 or (208) 558-7525. www.henrys-fork.com/.

Hyde's Last Chance Outfitters. Last Chance. Flies, tackle, and clothing. Inexpensive to moderate. (800) 428-8338. www.hydelodge.com.

The Grubsteak Market and Deli. Last Chance. The shy and sheepish co-owner is one of the best anglers on the Henry's Fork, ties and sells fine patterns. (208) 558-7399.

Linda B's Shuttles. Last Chance. Dropoff and pickup from all fly shops, lodging, put-ins, and take-outs. Linda is the best source of general information in Last Chance. (208) 558-9900 or cell phone (208) 390-1999.

Trouthunter. Last Chance. Rene Harrop, Rich Paini, and Jon Stiehl, owners. Now entering its fourth year, this shop has proved extraordinarily popular, perhaps because so many of its flies are tied by Rene and Bonnie Harrop (House of Harrop). Guides John McDaniel, Lynn Sessions, John Harrington, and other experienced guides can be booked through this shop. (208) 558-9900. www.trouthunt.com. E-mail: trout@fretel. com.

Where to Stay

A-Bar. Last Chance. Inexpensive. (208) 558-7358.

The Angler's Lodge. Last Chance. Nice lodge, but a little too close to the water. Moderate to expensive. (208) 558-9555. E-mail: feathrhk@vicon.net.

Elk Creek Ranch. North of Last Chance. Pretty and low-key, the attractive lodge and cabins are set among conifers well back from Route 20. Moderate. (208) 558-7404.

Henry's Fork Lodge. South of Last Chance. Superb accommodations on the river. Expensive but worth it. (208) 558-7953.

Hyde's Last Chance Lodge. Last Chance. Across from the A-Bar. Inexpensive to moderate. (800) 428-8338. www.hydelodge.com.

Pond's Resort. Last Chance. Inexpensive. (208) 558-7221.

Rentals. Rainbow Realty handles weekly, monthly, or season-long house and cabin rentals in the Island Park area. (800) 853-7420 or (208) 558-7116. www.rainbw.com.

Camping

U.S. Forest Service. Manages campgrounds on the Buffalo River opposite Pond's Resort, in Box Canyon off old U.S. Route 20, and at Riverside Campground, off Route 20 south of Osborne bridge.

Where to Eat

A-Bar. Last Chance. Inexpensive. Burgers and simple fare. Serves late. This is where the guides hang out. (208) 558-7358.

The Angler's Lodge. Last Chance. Moderate to expensive. (208) 558-9555. E-mail: feathrhk@vicon.net.

Elk Creek Ranch. North of Last Chance. Good, moderately priced food. (208) 558-7404.

Grubsteak Market and Deli. Best deli sandwiches in Island Park. Keeps fishermen's hours—open early and late.

Island Park Resort. Island Park. (208) 558-7281.

Mack's Inn. Island Park. On Route 20. An RV park with an inexpensive restaurant. (208) 558-7272.

Pond's Lodge. North of Last Chance. On Route 20. Big, convenient, serves late. Inexpensive. (208) 558-7221.

RESOURCES

Very detailed maps of the river, including access points and minor roads, are available at all the local fly shops.

The Henry's Fork Foundation. P.O. Box 61, Island Park, ID 83429. (208) 558-9041.

Island Park Chamber of Commerce. (208) 558-7751.

Retallic, Ken, and Rocky Barker. *A Fly Fisher's Guide to Idaho*. Portland, OR: Frank Amato Publications, 1996.

Ross, John. *Trout Unlimited's Guide to America's 100 Best Trout Streams*. Helena, MT: Falcon Publishing, 1999.

Tullis, Larry. *River Journal: The Henry's Fork*. Portland, OR: Frank Amato Publications, 1995.

CHAPTER NINETEEN

DENVER

Cindy Scholl

Anglers and authors often describe the South Platte River as Denver's Crown Jewel, and it has earned its status. When considering the populace of a major metropolitan city such as Denver and a world-class wild trout fishery within two hours' drive, the description is appropriate. Although this lovely piece of water has been used, abused, endangered, and dammed, it has prevailed like a prize workhorse. The river provides Denver with 80 percent of its water, all the while allowing anglers the world over some of the most challenging and rewarding trout fishing in the Rocky Mountains.

Recognized as the first trout stream in Colorado with designated catch-and-release areas, the South Platte was also recommended by the National Forest Service for wild and scenic designation. Its greatest triumph was when the EPA vetoed a proposed permit by the Denver Water Board to dam 30 miles of the river, including Cheesman Canyon. The victory was celebrated by conservationists, Trout Unlimited chapters, environmentalists, and dedicated fishermen. These groups had rallied to overcome what most thought was an insurmountable threat from the all-powerful water board. The skills and fine-tuned techniques necessary on the Platte will make an honest person of any veteran or aspiring fly angler.

SOUTH PLATTE MAIN STEM

The main stem of the South Platte is formed by the union of the South and Middle Forks, originating from snow-capped peaks of the Continental Divide some 14,000 feet in elevation. By the time it passes through Denver, it has descended close to 8,500 vertical feet and been dammed five times. Products of the dams, five reservoirs exist. Of the five, Cheesman Canyon and the Deckers area exhibit the heralded tailwaters so often attractive to fly fishers: Hatches are fecund, and big fish feed here. The South Platte between Spinney Mountain Reservoir and Eleven Mile

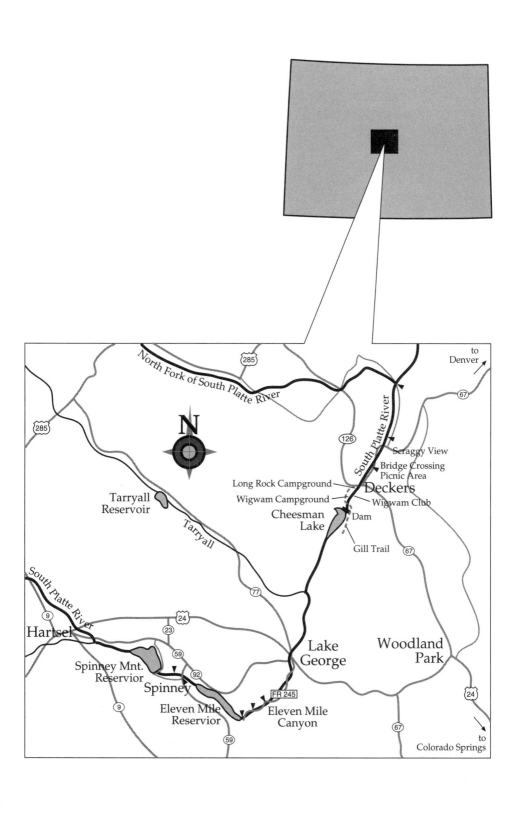

Canyon Reservoir is also awesome but entails a slightly longer drive from Denver.

DECKERS AREA, FROM THE WIGWAM CLUB TO SCRAGGY VIEW

Fellow guide, author, and friend Dana Rikimaru gave me an inscription in her first book, "Here's to all the beautiful places that fly-fishing takes you." She must have been referring to the majestic foothills and canyon roads that lead to the South Platte River. The drive out of Denver alone will serve as therapy to those wanting to escape the hustle and bustle of the city in search of angling opportunities.

The Platte River below Cheesman Canyon is bordered by crimson hillsides, Douglas firs, and stout ponderosa pines. It's as aesthetically pleasing to the eye as its rainbows and browns are in the hand. At a bend in the river below the canyon lies the small town of Deckers (blink and it's gone). Here the amenities include a small grocery store and fly shop, Flies and Lies, where you'll find all the necessary fishing supplies, up-to-date fishing information, and comfortable cabins for rent.

The stretch of river from the Wigwam Club to the Scraggy View Day Use area is gold medal water. The Colorado Division of Wildlife stocks numerous rainbows, but the browns are wild. The easy access to this river is part of what makes it so popular. Parking areas are plentiful and well marked, but expect them to be full on weekends—arrive early!

Except for a few intermittent meadows, most of the river is visible from the road. Crystal-clear water and slow, deep pools characterize much of the water. Rainbows inhabit the riffles and runs. If you're good at spotting fish, you'll increase your hookup odds tremendously, as I quickly learned on a recent outing with my friend Kris Tita, former president of the Colorado Women's Fly Fishers. While driving upriver in search of an opening, we spotted fish in a bend just below the road. Our rods had already been rigged with nymphs and were ready to go. We quietly crossed the river below where we'd seen the fish. Kris quickly landed a few nice 15-inch rainbows, and I managed one big 18-inch brown.

Wading in shallow areas is relatively easy, although I did experience some slippery spots. One word of caution: The flow is regulated, and water levels can exceed 1,000 cubic feet per second during May and June. Call one of the local fly shops for up-to-date water level information.

When fishing the canyon section just above Deckers, Route 126 takes you by the Lone Rock Campground just below the private Wigwam Club. Access the north side of the river from the campground, or cross the river in Deckers and drive back up on the south side.

Light (6X) tippet is recommended unless water flows are up and visibility is down. Double rig by tying a second fly on through the eye of the first fly or at the hook bend. Leave 12 to 16 inches of tippet between flies. Add enough weight to get the flies to the bottom. Soft lead is easiest to use when making adjustments according to speed and depth changes in the water. Your indicator should be double the depth of the water from your bottom fly. The key to fishing these pools and riffles is to use the high-stick nymphing method and keep all slack line off the water.

The Platte River's nutrient-rich environment is created in part by the constant temperatures and water flows of the Cheesman Dam. Fly sizes range from #18 through #26, with most imitations being in the #20s. Don't be surprised if during a heavy hatch not a single fish is rising. They often prefer nymphs and emergers to drys.

CHEESMAN CANYON

Cheesman Canyon is the jewel of the Platte River. I fished this stretch with Pat Dorsey, co-owner of the Blue Quill Angler fly shop in Evergreen and a seasoned South Platte guide. This section of the river is fairly remote and requires a short but exhilarating hike along the Gill Trail.

This trail serves as one means of access to Cheesman Canyon. An alternative is to drive to the reservoir and hike down to the water, but the dam trail is steep and dangerous. The Gill Trail is much safer. The Littleton chapter of Trout Unlimited has taken on the colossal project of renovating and rebuilding the trail. Much of the vegetation and the original path have been destroyed by heavy foot traffic. Stay on the path at all times.

Before hiking into the canyon, I suggest packing all fishing gear, including waders, boots, and lunch. The hike can be difficult in wading gear, although some eager beavers attempt it. The trail is well marked and fairly worn, although it may have some thin patches of ice during the winter months. The hike through the woods sets a relaxing tone for the rest of the day, and when Dorsey and I crested the top of the hill, I understood what the hoopla was all about. The sight of the 50-foot-wide blue ribbon of river flowing through the canyon below is breathtaking. The surroundings are truly wild and scenic. The water is so crystal clear that I could make out the granite-lined riverbed from high above.

Some 200 feet above the river, Dorsey sighted fish in the slow-moving boulder-filled pools below. He assured me that this was the "graduate water" of the Platte, and more than likely, the only fishermen here were skilled, well-seasoned anglers. The runs are longer, pools deeper, and fish more educated than what most anglers are accustomed to. Dorsey said most of the larger fish are caught on nymphs here.

After our descent, we geared up and waded into a pool at the base of the path. Dorsey offered me two flies, saying they'd be all I needed for the day: a #22 midge labeled the Mercury Midge, a fly he designed himself, and a #22 RS-2. I asked about the small size of the flies. He explained that the cold water coming out of the bottom of the dam is responsible for the fact that the naturals are small.

Dorsey directed me into a hole flanked by a car-size boulder, where he had spotted fish before I even wet my feet. His uncanny ability to spot fish left me feeling like a total neophyte. In the freestone waters of the Eagle River, where I guide, we read the water and cast accordingly. The usually tumbled, roiled water of the Eagle River, my home water, doesn't often allow for spotting fish.

Easing up next to me, Dorsey pointed his rod tip 2 inches above the water and said, "There they are." I felt sure that with one cast, my split shot and fluffy orange yarn indicator would spook every fish in the hole. I learned instantly that neatness counts. I did scare off a few, but after intense concentration, the figures came into view. Dorsey said I was in their feeding lanes but warned about microdrag in the slow water. It is paramount that all the line is off the water. He told me to look for the golf ball and set the hook. "Golf ball?" I thought to myself. "What was he talking about?" When the fish opens its jaws, he explained, you see a big, white mouth. I did just as I was told, and sure enough, an 18-inch rainbow took off upstream. I sighed with relief when he was netted safely and released.

My next encounter was in a small run, 16 inches deep and about 5 feet wide. I adjusted my weight and indicator and made a few short casts—making sure to pick up all my line—high-sticking my drift through the braided, almost impossibly shallow current. I wasn't sure whether I was casting to rocks or wild trout, but Dorsey had spotted them. Making out the long, sleek, undulating figures in the feeding lane was difficult, but to my surprise, my line suddenly tightened and the rod tip bent. This was no ordinary trout, but an athlete that tested all my fishing skills in a matter of seconds. The trout took the fly and shot across the river, running straight for a tangle of deadfall. Pulling up as firmly as I dared, fearing separation of fly from tippet, I turned him from the deadfall till he ran downstream. Dorsey netted a brawny, 20-inch, crimson-sided rainbow with shoulders too wide for my hand to grasp. It all happened so quickly that it took a moment to catch my breath.

Although we saw and caught a fair amount of large fish, Dorsey believes that the number of fish per mile has declined significantly and that whirling disease might be one of many factors involved. Barry Nehring, a fisheries biologist with the Colorado Division of Wildlife, says the South Platte has been hit heavily by whirling disease and the numbers of rainbows and browns have declined. The Platte is one of the few streams where studies indicate some survivors among rainbow fry. Whatever the cause of the decline, the Platte is a beautiful, memorable stream to fish. It carries the gold medal, catch-and-release title proudly, and we can only hope it stays so fine for years to come.

BELOW SPINNEY MOUNTAIN RESERVOIR

The 3-mile section below the Spinney Mountain Reservoir Dam is often referred to as the Dream Stream. It's famous for its lunker rainbows and browns measuring in the 16-inch-plus category. Similar in dynamics to Cheesman Canyon, it's also a tailwater. The major difference between the two reservoirs is that there are no canyon walls or huge boulders below Spinney. The river is fairly flat and easy to wade. It flows through an open meadow with few casting obstacles. I've found that when the Cheesman Canyon area isn't fishing well, angling seems better on Spinney, and vice versa. Your chances of catching a trout on a dry fly here are greater than in Cheesman Canyon. Spooky fish and no-see-um size flies will be your biggest challenges.

HATCHES, FLIES, AND BEST TIMES TO FISH

Cheesman Canyon and the Deckers area fish well year-round. Wait until midmorning during winter months, when the sun takes longer to rise in the canyon. Spring, summer, and fall are prime times. Expect crowds and fewer parking spaces. The Denver Water Board regulates the water flow. Exercise caution during May and June, when flows fluctuate and rise due to spring runoff. Water clarity may also decrease, making the fishing more challenging. During the winter, when flows are low, concentrate on the pools. A call to one of the local fly shops is suggested. The following are some of the best patterns:

January–February. Midges (#20–#26).

March–April. Midges (#20–#26), Blue-Winged Olives (#18–#22).

May. Midges (#20–#26), Blue-Winged Olives (#18–#22), caddis (#16–#18), scuds (#12–#16).

June. Midges (#20–#26), Blue-Winged Olives (#18–#22), caddis (#16–#20), Tricos (#20–#24), Pale Morning Duns (#18–#20), stoneflies (#10–#16), scuds (#12–#16).

July. Midges (#20–#26), caddis (#16–#20), Pale Morning Duns (#18–#20), ants (#18–#20), beetles (#18), hoppers (#10–#12).

August. Midges (#20–#26), Tricos (#20–#24), ants (#18–#20), beetles (#18), hoppers (#10–#12).

September. Midges (#20–#26), Blue-Winged Olives (#18–#22), caddis (#18–#20), Tricos (#20–#24).

October–December. Midges (#20–#26), Blue-Winged Olives (#18–#22).

IF YOU GO

To Cheesman Canyon and Deckers from the Denver International Airport, the drive is about two hours. Head south on Pena Boulevard to I-70 west. At I-225, turn south; the road will curve back to the west. At I-25, drive north to Hampden Avenue, and head west through town. Hampden turns into U.S. Route 285. Continue on Route 285 to Pine Junction. Turn south at Pine Junction onto Route 126. Drive 20 miles to the town of Deckers. From downtown Denver, take I-25 to Hampden Avenue and follow directions from there.

If you've decided to make the hike into Cheesman Canyon, the Gill Trail parking lot will be on your left 2.5 miles before you reach the town of Deckers.

To fish the section just below Deckers, turn left on Route 67. This stretch of road parallels the river. The parking and picnic areas are well marked.

From Colorado Springs, take U.S. Route 24 west to Woodland Park. Turn right (north) on Route 67 to Deckers. To reach the Gill Trail, turn left (west) on Route 126, and drive 2.5 miles to the Gill Trail parking lot.

To the Platte River below Spinney Mountain Reservoir, take I-25 south from Denver to U.S. Route 24. Take U.S. 24 west from Colorado Springs to the Spinney and Eleven Mile Reservoirs sign. Drive south on Route 23 to Route 592, and turn left (east). Take the next right, onto Route 59, and follow it to the parking lot.

Tackle Shops and Guides

The Blue Quill Angler. Evergreen. Located 3 miles off I-70 in Bergen Park. Jim and Martha Cannon and Pat Dorsey, proprietors. A full Orvis dealer, including equipment, tackle, and an enormous selection of flies. (303) 941-7517. www.bluequillangler.com.

The Complete Angler. Englewood. Bill Grems, proprietor. A fully equipped fly shop conveniently located one and a half blocks east of I-70 on Arapahoe Road in Englewood. (303) 858-8436.

The FlyFisher Ltd. Denver. Peter Dupont, proprietor. A full-service fly shop and Orvis dealer. Classes and guide service available. (303) 322-5014. www.theflyfisher.com.

Flies and Lies. Sedalia (Deckers). The only fly shop on the South Platte River. Shop owner Dick Johnson will fill you in on the latest fishing strategies and supply you with a few lies to wet your whistle. Stick around long enough, and you'll catch him building custom rods for clients at the back of the shop. He also carries quality fishing equipment and fishing licenses. (303) 647-2237. www.fliesnlies.com.

The Hatch Fly Shop. Pine Junction. Just off U.S. Route 285. Dan Hydinger, proprietor. A full selection of fly-fishing equipment and fly-tying materials. Guide service available. (303) 816-0487. www.Thehatch flyshop.com.

The Trout Fisher. Denver. David Padilla, proprietor. Complete line of equipment, clothing, and tying material. (303) 369-7970. www.thetrout fisher.com.

Where to Stay

Crystal Lake Lodge B&B. Pine. On the North Fork of the South Platte. Moderate. (303) 838-5253.

Deckers Cabins on the Platte. Deckers. Located directly on the river. Inexpensive to moderate. (303) 647-2237.

Platte River Cabins. Near Deckers. B&B on the North Fork of the South Platte twenty minutes from town. Quaint riverside cabins in a private setting. Expensive. (303) 838-9195.

Camping
Lone Rock Campground. Just up Route 126 from Deckers. Small RV spaces available. (303) 647-0440.
  Osprey and Ouzel Campgrounds. North of Deckers. (303) 647-2350.
  Platte River Campground. Deckers area. (303) 647-2350.
  Wigwam Campground. Deckers area. (303) 647-0440.

Where to Eat
The Buck Snort Saloon. Near Pine. An inexpensive local hangout. (303) 838-0284.
  Elk Creek Station. Fifteen miles west of Deckers. Good selection of moderately priced food. (303) 838-4450.
  Trout River Grill. Pine. Next to the Crystal River Lodge. Expensive. (303) 838-7688.

RESOURCES
South Platte Ranger District. (303) 275-5610.
Denver Chamber of Commerce. (303) 534-8500.
Colorado Atlas & Gazetteer. Yarmouth, ME: DeLorme Mapping Company. (207) 846-7000.
Bartholomew, Marty. *Flyfisher's Guide to Colorado.* Gallatin Gateway, MT: Wilderness Adventures Press, 1999.
Fothergill, Chuck, and Bob Sterling. *The Colorado Angling Guide.* Woody Creek, CO: Stream Stalker Publishing, 1989.
Hill, Roger. *Fly Fishing the South Platte River.* Boulder, CO: Pruett Publishing Company, 1991.
Ross, John. *Trout Unlimited's Guide to America's 100 Best Trout Streams.* Helena, MT: Falcon Press, 1999.

BLUE RIVER

Ann McIntosh

Whether you're a budget angler, a businessman with a couple extra days to fish, or on vacation, it's worthwhile to fish the Blue River. If you can, hire a local guide: You'll need one to lead you to the best holding places, which vary seasonally in what looks like equally productive water. He or she will also help you across some *very* stiff current.

As you drive along Route 9 next to the Blue, the inspiration for this river's name is evident: It looks as if a blue ribbon has been strung

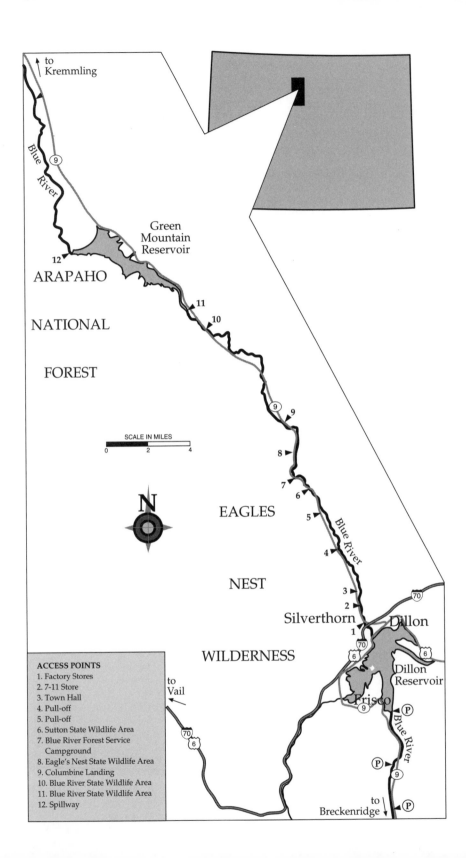

to
Kremmling

Blue
River

9

Green
Mountain
Reservoir

12

ARAPAHO

NATIONAL

FOREST

11

10

SCALE IN MILES

0   2   4

9   9

8

7

6

N

5

EAGLES

4

Blue River

NEST

3

2

WILDERNESS

70

Silverthorn   Dillon

1

70

6

Dillon
Reservoir

6

ACCESS POINTS
1. Factory Stores
2. 7-11 Store
3. Town Hall
4. Pull-off
5. Pull-off
6. Sutton State Wildlife Area
7. Blue River Forest Service
   Campground
8. Eagle's Nest State Wildlife Area
9. Columbine Landing
10. Blue River State Wildlife Area
11. Blue River State Wildlife Area
12. Spillway

to
Vail

70

6

Frisco

9

Blue River

P

P

9

to
Breckenridge

P

between the willows, dropped into narrow gorges, and threaded through sagebrush and cattle grasslands. The Blue flows about 45 miles from the town of Breckenridge northwest to the Colorado River at Kremmling. From the town of Breckenridge (County Route 3 to Kremmling), the water is designated as a gold medal trout stream, with catch-and-release and fly-fishing only sections spaced intermittently along it. Like many Colorado tailwaters, the Blue is subject to releases from dams along its length. The ideal release for trout fishing is 150 cubic feet per second.

Because of its approximately 9,000-foot elevation, the Blue contains the coldest water I've ever fished in the summer, and I believe it must rank among the coldest in Colorado. Water exits the dam between 34 and 37 degrees F, and during my mid-September stay, it never exceeded 54 degrees F. You'll see a lot of fishermen on the Blue with hoods up and gloves on.

My host on the Blue was Nick Doperalski, twice past president of the Gore Range Anglers chapter of Trout Unlimited. Doperalski has been the principal historian of the Blue, as well as the architect of the many large, legible, attractive public-access signs along the river. He explained that the Gore Range Anglers, the Colorado Division of Wildlife (CDOW), and the town of Silverthorne took a much-maligned river and in eight years made it a brown trout fishery with very good water quality. The Blue is important to local communities from an economic development stand-point. The Colorado Water Conservation Board, based in Denver, and local government officials spent countless hours negotiating a minimum flow from the dam (and its reaches) and finding support for stream improvement projects.

Beginning in 1988 Gore Range Anglers and Silverthorne put in more than $50,000 to improve the structure of the river in that town. They created fish condos: boulders, pockets, side eddies, and other places where trout could hold comfortably. They constructed a better pool-to-riffle ratio in what was already a wild brown trout fishery.

Only in the last twelve years, since the town section has been regulated as a catch-and-release area, has the Blue in Silverthorne prospered as a trophy trout fishery. The entire river is designated gold medal water, and all the brown trout in the publicly accessible sections are wild. On the 35-mile section from the Silverthorne town limits to the Colorado River, an angler may keep two trout more than 16 inches long. There is a strong kokanee salmon run in October.

For this chapter, I have divided the Blue into four sections, which I nicknamed the Fish 'n' Shop, catch-and-release water within the Silver-thorne town limits; the Wild Blue, the riffles and runs between Silver-thorne and Green Mountain Reservoir; the Blue Ribbon, highly visible, open, gentler water that flows through sagebrush and open range on mostly private land from 2 miles below the reservoir to Kremmling; and the Upper Blue, above Dillon Reservoir.

FISH 'N' SHOP SECTION

The trophy section of the river just below Dillon Reservoir is within easy walking distance of more than seventy-five outlet shops, ranging from Eddie Bauer to Donna Karan. Many anglers from Denver bring their families to Silverthorne and fish for trophy trout while their children and spouses spend their money. Some of the pools are named after the shops, such as the Nike Hole.

I first fished the Blue in mid-September. I was on the catch-and-release trophy section, which runs from the outflow of Dillon Dam to the Silverthorne town boundary. My guide was Greg Ward, an experienced local angler. Ward explained that brown trout do better than rainbows, which are not acclimated to the cold water. Both species like cold water, but rainbows do not spawn successfully in this very cold water. There is no attempt to stock rainbows, given their propensity to whirling disease, which the brown trout population stands a good chance to survive. Colorado has been the seat of controversy about whirling disease since the parasite that causes it was first discovered. At this writing, the state is continuing cleanup efforts in its hatcheries and fingerling stocking programs. Observers have noted that west of the Continental Divide, the prime waters hold fewer and fewer rainbows and are increasingly dominated by brown trout.

That first day, I caught two small browns on dry flies, and Ward netted a 14-inch brown; a bigger fish broke off his nymph. He explained that fishing along the town beats is very technical: You want a completely drift-free nymph at just the right depth in the water column and just the proper place in the current. Trout average 14 to 16 inches in this section, but there are many much larger fish. This reach also holds Arctic char that have been flushed through the dam. Many of these fish measure 20 inches or better.

Though the reach gets heavy pressure, being only an hour from Denver, and there are lots of savvy fish, an experienced fly fisher using the appropriate nymphs will do well. Nymphing is the name of the game here. Because of the cold water temperature, hatches are sporadic, and the trout prefer to take the nymphal stages of the bugs. Only when water spills over the top of the dam from late June through July does the water warm to a temperature that encourages emergences. The entire reach from the dam to Green Mountain Reservoir is affected.

In the section just below the dam, the fly of choice is the Mysis Shrimp (pronounced "micey"). This curved, white, flashback nymph imitates the *Mysis* shrimp that come out of Dillon Reservoir, where they were introduced many years ago.

Anglers on the Blue often fish with two flies—two nymphs or a dry fly and a dropper. They use large, visible strike indicators to detect the slightest pause in the drift. One fisherman, using what looked like a 2-

inch chunk of untreated lamb's wool, caught a number of fish that he said he wouldn't have detected with a conventional indicator.

I found myself challenged by the Fish 'n' Shop stretch. I spent the last day of my trip alone there and finally managed to land two 14-inch browns. But I'll admit, the weather was nasty, cold, and threatening, and being near the warmth and sustenance offered by the adjacent mall was not the least of my motives for staying near town.

WILD BLUE SECTION

The river drops 1,200 vertical feet from Silverthorne to Green Mountain Reservoir, creating a very strong current. The apparent water depth is deceptive and does not account for velocity. There were many places where the water was no more than knee-high, yet I couldn't have crossed without my two fishing buddies, one breaking the flow, the other offering a stiff forearm. Moreover, the altitude of the Blue (9,000 feet) is quite high, and winter weather lasts from about September 15 to July 4.

I spent most of my time fishing the Wild Blue from the access at the first major pulloff north of the Silverthorne, on Route 9 near mile marker 105.5. From the parking spot, a path leads across a short, flat stretch of land to good fishing up- or downstream. Doperalski caught two fish that afternoon, but I don't believe Greg Ward or I caught any. Doperalski admitted he couldn't quite figure out what was going on.

BLUE RIBBON SECTION

Doperalski gave me a tour of the full length of the Blue River from Silverthorne to Kremmling, where it joins the Colorado. When we set out, I was looking back at the new snow dust on Buffalo and Red Mountains in the Gore Range; as we grew closer to Kremmling, I became mesmerized by the gentler, rolling Williams range. Whereas the Wild Blue section has much public access, below Green River Reservoir in the Blue Ribbon, most of the water is privately owned or leased to private fishing clubs or lodges. One or two ranchers upriver from Kremmling will let you fish if you ask permission and return your fish to the river. If you're in the area, ask how to identify these landowners. There was so much pretty water as we drove along Route 9—long pools, riffles, oxbows—as to nearly make me want to poach.

The first 2 miles of the canyon below the output of the reservoir is public water. It can be accessed off Route 9 north of Power Plant Road below the dam. This section fishes best in October, when the browns come up to spawn in reaches below the dam. Even if you don't catch fish, it's worth a try. This is one of the most beautiful and secluded canyons in Colorado.

UPPER BLUE RIVER

Doperalski took me fishing with Terry Pitz (now a guide on the Florida coast) on the Upper Blue, above Dillon Reservoir between Breckenridge and Frisco. The water is only about 20 feet wide, but the current is strong. It was the best day's fishing I had on this trip. I felt as if I were on a classic small eastern trout stream. I caught twelve brown trout ranging from 12 to 16 inches on Dave Rothrock's Blue Quill emergers and duns (#18–#16) and on caddis emergers, nymphs, and drys.

Access the Upper Blue either at the Agapee Baptist Church or from the berm near its confluence with Swan Creek. Nearer to Breckenridge, get in upstream from County Route 3 (Coyne Valley Road).

HATCHES, FLIES, AND BEST TIMES TO FISH

The Blue River is a year-round fishery, especially below the dam in Silverthorne, since the tailwater runs hard and fast all year long. The lower Blue can ice up, but conditions vary from year to year, and the fish are always acclimated to the cold water. Anglers are seen on a regular basis on all good winter days. The nicest times to fish are between late April and early June (when runoff starts) and again between July 4 and November. The following lists some of the major hatches.

Mid-July–mid-August. Green drakes.

Mid-June–October. Caddis, small golden and small brown stoneflies.

Year-round. Sporadic hatches, including Red and Blue Quills, blue-winged olives, pale morning duns.

BLUE RIVER REGULATIONS

Regulations on the Blue are complex. They are spelled out in a regulations booklet provided with a nonresident fishing license, which costs from $5.25 for one day to $40 for a full year. They are available through CDOW offices or at local tackle shops.

BLUE RIVER ACCESS

The town of Silverthorne is purchasing leases along the river, establishing fishing access easements, and reselling the land to private owners. It's a well-thought-through plan that benefits all, driven by the vision of the town government.

Doperalski's CDOW signs are prevalent, well illustrated, and mark access points too numerous to list here. Each sign shows the public land, private land, public access to private land, and where you are.

Among the most attractive public-access points are Eagle's Nest State Wildlife Area and Columbine Landing. Also noteworthy are the Blue River Campground, and the two pulloffs downriver from it.

ALSO WORTH NOTING
Clinton Reservoir (11,200 feet altitude)
Small cutthroats. Fish from shore. Often ices out in mid-May.

Ten Mile Creek
Between Frisco and Copper Mountain. Due to pollution from mines, water quality is not the best.

North Ten Mile
A few miles upstream from Ten Mile, this is an excellent fishery, particularly for those willing to hike in a mile or so.

Upper Colorado River
This is gold medal catch-and-release water above Kremmling and below the town of Hot Sulphur Springs near Parshall. Only flies and artificial lures are permitted. These are the much-written-about sections leased by the CDOW: the Kemp-Breeze State Wildlife Areas and, below Byers Canyon, the Lone Buck and Paul Gilbert Units. Access these areas off U.S. Route 40 between Kremmling and Hot Sulphur Springs. Most local fly shops feature wading trips on this popular section of the Colorado. You can also fish from a raft from Pumphouse, west of Kremmling, to Dotsero.

IF YOU GO
Getting to Summit County and the Blue River from Denver is easy. Take I-70 west through the Eisenhower Tunnel. You'll come to the Dillon and Silverthorne exits, then the Frisco-Breckenridge exit. (After that, I-70 crosses Vail Pass to Vail and Avon, about two hours from Denver, and Glenwood Springs, about three hours from Denver).

Tackle Shops and Guides
In this area, float trips average $295 for two people and wade trips about $245 for two.

Blue River Anglers. Breckenridge. (970) 453-9171.

Breckenridge Outfitters. Breckenridge. An authorized Orvis dealer. (970) 453-4135.

Colorado River Anglers. Silverthorne. (970) 468-1836. www.river anglers.com. E-mail: CRAngler@Colorado.net.

Cutthroat Angler. Silverthorne. (970) 262-2878. www.fishcolorado .com. E-mail: anglers@fishcolorado.com.

Mountain Angler. Breckenridge. Jackson Streit, proprietor. A very reliable outfitter. (970) 453-1430. www.mountainangler.com.

Summit Guides. Keystone. Dale Fields, proprietor. Guide service only; flies included in trips. (970) 468-8945.

Where to Stay
Since this is a tourist destination, there are hundreds of choices of lodging, from expensive resorts to modestly priced B&Bs and motels. Call the Summit County Chamber of Commerce (see Resources, below) for listings and travel information. Prices range widely according to ski seasons, but most establishments have low off-season rates.

Camping
Colorado State Parks. (800) 678-CAMP.
National Park Service. (303) 969-2000.
USDA Forest Service. (303) 275-5350.
Colorado Association of Campgrounds. (303) 499-9343.

Where to Eat
From Silverthorne to Breckenridge, there are many fine restaurants featuring varied cuisine, some expensive, others moderate, as well as fast-food eateries easy to locate and far too numerous to list here. Look in the local tourist weekly newspapers for a full listing.

RESOURCES
Summit County Chamber of Commerce. Serves Silverthorne, Frisco, and Breckenridge. (970) 668-2051.

Bartholomew, Marty. *Flyfisher's Guide to Colorado.* Gallatin Gateway, MT: Wilderness Adventures Press, 1999.

Colorado Atlas & Gazetteer. Yarmouth, ME: DeLorme Mapping Company. (207) 846-7000.

Fothergill, Chuck, and Bob Sterling. *The Colorado Angling Guide.* Woody Creek, CO: Stream Stalker Publishing, 1989.

Hill, Roger. *Fly Fishing the South Platte River.* Boulder, CO: Pruett Publishing Company, 1991.

EAGLE RIVER

Ann McIntosh, with Kendrick Neubecker and Cindy Scholl

Soon after I went through the Eisenhower Tunnel west of Denver, I faced more than 150 miles of breathtaking trout water. The terrain looks like something from Zane Grey novels—contrasting shades of sandy gray gypsum rock and hard red minturn formation. After joining Dr. Anne C. Wentz, an old friend and new angler, in Beaver Creek, we fished the Eagle, as well as Brush Creek and the gold medal waters of Gore Creek near Vail. I even fit in a float trip on the Roaring Fork, catching a big

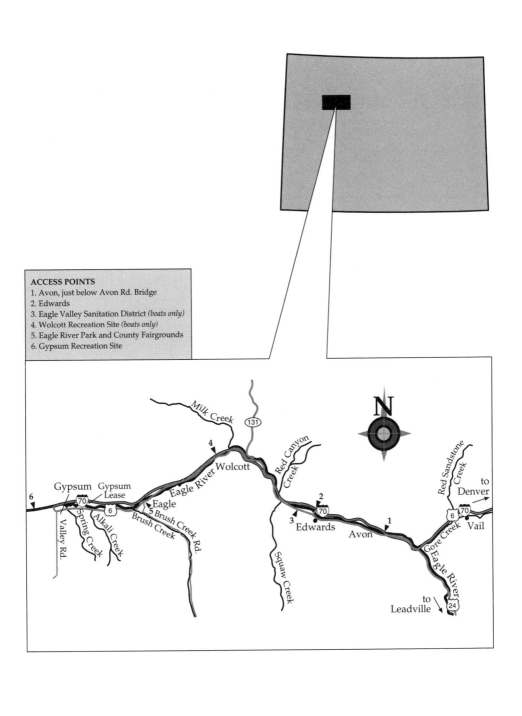

ACCESS POINTS
1. Avon, just below Avon Rd. Bridge
2. Edwards
3. Eagle Valley Sanitation District *(boats only)*
4. Wolcott Recreation Site *(boats only)*
5. Eagle River Park and County Fairgrounds
6. Gypsum Recreation Site

brown trout on a streamer that Pennsylvanian Jim Charron had designed to imitate alewives in the Delaware.

The Eagle originates near the Tennessee Pass of the Continental Divide, just above 10,000 feet. It flows 70 miles to Dotsero, where it joins the Colorado. The first day, I fished with Wentz and Ken Neubecker, an ardent Trout Unlimited leader. The weather was nasty: in the fifties, overcast, threatening rain. We first fished at the Fishing Park in Eagle, using Prince Nymphs and Beadhead Pheasant Tail Nymphs. Neither Wentz nor I caught anything, although Neubecker netted a brown seduced by a very fuzzy #14 Hare's Ear Nymph.

The Eagle is a typical freestone stream: unpredictable, but fortunately not subject to the releases from reservoirs that plague many western fisheries. Below Avon, the river averages 60 to 70 feet wide, the water flowing over rocks and big boulders that can be very slippery and are covered with silt in some reaches. The river becomes muddy below Wolcott after rainfall, when runoff from Alkali and Milk Creeks adds silt to the flow. I found studded, felt-soled boots and a wading staff essential. If you get caught in muddy or discolored water, switch to something like a big and flashy (#8–#10) Beadhead or Flashback Nymph.

A storm came up suddenly, so we ducked for lunch and a Colorado microbrew at a small restaurant in Eagle, an old-fashioned, western family community where no one locks car doors and people smile at visitors up and down the wide main street. Best of all is the Eagle Pharmacy—"the Nearly Everything Store"—which sells flies and other tackle, dry goods, hardware, and stationery, as well as drugstore items. (With the influx of motels, one can only hope that Eagle maintains its rural character.)

Over the next two days, I fished the Eagle at several access points. One of my favorites was a smooth, wide pool with willows on one bank, Douglas firs on the other, and rising fish in between. The most productive stretch for me was upstream, where I had the satisfaction of landing two nice browns on flies I had brought with me: a Blue Quill emerger and a Blue Dun tied by eastern angler and writer Dave Rothrock.

Were it not for the negative ecological effects of the local mine from the 1800s into the late 1970s, the Eagle might now be one of the gold medal trout waters of which Colorado is so proud. The mine was shut down more than two decades ago, but only in recent years have cleanup measures resulted in water with fewer contaminants and of a quality capable of sustaining trout. Today new developments present the biggest threats to the river.

Shannon Albeke, a fisheries manager with Colorado Division of Wildlife (CDOW), has calculated that there are about thirty-seven hundred trout per mile on the river downstream of Avon. Albeke used shocking data from an April 2000 count.

In 1995 the Eagle Valley chapter of Trout Unlimited initiated a letter-writing campaign and formed a partnership with the Eagle County commissioners, local guides, and the Vail Metropolitan Water District. The signators persuaded the CDOW not to stock the Eagle, due to the presence of whirling disease in Colorado hatchery-raised fish. This was a major achievement in the fight to keep diseased fish out of trout waters. The chapter has long-term goals to demonstrate that the river can support the natural reproduction of wild trout. Members are working with local municipal officials to produce guidelines for a uniform approach to river management.

HATCHES, FLIES, AND BEST TIMES TO FISH
The most reliable times to fish the Eagle are from mid-April to mid-May (two to three weeks before runoff) and from after July 4 (or whenever runoff wanes) through October. Least crowded times are March and April, as well as October and November. During the winter, some of the water may freeze over, but there is still a lot of activity on the water. Fly shops do good business with skiers who want a day to rest their legs.

Cindy Scholl cautions visiting anglers about fishing during runoff, in May and June. Do not wade during this period. If you want to fish, stick to dry land along the banks; the fish are right along the banks in the very shallow water. The following lists some of the major hatches and best patterns.

April–June. Yellow stones *(Isoperla)*, golden stones *(Acroneuria)*, blue-winged olives *(Baetis)*, Grannom caddis *(Brachycentrus)*, black midges, olive midges. A Parachute Adams #18 can be particularly effective. The Grannom caddis hatch is amazing, peaking on the river in late May to early June. Try soft-hackle wets for caddis imitations whenever caddis are around. A Green and Brown Spent Caddis is also a good choice.

June–September. Salmon flies, Red Quills, pale morning duns, green drakes, western sedges *(Rhyacophila)*, small olive sedges. Try dry stonefly patterns near the shore.

If there isn't activity on top of the water, Scholl recommends trailing a caddis Breadcrust from a dry or sinking it to the bottom. Elk Hair Caddis, as well as brown, cream, and green caddis, should be in your fly box. Scholl also advises anglers to carry Pheasant Tail and Prince Nymphs (#14–#16) throughout the year.

September–October. Blue-winged olives (#20), various caddisflies: spotted sedges, fall sedges, small olive sedges, black midges, olive midges.

November–March. Blue-winged olives (#20), black midges, olive midges, small olive sedges (caddis).

ACCESS
In addition to the map in this chapter, the Eagle River Public Access Map, available at all fly shops, is a good map detailing public access, including

the BLM and the CDOW leases. There are a number of public pulloffs along U.S. Route 6, which follows the Eagle (see map).

ALSO WORTH NOTING
Roaring Fork and Frying Pan
Two notable rivers a couple hours farther from Denver are the Roaring Fork and the Frying Pan. Enough has been written about these fisheries to fill several books. If you want to fish them, the fly shops listed here can refer you to others farther west. Both of these rivers can be fished in the winter.

Gore Creek and East Brush Creek
If you're in the area during runoff, when the Eagle is unfishable, or if you prefer to fish farther from civilization, try one of the Eagle's productive tributaries, such as Gore Creek or East Brush Creek.

Gore Creek is gold medal water, a designation awarded by CDOW to waters that have high-quality aquatic habitat and yield a high percentage of trout 14 inches or longer. Some gold medal waters are stocked; others contain a combination of stocked and streambred fish. The stream is only about 25 feet wide, with plenty of willows to stop your backcast. A bike path runs along the stream by the golf course, offering frequent access to the water, and there is a pulloff at Gore's confluence with the Eagle at Exit 180 (East Vail) off I-70 onto U.S. Routes 6 and 24. There is also an East Vail pulloff above the Vail Golf Course, just off I-70.

East Brush Creek is a high meadow stream. During my stay, Neubecker and I drove from Eagle into the White River National Forest, following the winding dirt road that runs along Brush Creek. We parked at the Yeoman Park Campground and waded the small water upstream to a beaver dam, making tight casts between overhanging willows. Sneaky though we were, between retrieving flies from bushes and the impact of our lines on the water, we figured we must have spooked trout for 100 yards.

Poking around under little deadfalls for snagged nymphs, I realized I'd be better off fishing this lovely spot when the fish were rising visibly midstream. There are deep cuts under the banks where brookies can hide and never be reached by anglers. If I lived in the area, I'd probably fish these small, wild meadow streams, away from the crowds, far more frequently than I would the larger waters. It's the kind of stream best fished alone, given time to sink into the feeling of freedom and deep-breath spirituality brought on by such near-wilderness landscape.

Upper East Brush Creek, from the fork going left up to Yeoman Park Campground, has recently been acquired by the state and is now public. Sylvan Lakes (the fork to the right) has cabins and is open year-round for lake fishing. For information on the cabins, call (800) 678-2267. The campground is about 13 miles from Eagle, Lake Sylvan 15 miles.

IF YOU GO
Drive about two hours west from the Denver Airport on I-70, and you'll reach the Vail, Avon, and Eagle exits. There is an airport in Eagle that's open during ski season; you can fly nonstop to Eagle from Chicago, Dallas, and Los Angeles.

Tackle Shops and Guides
The following shops provide tackle and flies, as well as guide service on the Eagle, Roaring Fork, Frying Pan, and Colorado Rivers. Float trips average $295 for two people and wade trips $245 a day for two.

Eagle Pharmacy. Eagle. "The Nearly Everything Store." The *perfect* resource for a true budget angler!

Eagle River Anglers. Eagle. Bob and Kim Nock. Destination shop that also offers float trips. (970) 328-2323.

Fly Fishing Outfitters. Avon. Billy Perry, proprietor. Orvis authorized dealer. (970) 476-3474 or (800) 595-8090. www.flyfishingoutfitters.net. E-mail: fish@vail.net.

Gorsuch Outfitters. Edwards. (877) 926-0900 or (970) 926-0900. www.gorsuch-outfitters.com. E-mail: flyfish@vail.net.

Cindy Scholl. Guide. Fish with the best! (970) 876-0434. E-mail: cinbadscholl@aol.com.

Vail Fishing Guides & Gore Creek Fly Fishermen. Vail. (970) 476-3296. www.gorecreekflyfisherman.com. E-mail: info@gorecreekflyfisherman.com.

Where to Stay
Best Western. Eagle. Inexpensive. (800) 328-6316.

Comfort Inn. Avon. Moderate to expensive. (970) 949-5511.

Comfort Inn. Eagle. Moderate. (970) 328-7878.

Eagle River Inn. Minturn. Inexpensive. (970) 827-5761.

Prairie Moon Motel. Eagle. Moderate. (970) 328-6680.

The Wolcott Inn B&B. Wolcott, near Eagle. Very charming. (970) 926-5463.

Camping
BLM Campground. Wolcott. Just below town along the river.

Gypsum BLM Campground. Gypsum. Just west of town off the frontage road. Good fishing access and a pedestrian easement on the south and north sides of the river. (307) 775-6256.

Where to Eat
Back Alley Pizza and Ice Cream Parlor. Eagle. Wonderful lunch place. No reservations.

Brenner's. Eagle. Inexpensive, varied cuisine. No reservations.

Brush Creek Saloon. Eagle. Good for a beer and burger. No reservations.

The Eagle Vail Cafe. Avon. At junction of Routes 6 and 24. Moderate. (970) 949-6393.

The Gas House. Edwards, just west of Avon. Fabulous inexpensive local restaurant and bar, with all the quail you can eat for under $10. (I took home a few for the next day's float trip.)

Fiesta's. Edwards. In Edwards Plaza. Good, reasonably priced Mexican food. (970) 926-2121.

The Left Bank. Vail. Probably the best restaurant in town. Expensive. (970) 476-3696.

The Wolcott Grocery. Wolcott. A popular hangout with tourists, fishermen, and rafters.

RESOURCES

Avon Chamber of Commerce. (970) 949-5189.

Eagle Valley Chamber of Commerce and Eagle Visitors Information Center. (970) 328-5220.

Vail Visitor Center. (970) 479-1394.

Bartholomew, Marty. *Flyfisher's Guide to Colorado.* Gallatin Gateway, MT: Wilderness Adventures Press, 1999.

Colorado Atlas & Gazetteer. Yarmouth, ME: DeLorme Mapping Company, (207) 846-7000.

Fothergill, Chuck, and Bob Sterling. *The Colorado Angling Guide.* Woody Creek, CO: Stream Stalker Publishing, 1989.

PART SIX

The Southern Rockies and the Southwest

CHAPTER TWENTY

ALBUQUERQUE AND SANTA FE, NEW MEXICO

SAN JUAN RIVER

Ti Piper

Located in northern New Mexico in the Four Corners Region, where Colorado, Arizona, Utah, and New Mexico touch, the San Juan River starts high in the mountains of Colorado. Draining south into New Mexico, forty years ago it was a warm-water river—full of razorback suckers, humpback chubs, and giant predator pikeminnows.

In 1962 Navajo Dam was finished, and a world-class, high desert trout fishery resulted. Navajo Lake is used for flood control, water management, and water for the Navajo nation. Water out of the dam is cold and normally clear. It provides enough nutrients to support a vigorous aquatic plant food base. These photosynthetic organisms support an incredible, but mostly tiny, invertebrate community. Cold water, about 42 degrees F year-round, holds plenty of dissolved oxygen.

Cactus are here year-round. The bald eagle is a winter resident. Summertime brings swallows and bats. There are resident, not-quite-tame deer, obnoxious beavers, great blue herons, quail, coyotes, mountain lions, and a hardy home population of ducks and geese. Rattlesnakes, too, though I've seen more in my house (one) than on the river (none).

Thick groves of willows line the wet bank, with junipers and piñons behind the riverside green. River meadows sport giant cottonwoods. And everywhere you gaze, there are pipes, tanks, condensers, and pump-jacks, for this is big-time oil and natural gas country.

For New Mexico, the San Juan is a big river. Flows range from 500 (low) to 2,000 (moderate) to 5,000 plus (high) cubic feet per second. At low to moderate flows, the river is mostly wadable but rarely crossable. Even at low flows there is good holding and feeding cover. The river provides decent spawning patches, although whatever spawning there is adds little to the catchable fish population.

For 6 miles below Navajo Dam, the San Juan River is a tailwater full

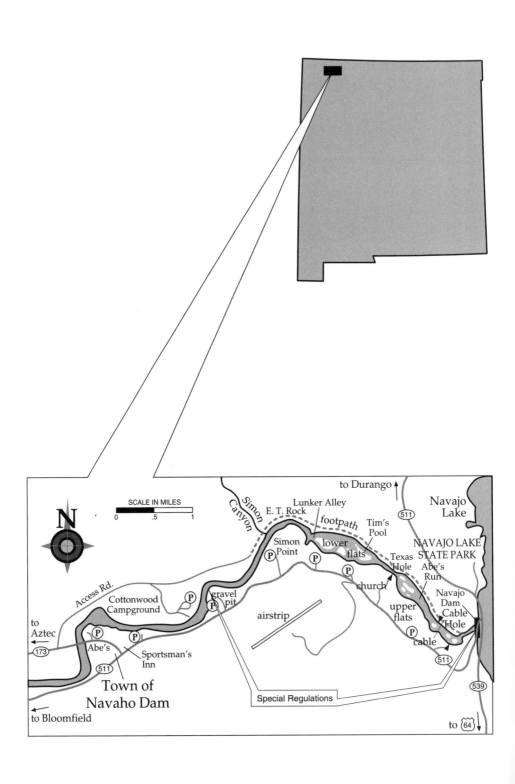

of stream-raised rainbow trout. Much of the fishing is in close; long casts are not necessary. Much of it is fishing fine: #22 flies and 5X tippets.

The San Juan is a hatchery-supported fishery of big, stream-raised—but not streambred—rainbow trout. The New Mexico Department of Game and Fish (NMDG&F) stocks thousands of fingerling rainbows. Some occasional cutthroat-marked fish show up from earlier stockings. There are browns farther downriver. Fish grow quickly in this river and are numerous and big, averaging 16 inches.

The river has had the parasite that causes whirling disease for some years. Because this is a hatchery-supported river, and because the disease has been managed for decades, it seems likely that the river will continue to produce big trout and excellent fishing.

THE TEXAS HOLE

The most famous spot on the river, where all the upper side channels reconvene, is called the Texas Hole. Some ten thousand catchable trout live in and down from the Texas Hole. The area features a large paved parking lot, shaded picnic tables, maintained outhouses, fishing access for the disabled, and on most nice days, a lot of people. The New Mexico State Parks access sign to the Texas Hole says San Juan Point. A small church also marks the turnoff.

Even with the crowds, the Texas Hole should be your first stop. It's where the guides launch their boats. Many wading anglers never get more than ten minutes from the parking lot, catching big rainbows on tiny flies all day long. There is also good access for those wanting to work either upstream or down. First-timers should stop and talk to anglers who just came off the river. They'll show you their flies and how they rig their leaders and strike indicators. Don't miss the local knowledge available at the Texas Hole parking lot.

Driving *upstream* from the Texas Hole turnoff, you'll find well-marked parking areas with ten-minute trails leading to the upper part of the river. These reaches include lots of braided channels, some big, long riffles, the main channel, and a large catch-and-release area below the dam. The areas farthest from the parking lots are the least crowded.

Driving *downstream* from the Texas Hole turnoff, you'll also find well-marked parking areas within a ten-minute walk of the river. There are fewer braided channels in this stretch, but many good fishing opportunities. Unlike the water above the Texas Hole, guideboats hold in prime spots all day long.

The guideboats take out at the lower end of the 3½ miles of special trout water. The NMDG&F has two public fishing access points below the state park's Cottonwood Campground. This water, from which fish can be taken by bait, lure, or fly, is stocked with 10- to 12-inch hatchery fish. A small group of hard-core fly anglers fishes these so-called bait waters. They hold some *huge* trout and a diverse population of caddis and mayflies.

TACKLE AND EQUIPMENT

A standard 8½-foot, 5-weight outfit is fine on the San Juan. Light-line folks covet their 3-weights, which will do until the wind comes or it's Woolly Bugger time.

Your knots will be tested, so take care when tying on terminal tackle. A water bottle, sunscreen, sunglasses, long-sleeved shirt, and fishing cap are all required for high-altitude fishing.

A wading staff is handy and a net an asset. A standard trout net will be a hassle with big fish, so use a short-handled, wide-gap net.

Wear chest waders. The water is 42 degrees F year-round; neoprenes are common. Others prefer layering fleece or other synthetics with breathable waders. Make sure your wading shoes do not constrict your feet.

Rocks, pebbles, and coarse sands make up much of the San Juan's floor. Wading gear with felt bottoms is usually adequate. The exception is a set of side channels above the Kiddie Pool (above the Texas Hole in the side channels), many of which are bottomed with a goose-grease-type flooring; be careful or use cleats.

HATCHES, FLIES, AND BEST TIMES TO FISH

Expect low flows from July through winter and into spring. Sometime in spring, depending on snowpack, reservoir levels, and runoff, flows will increase to medium or high levels. Anglers fishing from boats, or in the back channels, can have record days.

During rare wet years, expect high flows March through July. Low flows will occur from August through winter and into the next spring. Rarely will you see more than a modest change on a given day. This is not a river where you have to worry about quick, dangerous flow increases.

Some years, there are about three months of mildly to very murky water sometime between fall and spring. Other times, the river is clear all year.

Foam line fishing at the upper end of the Texas Hole can be amazing. You can fish for vertically rising fish, the more classic head-and-tail horizontally rising fish, or fish 2, 3, or 5 feet beneath the foam line.

Snouts rising in the foam line indicate fish rising vertically, head up and body vertical in the water. Slurping in the target insect, they get a bonus of a dozen or more midges or mayflies that happen to be in the suck zone. They're fun to watch, but angling for these fish, even from a boat, can be very difficult.

Rainbows rising in the foam line, showing their classic horizontal posture, are best fished with an emerger. Note that one hour's emerger may resemble a dry, while the next hour's emerger may be closer to a nymph. It pays to keep experimenting. Anglers have been known to fish the foam line for hours—until they need help getting back to shore. The beginnings of hypothermia, even in July and August, have caused many a strong angler's legs to collapse.

More productive, at least in terms of catching fish, is using the foam line as a fish locator. Majorities of the run's fish are feeding 3, 4, or 5 feet beneath the surface risers. You need a bobber (indicator), two tiny flies, miniature split shot, and the ability to mend, mend, and mend. The bobber can be CDC, poly yarn, a dry fly, or a small pegged bobber. A poly yarn strike indicator is most popular, but a small orange pegged bobber is another favorite.

Even with #18 or #22 flies, today's modern 5X tippet is good enough to catch large San Juan trout. Going to #24 or #26 necessitates 6X or 7X tippet. First-timers should stick with 5X and learn the gentle slip strike needed to keep from breaking off large trout. First-timers should also hire a guide, as San Juan tactics are significantly different from those used on other tailwaters.

March 21–June 21. There will be very low flows in dry years, with moderate to high flows May through June in wet years. There will be only light pressure on most days, moderate pressure on nice weekends. During high flows, expect very low pressure. Patterns that almost always work include midges, some *Baetis* (Blue-Winged Olives #20), eggs, leeches, and San Juan Worms. On long daylight days, the best fishing is from first light to dark.

June 21–September 21. Expect low flows in dry years and moderate to high flows through early July in wet years. Early-season high flows can be murky. One of the best times to be on the river is after the river drops down from really high flows, before the rest of the world has gotten the news. The most effective patterns include midges, some *Baetis*, *Ephemerella* (Pale Morning Duns tied sparsely on #18 hooks), eggs, leeches, and San Juan Worms. Again, on long daylight days, the best fishing is from first light to dark.

September 21–December 21. The flow is low and occasionally murky. You can expect fewer anglers, but there will be crowds on warm weekends. Any nice day to be outside is a good day to be fishing the San Juan, but fishing is best from 10 A.M. to 4 P.M. During this period, midges, *Baetis*, *Ephemerella*, leeches, San Juan Worms, and egg patterns work.

December 21–March 21. Expect very low flows. March brings wind, few anglers, and a very productive time to catch San Juan rainbows. On these short daylight days, 10 A.M. to 4 P.M. is the best fishing window. San Juan Worms, egg flies, and leech patterns all produce fish and allow you to use heavier tippets. Leeches are effective when the sun is off the water. Mayflies *Baetis* and *Ephemerella* are covered by standard ties, with the edge going to emergers. Midges are copied by flies so little you can fit $250 worth in a shot glass. Sizes are as tiny as #26. For both the little mayflies and the midges, trailing shuck patterns may attract more fish.

REGULATIONS

The quarter mile below the dam is regulated as catch-and-release water; the lower end is marked by a thick cable. Only single barbless hooks are allowed here, and bait and plastic imitations are prohibited.

On the next 3½ miles, only single barbless hooks are allowed; no bait or plastic imitations. Anglers may keep one fish 20 inches or longer. If you keep a fish, you must stop fishing the area at once. You may, however, still fish the upper catch-and-release water or down below in the regular regulation water.

The regular regulation water is open to all legal forms of bait, lures, or fly fishing. The limit is five fish per day, only two of which may have cutthroat markings.

Annual NMDG&F licenses are issued starting April 1. A five-day nonresident fishing license is $17, one day is $9, and annual is $40. A New Mexico State Parks San Juan day-use permit is required on each vehicle ($4 per day, $10 annual). These costs may change; check the website listed under Resources below or telephone for updates.

ACCESS

The river is public and fishable from below the dam spillway downstream more than 6 river miles to the lower NMDG&F boat access. Below this point, ownership of the stream bottom and the streambank is in dispute. *Do not trespass.* People have been shot at; boats have been wrecked. Some private access is available to this water. Ask at the fly shops.

A paved state road, Route 511, parallels the south side of the river. A maintained gravel road parallels the lower half of the north side. A footpath continues upstream to the spillway from the end of the gravel road.

Access is easy. There are no dangerous canyons, rock climbing, or half-day hikes necessary to get to the water. Parking areas are signed. Garbage cans and handicapped-accessible outhouses are available at most parking lots.

ALSO WORTH NOTING

Jicarilla Apache Reservation

The reservation has good trout lakes. About an hour's drive east of the San Juan River, these trout lakes have wonderful *Callibaetis*, caddis, and midge action. Stone Lake in particular can be well worth the cost of a Jicarilla day permit, available at the Best Western in Dulce, (505) 759-3663, for $11 a day. These waters are on the way for anglers driving between Albuquerque and the San Juan.

Brazos River

For a more private experience, the upper meadows of the Brazos River are amazing. This is elk-country fishing in streams full of small brook trout and large rainbows. At this altitude, spring fishing is nonexistent. Summer is the time for multiple hatches. Fall brings low flows and small flies. In a rough winter, you can't get there in a snowmobile. The Reel Life (see Tackle Shops and Guides, below) offers guided fishing on private water on the Brazos.

Jemez River

For public waters close to Albuquerque, I recommend the Jemez. Only ninety minutes from the north side of town, this is a wild brown trout and stocked rainbow fishery. Access is either paved or good gravel. The waters are small—only 10 to 25 feet wide. Some call them rivers, some call them creeks; however you describe them, they offer great spring stonefly hatches and summer evening hatches (see hatches for the San Juan).

IF YOU GO

Most visitors fly the major airlines to Albuquerque, rent a car, and drive north to fish. You can also fly to Farmington, Durango, or Santa Fe and rent a vehicle.

From the Albuquerque Airport, turn left (west) on Gibson Avenue, and get in the right lane. The freeway, I-25, is less than a mile west. Enter northbound I-25, and drive north for 20 miles. Take Exit 242, turn left (west), and cross over the freeway. You are now on Route 44, which will take you close to the trout fishing. But first you've got a mile of gas stations, fast food, and convenience stores in front of you. Stock up on refreshments, and check the gas gauge and tires.

Continue north on Route 44 for 175 miles. Don't think the wide open spaces means no state police. *Be careful.* Be alert. There are gas stations with convenience stores every 30 to 40 miles. After about 175 miles, you'll cross the San Juan River into Bloomfield.

Route 44 ends in Bloomfield. Turn right (east) on U.S. Route 64. At this corner, there is a good-size grocery store. Go east on U.S. Route 64 for about 10 miles, and again cross the San Juan. Continue east for 1.5 miles, and turn left (north) on poorly marked Route 511. Continue on Route 511. After 8 miles, you'll be at the downstream end of the public fishing water, right in the middle of the lodges, outfitters, and restaurants.

Tackle Shops and Guides

On the San Juan River, most of the tackle shops also offer lodging and food.

Duranglers. Durango, Colorado. Fly-fishing stores on the San Juan and in Durango. Guided trips. (888) 347-4346. www.duranglers.com.

Float 'n Fish. Navajo Dam. A large fly-fishing store. Guided trips. (505) 632-5385.

The Reel Life. Albuquerque and Santa Fe. Manuel Monasterio, proprietor. Full-service Orvis-endorsed fly shops. (888) 268-FISH. www.the reellife.com.

T. J. Jimerson. Navajo Dam. Guided trips. (800) 669-3566. www.four cornersguideservice.com.

Where to Stay and Where to Eat

In San Juan territory, there is little distinction between lodging and eateries.

Abe's. Navajo Dam. Inexpensive units with kitchenettes. Restaurant, bar, tackle, and guided trips. Amenities include a convenience store, gas stations, and RV hookups. (505) 632-2194. www.sanjuanriver.com.

Enchanted Hideaway. Navajo Dam. Four medium to large units with two to three bedrooms and kitchenettes. Moderate. (505) 632-2634. Luna tuna@cyberport.com.

Rainbow Lodge. Navajo Dam. Fly-fishing tackle and guided trips. B&B, meals, four-person cabins. (888) 328-1858. www.sanjuanfishing.com.

Rizuto's San Juan River Lodge. Navajo Dam. A fly-fishing store. Guided trips. Eight B&B units and a delicatessen. Inexpensive. (505) 632-1411. www.rizutos.com.

Soaring Eagle Lodge. Navajo Dam. On private water. A fly-fishing store, guided trips, four-person cabins, meals. (800) 866-2719. www.san juanflyfishing.com.

Sportsman Inn. Navajo Dam. Convenience store, tackle, gas, restaurant, bar, guided trips, RV park, trailer rental. (505) 632-3271.

Camping

Cottonwood Campground and Pine River Campground. New Mexico State Parks. (505) 632-2278. www.newmexico.org.

RESOURCES

Mike Mora has one of the best San Juan River webpages at www.ifly 4trout.com.

New Mexico Tourism Department. Free maps and vacation guide. (800) 733-6396. www.newmexico.org.

New Mexico Department of Game and Fish. Free fishing map and regulations. (505) 827-7911 or (877) 2GO-FISH. www.gmfsh.state.nm.us/.

Martin, Craig, ed. *Fly Fishing in Northern New Mexico.* Albuquerque, NM: University of New Mexico Press, 1992.

Piper, Ti. *Fishing in New Mexico.* Albuquerque, NM: University of New Mexico Press, 1994.

CHAPTER TWENTY-ONE

SALT LAKE CITY

PROVO AND GREEN RIVERS

Ann McIntosh

Anglers with business in Salt Lake City should take along a fly rod. The urban area boasts quality trout water nearer to it than to any city in the Rockies, and much of it can be fished throughout the year. The Provo is less than an hour from downtown, while the Weber River, Strawberry, and Currant Creek are within ninety minutes. The renowned Green River is only three and a half hours east, and the Jones Hole, a sprightly mountain spring creek, is near the Green. Below Price, 150 miles south of Salt Lake, Cottonwood and Huntington Creeks offer fabulous pocket water fishing. Contact area fly shops for information on any of these other waters.

PROVO RIVER

Given its plentiful population of large wild brown trout, the Provo is finally receiving long overdue attention. By western standards, the Provo is not a big river, averaging 65 feet wide in its middle and lower sections, but it's a strong tailwater, rich with bug life and muscular browns. Only fingerling rainbows are stocked, and protective regulations limit the angler's take to two trout under 15 inches on flies or artificial lures. The river has three distinct sections.

Upper Provo

The upper reaches of the Provo are freestone, flowing off the Uinta Mountains east of Salt Lake to the Jordanelle Reservoir. I did not fish this stretch, much of which is privately owned. It is most productive after runoff, beginning in early July, and it fishes well in autumn.

Middle Provo

The middle Provo flows through the Heber Valley between the Jordanelle and Deer Creek Reservoirs, south of Park City and southeast of

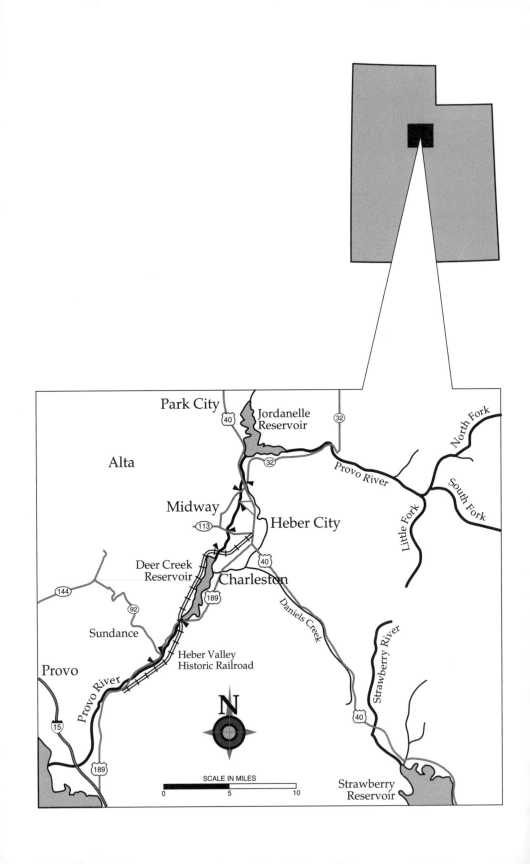

Salt Lake. I was able to put myself on an accessible reach within two hours of stepping off the airplane one day in late August. Following directions from a local fly shop, I parked where the Heber Valley Historic Railroad crosses Route 113 (between Midway and Charleston, a couple miles west of Heber City). From there, I followed the railroad tracks up to the river.

The surroundings were pleasant: Cattle pastures glowed golden under the late-afternoon summer sun; a little spring creek ran through watercress in the field to my left; pickups looked tiny as they sped across country roads a mile or so away. The *whooooo-hoo* of the historic railway's whistle sounded in the distance as I skidded down to the water.

I tied on a #12 Stimulator and watched for rising fish. Although I detected no surface feeding, a lively 14-inch brown took my fly in the trestle pool. I waded upstream, still noting only a few rises, alternating between the Stimulator and subsurface patterns. This water features long runs, a few slack pools, riffles here and there. Between 5 and 7 P.M., I landed three 17-inch browns and missed several others—a good afternoon for a visiting angler alone on unfamiliar water.

Pete Idstrom, an experienced local guide, took me back to the middle Provo a few days later. We entered the water above the site of my initial foray, where the river was wider and shallower, slowed by rocks, grass islands, and angular turns. On my third or fourth cast, a ginger caddis produced an 18-inch rainbow. It was a strong fish. Idstrom judged it had been in the river four years.

That rainbow turned out not to be a harbinger of fish to come. The action was slow that day, and we covered more than a mile and a half of water in a few hours. The stream gradient is very gentle, and only once did I, an angler very respectful of the power of western tailwaters, need help crossing. There are long runs and riffles, deep pools cut beneath the grassy banks, and a few sections of fast water. Often the river divides into two channels, making a convenient way to fish near another angler. Idstrom and I often split up, each of us fishing one channel.

The river's course makes frequent changes of direction in the reaches we fished. It washes over stony rubble into deep corner pools, then turns and levels off into shallow runs. Idstrom explained that fish often feed in the skinny water at the bottom of the washes; anglers should work these shallows carefully.

The middle Provo between Jordanelle and Deer Creek Reservoirs is in the process of being restored to its original blue-ribbon status. It was subject to severe dredging and channelization during the post–World War II flood-control period. Fishing will likely be a bit spotty in the muddied waters where construction is happening; when the water is clear, however, this stretch produces respectable numbers of trout.

Middle Provo Access
- Heber Railroad. Take U.S. Route 40 south from Park City to Heber City. Turn right at the south end of Heber City on U.S. Route 189, and make another right at the little community of Charleston. Drive north for a mile or so, and park where the railroad tracks cross the road. Walk up the tracks to the railroad trestle.
- From the center of town in Heber City, drive west on 100 South. Go about 1.8 miles, turn right on a dirt road before the bridge, and park. Or, turn left on another dirt road just across the bridge, and park at the water treatment plant.

Lower Provo

The lower Provo can be accessed along U.S. Route 189, southwest of Heber City. The special regulations on the lower section begin at Deer Creek Reservoir and end at the Olmstead Diversion Dam. This section is sometimes maligned for its crowds. But a "crowd" on the Provo seems to mean four or five anglers fishing within 20 yards of one another. Along the popular canyon stretch, where the river runs along U.S. Route 189 near the entrance to Sundance (Robert Redford's renowned film festival site), anglers stand much closer together than necessary, with stretches of quality water running past them undisturbed at either end.

I fished the lower Provo with Stu Asahina, then president of the Stonefly Society, the oldest and largest Trout Unlimited chapter in Utah. We met at a pulloff on Route 189 below Deer Creek Reservoir, parked at the public lot below the dam, and walked down a dirt road past private camps with trailers and cottages to the water. Although the camps are private, most owners permit anglers to cross their land to the water.

Asahina was determined that I catch one of the 6-pound browns for which this stretch is famous. The river was running high and strong and was certainly not something I could cross alone. As it turned out, we didn't need to venture to the other side. Asahina assured me that anglers usually fish from one side or the other, seldom crossing.

I began fishing deep, as Asahina had rigged up a dropper rig featuring a sowbug, a Flashback Olive Nymph, and lots of split shot. First we covered water close to the near bank, casting directly up and quartering downstream. Then we inched out, fishing until we reached mid-river, throwing line upstream in the channels and under the brush on the far side. Six times my nymph stopped, I raised the rod tip, and found myself into a heavy fish. Six times I set the hook, and five times I came up empty—even with 4X tippet! Taking line like submarines, these fish left me agape.

After each loss, I turned to Asahina for a clue. He just chuckled and rerigged my line. Then he explained that Provo trout are conditioned in very strong current and grow large and muscular quickly. He assured me that even experts have trouble hooking and holding them until they get the knack of it.

Hatches, Flies, and Best Times to Fish

The middle and lower Provo can be fished 365 days a year. Winter flow rates are low—150 cubic feet per second—resulting in easy wading and fishable water. Skiers vacationing at Alta, Deer Valley, Snowbird, and Sundance often take a day to rest their legs and fish the Provo.

The flow was about 300 cubic feet per second in early September; the river is wadable up to 400 cubic feet per second. In April, the water level is raised to accommodate farmers, the higher level coinciding with runoff season.

There are prolific blue-winged olive hatches during the spring and fall. During the winter months (November–March), midges and midge larva patterns are effective. Pheasant Tail Nymphs and sowbugs work well. During the high-water spring months (April–May), use nymphs—Pheasant Tails, Brassies, and Hare's Ears in smaller sizes (#18–#20)—and streamers, unless surface feeding is evident.

June through mid-July brings a good emergence of pale morning duns, and by July caddis are on the water, closely followed by terrestrials. In late September and October, *Baetis* dominate again.

GREEN RIVER

As he drove me to Currant Creek, a wild trout tributary of the Strawberry River, Steve Matheson, brother of former governor Scott Matheson, observed: "Utah is the most scenic state in the United States. The variety of landscape is unique and its superlatives are earned and deserved."

If you approach the Green via the Flaming Gorge and Red Canyon from the south, taking U.S. Route 40 east to U.S. Route 191 north, you will see why this statement is valid. There are brightly striped sandstone buttes stratified in a rainbow of color, vast grasslands, the dramatic Pinnacles rocks near the Strawberry River, and deep valleys of blue-black evergreens.

Thousands of words have been written about the Green River and its Flaming Gorge, renowned for extraordinary numbers of large rainbow trout. The most reliable information is found in Larry Tullis's *Green River Journal,* which includes color photographs, a river map, a hatch chart, and detailed discussions of the water and how to fish it. Rather than repeat what Tullis has written, this section will target wading fishermen and anglers who rent rafts. Naturally, you will catch more fish if you hire a guide and drift the water.

I strongly advocate hiring a guide your first time on the Green. This is a complex fishery, and the trout see hundreds of anglers daily. By taking a float trip first, you will see how wary the fish are and understand

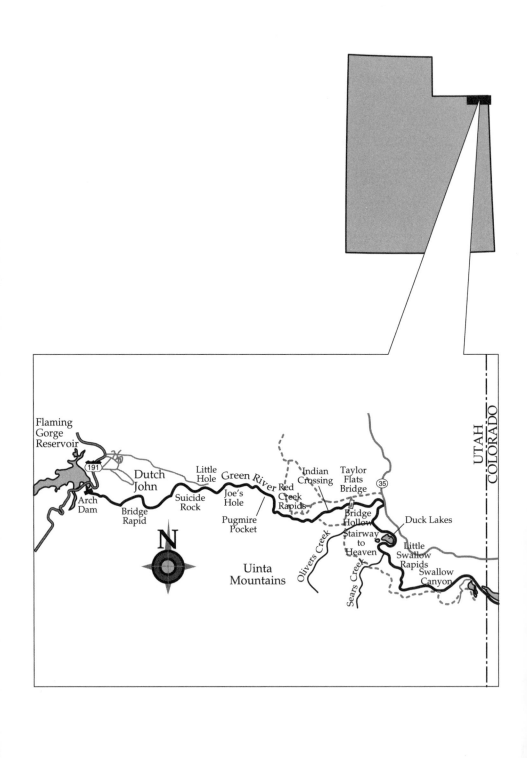

the advantages of approaching them from a boat—undetected and well outside their feeding lanes. The guide can also show you good spots to wade on your own. He or she will familiarize you with effective flies and the millions of aquatic insects that crawl in the vegetation.

The Green is divided into three sections, known as A, B, and C. Stu Handy, my float trip guide and one of seven guides who has worked on the river for more than a decade, estimates that there are eight thousand to ten thousand fish per mile in section A, and six thousand to eight thousand in section B. Twenty years ago, the river boasted twenty-one thousand fish per mile. But according to Emmett Heath, the guru of the Green, that was too many fish for the river. The numbers have leveled off, and now the system is balanced. And of course, the fish are more educated.

Anglers can rent rafts from the Flaming Gorge Lodge, which also provides a shuttle service. Neither Stu Handy nor Emmett Heath advocate float tubes. They have witnessed several drowning accidents, the result of strong current swirls and eddies caused by hidden boulders pulling float tubers underwater.

Of the three sections of the Green, A and B provide the best fishing for wading anglers. A hiking trail runs the length of section A, from the dam to Little Hole, beside the scenic red canyon. This section has the greatest concentration of fish, predominantly rainbows. To reach good fishing, you should hike down 3 miles from the dam; even there, the canyon walls are steep, and there is little room for a backcast. If you explore this section, Handy suggests waiting until noon to begin, after the boats have disappeared downriver.

While there are always anglers in the riffles at Little Hole (the lower end of section A), the most rewarding fishing is between Dripping Springs and Diving Board Rapid. Handy suggests walking upstream for at least a mile and a quarter before even stringing up a rod. When accessible water is reached, fish its edges and back eddies wherever possible. If you are with a friend, spot fish for one another; this strategy will save hours of fruitless blind casting. And when the float boat traffic comes through between 2 and 4 P.M., take a lunch break and wait for the pressure to abate. Then fish back downstream until dark.

At Dripping Springs, I sight-cast nymphs to browns ranging from 16 to 20 inches. The water was crystal clear, the fish finicky as could be, while they finned gently in the slimy green vegetation, apparently nibbling on tiny scuds. I managed to land one 13-inch brown on a #18 tungsten beadhead olive nymph. There were several more fish I could see but not interest. When Handy showed me the number and size of the scuds and sowbugs in a handful of river weed, I comprehended the degree of competition. This was sight-nymphing at its most difficult: drifting tiny underwater flies delicately past nervous trout.

That evening I met Martin Walker, an Englishman who had learned to fish on the Itchen and the Test. He was spending a week fishing section A. Thus far, he had averaged six to twelve fish per day. I told him about the bugs crawling in the wad of weeds Handy showed me, and he described similar creatures, even as he vowed to tie flies to match them.

The next evening, Walker reported taking eighteen trout in the 14- to 20-inch range. Based on careful observation his first day, he had tied up #20 scuds and #22 Griffith's Gnats. Supplementing these with Pheasant Tail Nymphs, he was able to fool a surprising number of wild fish, landing nearly as many as we did on our float trip the same day.

Section B, the 8 miles from Little Hole to Indian Crossing, holds a larger number of browns than rainbows, and pools as big as hockey rinks are known for huge, selective fish. Handy and I spotted two that were so big they looked like small porpoises.

Anglers can hike down from Little Hole about 2 miles, traversing a steep hill and walking along flat sections to productive riffles and deep pools. The trail is not as improved as the one along section A, however, and Handy recommends renting a raft and camping at one of the sites on the banks of section B.

Another option is to wade upstream from Indian Crossing (the B takeout) toward Red Creek, fishing terrestrials and nymphs along the undercut grassy banks. Handy is a proponent of this strategy, saying that very few anglers try it. The day we floated, we couldn't fish this section; rain had washed the red siltation for which Red Creek is named into the river. Before you commit to this stretch, make sure Red Creek is not blown out.

Hatches, Flies, and Best Times to Fish

The best time for wading is in April and May. Even with the heavy flows, there is always good shallow water to wade. Also, the high spring flow, which can reach 4,600 cubic feet per second, abates. The summer, fall, and winter flows are fishable, ranging from 1,200 to 3,000 cubic feet per second.

The Green is not primarily a dry-fly fishery, although when hatches occur, they can be *very* heavy. Terrestrials and aquatic insects make up the bulk of trout food. Anglers should carry a supply of large (#10–#6) ants, beetles, hoppers, and crickets, best purchased locally or tied after viewing local patterns. Huge Chernobyl Ants and inch-long foam cicadas are favorite local patterns that have begun to find their way east—if only as highly visible strike indicators.

The most sustained hatch on the Green are *Baetis*—the central event of the spring and fall seasons—but pale morning duns, some mayflies, and caddis have their moments. Your fly box should include lots of small stuff: midges, Serendipities (#20–#24), biot nymphs, scuds, RS2s, Brassies, aquatic worms. Tullis's *Green River Journal* and local fly shops have detailed lists of effective flies.

IF YOU GO

The middle and lower sections of the Provo River are about one hour from Salt Lake City. Take I-80 east to U.S. Route 40 south to Heber City and U.S. Route 189.

The shortest route to the Green is via I-80 east. Take I-80 into Wyoming, then turn south on U.S. Route 191 and follow it back into Utah to Dutch John.

Tackle Shops and Guides

All provide guide services and float trips on the Green River.

Angler's Inn. Salt Lake City. (801) 466-3927. www.anglersfly.com.

Fish Tech Outfitters. Salt Lake City. (801) 272-8808.

Flaming Gorge Lodge & Fly Shop. Dutch John. Float trips, raft rentals ($45 a day), shuttle service. (435) 889-3773. www.fglodge.com.

High Country Flyfishers. North Salt Lake. (801) 936-9825 or (800) 397-1629. www.hcff.com/home.htm.

Jan's Mountain Outfitters. Park City. (435) 649-4949. www.jans.com/flyfish.html.

Spinner Fall Fly Shop. Salt Lake City. Tackle and guided trips. (801) 466-5801. www.spinnerfall.com. E-mail: info@spinnerfall.com.

Trout Bum 2. Park City. (435) 658-1166.

Trout Creek Flies. Dutch John. Dennis Breer, proprietor. (800) 835-4551 or (435) 889-3735. www.fishgreenriver.com/.

Western Rivers Flyfisher. Salt Lake City. Andy Fitzhugh and Jon Hodge, managers. (801) 521-6424. www.wrflyfisher.com.

Where to Stay

If you don't stay in Salt Lake but wish to be in the area, I recommend Park City. Accommodations in Heber City are basic and inexpensive. Call (801) 654-3666 for visitor information.

Old Town Guest House B&B. Park City. Debra Lovci, an angler, is hostess. Moderate. (435) 649-3320.

Flaming Gorge Lodge. Dutch John. Inexpensive. (435) 889-3773.

Red Canyon Lodge. Near Dutch John. Inexpensive. (435) 889-3759.

Camping

Public campgrounds. Near the Provo and Green Rivers, as well as sites on the Green. (800) 280-2267.

Where to Eat.

There are excellent restaurants in Salt Lake and in Park City. Here are a few moderate to expensively priced gems. Heber City also has several fast-food eateries.

Chimayo. Park City. Fabulous southwestern and Mexican food. Expensive. (435) 649-6222.

Cicero's. Park City. An old local favorite. Moderate to expensive. (435) 649-5044.

Lakota. Park City. Good food, open late. Moderate. (435) 658-3400.

Zoom. Park City. Owned by Robert Redford. Expensive but worth it. (435) 649-9108.

Memphis Jake's Smokehouse and BBQ. Heber City. Popular locally. No reservations.

RESOURCES

Park City Chamber of Commerce. (800) 453-1360.

Utah Fishing & Outdoors. (800) 366-UTAH.

Bed & Breakfast Inns of Utah. (801) 645-8068.

DeMoux, Jim. *Flyfisher's Guide to Utah.* Gallatine Gateway, MT: Wilderness Adventures Press, 2001.

Tullis, Larry. *Green River Journal.* Portland, OR: Frank Amato Publications, 1993. (800) 541-9498.

Utah Travel Guide. Utah Travel Council. (800) 200-1160.

CHAPTER TWENTY-TWO

PHOENIX

COLORADO RIVER AT LEES FERRY, OAK CREEK, AND CANYON CREEK

John Rohmer

Somewhat surpisingly, there are trout streams within a few hours of Phoenix in this desert state. The most worthwhile fishery is the well-known one at Lees Ferry on the Colorado, a nationally recognized big-river experience. The two other streams described here are closer to the urban area and provide excellent trout fishing experiences.

LEES FERRY

Arizona's fast-growing metropolitan areas depend on stored water from the few sources available. Water is as precious as gold in this arid desert state. Dams on the major rivers retain the precious water during the wetter years for use in the future. Glen Canyon Dam is the uppermost barrier on the Colorado River and forms 186-mile-long Lake Powell behind it. When the dam was completed in 1963, it not only tamed the mighty Colorado, it also formed one of the West's premier tailwater fisheries. The normally muddy, turbid waters were transformed into a beautiful emerald green river with a constant temperature between 45 and 48 degrees F—perfect for trout!

The 15-mile-long stretch of fishing water is known as Lees Ferry, the origination point of all river trips through the Grand Canyon. The rafters head downstream through the Grand Canyon . . . while the anglers head upstream, winding through the beautiful towering cliffs of Glen Canyon for some of the best rainbow trout fishing in the lower United States. For someone unaccustomed to the wonders of Arizona, the trip upstream is a unique journey in itself, whether or not you string up a rod. The clear emerald water contrasts greatly with the sheer red sandstone cliffs that soar over 1,000 feet straight up from the river's edge. In the winter months,

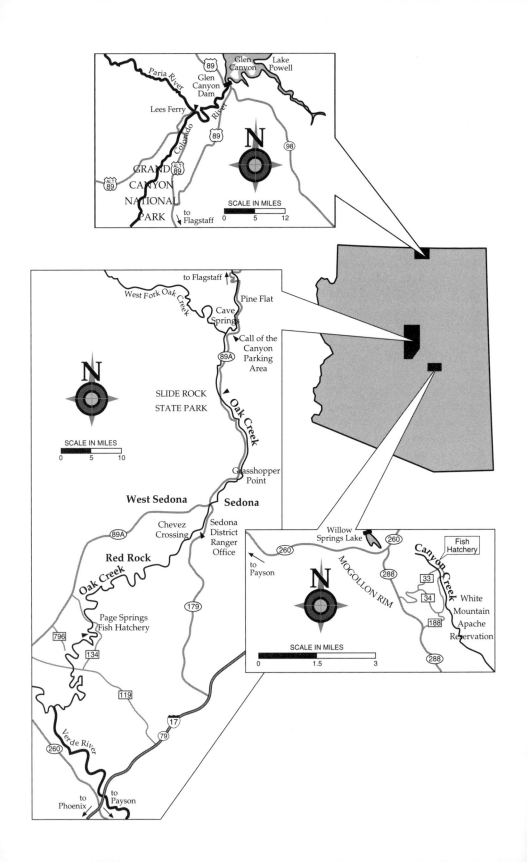

peregrine falcons soar along the cliff walls, along with bald eagles, geese, and numerous species of ducks. The California condor was introduced within the past few years just downstream from the ferry and may soon be venturing upstream. For the angler, however, rainbow trout are the main attraction. Trout here average 16 to 17 inches, with 20-inch fish not uncommon. A little patience and observation will get you into the best fish. Constant blind casting will push the bigger fish into the depths and safety of the river.

The 15-mile stretch has a regulation "prohibiting the killing of any fish over 16 inches." Two fish 16 inches or smaller may be kept, but most anglers observe catch-and-release as standard practice. The rainbows here are fall spawners, and winter months can be very productive for the fly fisher. From October through March, the spawning rainbows congregate on the many gravel bars to perform their mating ritual. This is a good time for sight fishing to large fish, fish with gorgeous red sides and deep bellies.

In the past, the water was stocked annually to keep the river supplied with fish, but since 1996 flows from Glen Canyon have been high enough with minimal fluctuation to allow good spawns, and the river is starting to experience a more wild status.

Lees Ferry is big water, with normal flows from 8,000 to 13,000 cubic feet per second in the morning and 17,000 to 21,000 cubic feet per second in the evenings. The water flows are determined by the power demands of the metropolitan areas of the larger western cities. Higher flows are in the summer months, when power demands increase to keep city folks comfortable in their air-conditioned environments.

I prefer a fairly fast-action 5- to 6-weight 9-foot fly rod that can handle a couple flies, split shot, and an indicator. The 9-foot length makes it easier to mend line on the longer drifts that are sometimes needed. Recently, I've been seeing longer rods in use, which make mending line easier.

If you are planning a trip, it's advisable to hire a guide, at least for the first day, to show you the river channels, where to fish, and proper technique. Several good guide services operate on the river and offer boat rentals for the "do-it-yourself" experience.

No matter what time of the year you choose to go to Lees Ferry, it's a "must see" for any trout fisher coming to Arizona. You'll get to see water that is unlike anything else you've experienced, and with any luck, you'll catch a few fish as well.

Hatches, Flies, and Best Times to Fish

With the constant water temperatures, introductions of aquatic insects have failed. As a result, the fly fisher will not have to worry about matching the hatch, except for the prolific midges that have become so abundant in the last few years.

Scuds and aquatic worms have been the main food sources for years. Patterns that match them fish well all year long. Egg patterns are preferred by the trout during the spawn. With the more consistent water flows, midge imitations have become a welcome addition to the fly fisher's options. Snouts poking through the surface film are a major attraction for mini-fly addicts. One can throw small drys to large trout actively feeding on midge emergers, adults, or spinners. Fishing midge patterns makes it possible to use lighter (3- and 4-weight) fly rods. Fishing the dead drift with an indicator is always productive, but I'll take light dry-fly action any day.

More than forty different Chironomid species have been documented on the river, and it's amazing how particular the trout can be when keying on them. Chironomid larvae and pupae are fished successfully under a large dry fly in shallow water conditions. They can also be used as a second fly in indicator fishing. Every so often, you will get a surprise taker on a big dry fly. During the summer months, hoppers can be a bonus for the topwater fly fisher.

The river fishes well year-round, with the best weather conditions in spring and fall. Fish are in normal feeding mode, and dead-drift nymphing with a floating fly line works well. The trout are always in good shape and fight strongest during this time.

The winter months offer the best shot at big fish. This is the time to sight-fish for large spawners. Summer probably has the best fishing of all, but it can get hot. You may forget it while on the river, but this is still Arizona, and 100 degrees F or higher temperatures are common.

Some of the best underwater patterns include scuds in orange, tan, pink, and amber (#16–#12); egg patterns in chartreuse, pink, cheese, and natural egg color; large and micro-midge patterns; Zebra midges in black, brown, and maroon (#18–#14); San Juan Worms (#18–#12); Yellow Pheasant Tails (#20); and WD-40s (#20–#24) in gray, black, chocolate, cream, olive, and yellow.

The most effective dry flies are Unbelievables (#16), Royal Wulffs (#16–#12), Parachute Adamses (#2), Griffith's Gnats (#18–#20), Irresistibles (#16–#12), hoppers (#8–#12), and cicadas (#8).

OAK CREEK

Driving through the red-rock country of Sedona, you can see why this area has become one of the major tourist attractions in the Southwest. It's hard to believe these beautiful red boulder mountains and juniper pines are just two hours from the hustle and bustle of downtown Phoenix. All this beauty and a nice trout stream to boot.

Oak Creek spews from below the western edge of the Mogollon Rim country and flows southward through the town of Sedona, emptying into the Verde River. This scenic water is paralleled at times by Route 89A.

During the warm summer months, it can become crowded with picnickers, hikers, and people wanting to escape the summer's often relentless heat. Even though the road is close to the stream, access is limited to places where you can hike down to the water. A few turnoffs have trails leading down to the creek, and these are good places to start. From there, your fishing will be limited only by the amount of time you can devote to fishing the next pool or riffle. Often the stream is deep in a canyon, and a little hiking can get you into some areas that are not fished as heavily as others. Other times your path will be blocked by a huge boulder or canyon wall, and your only alternatives are to climb over or backtrack and find another way down.

Upper Oak Creek is faster pocket water, and water temperatures are usually colder. Stocked rainbow trout dominate the water here. There are a few streambred browns and holdover rainbows. The section from Junipine to Call of the Canyon Crossing is catch-and-release water, with only barbless hooks permitted. Farther downstream, the water slows and water temperatures climb until the creek empties into the Verde River. This area is your best bet for a nice streambred brown.

If you have a little more time and feel adventurous, try the West Fork of Oak Creek. This smaller water enters Oak Creek from the west and is under catch-and-release regulations. It's a wild stream and receives no supplemental stocking of rainbows; consequently, it's dominated by brown trout. Making the West Fork a future catch-and-release stream for the native Gila trout is being given some consideration. It would be great to have a stream close to Phoenix where you can catch one of only two trout native to Arizona. Let's hope the project will succeed.

Hatches, Flies, and Best Times to Fish
The best time of the year to fish Oak Creek and its West Fork is early after spring runoff has subsided into late spring. During summer, the flows diminish, the browns become skittish, and your success ratio will drop. Fall can be productive when the browns are reproducing. The angler often has a one-cast shot, and it can be a lot of fun.

I don't target actively spawning browns, but there are usually enough smaller egg eaters downstream to make things interesting. Just make sure that if you do hook one of the spawners, handle it carefully and return it to the water. These fish are the future of the fishery.

The stream has an abundance of insect life, and the trout—rainbows and browns alike—will rise to a dry fly readily. *Baetis* hatches are common on the stream from early spring through fall and early winter. There is a good small black stonefly hatch early in the season, and later small golden stones come off as well.

Tan caddis seem to work on the stream any time of the year. These fish can be exceptionally difficult to fool, especially later in the season, when the water thins and fish spook from the shadow of a big oak leaf falling to the water. Tippet (6X) on a 10- to 12-foot leader is the norm. Don't expect more than one shot at a decent fish. Make that first cast count.

CANYON CREEK

Only two and a half hours from Phoenix, Canyon Creek emerges from the face of the Mogollon Rim, the giant rock wall stretching halfway across central Arizona. The stream flows southward through the giant ponderosa pines of the Apache-Sitgreaves National Forest, through the red sandstone country of the White Mountain Apaches, emptying into the Salt River some 50 miles downstream. Fly fishers are concerned mainly with the upper 6 miles of water. This section is state land and is governed by the Arizona Game and Fish Department as blue ribbon quality water. This means that special regulations are in effect.

Earlier conservation work by Arizona Game and Fish, the U.S. Forest Service, Trout Unlimited, and local anglers has greatly enriched the stream and helped keep it a viable natural fishery. Fences have ensured that no cattle would beat down the banks and foul the water. Trees were planted to help maintain adequate cool temperatures in the middle of Arizona's hot summer months, and instream structures are in place today. During summer months, the streambed has a good cover of watercress and enough pockets and riffles to make it interesting for even the most proficient angler.

One of the beauties of Canyon Creek is the willingness of the browns to take a dry fly. A huge swarm of mayflies hovering overhead is not a necessity to get the browns looking up. It seems as though they are always looking up, except a few times during early spring runoff. That's the time to fish a weighted Bugger or stonefly nymph on 3X tippet. The high, off-colored water usually lasts into May, depending on the severity of winter.

During the summer, the water is gin clear, and 6X tippet and a good cast are imperative. It's 3-weight water, and a floating line is all you need. I generally fish dry through the first pass and then go back through with a nymph. Another alternative is a dry fly and dropper rig.

It always surprises me how many fish you'll pick up going back through again with a different rigging. I am sure I hamper my own success rate a bit by starting strictly on top, but giving the fish just one option and hoping it's the right one is more fun.

Brown trout are definitely more challenging, especially in skinny water. I've seen the telltale wake of a big brown all too often. Even with the most careful approach, you'll spook some of these fish. You'll have the most success with a soft, 50-foot upstream cast using a 10- to 12-foot leader. The trick is getting to know the holding areas and where the fish should be at that time of day before you make your first cast. It may be the only cast you get.

Fall is the best time to sight-fish for big browns. Spawning usually starts at the end of September and is a great time for the angler to see how many big fish he or she has fished over all summer and never knew it. It always amazes me how a big brown can live and flourish in a small stream and never be seen.

I usually don't fish to actively spawning fish, but there are some times that I can't resist tempting one to a fly . . . only to release her carefully to assure future fishing. It's also nice to just sit and watch big fish. You'll be surprised how much you can learn by not disturbing the water.

Hatches, Flies, and Best Times to Fish

The stream is rich in insect life. *Baetis* constitute the majority of mayflies, *Hydropsyche* make up the bulk of the caddis, and a smattering of stonefly husks will be seen in early spring. Hoppers are the pattern of choice in the summer, with ants, beetles, crickets, and cicadas working as well. Browns can usually be fooled with a good imitation of these, along with a Royal Wulff, Stimulator, or Parachute Adams pattern (#20–#12), depending on the time of year.

Canyon Creek Regulations

Currently, regulations split the stream into two sections. The upper is tighter water, with more brush and slightly steeper grade. It has a four-fish limit, with bait allowed. Arizona Game and Fish stocks it regularly during summer months with rainbow trout from its hatchery at the headwaters of the creek. This section is managed as a put-and-take fishery, as many of the state's waters are. It has nice campgrounds close by and is frequented heavily by families and valley residents looking to get away from the heat. Rainbows rule the roost in this section, and the state stocks enough to make sure everyone can feel the tug of a feisty 9-incher, with a few larger trout mixed in.

The lower section is managed as catch-and-release water and is dominated by brown trout. Even though Arizona has been suffering a drought for the past few years, there has been enough water for the browns to spawn successfully. Tiny fingerlings can be seen in the shallows and hiding in the watercress, keeping the future of Canyon Creek bright. The browns have plenty of cover—downed logs and uprooted trees appear throughout the streambed.

IF YOU GO
Lees Ferry

To reach Lees Ferry from Phoenix, take I-17 north to Flagstaff. Follow U.S. Route 89 north from Flagstaff to Alternate Route 89 (89A), and take this to Marble Canyon. Lees Ferry is 5 miles upstream from the Navajo bridge crossing the Colorado River.

Tackle Shops and Guides
Alta Vista Classic Anglers. Phoenix. (602) 277-3111.
Arizona Flyfishing. Tempe. (480) 730-6808. www.azflyfishing.com.
4 J's Troutfitters. Scottsdale. (480) 905-1400.
On the Creek Outfitters. Sedona. (520) 203-9973.
Scottsdale Flyfishing. Scottsdale. (480) 368-9280.
There are a number of guide services available to float the canyon, but the two listed here are the most experienced. Both have been in service since the early 1980s and have extensive knowledge of river conditions and fishing.
Lee's Ferry Anglers. Marble Canyon. $300 a day for two people. (520) 355-2261 or (800) 962-9755.
Marble Canyon Guide Service. Marble Canyon. $300 a day for two people. (520) 355-2245 or (800) 533-7339.

Where to Stay and Where to Eat
All the lodgings below serve breakfast, lunch, and dinner and are moderately priced.
Cliff Dwellers Lodge. Marble Canyon. (800) 433-2543.
Marble Canyon Lodge. Marble Canyon. (800) 726-1789.
Vermillion Cliffs. Marble Canyon. (520) 355-2231.

Oak Creek
To reach Oak Creek, take I-17 north from Phoenix to the Sedona turnoff, Route 179. At Sedona, take 89A north, and follow until you see the stream.

Tackle Shops and Guides
Arizona Flyfishing. Tempe. Fifteen minutes from the airport. Knowledgeable and helpful staff. (480) 730-6808. www.azflyfishing.com.

Where to Stay
Don Hoel's Cabins. Two and a half miles above Slide Rock State Park. Moderately priced cabins. (800) 292-4635.
Red Rock Lodge. Inexpensive to moderate cabins. (520) 282-3591.

Where to Eat
Junipine. Breakfast, lunch, dinner menu. (520) 742-7463.
Garlands at Oak Creek Lodge. Moderate to expensive limited seating dinner menu. (520) 282-3343.

Canyon Creek
From Phoenix, take Route 87 north to Payson. Take Route 260 east from Payson, up the Mogollon Rim past Willow Springs Lake, turn right (south) on Young Heber Road Route 288 south and follow the signs to the stream.

Tackle Shops and Guides
There are no fly shops in the area, so check with Arizona Flyfishing in Tempe for the latest report. (480) 730-6808. www.azflyfishing.com.

Where to Stay
Rustic Rim Hideaway. Forest Lakes. Inexpensive to moderately priced cabins. (520) 535-9030.
Village at Christopher Creek. Moderate to expensive cabins on the creek. (800) 950-6910.

Where to Eat
Rim Cafe. Forest Lakes. Breakfast and lunch. No reservations. (520) 535-4007.

RESOURCES

Meck, Charles, and John Rohmer. *Arizona Trout Streams and Their Hatches.* Woodstock, VT: Backcountry Guides, 1998.

Arizona Atlas & Gazetteer. Yarmouth, ME: DeLorme Mapping Company. (207) 846-7000.

CHAPTER TWENTY-THREE

RENO, NEVADA

TRUCKEE AND LITTLE TRUCKEE RIVERS

Ralph Cutter

TRUCKEE RIVER

Reno was born on the banks of the Truckee River in the early 1800s. Nestled against the eastern flanks of the Sierra Nevada, it was the obvious place for westward immigrants to feed their stock, repair wagons, and take an extended power nap before beating themselves silly against the granite rampart between them and the California Dream. Reno was also an obvious place to fish.

Cutthroat trout the size of children finned in the shade of riverside cottonwoods, and it was popular sport to wade and fish the silky cool waters of this desert stream. In the days before graphite rods, triangle tapers, and Orvis-endorsed sport utility vehicles (SUVs), all one needed was a stout club and a gunnysack to catch a mess.

The Truckee is an exotic river. It is an oddity in the world of rivers, because it flows not to the ocean, but into a land-bound lake. Pyramid Lake is the last vestige of a vast inland sea that once mated with the ocean through the Snake River system. Via this conduit, anadromous trout migrated into the Lahontan Sea, only to become landlocked when the waters receded and volcanic upwellings blocked access to the Pacific. These fish evolved into the famous Lahontan cutthroat.

When Fremont brought his exploration team to the shores of Pyramid Lake in 1844, he discovered the greatest freshwater fishery on the face of the earth. Hundreds of thousands of giant cutthroats, many over 20 pounds, and not just a few twice that size, thrived in the food-rich waters at the Truckee River's terminus.

One hundred years later, the nascent Bureau of Reclamation tamed the Truckee. The bureau diverted the river at Derby Dam to irrigate the desert and grow cattle feed. At the grand opening of the dam, thousands

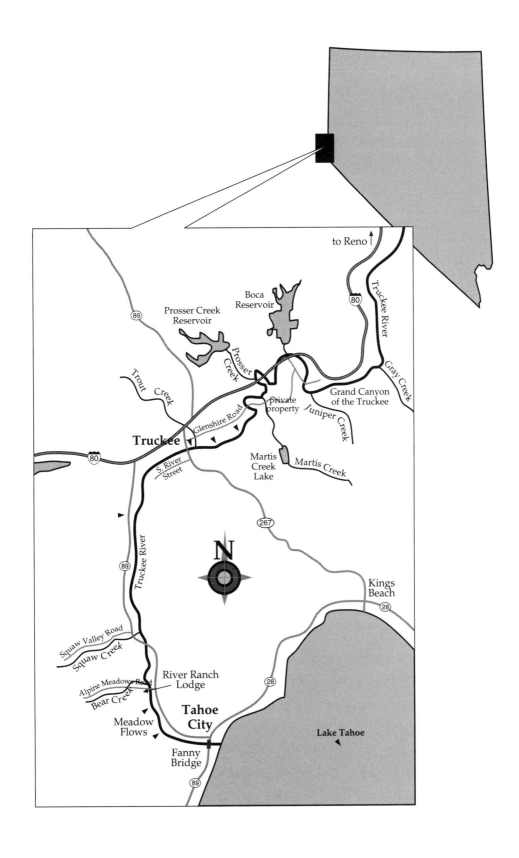

of stranded cutthroats lay flopping on the desiccated riverbed. Onlookers rushed into the mud and with wild cries of joy, clubbed the fish dead. Pyramid's trout population quickly succumbed to the increased salinity of the lake and lack of access to spawning beds. Downstream of Pyramid Lake, Winnemucca Lake, site of the country's first national wildlife refuge, which had hosted what was possibly the largest concentration of waterfowl on the continent, dried up. A remnant population of Lahontan cutthroat in Lake Tahoe succumbed to commercial harvest, timbering practices, and the introduction of exotic trout species.

A viable cutthroat fishery has been reestablished in Pyramid Lake and various parts of the Truckee watershed, but it is a mere whisper of its former greatness. Few cutts are caught in the Truckee, and it's only the rare and exceptional Pyramid fish that might top 15 pounds.

Today fishing the Truckee with a club would be considered gauche, and genuine canvas gunnysacks are hard to find. The river is better addressed with a 5-weight, 9-foot rod and a floating line.

Hatches, Flies, and Best Times to Fish

After spring runoff, the best fishing is found in June and July. Almost every night will bring trout rising and a smorgasbord of bugs in the air. A quick look at the hatch chart will show you that your fly box had better be filled with a variety of patterns, ranging from size eight green drake emergers to size twenty midges.

By midsummer, the Reno hatches will have largely come and gone, and most of the insects will be freshly born and almost invisible to the human eye. The best bet is to head into the mountains, where the air will be clear and the water cool and inviting. Near the town of Truckee, California, at 6,000 feet, the river will host early-morning hatches of Tricos, and the midmorning calm will be broken by the occasional detonation of rainbows and large brown trout inhaling unfortunate grasshoppers.

As the water temperature creeps into the seventies, midday fishing gets pretty boring on the Truckee, and many locals migrate to the shores of nearby Martis Creek Lake, in California, to strip scuds or damsel nymphs. Martis is a veritable fish stew, where you can catch three kinds of trout, sunfish, and half a dozen nongame species on a fly. You must release all fish in Martis Creek. The food supply is boundless; its trout reach considerable proportions. The lake usually fishes poorly in midsummer.

After midnight, hard-core anglers return to the Truckee with heavy tippets, big poppers, and 3/0 streamers—any fly that makes a commotion will do. The night belongs to lunker browns, which range from their lairs in search of planted trout, big crayfish, and chipmunks. Expect fish over 5 pounds. There are enough 30-inch-plus browns in the river to keep the gambler in all of us away from the downriver slot machines.

LAKES

Proper Name	Common Name	Sub Adult	Adult	Size	May	Jun	Jul	Aug	Sep	Oct
Callibaetis	Speckled Dun Mayfly	Pheasant Tail	BiVisible Dun Grey Cripple	12–18	**	***	**	*	*	**
Siphlonurus	Grey Drake Mayfly	Birds Nest	BiVisible Dun Grey Cripple	10–12	*	***	*	*	*	*
Caenis	Snowflake Dun Mayfly	Pheasant Tail	Sparkle Dun	20–22	*	**	***	**	*	
Tricorythodes	Trico Mayfly	Pheasant Tail	BiVisible Dun	20–22	*	**	***	**	*	*
Phryganea	Motor Boat Caddis	Teichert Caddis	E/C Caddis	10		**	***	***	*	
Mystacides	Black Dancer Caddisfly	Pheasant Tail Birds Nest	E/C Caddis	14–16		**	***	*		
Zygoptera	Damselfly	Marabou Damsel	Braided Butt Damsel	8–14	**	***	***	**	**	*
Anisoptera	Dragonfly	Geirach Dragon		6–10	**	***	***	***	**	
Chironomus	Blood Midge	Brassie	Martis Midge	14	***	***	**	*	*	**
Gammarus	Scud	Birds Nest	Birds Nest	10–16		*	**	***	***	**
Various	Snail	Floating snail	Floating snail	6–16		*	**	***	***	***

*** Main Hatches   ** Minor Hatches   * Sporadic Hatches

RIVERS

Proper Name	Common Name	Sub Adult	Adult	Size	May	Jun	Jul	Aug	Sep	Oct
Ameletus	Slate Wing Dun Mayfly	Birds Nest Pheasant Tail	Brown Cripple	10–12	**					
Heptagenia	Blue-Winged Olive Mayfly	Soft Hackle Birds Nest	BiVisible Dun Cripple	12–16	**	*				
Rhithrogenia	March Brown Mayfly	Soft Hackle Birds Nest	BiVisible Dun Cripple	12–14	**					
Epeorus	Sulfer Mayfly	Pheasant Tail GR Hare's Ear	BiVisible Dun Humpy	14–18		***	**			
Cinygmula/ Cinygma	Red Quill Mayfly	Birds Nest GR Hare's Ear	BiVisible Dun Humpy	16/18	**	**	*			
Baetis	Blue-Winged Olive Mayfly	Pheasant Tail GR Hare's Ear	BiVisible Dun	18–24	***	*	*	*	*	***
Paraleptophlebia	Mahogany Dun Mayfly	Pheasant Tail GR Hare's Ear	BiVisible Dun Cripple	14–18	**	**	*			
E. Tibialis	Creamy Orange Mayfly	Birds Nest Pheasant Tail GR Hare's Ear	BiVisible Dun Cripple Humpy	14–16	**	***	**	*		

LITTLE TRUCKEE RIVER

It may not be as exciting as a 15-pound brown on a popper, but a better bet might be to head to one of the smaller streams, such as the Little Truckee, in search of light-line, dry-fly action. The tailwater fishery on the Little Truckee River below Stampede Reservoir can serve up world-class fishing even through the heat of summer. In early August, you might

RIVERS, *continued*

Proper Name	Common Name	Sub Adult	Adult	Size	May	Jun	Jul	Aug	Sep	Oct
E. Flavilinea	Flav Mayfly	Birds Nest GR Hare's Ear	Green Cripple Humpy	12–14		**	**			
E. Infrequens E. Inermis	Pale Morning Dun Mayfly	Birds Nest Pheasant Tail GR Hare's Ear	BiVisible Dun Tan Cripple Humpy	14–16 18	**	***	***	*		
Drunella Grandis	Green Drake Mayfly	Birds Nest GR Hare's Ear	BiVisible Dun Humpy	10	*	***	*			
Rhyacophila	Green Sedge Caddisfly	Rockworm Sparkle Caddis	E/C Caddis Z Wing Caddis	12–18	*	***	***	**	*	
Hydropsyche	Spotted Sedge Caddisfly	Rockworm Sparkle Caddis	E/C Caddis Z Wing Caddis	12–18	*	***	***	**	*	
Glossosoma	Saddle Case Caddisfly	Rockworm Birds Nest	Bird Nest E/C Caddis	16–18	*	***	***	*		
Brachycentrus	Grannom Caddisfly	Pheasant Tail	Birds Nest E/C Caddis	10–18		**	**	**		
Dicosmoecus	October Caddis	Red Squirrel	Madam X Stimulator	6–8					**	***

*** Main Hatches   ** Minor Hatches   * Sporadic Hatches

encounter Tricos in the early morning and, as the day warms, pale morning duns, *Paraleptophlebias*, *Flavilineas*, and a smattering of *Hydropsyche* caddis. Terrestrials include huge carpenter ants, hoppers, and yellow jackets. The evenings often host intense midge, *Epeorus* mayfly, and *Glossosoma* caddisfly hatches. Throughout the day and evening, you'll likely see the eyes and mouths of selective trout as they gulp down drifting bugs.

ALSO WORTH NOTING

Don't overlook the small creeks that cross Route 89 north of Truckee: Prosser Creek, Alder Creek, Sagehen Creek, and the upper Little Truckee River all play host to fun populations of brookies, browns, and rainbows. If you want to catch lots of trout, try Ophir Creek as it meanders through Sheep Flat off Nevada Route 431 one mile west of the Mount Rose summit. Follow the creek a mile or two downstream of the highway, and fish your way back to the car. The little rivulet simply teems with tiny, voracious brook trout—just perfect for a 1- or 2-weight rod.

No matter where you fish, you'll need to get a California or Nevada fishing license, stock up on local patterns, and catch the latest fishing news.

IF YOU GO

From Reno, take U.S. 80 south to the river, as shown on the map for this chapter.

If you're approaching the Truckee from California, take I-80 through Sacramento to the town of Truckee, roughly 200 miles. Access the river from Route 89 or Glenshire Road. The Little Truckee is off I-80, north of Truckee.

Tackle Shops and Guides

California School of Flyfishing. Truckee. Lisa and chapter author Ralph Cutter, owners. This is not actually a fly shop, but it does provide guides and information. Before a trip, check out www.flyline.com for up-to-the-minute Truckee-area hatches and fishing conditions. The website has hundreds of scanned fly patterns with tying recipes and information on how to fish the local waters. (530) 587-7005.

Frank Pisciotta. Reno. Guide service. (530) 587-4844. E-mail: cyberfly @hooked.net.

The Reno Fly Shop. Reno. The area's only full-service fly shop. Extensive selection of flies and gear. Reliable guides and knowledgeable staff. (775) 827-0600.

Truckee River Outfitters. Truckee. An arm of Reno Fly Shop (above). (530) 582-0900.

A word of caution: The Reno-Truckee area hosts a few duplicitous "guides" who specialize in swindling tourists. These scam artists flash California Department of Fish and Game guide's licenses but do *not* have the necessary insurance and permits to guide on Army Corps or National Forest properties, virtually all of the region's trout water. Protect the fishery and yourself: Ask to see a copy of the guide's federal use permit before handing over any cash. Immediately report any violators to the Tahoe National Forest Service at (530) 587-3558.

Where to Stay
In Truckee

Alpine Village Motel. Truckee. At I-80 and Donner Overpass. Moderate. (530) 587-3801.

Best Western. Just south of Truckee. On California Route 267. Moderate. (800) 528-1234.

Richardson House. Truckee. B&B in an ideal location. Moderate. (530) 587-5388.

Super 8 Lodge. Truckee. Moderate. (800) 800-8000.

Truckee Hotel. Truckee. 1900s decor. (530) 587-4444.

In Reno

Atlantis Hotel. Reno. Moderate to expensive. (800) 723-6500.

The Nugget. Sparks. Moderate to expensive. (800) 648-1177.

The Peppermill. Reno. Moderate to expensive. (800) 282-2444.

Silver Legacy. Reno. Moderate to expensive. (800) 687-8733.

Camping

Donner Memorial State Park. (800) 444-7275.

Goose Meadows, Granite Flat, and Silver Creek Campgrounds. (800) 280-CAMP.

Where to Eat
In Truckee or Tahoe City

Cottonwood. Truckee. Eat on the deck overlooking the river and enjoy the caddisflies as they flip out in your wine. Moderate. (530) 587-5711.

Donner Lake Kitchen. Truckee. Great breakfast place, serving the best huevos rancheros this side of Mazatlan. Don't plan on lunch. No reservations. (530) 587-3119.

Hacienda del Lago. Tahoe City. In the Boatworks Mall. Great Mexican food. (530) 583-0358.

Pizza Junction. Truckee. On Donner Pass Road in the Gateway section. Pool tables, video arcade, pretty good pizza, and very good beer. Inexpensive. (530) 587-7411.

Squeeze Inn. Truckee. This small, claustrophobic breakfast nook buried in Old Town's "commercial row" serves mountainous omelets in a staggering number of varieties. Plan on standing in line to get a table. Inexpensive. No reservations. (530) 587-9814.

Sweets. Truckee. No Truckee meal would be complete without an after-dinner stroll along the historic Old Town storefronts and a stop here for some killer homemade fudge or brittle.

Taco Station. Truckee. The best burritos in the known world. Inexpensive. (530) 587-8226.

Wild Cherries. Truckee. On Donner Pass Road between the firehouse and high school. A healthy breakfast alternative. The fare leans toward fruit, granola, waffles, and specialty coffees. (530) 582-5602.

In Reno

Adele's. Reno. French restaurant. Moderate to expensive. (775) 333-6503.

Bertha Miranda's. Reno. Mexican food. (775) 786-9697.

Famous Murphy's. Reno. American fare. (775) 827-4111.

Harrah's Steak House. Reno. American fare. Moderate. (775) 786-3232.

Kyoto. Reno. Japanese food. Moderate to expensive. (775) 825-9686.

Luciano's. Reno. Italian. Moderate. (775) 322-7373.

Palaise de Jade. Reno. Chinese. Moderate. (775) 827-5233.

Rapscallian. Reno. Seafood. Moderate to expensive. (775) 323-1211.

Santa Fe Hotel. Reno. Moderate to expensive. (775) 323-1891.

RESOURCES

Truckee Chamber of Commerce. (530) 587-2757.

Cutter, Ralph. *Sierra Trout Guide.* Portland, OR: Amato Publications, 1991. Describes two thousand lakes and 1,700 miles of trout streams in the Sierra Nevada. Extensive coverage of fly fishing, fisheries, and entomology.

Dickerson, Richard. *Nevada Anglers Guide: Fish Tails in the Sagebrush.* Portland, OR: Amato Publications, 1997. A complete fishing guide to the state, with many personal anecdotes.

Stanley, Dave, and Jeff Cavender. *Dave Stanley's No Nonsense Guide to Fishing Nevada.* David Marketing Communications, 1997. A down-and-dirty "just-the-facts" guide to Nevada's best fly-fishing opportunities. Includes hatches, fly suggestions, and maps. A must-have. Order directly from the Reno Fly Shop. (775) 827-0600.

PART SEVEN

The West Coast

CHAPTER TWENTY-FOUR

SEATTLE

SNOQUALMIE AND YAKIMA RIVERS

Adem Tepedelen

Many fly fishers who moved to the Emerald City with the high-tech boom of the 1990s discovered that this bustling metropolis, wedged between the island-dotted beauty of Puget Sound and the craggy, majestic Cascade Mountains, has much to offer the ambitious angler. Hidden in the shadow of western Washington's anadromous fishery are two rivers that can stand up to the excellence of any of the best wild trout fisheries west of the Mississippi: The Snoqualmie and Yakima Rivers, flowing down opposite sides of the Cascades, provide year-round opportunities to catch wild trout in a variety of stunning settings.

Though both rivers draw clear, cold water from the snowy reaches of Snoqualmie Pass, they flow through distinctly different climates and terrain. The Snoqualmie descends the lush western slope and ultimately empties into Puget Sound, while the Yakima coasts eastward across the dry eastern plateau to its confluence with the Columbia River in Richland. There are many differences in the fishing experience each offers. The Snoqualmie provides a small-stream adventure less than an hour from Seattle; the Yakima is a bit farther away and offers larger fish in an astounding variety of terrain.

If you're visiting Seattle for the weekend and are looking for a quick escape from the city, spend an afternoon catching feisty cutthroats on the Snoqualmie forks in the shadow of the Cascades and be back in time for dinner. If you have more time and want a multiday adventure, a float down the Yakima will give you access to many miles of a broad, beautiful river that holds a healthy population of sizable rainbows. Both rivers have a few things all anglers can appreciate: plenty of easy access, a minimal amount of required gear, and lots of beautiful, wild fish.

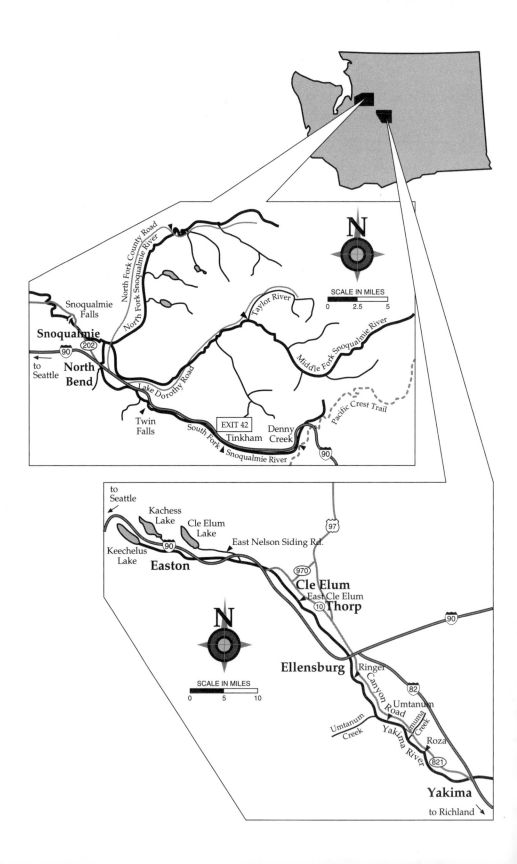

SNOQUALMIE RIVER

On a sunny day in Seattle, the Cascade Mountains fill the eastern skyline with a seamless, jagged line of craggy, snow-covered peaks. At the base of this majestic range sits the tiny town of North Bend, where the three forks—North, Middle, and South—that constitute the trout fishery of the Snoqualmie coalesce into a broad, slow-moving river that plunges 268 feet over Snoqualmie Falls. Below the falls, the Snoqualmie is a respectable salmon and steelhead fishery, but above it, cutthroats, rainbows, and their hyrids, "cuttbows," as well as a smattering of eastern brookies, provide most of the action.

The forks begin as small, snow-fed creeks near the Pacific Crest Trail along the spine of the Cascades and tumble through lush, rocky terrain before flattening out in the foothills surrounding North Bend. Forests of Douglas fir crowd the rising Cascades, and pale, thin alders line the forks as they amble down through the valleys. Because this area receives a lot of snow and rain, it's a wonderland of thick forests, berry-covered bushes, huge ferns, and bright wildflowers.

The three forks are perhaps the most unsung and underrated trout streams in western Washington, frequently passed over by fly fishers heading across Snoqualmie Pass to the mighty Yakima on the eastern slope of the Cascades. These rocky streams are brimming with plenty of little beauties in the 6- to 10-inch range, though it's not uncommon to hook a colorful 12-inch native cutthroat or crimson-striped rainbow. The fish are all native or streambred, as the river hasn't been stocked in more than twenty years.

Unless you're accessing one of the forks via a man-made trail, of which there are plenty, be prepared to push through some brush. A few breaths of the heady, intoxicating scents that fill these woods—vine-ripened berries, wildflowers, spicy firs, and the dark, moist soil—are worth any scrapes or scratches you might experience along the way.

If you have only a few hours and want to get into fish quickly and easily, there are several public accesses within North Bend's city limits. There is decent fishing in the flat, deep pools and brushy, undercut banks; however, the better angling and purest water are farther east, in the mountains.

Although its close proximity to the Seattle-Tacoma area makes the Snoqualmie a convenient getaway, it's the fast fishing and gorgeous setting that truly make it special. Western Washington may not have a reputation for quality trout streams, but this frequently overlooked beauty is well worth seeking out and exploring.

South Fork of the Snoqualmie

The South Fork is the most accessible of the three forks and has the best fishing. Though much of the South Fork parallels busy I-90, there are numerous places where the rush of the highway is inaudible.

An excellent place to start fishing is a mile from Exit 34 off I-90. Take a right onto 468th Street SE off the exit and head south. Go just past the sign for Twin Falls, and park near the bridge. The stretch from the bridge to the Twin Falls trailhead, about half a mile, is rife with prime pocket water. Every place that looks like it holds fish does. Long, slow, deep pools contain big, cautious fish, and swirling eddies are chock full of voracious smaller guys—all of them greedy to snap up dry flies. There are several houses along the river in this section, but wading in the river presents no trespassing problems.

You can find additional access points at Olallie State Park off Exit 38, Tinkham Campground at Exit 42, and Exit 47, Denny Creek and Asahel. A short, light rod is recommended for the entire South Fork, as the cover is often heavy and the stream is mostly narrow.

In these upper reaches, you can fish for wild cutthroats through the small pockets and the deeper pools undercutting rock facings and flowing past huge boulders. Don't be fooled by the diminutive size of the South Fork at this higher elevation—it holds fish in every little nook and cranny. The fish are smaller up here, but no less beautiful or frisky, and there are a few trout up to 11 inches in some of the deeper pools.

The wild cutts are wily little fish that are as sporty as they are gorgeous. They are also renowned for their ability to spit out barbless hooks. For every two fish you'll hook, you'll lose at least one. Keep in mind, too, that late in summer when lack of rain causes the river to drop to its lowest level, the fish are easily spooked in shallow water. Overhanging brush and branches will help break up direct sunlight and mask your shadow, but stealth is required.

The lush mountain setting of the upper reaches of the South Fork is magical, and on a hot summer day, it's a mere hour's drive from Seattle to the cool air. If you camp at Denny Creek, there are plenty of trails, falls, and alpine lakes to explore when you're not fishing.

Middle Fork of the Snoqualmie

The Middle Fork is the biggest of the three forks and therefore the most popular with anglers. Many of the locals picnic and swim in the upstream reaches, where you might also encounter kayakers. Nonetheless, there is plenty of great fishing in the upper water.

To get to the upper reaches, take Exit 34 off I-90 and go left on 468th SE (Edgewick). Follow this road for about a mile, and then go right on Middle Fork Road SE, which eventually turns into Lake Dorothy Road, a rough gravel road that follows the Middle Fork fairly closely for more than 15 miles. There are several pullouts along the way. Drive at least 8 or 9 miles up to get away from the crowds and into the best fish.

The Middle Fork is a broader river than the South Fork. Its pools are deeper and riffles faster in some areas. There's also more room to cast, as gravel banks provide relief from the dense foliage surrounding the river.

The Middle Fork has some primitive forest service campgrounds along the upper reaches, an excellent destination if you're interested in escaping the crowds and roughing it for a few days. One of its tributaries, the Taylor River, is a great pocket water stream, tucked into a dense fir forest just below the imposing Cascades.

North Fork of the Snoqualmie

The least accessible of the three forks of the Snoqualmie, the North Fork, can be reached by following the county road north through North Bend. After a few miles, it forks off to the left and becomes a rough gravel road that runs through a Weyerhauser tree farm. You'll need to buy a pass from Weyerhauser to access the area, but it's well worth it if you live nearby, as it also gives you access to several alpine lakes and other streams.

The first access point to the North Fork from this road is 8 or 9 miles upstream, where the road crosses the water. The road then follows the stream a little more closely for the next few miles. You'll encounter few other anglers in this area. Overnight camping is not allowed in the area, but an early start will enable a full day of fishing.

In its upper reaches, the North Fork is relatively narrow, with nice deep pools and bountiful riffles. Many of the pockets are short and swift, but well-placed flies can root out hungry fish. The gravel banks revealed in the summer provide area away from the thick brush and allow for long, unfettered casts. The meadows surrounding the upper reaches of the North Fork are thick with huckleberry bushes, and though black bears in the area are fond of the fat purple berries, they are extremely shy and rarely encountered. You're far more likely to spot a herd of elk or a couple of black-tailed deer.

Hatches, Flies, and Best Times to Fish

Part of what makes fishing the three forks of the Snoqualmie so appealing is that the fish, for the most part, are not picky. They readily gobble dry flies from June through October, even when there is no hatch. I'll admit that there have been a few occasions when I've encountered hatches where the trout became selective. However, the first time I fished each of the forks, I had no trouble connecting with fish. There are plenty of insects and lots of hungry fish.

The hatches on the Snoqualmie are similar to those that occur on many eastern Washington rivers. There are plenty of midge hatches all year long, and trout frequently key into these late on summer evenings.

Caddis make up the majority of the hatches and are omnipresent from the beginning of June through late fall. There is a brief October caddis hatch. During the heat of the summer, there's some hopper action, but nothing like what takes place on the Yakima. Some pale morning dun hatches also occur throughout the summer.

Caddis patterns (#12–#18) are consistent Snoqualmie trout pleasers; I've had good success with Olive Body Elk Hairs, but most elk hair variations work just fine. An angling friend ties an X-Caddis variant, with a shiny blue-green body and tail, that does equally well on the surface or in the film at the end of a downstream cast. Standard attractors such as Adamses, Irresistibles, Humpies, Royal Wulffs, or Stimulators (#12–#14) work well. In the late summer and fall, when the water is low and the trout are spooky, a Parachute Adams or Pale Morning Dun (#16–#18) will do the trick.

As on any trout river, there are times when the fish key into specific hatches—including emerging caddis and spinners—but more often than not, they actively take any of the well-presented imitations mentioned above. If no insects are hatching and the fish are refusing to rise, small beadhead nymphs (# 14–#18), Hare's Ears, Prince Nymphs, and most caddis larva or nymph imitations are worth a try.

In the heat of the summer, when the sun doesn't set until after 9 P.M., the best fishing occurs in the late afternoon and evening. Toward the fall, as the days get shorter and cooler, fishing is consistent and productive throughout the day.

Snoqualmie Regulations

All three forks are open year-round, but like many mountain streams affected by cold spring and summer snow runoff, they usually fall into good shape by July and continue to be very active well into the Northwest's October Indian summer. You may encounter rain and fluctuating water levels in October, but until the heavy rains set in and the rivers bloat, quality fishing continues late into the fall. The Middle Fork is catch-and-release year-round, but the South and North Forks are catch-and-release only from November 1 to May 31.

YAKIMA RIVER

Born of the same Cascade waters as the Snoqualmie, but flowing east rather than west, the Yakima River could hardly be more different from its delicate west-slope sister. Drawing its strength from three impoundments—Kachess, Keechelus, and Cle Elum Lakes—this tailwater fishery is as robust and rugged as the Snoqualmie is precious. And whereas the Snoqualmie is subject to the frequent fluctuations brought by the heavy rainfall that soaks western Washington throughout much of the year, the Yakima is affected more by seasonal releases from the dams in its headwaters, to meet the irrigation needs of farmers in the Yakima Valley, rather than by precipitation.

The 75 miles of prime fishing water—from the Easton Dam to Roza Dam—are open to anglers year-round, and each of the four seasons brings vastly different conditions and possibilities. The river changes character gradually on its southeastern journey, going from the high-altitude pine forests near Easton, where it's still a stream, to the twisting hardwood-covered banks near Cle Elum, to the dry plains of the Kittitas Valley, where it flattens and descends into a canyon south of Ellensburg. Several major tributaries, such as the Cle Elum and the Teanaway, hook up with it along the way, greatly influencing flows and clarity throughout the year and turning the Yakima into a sizable river.

Regulated as a catch-and-release fishery in this 75-mile section, the Yakima has thrived and gained a reputation as arguably Washington's finest trout fishery, where anglers have the chance to hook 18-inch rainbows, as well as the occasional cutthroat and cuttbow, on dry flies eight months of the year. However, it's also one of the state's most challenging and intimidating rivers, requiring successful anglers to be well-informed and resourceful. Knowing when to fish what parts of the river is essential to any successful trip to Yakima.

Crystal Springs to Cle Elum

Before the Yakima reaches its confluence with the Cle Elum River, just west of the town of Cle Elum, it's a stream that ambles briskly through mountainous, high-elevation terrain where pine trees and other conifers grip the dry soil.

That all changes when the summer dam releases create a torrent. Too cold and snowpacked to fish in the winter and spring, too swift in the summer, the river hosts lively little rainbows, cutthroats, and brookies eager to rise to dry flies in the fall once irrigation flows have subsided.

Access is somewhat limited in this area, but the first place worth stopping when traveling east is Crystal Springs Campground at Exit 62, just off I-90, which roughly parallels the Yakima to the town of Cle Elum. Here you'll find the Yakima a lot like the Snoqualmie, with plenty of pocket water, shallow riffles, and the occasional sweeping, undercut bank. Fish are small, but the dense forest setting and crisp air make for a great small-stream experience, and you're unlikely to see many anglers.

Catch-and-release regulations don't begin until 10 miles downstream at the Easton Dam, but you are nonetheless required to use only artificial flies and lures. Continuing east on I-90, take Exit 78, Golf Course Road. Take two left turns, and follow Nelson Siding Road (heading west alongside I-90) to a clearly marked state fishing access site at the road's end. You can park here and wade or launch a boat or pontoon, though logjams and sweepers make it a tricky and potentially hazardous float for the inexperienced.

Thanks to the addition of flows from Kachess Lake, the Yakima has grown in size at this point, though it's still quite wadable and now holds larger fish. Twelve-inchers are common, and it's not unusual to land a 16- or 17-inch fish on a high-floating Stimulator in the fall when the October caddis are hatching.

Once the Cle Elum River (which is a good trout fishery during its June 1 to October 31 season) enters, the Yakima starts to take on the characteristics that define it as it rolls toward the central Washington plains. The curves soften, it spreads out, and giant cottonwoods take the place of the conifers along its banks.

Get off at Cle Elum Exit 84 toward town, take a right following the sign to South Cle Elum, and you'll find another access point at a bridge where you can park and wade or launch a boat or raft. Since the river is much broader here and can accommodate higher flows, the area can be fished from the banks all year, but it's best for wading in the spring when the golden stones are shaking hungry 'bows out of their winter doldrums. It also fishes well in the fall, when the irrigation flows subside and the blue-winged olive hatch occurs every afternoon like clockwork.

Cle Elum to Ellensburg

Like a magical divider between lush, rain-soaked western Washington and the dry, high plains just across the mountains, both the terrain and climate begin to change drastically between Cle Elum and Ellensburg. On a given day, it may be raining and gray in Seattle and dry and sunny east of Cle Elum. Don't let foul weather in Seattle deter you from a trek across Snoqualmie Pass to the Yakima. Past Cle Elum, the Yakima separates itself from I-90, and access is along Routes 970 and 10.

As the Yakima travels beyond Cle Elum's city limits and the tall cottonwoods begin to thin, it enters a canyon best reached by wading anglers taking Iron Horse Trail. Walk along this trail to access boulder-studded banks where you can entice big fish from their lairs with well-placed streamers.

Beyond the steep walls of this upper canyon, the terrain opens up, and farms frame both banks. Because there aren't many public-access points, this section is most successfully fished year-round from a drift boat or pontoon raft; there are put-ins just east of Cle Elum and take-outs at the Thorp bridge and farther down just before a diversion dam, where you *must* exit the river. Floating anglers need to beware of a wasteway flume discharging blasts of water on the right bank. Watch for it once you cross under the power lines, and stay on the left.

Ellensburg to Roza Dam

The ultimate destination for most anglers is the Yakima Canyon, a few miles south of Ellensburg and accessible via Route 821. When locals talk of fishing the Yakima, they are generally talking about this section. Considering the quality of fishing throughout the 75 miles of catch-and-release water, you probably wonder what it is about this particular section that makes it so special.

The reasons read like a fly fisher's dream river: big, wild fish, and lots of 'em; 20 miles of nearly uninterrupted access; an absolutely gorgeous setting; and dry-fly action eight months of the year. Sound too good to be true? Well, it sort of is. Depending on what time of year you fish, it can be as vexing as it is heavenly.

The Yakima is wide through the canyon, and its personality and characteristics change with the seasons. When the high irrigation flows of summer swell the river, it's difficult to fish from the banks, but those who float it cast Pale Morning Duns, caddis imitations, and hoppers up toward the brush- and grass-covered banks where big fish feed.

In the fall and winter, greatly diminished flows are a dream for wading anglers. The low, clear water allows you to detect the variety of structures in the river where fish hold. Cast tiny Blue-Winged Olives (*Baetis*) to sippers hiding in fishy rock gardens from September to November, and stir up strikes in January and February with a variety of nymphs in those same spots.

Spring may be the most unpredictable, though not necessarily unproductive, season in the canyon. Rainfall and snowmelt in tributaries such as the Swauk and Teanaway Rivers and Wilson Creek frequently swell and discolor the Yakima. Timing is everything, and checking the river's vital signs—cubic feet per second and coloration—on the Internet before you travel to the canyon in the spring is recommended. Hit it just right, and you might find yourself casting a bushy March Brown imitation to active risers. Hit it wrong, and you might find yourself staring at a blown-out river whose color could best be described as march brown.

Floating is the preferred method of fishing the canyon year-round, though bank anglers should not be discouraged; I've landed some of my biggest fish standing on the bank and casting upstream into the foam lines that run a few feet off the grass-lined banks. Nevertheless, there's no denying that you have more access to terrific water fishing from a boat.

Floaters don't *always* have the advantage, though. There's a serious "rubber hatch" throughout the summer that finds hundreds of beer-swilling locals in rubber rafts and inner tubes cruising the same stretch favored by anglers. Though they tend to stick to the middle of the river, while the trout are found close to the banks, be prepared to be asked dozens of times if you've caught anything.

Despite the distractions, a float down the Yakima Canyon is still a day well spent. Eagles, elk, deer, bighorn sheep, and coyotes inhabit the steep, grassy ridges above the river, and blue herons, otters, ducks, and geese are fellow floaters. The stunning scenery is certainly equal to the excellence of the angling in the canyon, and whether you're in a boat or on foot, fishing this part of the Yakima will definitely be a memorable experience.

Hatches, Flies, and Best Times to Fish

This is a fertile, healthy river that supports rich and diverse insect life. These hatches emerge on different sections of the river, but most early-season hatches occur in the canyon first, where the water temperature warms a little earlier than in the upper reaches.

January–February. Midges constitute the only hatches in these cold, snowy months. River temperatures run in the thirties, and the fish are sluggish. Try working beadhead nymphs (#12–#20)—Hare's Ear, Zug Bug, Prince, Brassies—and big stonefly nymphs (#6–#10).

March. Dry-fly action begins in earnest with a hatch of golden stoneflies, and a big Stimulator (#8–#12) will entice fish. If the weather warms, look for a *Baetis* hatch (#20) in the heat of the day.

April. March brown mayflies (#12–#14) show up in April and can continue through early May, depending on water temperatures. Watch for a hatch during the heat of the day. Try a Pheasant Tail Nymph (#14–#16) dropper if rising fish are being picky. *Baetis* will also hatch this month during the warmest part of the day.

May. You might need a scorecard to keep track of all the hatches in May: march browns, caddis (#14–#16 olive and tan), pale morning duns (imitated by #16–#18 parachute or Compara-dun patterns), and *Baetis*.

June. More of the same, with caddis being the food of choice for increasingly fat trout that simply feast on the enormous evening hatches. Pale morning duns and *Baetis* (on cooler days) are still good bets, and yellow sallies (use a #14 Yellow Stimulator or #12 Bright Yellow Elk Hair Caddis) are a staple in the area around Cle Elum.

July. Pale Morning Dun, caddis, and Yellow Sally patterns continue to work throughout the day, with major hatches occurring in the evening. Terrestrials are the big news in July, and hopper (#10–#12), ant, beetle, and bee patterns tossed in tight to the bank will draw ferocious strikes.

August. Hoppers in the heat of the day; caddis in the evening.

September. Once flows drop in the middle of the month, the river is perfect for wading. Caddis hatches continue, hoppers are still great, and *Baetis* return as the water temperatures cool toward October. A gray stonefly (use a #10–#12 Black or Gray Stimulator) appears in the canyon and causes a lot of commotion. An October caddis (#8 Orange Stimulator) hatch, mostly in the upper section, also stirs things up.

October. With the summer crowds a distant memory, like clockwork *Baetis* provides reliable hatches from 11 A.M. to 4 P.M. The window tightens closer to November. Light cahills (#14) frequently appear at this time and offer feeding trout a slightly larger meal. Light tippets and skillful presentations are musts for these sipping risers.

November–December. Depending on the weather, you might get some brief *Baetis* hatches in the warmth of the afternoon in early November, but once the snow begins to blanket the banks, it's back to midges and nymphing until March.

Yakima Regulations
From the Easton Dam to the Roza Dam, the Yakima is catch-and-release, and only artificial flies or lures are permitted. No floating devices with motors are allowed.

IF YOU GO
Snoqualmie River
The three upper forks of the Snoqualmie are conveniently located near North Bend, 30 miles from downtown Seattle via I-90 east. North Bend, nestled at the base of the Cascade Mountains, lies at the confluence of the forks. It's an excellent place to begin your quest for Snoqualmie cutthroats and rainbows. From I-90, take Exit 27, 31, or 34, depending on which fork you want to fish. Exit 31 will lead you to the downtown of tiny North Bend, approximately a mile north of the interstate.

Tackle Shops and Guides
Make sure you stock up in Seattle and Issaquah, just off I-90 on the way to North Bend, as there is no place to buy flies and gear in North Bend.

Creekside Angling Company. Issaquah. Plenty of supplies and a helpful, friendly staff. (425) 392-3800. www.creeksideangling.com.

Outdoor Emporium. Seattle. Lots of equipment for the budget-minded angler. (206) 624-6550.

Patrick's Fly Shop. Seattle. Fly-tying supplies and guide service. (206) 325-8988 or (800) 398-7693.

Where to Stay
Since the Snoqualmie is close to Seattle, it's an ideal destination for day trips. However, there are a decent motel in North Bend, an exquisite lodge in nearby Snoqualmie, and a few places to camp along the Middle and South Forks.

Edgewick Inn. North Bend. Just off Exit 34 and convenient to both the Middle and South Forks. Restaurant nearby. Inexpensive. (425) 888-9000.

The Salish Lodge. Snoqualmie. Deluxe lodge overlooking Snoqualmie Falls and convenient to the North Fork. Lounge and restaurant. Expensive. (425) 888-2556.

Camping

Mount Baker–Snoqualmie National Forest Ranger Station. North Bend. Plenty of maps and information for camping along the South Fork. (425) 888-1421. www.fs.fed.us/r6/mbs.

Taylor River and Dingford Creek. Two primitive Forest Service campgrounds along the upper reaches of the Middle Fork.

Where to Eat

Ken's. North Bend. Near the Edgewick Inn. Inexpensive. (425) 888-3322.

Mar-T Cafe. North Bend. Home of "Twin Peaks" pie, named for the TV show. Simple diner-style meals and good pie. Inexpensive. (425) 888-1221.

The Salish Lodge. Snoqualmie. In the lodge overlooking Snoqualmie Falls. Expensive. (425) 888-2556.

Yakima River

Since the Yakima is only two to three hours from Seattle, depending on what part you fish, it's a great destination for either a long day trip or an overnight excursion. I-90 pretty much follows the river to Ellensburg, and there are plenty of services along the way.

Tackle Shops and Guides

The Yakima is a big river from Cle Elum down through the Yakima Canyon, and if you have the time, money, and inclination, a guided trip is a good way to fish it for the first time, especially during the summer when flows are high.

Cooper's Fly Shop & Pro Guide Service. Ellensburg. Good source for local information and guide service. (509) 962-5259.

The Evening Hatch Guide Service. Ellensburg. Knowledgeable local guides. (509) 962-5959. theeveninghatch.com.

Worley Bugger Fly Co. Ellensburg. This started as a website—still an excellent source of up-to-the-minute information—and has blossomed into a fantastic fly shop and guide service. (509) 962-2033. www.worley buggerflyco.com.

Most area fly shops don't sell licenses, so you have to pick one up at any of the locations listed below. More information is available from the Washington Department of Fish and Wildlife. www.wa.gov/wdfw.

Seattle. Chubby & Tubby, Fred Meyer, Big 5, Gart Sport, GI Joe's (all have multiple locations in the Seattle area).

North Bend. Ace Hardware. (425) 888-1242.

Cle Elum. Cle Elum Farm & Home Supply. (509) 674-7104. Coast to Coast Hardware. (509) 674-4466.

Ellensburg. Bi-Mart. (509) 925-6971. Pioneer Pantry. (509) 962-8107.

Where to Stay

Cle Elum has one main street, and all the services are located along it. Take Exit 109 off I-90 to reach the motels and many other services located in this area.

Best Western Ellensburg Inn. Ellensburg. One of several motels just off I-90 and within a couple miles of the Yakima. Moderate. (509) 925-9801.

Super 8. Ellensburg. Inexpensive accommodations just off I-90 at Exit 109. (509) 962-6888.

Timber Lodge Inn. Cle Elum. You can walk to the Yakima from this comfortable motel. Moderate. (509) 674-5966.

Camping

National Forest Service campgrounds. Many in the Cle Elum area, but none next to the river. Wenatchee National Forest. (509) 674-4411. www.fs.fed.us/r6/wenatchee/recreate/reports.html.

Along the Yakima in the Ellensburg area. This is much easier. There are free public sites in the canyon at Umtanum and "The Slab," a few miles downstream.

Ellensburg KOA. On the Yakima. Restrooms, hot showers, a store, laundry, RV hookups, and tent sites. (509) 925-9319.

Where to Eat

Bar-14 Ranch House Restaurant. Ellensburg. Just off I-90 at Exit 109. Good, stick-to-your-ribs food. Inexpensive. (509) 962-6222.

Mama Vallone's Steak House & Inn. Cle Elum. If you feel like treating yourself after a long day of fishing, this is the place to go. Moderate. (509) 674-5174.

Rodeo City Bar-B-Q. Ellensburg. Locally acclaimed barbecue joint. Inexpensive. (509) 962-2727.

RESOURCES

Probasco, Steve. *River Journal: Yakima River.* Portland, OR: Frank Amato Publications, 1994.

Ross, John. *Trout Unlimited's Guide to America's 100 Best Trout Streams.* Helena, MT: Falcon Publishing, 1999.

Thomas, Greg. *Fly Fisher's Guide to Washington.* Gallatin Gateway, MT: Wilderness Adventures Press, 1999.

Washington State Atlas & Gazetteer. Yarmouth, ME: DeLorme Mapping Company. (207) 846-7000.

CHAPTER TWENTY-FIVE

PORTLAND, OREGON

DESCHUTES, CROOKED, AND METOLIUS RIVERS

Ann McIntosh, with David Nolte

I left Baltimore in mid-March in subfreezing temperatures to be welcomed in Portland by cherry blossoms, forsythia, and daffodils gracing green lawns. These lush conditions prevailed as I left the city and ascended the Cascade Mountains. East of the Cascades, everything changed dramatically; I drove out of a dripping evergreen rainforest onto a sagebrush desert. I had entered the rain shadow: Annual rainfall on the western side of the mountains is 40 inches, whereas on the eastern slopes it's only 10 inches.

Year-round fishing is possible in much of Oregon, but the Deschutes, Crooked, and Metolius Rivers offer opportunities to catch wild fish within three hours of Portland. These fisheries don't freeze over, making them a destination for cabin-feverish anglers from Wyoming, Montana, and Colorado, as well as West Coast regulars and eastern visitors.

Each river can be fished on your own, without a guide, but advice from local anglers and fly shops is essential. Nourished by the plankton-rich water in reservoirs feeding these rivers, the fish are healthy and very strong, fit from living in the swift river current. Hatches are multiple and complex.

DESCHUTES RIVER

For nearly four million years, the Deschutes River ("river of falls") has deepened its canyon through lava flows—a wide, slate-gray stripe at the base of black basalt and sharp, burnt sienna scree. A haven for both steelhead and native rainbows (also known as redbands or redsides), the river flows north for 200 miles, from its headwaters in the Cascades to the Columbia River. The most productive water is the last 100 miles downstream from Pelton Dam.

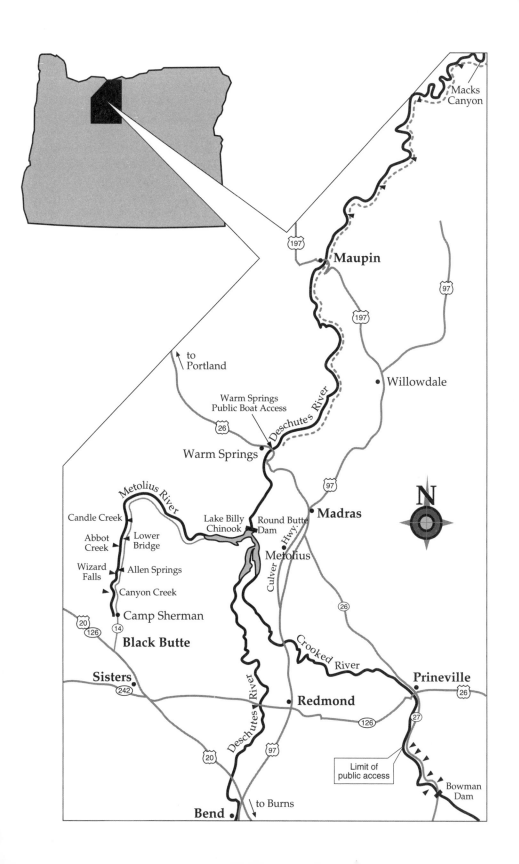

Macks
Canyon

197

Maupin

197

Willowdale

97

to
Portland

Warm Springs
Public Boat Access

Deschutes River

26

Warm Springs

97

Metolius River

Candle Creek

Lake Billy
Chinook

Round Butte
Dam

Madras

N

Abbot
Creek

Lower
Bridge

Allen Springs

Metolius

Culver Hwy.

Wizard
Falls

Canyon Creek

Camp Sherman

20

126

14

Black Butte

26

Crooked River

Prineville

26

Sisters

242

Deschutes River

Redmond

126

27

20

97

Limit of
public access

Bowman
Dam

Bend

to Burns

The river has magnificent hatches year-round, and throughout the year, salmonids feed in the Deschutes. It is perhaps best known for the summer steelhead run, which begins in early August at the mouth of the river and continues until December 31. But the Deschutes is at its most sporting during salmon fly season in late May and early June, with the reckless redbands leaping throughout the upper river.

Outdoor writer George Strakes describes blizzards of caddis from 2 to 9 P.M. from the end of July through August, when the fish are all looking up and will take Adams soft-hackles with abandon. In winter and spring, the Deschutes is primarily a nymph fishery.

The river is open for year-round fishing from its mouth to the Confederated Tribes of the Warms Springs boundary about 70 miles upstream; the upper section opens the last Saturday in April. Generally speaking, the river above Sherars Falls provides the best trout fishing, while the 44-mile stretch below the falls is better for steelhead. A road follows the river for 30 miles from the locked gate above Maupin downstream to Sherars Falls. There is easy access along this stretch.

An estimated thirteen hundred trout per mile swim in the waters between Sherars Falls and Pelton Dam; the majority are native Deschutes redside (redband) rainbows. As Mark Bachmann, owner of the Fly Fishing Shop in Welches, explained to me, redsides are "desert redbands"— native fish that dominate all Oregon fisheries east of the Cascades, having laid their claim before coastal rainbows.

These fish, like brown trout, are selective insectivores. Redbands feed on top in certain areas at certain times. Anglers focus on careful presentations in back eddies, dropping their flies in the foam line. Most of the redbands I caught were hooked in back eddies where fish were resting near the bank.

Most redsides are in the 8- to 15-inch range, although a few reach 20 inches. Oregon Trout played a part in the establishment of a slot limit on the Deschutes: Only two trout between 10 and 13 inches may be kept—just right for a camper's supper. A combination of this lack of pressure and stable river flows results in an increasing number of large fish. Since the 1930s Oregon Fish and Wildlife has prohibited fishing the Deschutes from any kind of flotation device. Boats are used only to transport anglers to productive reaches. Once there, they anchor, get out, and wade. This regulation results in masses of water over which a fly line never passes, providing safe havens for fish.

When I fished the Deschutes in March, I caught numerous redbands and a few brown trout—all in the 12- to 16-inch range. I floated for about 8 miles with George Strakes and his fishing buddy Dan Thomas. We put in at the Pine Tree access and took out at Beavertail. The river was flowing at 5,600 cubic feet per second (optimum flow for anglers is 3,500 to

4,200), but the water was clear and fishable at 48 degrees F. The temperature was balmy, with no wind or rain.

The first fish I caught was a 12-inch redside that took Strakes's March Brown nymph, and the second one succumbed to a big golden stonefly nymph tied by Pennsylvania tier Randy Buchanan. The guys had good luck using a Butch's Bug—a big, black, ugly stonefly nymph with long rubber legs.

We drifted the river looking for fish, but an angler could also walk or inch along slowly in a car, stopping frequently to look for rising fish in back eddies. Often we walked on banks high above the water, sliding down scree slopes to cast a fly in appealing backwaters. Strakes cautioned me that except during the salmon fly and summer caddis hatches, an angler shouldn't expect to take numerous fish in a day on the Deschutes. But I can attest that what you do hook will be quality wild trout: Redside rainbows are muscular and hard to subdue. To my surprise (not to mention that of my fellow anglers), the largest fish of the day was taken by me on a crayfish pattern tied by Pennsylvanian Ed Kraft.

A 5/6-weight 8½- to 9-foot rod is good for trout, while a 7- to 9-weight or a Spey rod is appropriate for steelhead. The Deschutes River rocks are slippery. Cleated, felt-soled boots and a wading staff are advised. This is big, strong water. The good news is that you don't have to move far to find fish.

David Nolte, former director of special projects for Trout Unlimited, likes to divide the Deschutes into three sections: upper, middle, and lower.

Upper Deschutes

The upper Deschutes runs from the headwaters at Lava Lake to Bend. The Deschutes starts as a classic small trout stream with easy wading. This is the least fished section of the river and provides the coolest water, creating excellent habitat for brook and brown trout, kokanee salmon, whitefish, and native redbands.

The upper section flows through meadows and pine, cutting into banks and creating oxbow twists and turns. Two large reservoirs, Crane Prairie and Wickiup, provide trophy stillwater trout angling. These reservoirs change the flow, and the small classic trout stream becomes a large river with opportunity for large brown trout.

Groups such as Trout Unlimited chapters, Federation of Fly Fishers clubs, American Rivers, and Oregon Trout are working closely with local, state, and federal agencies, as well as the Confederated Tribes of Warm Springs and Portland General Electric, in a comprehensive effort to restore anadromous salmonids in the upper Deschutes basin. Habitat restoration and the creation of a fish passage over Pelton–Round Butte Dams are the primary projects.

Middle Deschutes
The middle section is from Bend to Lake Billy Chinook. Here the water varies from 30 to 60 feet wide and holds brown and redband trout. The water moves slower than in the upper reaches and sometimes the flow is extremely low—especially from spring to early fall—as a result of irrigation demands. The redbands tend to occupy the faster water, and the browns dominate the slower reaches. Access is through Cline Falls State Park and Bureau of Land Management–managed public lands that parallel portions of the river.

Lower Deschutes
The 100 miles from the outflow of Lake Billy Chinook at Pelton Dam to the Columbia River constitute the lower Deschutes. This water ranges from 100 to 150 feet wide and is best known for steelhead. However, an estimated thirteen hundred trout per mile forage here, with the largest concentrations of redbands (two thousand per mile) between Warm Springs and North Junction. There are also spring and fall chinook salmon runs in this part of the river.

Hatches, Flies, and Best Times to Fish
Much has been written about the Deschutes and its insects (see Resources, below), so I mention only the major standbys here. Year-round major hatches and reliable flies include five subspecies of *Baetis*, caddisfly and stonefly nymphs, and midges. Major periodic hatches include the salmon fly (#4–#6) (*Pteronarcys californica*), golden stonefly (#8–#10) (*Hesperoperla pacifica*) nymphs, pale morning duns (July–September), and caddisflies (late July–August).
     Michael Crutcher, a Deschutes regular, claims that a weighted Hare's Ear Nymph (#12–#14), Elk Hair Caddis (#14–#16) (middays in March), and Parachute Adams (#14–#16) are the three inexpendable flies for the Deschutes.

CROOKED RIVER
The best fishing on the Crooked River—a major tributary of the Deschutes, which it joins near Lake Billy Chinook—is the 12-mile stretch running beside Route 27 between Bowman Dam (on Prineville Reservoir) and the town of Prineville. It is not uncommon to see eagles soaring near the rim of the canyon that cradles the river as it emerges out of deep lava-rock walls highlighted by an unusual spectrum of lichens. This is a very inviting piece of water, totally accessible to a visiting angler. It offers an extraordinary combination of easy access, breathtaking scenery, and more than three thousand redbands per mile. Add these advantages to an abundance of mountain whitefish (although the trout outnumber them

two to one), and you have one of the best year-round fisheries in Oregon. If you happen to be a beginner, this tailwater can be a confidence builder.

Like the Deschutes, the Crooked can be divided into three distinct sections: the headwaters, located mostly in Ochoco National Forest; the middle, largely unfishable section between the national forest boundary and Prineville Reservoir; and the tailwater, between Bowman Dam and Prineville. Downstream (north) of Prineville, access is limited and the trout population nearly disappears.

The headwater areas (not on map; see Resources, below, for map source) in the Ochoco Mountains have several small meadow stream tributaries, pretty water shaded by ponderosa pine, willow, and aspen. The most notable are Deep Creek and Mill Creek. The adventurous angler will find excellent fishing and few other anglers here. Mill Creek Wilderness provides an opportunity to take dozens of redbands in a single afternoon.

The middle portions of the river, from the U.S. Forest Service boundary to the Prineville Reservoir, have been severely damaged by irrigation withdrawals and more than 120 years of grazing. Today local landowners, the Crooked River Watershed Council, and conservation groups such as Trout Unlimited are working to restore the river. Habitat must be improved to elicit the return of redbands and ensure future runs of steelhead and salmon.

Nearly all 12 miles of the tailwater can be accessed by anglers, along Route 27, which runs on the east side of the river from Prineville to the dam. The river flows between 30 and 250 cubic feet per second, depending on the season. After it plunges from the dam, the river widens and is easy to cross and to wade from either side. There are seven small public campgrounds on Route 27 in this stretch, each providing twenty-five primitive sites. Anglers can park at these or at smaller pulloffs along the highway.

Hatches, Flies, and Best Times to Fish

Nymphs (#16) in patterns such as Hare's Ears, Pheasant Tails, or beadheads will do the trick. Successful dry-fly patterns include Elk Hair Caddis, mosquitoes, Renegades, or Adamses.

Nymphs will produce year-round, but the discerning angler looks for hatches. The dry-fly action can be blazing. Hitting the river in late July, Dave Nolte caught more than one hundred fish in an hour on a #16 caddis. The fish averaged 10 inches, with a few exceeding 16 inches. Fish are evenly and plentifully distributed throughout this stretch.

Hatches generally follow the schedule of those on the Deschutes. The Crooked tailwater is noted for scuds, especially immediately below the dam. A #18 Orange Scud fished over weed beds with a floating line (no weight, no strike indicator) can produce fine fish stories.

Don't be concerned if the Crooked looks like a big swatch of double-mocha coffee. The discoloration is the result of large amounts of suspended fine sediment. Though silt does inhibit insect propagation, many fish will have no trouble finding your flies.

METOLIUS RIVER

The Metolius is one of the largest spring-fed rivers in the United States. It is surely a candidate for the most beautiful small river I've ever seen, and visiting anglers must see and fish it at least once—the scenery alone is worth it.

The river bursts from a spring surrounded by ponderosa pine at the base of Black Butte near Camp Sherman. Throughout its course, the Metolius defines "bottle green." Shades range from aquamarine in the deep chutes to royal blue in pine-shaded back eddies. You can usually see to the bottom, more than 10 feet down.

After concentrated efforts by Trout Unlimited, Central Oregon Fly-fishers, and Oregon Trout, the Metolius is now managed as a wild trout stream. It has not been stocked since 1996 and is open to catch-and-release fishing year-round.

Although it is only 30 to 40 feet wide, the river's gradient and very cold temperatures (midforties Fahrenheit) limit trout habitat. It is now believed that large wood is important to the river. Big trees, such as old-growth ponderosa pine, fall into the water and redirect currents. This creates side channels, gravel, islands, shelter, and pools. Trout Unlimited members and others are constructing instream habitat for trout. Although the count of redbands is only about one hundred per mile, there have been encouraging signs of increased population since stocking was discontinued.

The Metolius's cold water provides the finest habitat in the country for bull trout *(Salvalinus confluentis)*. This char species is now making a comeback after near extinction in the mid-1980s, thanks to a wide range of partners, including the National Fish and Wildlife Foundation, Trout Unlimited, and the Bring Back the Natives program. These monster fish range from 5 to 20 pounds; the average fish is in the 5- to 6-pound range, and catches of 8- to 10-pound fish are possible.

Because of its strong current and considerable depth, little wading is possible on the Metolius, which is best fished from or near its banks. The water is dominated by fast riffles and runs that don't lend themselves to dry-fly fishing, and the lack of cover makes fish reluctant to rise.

Many Metolius regulars recommend fishing long (12- to 15-foot) leaders with fluorocarbon tippets on a slack line downstream. The use of lead or split shot is prohibited, so anglers often use weighted stoneflies to get to the bottom. For visitors, I recommend a trip with the guide John Judy (under Tackle Shops and Guides, below). This can be mystifying water if you want to find bull trout.

Hatches, Flies, and Best Times to Fish

The best time to fish drys is during the green drake hatch in May, the golden stonefly hatch in early July, and the October caddis emergence. Overall, however, beadhead nymphs are more productive than drys.

Bull trout hang near the bottom, and the best flies to use for them are sculpin and minnow imitations, Woolly Buggers, #10 Clouser Foxee Redd, and large streamers. John Judy, master guide, author, and bull trout expert, recommends light-colored streamers, which you can see deep down in the current.

ACCESS TO THE DESCHUTES, CROOKED, AND METOLIUS

The Deschutes, Crooked, and Metolius all are easy to access. There are many pulloffs along the Deschutes between Maupin and Macks Canyon. Access to the Metolius is readily available on roads and trails from Camp Sherman to Lake Billy Chinook.

IF YOU GO

From the Portland Airport, take I-205 south toward Gresham, then head east on U.S. Route 26 toward Sandy and Welches. Turn left (east) on Route 216, and follow to U.S. Route 197. Turn right on Route 197 to Maupin. Here you can access the lower Deschutes.

To reach the middle and upper Deschutes, continue on U.S. Route 197 from Maupin to U.S. Route 97. Go south to Madras, then head west on Route 26 to Warm Springs to access the middle section, and continue on toward Bend for the upper waters.

To reach the Crooked River, follow the above directions to Madras. Continue south to U.S. Route 26, and turn left (east) toward Prineville. At Prineville, take Route 27 south to reach the Prineville Reservoir.

To reach the Metolius, follow the above directions to Madras. Continue south on U.S. Route 97 to Redmond, then head west on Route 126 and go right on Route 14 to Camp Sherman.

Tackle Shops and Guides

For the Deschutes River

The Fly Fishing Shop. Welches (between Portland and Maupin). Mark Bachmann, co-owner. (503) 622-4607.

Deschutes Canyon Fly Shop. Maupin. John Smeraglio, proprietor. (503) 395-2565.

Deschutes River Outfitters. Bend. (541) 388-8191.

The Fly Box. Bend. (541) 388-3330.

Fly and Field Outfitters. Bend. (541) 308-1616.

The Hook Fly Shop. Sunriver. (541) 593-2358.

Kaufman's Streamborn. Portland. Lodge for rent at Maupin. (800) 442-4359.

The Patient Angler. Bend. (541) 389-6208.

For the Crooked River
  Fin 'n Feather. Prineville. (541) 447-8691.

For the Metolius River
  Camp Sherman Store. Camp Sherman. (541) 595-6711.
  The Fly Fishers Place. Sisters. (541) 549-3474.
  John Judy Flyfishing. Camp Sherman. A master guide. (541) 595-2073.

Where to Stay
  C&J's Lodge. Maupin. Carroll and Judy White, proprietors. Inexpensive. (541) 395-2404.
  Deschutes Motel. Maupin. Moderate. (541) 395-2626.
  Deschutes River Lodge. Near Redmond. Jeanene and Dick Stentz, hosts. Magnificent view of the Sisters, overlooking the upper Deschutes. Expensive. (541) 923-4701.
  The Oasis. Maupin. Mike McLucas, proprietor and guide. Nice, clean cabins. Moderate. (541) 395-2611.
  Bend and Redmond. For information on the many motels and B&Bs here, contact the Central Oregon Visitors Association. (800) 800-8334.

Camping
  On the Metolius. Seven beautiful campsites in ponderosa pine groves between Camp Sherman and Candle Creek. First-come, first-served. Small fee.
  Along the Deschutes. Thirty drive-in and fifty walk-in or boat-in campsites. Call for reservations and information. (800) 452-5687.
  On the Crooked River. Seven small (twenty-five-site) public Bureau of Land Management (BLM) campgrounds on Route 27. Call BLM in Prinesville. (541) 416-6700.

Where to Eat
  Deschutes River Inn. Maupin. Inexpensive. (541) 395-2468.
  The Oasis. Maupin. Inexpensive. (541) 395-2611.
  The Kokanee Cafe. Camp Sherman. Inexpensive. (541) 595-6420.
  Rainbow Grill. Maupin. Bar and late-night fare. No reservations.
  Bend area. This destination resort area offers many fine eating opportunities.

RESOURCES
  Oregon Department of Fish and Wildlife. Licenses and regulations. (503) 229-5403.
  To purchase a map ($4) of the Ochoco National Forest, location of the headwaters of the Crooked River, contact Supervisor's Office, P.O. Box 490, Prineville, OR 97754.

Huber, John. *Flyfisher's Guide to Oregon.* Gallatin Gateway, MT: Wilderness Adventures Press, 2000.

Hughes, Dave. *Deschutes.* Portland, OR: Frank Amato Publications, 1990.

Judy, John. *Slack Line Fly Fishing.* Harrisburg, PA: Stackpole Books, 1994.

Oregon Atlas & Gazetteer. Yarmouth, ME: DeLorme Mapping Company. (207) 846-7000.

Richmond, Scott. *Fishing in Oregon's Deschutes River.* Scappoose, OR: Flying Pencil Publications, 1993.

Ross, John. *Trout Unlimited's Guide to America's 100 Best Trout Streams.* Helena, MT: Falcon Publishing, 1999.

Sheehan, Madelynne Diness, and Dan Casali. *Fishing in Oregon.* Scappoose, OR: Flying Pencil Publications, 1995. (503) 543-7171.

Teel, Harry. *No Nonsense Guide to Fly Fishing Central and Southeastern Oregon.* Sisters, OR: David Marketing Communications, 1998.

CHAPTER TWENTY-SIX

SAN FRANCISCO

LOWER SACRAMENTO RIVER, PUTAH CREEK, AND STANISLAUS RIVER

Stephen D. Trafton

Visitors to the Bay Area, whether sightseers jammed onto a San Francisco cable car, high-tech executives scheming in Silicon Valley, or academics making a pilgrimage to Berkeley, inevitably come into contact with the Bay. San Francisco Bay is the reason that this area was settled, the reason the city is so picturesque, and the reason that visitors will, inevitably, become embroiled in a traffic jam at one of its bridges.

San Francisco Bay is also the spot at which California's two greatest river systems, the Sacramento and the San Joaquin, first mingle with salt water before reaching the Pacific at the Golden Gate. These two rivers drain more than 300 miles of the Central Valley, California's fertile heartland surrounded on all sides by rugged mountains. The combined drainages encompass one of the richest repositories of trout anywhere in the country. This chapter describes but a small sampling of what this extraordinary system has to offer.

LOWER SACRAMENTO RIVER

The fingers of the Sacramento River's headwaters reach high into the alpine ice of Mount Shasta, ranging almost to Oregon and Nevada in their search for water. They gather to form legendary trout fisheries—Hat Creek, the McCloud, and the Pit, among others—before they join to form the Sacramento River at the head of the Central Valley. In 1942 the completion of the Shasta Dam (and its downstream neighbor, Keswick Dam) near the small city of Redding formed Shasta Lake and became the northern capstone of the Central Valley Project, providing controlled water to countless users throughout the state.

Shasta Dam also irreversibly blocked fish passage to thousands of

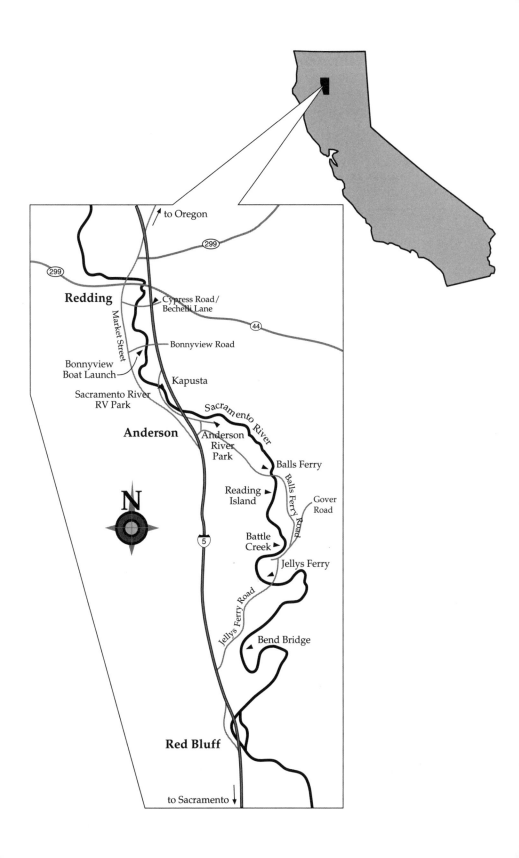

miles of headwater spawning and rearing waters, thus reducing one of the world's most prolific chinook salmon fisheries to a hatchery-dependent remnant of its former self. But a kernel of gold can be extracted from the wreckage: Shasta Dam also created a tailwater trout fishery to rival any in the country.

In California anglers' lexicon, there are two Sacramento Rivers: the Upper Sac and the Lower Sac, separated by Shasta Lake. The latter river, our subject here, is a broad, powerful river flowing from Redding through the fields and woodlands of the upper Central Valley to the town of Red Bluff. Although the sheer scale of the river can be intimidating and the urban surroundings of Redding are less than bucolic, anglers should eschew a costly, scenic drift boat ride and don their waders. The river has many lifetimes' worth of riffles, back channels, and pools for the shore-bound wading angler to explore. Even better, the Lower Sac is open year-round.

Unfortunately, the enormous demand for water in the hot season ensures that the river usually cannot be waded in the summer. From mid-September through mid to late April, however, releases from Keswick Dam are usually between 4,000 and 8,000 cubic feet per second (call a fly shop to check flows), providing good wading in fishable water.

Although many of America's famous tailwaters provide non-native trout with habitat where warm-water denizens once held sway, cold flows from Shasta Lake have provided a measure of thermal stability in an already rich native trout fishery. The trout in your net is the native coastal rainbow trout (*Oncorhynchus mykiss*) of the Sacramento and San Joaquin drainages. Its ancestry may contain a hint of redband rainbow, or it may—particularly if it is large—be a steelhead.

Although hatchery fish are planted in places throughout the system, that misfortune has not yet diluted nature's marvelous genetic formula that produces both resident and oceangoing fish from the same species in the same river. The Sacramento rainbow is a sensational physical specimen, subsisting grandly on a fantastic array of trout delicacies and—one theory maintains—maintaining its fighting fitness during a long summer of swimming in the monstrous flows released from the dam. This rainbow is a thoroughly admirable fish, well worth any angler's trip.

The Lower Sac is a big river and holds big fish. Although inflated reports of size have made the 18-incher commonplace all around the country, on these waters reports of fish that size (and much larger) are likely to be legitimate. Gear should reflect the size of the water and the quarry. A 9-foot, 6-weight rod is ideal for casting in the wind, mending line, and fighting big trout, although a 5-weight will suffice.

Reels must have adequate drag and plenty of backing. Tippet selection should be dictated by the fish: 3X if you can get away with it, but anything lighter than 5X is inviting disaster. Lightweight waders, with insulating layers according to the air temperature, are fine. Boots should be felt-soled, and a wading staff will give you that extra dose of courage to forge out into the thick of the current.

Hatches, Flies, and Best Times to Fish

The Lower Sac supports prolific insect life. Caddis in the spring and fall and *Baetis* in the winter provide fine dry-fly fishing, but the methodical nymph angler, patiently experimenting with various combinations of flies, weights, and indicators, reaps the greatest rewards.

The river's most memorable feeding phenomenon occurs each autumn when the chinook salmon return and disperse in the riffles to spawn. The heroic sight of mighty salmon swimming past your legs, leaping and fighting in the shallows, drifting in the current nearly dead, or rotting on the bank in pungent heaps is almost distraction enough to make you forget to cast out a tiny yarn salmon egg imitation. Have a good supply of Glo-Bugs (pink #16, although others will swear by different combinations of size and color), in addition to a solid assortment of caddis pupae, mayfly nymphs, and standard dry flies like Elk Hair Caddis and Adamses (#12–#18).

All three of the rivers described in this chapter offer outstanding "omelette" (salmon or trout egg imitation) fishing, be it during salmon runs or at trout spawning time. This is an opportunity to be taken cautiously and in moderation. Catching trout feeding on eggs is legitimate; provoking spawning fish, snagging them, or harassing them is not. Break off the big salmon that you accidentally hook and leave spawners alone. Streamside etiquette applies to the fish as well as to fellow anglers.

Lower Sacramento Access

At Redding, take the Cypress Avenue exit off I-5, turn left under the freeway, and proceed to Bechelli Lane. Turn right and drive to the parking lot. The varied waters of Turtle Bay, as this section of the river is known, will provide an introduction to the Lower Sac's offerings.

Further exploration to access points along Market Street, Balls Ferry Road, and Jellys Ferry Road will reveal more access and new water. It's 215 miles, about three hours, to the Lower Sacramento from San Francisco. The access points shown on the map are all within easy reach.

PUTAH CREEK

If the three-hour drive to Redding is too far for your allocated fishing time, then Putah Creek, an hour and a half from San Francisco (traffic allowing), will serve the visiting angler's needs. Putah Creek is a tributary of the Sacramento flowing from the mountains separating the Napa and Central Valleys. Its rainbows are the same noble fish that delight anglers on the Sacramento, augmented by hatchery fish. A few wily and very large browns also live here.

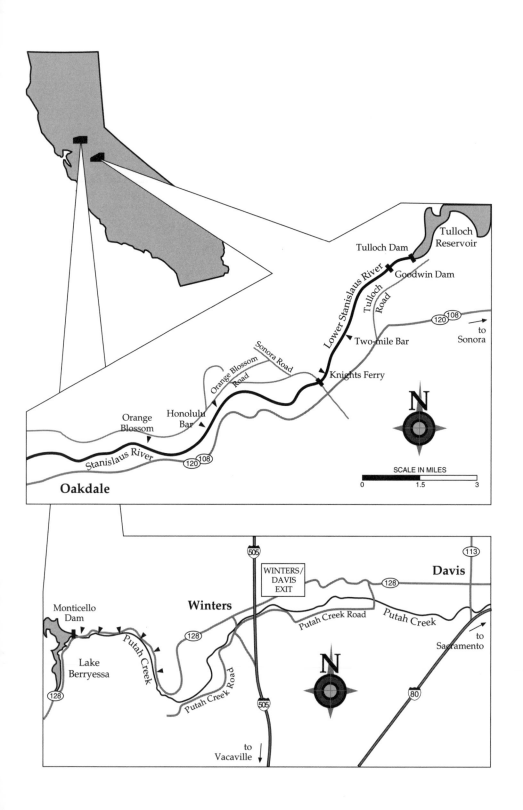

The setting is that of a California impressionist painter's landscape: bare, rolling, suntanned hills spotted with trees, a steep valley, and a shaded stream dark enough to be faintly mysterious. Despite the predictable crowds of anglers, Putah Creek is a quintessential California angling experience.

The fact that a creek as small as Putah has been dammed to form massive Lake Berryessa is emblematic of the insatiable thirst of the Central Valley. Ironically, however, Monticello Dam may be the reason that a trout fishery still exists in Putah's lower reach. If western anglers must often count their blessings wherever accidents of water policy provide them, then the tailwater trout fishery of Putah Creek is one of those blessings.

Putah is small and deep, characterized by broken pocket water interspersed with long, slow pools. Successful anglers look for the slots behind boulders and the holding water at the heads and tails of pools and ply them with nymphs, fished with or without indicators. More difficult fishing can be had in the slower pools or the long flat-water sections of the creek, which often lack obvious features but can reward the patient nymph or streamer angler with enormous trout.

Nine-foot rods for line weights 3 to 5 are ideal for Putah. Although this is a small stream, there are exceptionally large fish here. Wading is essential to cover the water, which is very cold; bring waders, felt soles, and a staff for negotiating the deep water.

Hatches, Flies, and Best Times to Fish

In general, light tippets (5X–7X) and small flies are productive on Putah. The creek is rich in insect life, and #18–#22 mayfly and midge imitations like Brassies, Pheasant Tails, and Copper Johns work well. As always, getting the fly to the fish, which means spending as much time experimenting with weight and indicators as it does changing flies, is essential. So are absolutely drag-free drifts.

Canny anglers will set the hook at the merest hesitation of line or indicator; these fish eat well and see many flies. Surface activity does occur, so be prepared with basic mayfly and midge imitations. Take a few buggy streamers along as well, and in the early spring, the Glo-Bugs that work on the Sacramento can be deadly. In general, though, Putah is a nymphing stream.

Putah is open year-round, although during the summer it suffers from the same high flow problems as the Lower Sacramento. From November through the end of April, Putah is fishable at 50 to 200 cubic feet per second. Call the fly shops to check flows. During this time, the water is restricted to barbless flies and catch-and-release. These protective policies, combined with the fact that the creek is easy to reach, has outstanding access, and is filled with big trout, leave the visiting angler no excuse not to cut short his or her meeting, cancel dinner plans, and go fishing. A coastal rainbow caught and released in the cool of a winter evening on Putah provides far more potent sustenance than does yet another plate of "authentic" crab and sourdough bread in the big city.

Putah Access

Shortly after the town of Winters, heading west on Route 128, Putah Creek will come into view, at this point a virtual slough. Shortly thereafter, the first of five anglers' parking lots will appear, all of which are on the left. Park at one of these (fee required) or at any of the obvious turnouts along the road. There is also parking at the bridge just below the dam. It is 75 miles, a little over an hour, from San Francisco to Putah Creek.

STANISLAUS RIVER

The mighty San Joaquin River, fed by the snows of the Sierra Nevada through a handful of watersheds that are great rivers in their own right, drains much of the Central Valley south of the Bay. The Stanislaus River is one of its major tributaries. Although it sacrifices far more than the proverbial pound of flesh in its journey to the San Joaquin, its waters harnessed, impounded, and piped through mountains to other basins, the "Stan" and its cold-water fishery persist and flourish.

Access to much of the Stanislaus is limited, but the section below Tulloch Lake Reservoir has several miles of public water maintained by the U.S. Army Corps of Engineers. Combine the facts that the Stan is only two and a half hours from San Francisco and that it is usually fishable in the summer, when the faucets are running at full force on the Lower Sacramento and Putah, and the angler has no reason to board a plane for the Bay Area without a rod and reel.

The lower Stanislaus, rarely more than a large stream, flows through extremely rugged country, often at the foot of vertiginous precipices and through tight gorges. Fishable water abounds for the angler who prefers to keep the car within reach, while the adventurous who enjoy bushwhacking, rock scrambling, rattlesnake encounters, and the expectant attentions of circling buzzards can risk themselves for days on this water. There are numerous steep whitewater drops leading to deep pools, but shallower riffles also occur. The trout are the same coastal rainbows found in the Sacramento system, and you can—if you are willing to accept the possibility of some hatchery influence—feel satisfied that the trout you bring to hand is a native Californian.

A 9-foot, 5-weight rod is ideal for the Stanislaus, and although there will probably be no need for backing, a solid drag is advisable. Tippets (3X–5X), waders, and felt-soled boots round out your equipment needs. Those would-be commandos seeking adventure amidst the Stan's steep canyons are advised to remember the old Marine Corps adage: "It's easy to be hard, but it's hard to be smart." Carry food and, above all, water and sunscreen. Summertime temperatures along the river can be scorching.

Hatches, Flies, and Best Times to Fish
Techniques for the Stan are straightforward. Nymphing with plenty of weight, with or without an indicator, will almost always bring results. Standard patterns such as Prince Nymphs and A.P.s work well, but if I could use only one fly, I would choose a Hare's Ear.

Dry-fly action can be good, too: Imitate the mayfly and caddis hatches with the usual suspects, but don't wait until rising fish appear to try drys. Prospecting with Stimulators, Humpies, and grasshopper patterns can produce zealous assaults from the local trout. This stretch of the river is below any barriers to fish passage. Consequently, during the fall through late-winter seasons, some of the hardy survivors of the San Joaquin's decimated chinook salmon runs appear in the Stan. Glo-Bug fishing for opportunistic rainbows can be sensational, and the possibility of hooking a steelhead adds piquancy to the experience.

The deep pools are well worth the time spent dredging them with Woolly Buggers and other streamers, especially those imitating juvenile salmon. Anglers should beware of targeting the Stan during the salmon run. The river's only annual closure runs from mid-October through the end of December to protect the bulk of the spawning run.

Like the Lower Sacramento and Putah, the Stanislaus is a tailwater. Although summer flows are generally fishable (and the river can be fished throughout most of the year), the flows are subject to extreme fluctuations at any given time, especially in the early summer when heavy snowmelt in the mountains can force dam operators to flush water out of reservoirs to make room for incoming runoff. Flows of 400 to 700 cubic feet per second are ideal. Call fly shops to check flows.

Trout Unlimited and other conservation organizations are currently involved in a complicated relicensing effort covering most of the Stanislaus watershed, and anglers can bide their time in the hope that more stable flow regimes will someday be reestablished, albeit artificially, on this great river.

Stanislaus Access
A few miles east of Oakdale on Route 120, follow the signs to Knight's Ferry Park and the Stanislaus River to the Army Corps parking lot. Or, continue on Route 120 east to the Tulloch Lake South Shore sign. Either follow the signs to Tulloch Lake Reservoir (access to the river is very limited by terrain and private property) or return west on Route 120 for a short distance to the Two Mile Bar Recreation Area sign on the right. Follow the road to the Army Corps parking lot. This lot and the downstream lot are open from 6 A.M. to 9 P.M.

The Lower Sacramento, Putah Creek, and Stanislaus, as well as northern California rivers farther afield, provide visiting anglers with enough angling opportunities to sustain many trips to the Bay Area. They are representative of the wealth of California's natural resources and of the multiple-use burden that the Golden State's tremendous growth demands of its resources. These waters and their resilient trout and salmon bear their burden well. Given the opportunity, and with the help of Trout Unlimited and other conservation organizations, it is hoped that they will continue to do so for decades to come.

ALSO WORTH NOTING
The Upper Sacramento River is less than an hour north of Redding, and other nationally famous streams such as Hat Creek and the McCloud are within one to two hours of Redding.

If you're willing to drive farther east from the lower Stanislaus, Routes 120 and 108 lead into the heart of the Sierra Nevada range. The forks of the Stanislaus are lovely havens for wild trout. The splendors—and not inconsequential trout fisheries—of Yosemite National Park await only a couple hours beyond Oakdale.

IF YOU GO
Lower Sacramento River
From the Bay Area, take I-80 east to I-505 north ("the Cutoff") to I-5 north to Redding.

Tackle Shops and Guides
Check conditions and buy licenses and flies before you leave the Bay Area.

A-1 Fish. Oakland. (510) 832-0731.

Angling Arts. San Francisco. Charles P. Anthony, owner. (415) 863-8426.

Fly Fishing Outfitters. San Francisco. (415) 781-3474.

The Fly Shop. Redding. This is an internationally respected fly shop that provides local advice and hosts numerous trips to fresh- and saltwater destinations throughout the year. (530) 222-3555.

Fish First! Albany. Take the Albany/Buchanan Street exit off I-80 on the way to the Sacramento and Putah (and it's only a short detour for those headed to the Stanislaus). Equipment, a superb selection of local fly patterns, and the latest information on flows, hatches, and conditions for the entire northern half of the state. Guide services on the Lower Sac and Putah Creek from the shop's Albany and Chico locations. (510) 526-1937. www.fishfirst.com.

Where to Stay
Redding offers the full range of chain motels, plus dozens of alternatives to suit all tastes and budgets. La Quinta, Howard Johnson Express, and Best Western, among others, are located on Cypress Avenue within minutes of the river parking area and generally have rooms in all price ranges.

Camping
Limited in the immediate area. Call the Redding Chamber of Commerce (see Resources, below).

Where to Eat
   Jack's Grill. Redding. Steaks worthy of the river's fishing. Moderate. (530) 241-9705.
   Big Red's Bar-B-Q. Redding. Solid carnivorous fare. Inexpensive. (530) 221-7427.
   Black Bear Diner. Redding. Inexpensive to moderate. Good for breakfast or lunch. (530) 221-7600.
   Cedar Tree Café. Redding. Inexpensive to moderate. Another good choice for breakfast or lunch. (530) 221-4157.

Putah Creek
From the Bay Area, take I-80 east to I-505 north. Get off at Route 128 west, the Winters/Davis exit (don't take the Putah Creek Road exit). Follow Route 128 west toward Lake Berryessa. Shortly after the town of Winters, Putah Creek will come into view.

Tackle Shops and Guides
   Fly Fishing Unlimited. Vacaville. (707) 446-0760. www.flyfishing unlimited.com. Also use San Fransisco area shops listed above.

Where to Stay
I advise anglers fishing Putah to stay in the Bay Area. If you want to be closer to the water, Vacaville offers a wide variety of chain motels.

Camping
   Canyon Creek Resort. Monticello Dam.

Where to Eat
   Murillo's. Vacaville. If you fish late and want to eat before you get back to the Bay Area, try one of the two locations. Good Mexican food. Inexpensive. No reservations. (707) 448-3395 or (707) 447-3704.

In-n-Out Burger. Inexpensive eateries along I-80. A true California institution. Originally confined to Southern California, this chain has spread north, to the delight of all hamburger aficionados.

Stanislaus River

From the Bay Area, take I-580 east to I-205 east to Route 120 east (following signs for Yosemite National Park) through Oakdale. Then follow the directions under Stanislaus Access, above.

Tackle Shops and Guides

Use shops in the San Francisco area listed above for the Sacramento River.

Where to Stay

Oakdale is the last sizable town on the road east to Yosemite. It has numerous hotels and restaurants to suit all tastes and budgets.

Where to Eat

The Cocina Michoacana. Oakdale. Solid Mexican food and cold beer for tired anglers. Inexpensive to moderate. (209) 848-3818.

Fruit and vegetable stands. Stop at these stands that line Route 120 as you head toward the mountains. The local delicacies have been nurtured by the same water that you will soon fish, and they, like the Stan's fishery, are undeniably superb.

RESOURCES

Redding Chamber of Commerce. (530) 225-4433. redding.area guides.net.

Vacaville Chamber of Commerce. (707) 448-6424.

Oakdale Visitors' Bureau. (209) 847-2244. Twenty-four-hour recording. (209) 848-9484.

Cal Trout. 870 Market St., Suite 859, San Francisco, CA 94102. (415) 392-8887. A local trout conservation and information group.

Norman, Seth. *A Flyfishers' Guide to Northern California.* Gallatin Gateway, MT: Wilderness Adventures Press, 1997.

Northern California Atlas & Gazetteer. Yarmouth, ME: DeLorme Mapping Company. (207) 846-7000.

Very good, detailed map of the Sacramento River. StreamTime Fishing Access Maps, P.O. Box 991536, Redding, CA 96099. (916) 244-0310.

CHAPTER TWENTY-SEVEN

LOS ANGELES

PIRU CREEK

Conrad L. Ricketts

When you think of Los Angeles, certain things come to mind: a city on the edge of a desert, film stars, palm trees, highway gridlock, but not wild trout—but . . . yes, wild trout. Los Angeles has one of the best urban wild trout fisheries of any metropolitan city in the United States, so the next time you come to the City of Angels, bring your fly rod. The season is year-round, and there are five streams within one to three hours of downtown. My favorite is Piru Creek.

Stepping into Piru and stalking its trout is stepping back in time. Before the lakes and dams were built, Piru ran to the Pacific Ocean and was an ancient steelhead run.

Piru is an Indian name meaning "a place of reeds." The area was inhabited by the Chumash Indians dating back to 3000 B.C. In 500 A.D. the Tataviam Indians ("dwellers of the sunny hills") moved in. They built more than twenty-five villages. Archaeologists have cataloged eight of them along the riverbanks.

In 1769 the Spanish explorer Don Gaspar followed its course, and in 1821 the Hudson Bay Company sent in French fur trappers. Gold was found in 1842, six years before Sutter's Mill. Col. John C. Frémont accepted the surrender of California from Mexico while camped at its headwaters, and in 1849 John W. Audubon (son of the renowned John James Audubon) put it on paper while on a federally sponsored mapping expedition.

Today, less than one hour from Los Angeles's downtown skyscrapers, Piru Creek is an example of what urban wild trout fisheries can be—thanks to the hard work and stewardship of the Sierra Pacific Flyfishers, Cal Trout, and the California Department of Fish and Game's wild trout program.

The best fly fishing is found in the wild trout section. This part of the stream is like doing nine holes. It's only one and a half miles long, and you

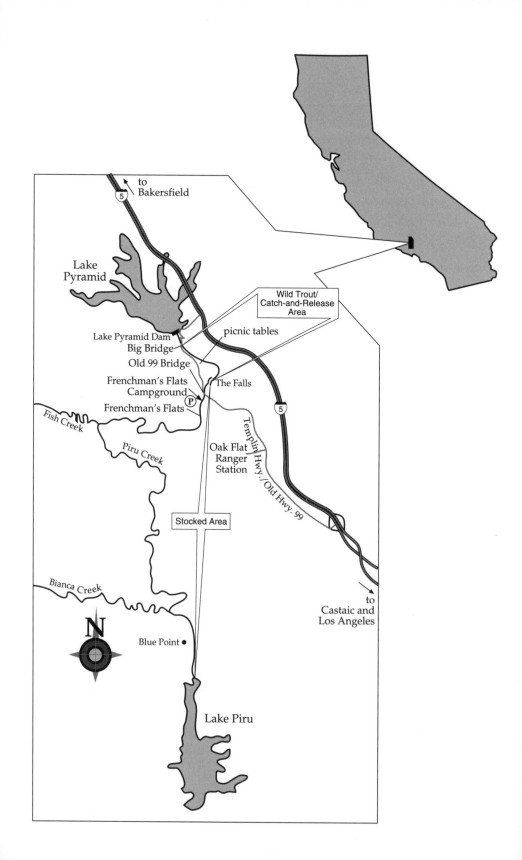

to
Bakersfield

Lake
Pyramid

Wild Trout/
Catch-and-Release
Area

Lake Pyramid Dam
Big Bridge
Old 99 Bridge

picnic tables

Frenchman's Flats
Campground
Frenchman's Flats

The Falls

Fish Creek

Piru Creek

Templin Hwy./Old Hwy. 99

Oak Flat
Ranger
Station

Stocked Area

Bianca Creek

to
Castaic and
Los Angeles

N

Blue Point

Lake Piru

can be on the stream in the morning and back to the office for a noon meeting. If there's no office to go to, you've got another 13 miles of stocked stream to explore. This is fast action fishing for rainbows in the 6- to 10-inch size.

With over six thousand trout per mile, Piru can be fished year-round. It is the tailwater of Lake Pyramid and the headwaters of Lake Piru. It flows 14½ miles through steep, narrow canyons with wide floors. The stream drains south from the center of the mountains known as the Transverse Ranges. The streambed is narrow, often no more than 20 to 40 feet wide, and is made up of long runs of riffles, deep pools, pocket water, and stretches of slow-moving flat water.

Since Piru is a tailwater, water temperatures are constant within the first 3 miles. There are times when the water can be rich in nutrients and plankton. This makes for a healthy population of aquatic insects, and the crayfish are so large that the locals call them lobsters. An agreement with the Department of Water Resources ensures a minimum flow from the dam of 5 cubic feet per second in the winter and 20 in the summer.

This is not the place to be fishing during a thunderstorm. The narrow canyon walls concentrate the runoff and can produce flows up to 10,000 cubic feet per second. The creek channel below the reservoir is made up of sandstone, huge boulders, and exposed bedrock. The stream is lined with alders, sycamores, cottonwoods, and willows. Cattails and an abundance of aquatic plants provide excellent cover. The average size is in the 6- to 8-inch class, with a large number of rainbows that are 9 and 10 inches. In the deep pools and holes, you can find 14- and 15-inch wild trout, which would be trophy size for this stream.

The wild trout are shy and spooky, and when fishing this stream, stalking is the order of the day. Wear clothing that blends in with the background and a good pair of polarized sunglasses. Long stretches of the stream are lined with an overhanging canopy. To get a good cast, you'll need chest waders and felt-soled boots. Short rods, 6½ to 7½ feet in 3- to 4-weight, were built for this type of work. Use long leaders and a fine tippet, 10 to 15 feet tapering down to 6X or 7X.

Start walking upstream far enough away from the bank to keep concealed. Take time to watch the water for trout rising or holding in feeding lies. When you spot a trout, enter the water well downstream of the fish and work your way slowly upstream, being careful not to alarm it by pushing surface waves in front of you. The best presentation is upstream with a curve cast. This is done by flipping your wrist over sharply (to the right for a right curve or left for a left curve) on your forward cast. For more of a curve, put some forearm motion to it. This will prevent spooking the fish by throwing line over its back, and it works well in tight places.

When you find yourself directly across from a fish, position yourself slightly downstream, and cast across and upstream. If you don't get a strike, point the rod tip back to its first position and make an upstream roll cast. The fly will scoot into the air and travel to the first point where it entered the water. The upstream roll cast is one of the best techniques on Piru Creek because of the riparian vegetation that lines most of the stream. Dry-fly action takes place early or late in the day. When the sun is fully on the water, switch to a nymph.

The water flows on Piru Creek are slow enough throughout most of the year that the trout do not find themselves in a balancing act between calories and energy. This means they will be feeding on food drifting in the current and will be active rather than holding on the bottom. Use lightly weighted nymphs that float above the surface bottom, or grease the tippet and fish the nymph within the surface film. This not only will produce some explosive strikes, but will keep you from going mad during the summer and winter when long filaments of green algae will grab anything bouncing along the bottom.

When fishing Piru Creek in the summer, keep your eyes open for poison oak, stinging nettles, and rattlesnakes. Bring insect repellent; the blackflies will be far more troublesome than the rattlesnakes.

What makes Piru Creek and the other Southern California rivers so unique is how uncrowded they are if you walk just a bit. In summer, weekdays are the best times to fish. You can often spend an entire day and come across only three or four anglers, and in winter, you'll find miles of stream for just you and the trout.

Like most urban wild trout streams, Piru has an effect on you. At the parking lot and as far as you can drag an ice cooler, you'll find trash and graffiti. Go farther than that, and you'll fish the stream as it has been for thousands of years.

HATCHES, FLIES, AND BEST TIMES TO FISH

Two things can be said about Piru Creek hatches: As on most tailwater streams, the aquatic insects are small (#16–#28), and you won't need a box filled with every fly known to man. The most abundant aquatic insects are the caddisflies (Trichoptera), including the spotted sedge *(Hydropsyche)*. Good nymph patterns are the Latex Caddis Larva and Green Rockworm (#16–#20).

For the dry fly, nothing beats the Elk Hair Caddis in olive, brown, and yellow (#16–#22). The tube-case caddis *(Micrasema)* will be found throughout the drainage. Nymphs like the Strawman and Tan Caddis (#14–#18) are good producers, and drys like the Henryville Special and Fluttering Caddis (#16–#18) are also among the best choices.

Although not as abundant, patterns that imitate other caddis hatches are the Net-Spinning Caddis, Western Water Sedge, and Speckled Peter. Nymphs like Zug Bugs, Pheasant Tails, and Brassies (#18–#22) are good imitations. If you like to tie, make sure you've got lots of LaFontaine's Emergent Sparkle Pupae, deadly on Piru trout.

Mayfly selection is simple. The two predominant bugs are the small blue-winged olive *(Baetis tricaudatus)* and the Trico. Stream samples show that the most common invertebrate found is a bug best imitated by a Blue-Winged Olive Nymph. Patterns should include the Little Olive Nymph, Gold-Ribbed Hare's Ear, and *Baetis* Compara-nymph (#16–#22). Drys include the Little Olive Parachute, *Baetis* Compara-dun, and Olive No-Hackle (#16–#24). Trico hatches can be mind-boggling on the stream, so put some Trico Thorax and Sparkle Wing Tricos in your box (#20–#28).

Because Piru Creek is at a low elevation and Southern California winters are very mild, hatches of caddisflies and mayflies can happen any day of the year. All it takes is for the sun to come out and warm the water to 45 to 50 degrees F. But not all days are like the Rose Bowl Parade; that's why God made the midge (Chironomid). You'll find it hatching on the cold days of winter when nothing else will. The best nymph patterns are the Serendipity in red and the Ascending Midge Pupa (#20–#28). For adult midges, use Griffith's Gnats (#18–#22).

If tying on small flies and nymphs is not your cup of tea, and you're after the biggest trout in the stream, then grab a 6-weight, put on a 5-foot, 4X tippet, tie on a blood red crayfish (#1/0–#8), and hold on.

REGULATIONS

A California fishing license is required for anyone over age sixteen, and it must be displayed by attaching it to outer clothing at or above the waist-line. Fishing hours are from one hour before sunrise to one hour after sunset, year-round. The daily limit in the stocked section is five fish per day and is open to all legal tackle. The wild trout section is a catch-and-release, zero-limit fishery, restricted to barbless hooks, artificial flies, or lures. No bait fishing is allowed. To report poachers or polluters, call CalTip at (800) 952-5400.

ACCESS

To get to Piru Creek, take I-5 to the Templin Highway (old Route 99) turnoff, about 7 miles north of Castaic. At the end of the Templin High-way, you come to a locked gate and parking area adjacent to Frenchman's Flats Campground. Park here and walk to the stream. A $5 parking fee is required. The permit can be bought at local stores in Castaic.

To fish the wild trout section, walk upstream on the paved road 1⅓ miles to the waterfalls. Wade in the stream from the falls upstream to the Big bridge. This is the 1½-mile-long wild trout catch-and-release section.

Past the Big bridge upstream to Lake Pyramid Dam is a restricted, no-trespassing area. Once you reach the falls, cross over to the far bank and start fishing upstream. Trails parallel the stream, but the terrain can be difficult in spots.

In the 1⅓ miles from the falls downstream to Frenchman's Flats Campground, the California Department of Fish and Game stocks ten thousand to twelve thousand trout per year in the 7- to 9-inch class. This part of the stream flows through a wide canyon floor and is made up of pocket water, small riffles, and pools.

Starting from the campground, Piru Creek runs downstream for 11½ miles into Lake Piru. A trail follows the stream for several miles, and from there you start boulder hopping and working your way through dense shrubs. The fishing can be quite good in spring, fall, and early winter. But don't let the dog days of summer fool you; Southern California streams are unique. In the heat of midday, the relative humidity drops so low that the streams act like giant evaporated coolers, causing the water temperature to drop several degrees. You'll find long stretches of pocket water and large boulders obstructing the flow, creating deep pools, as the stream winds through canyon narrows. This section has a mix of wild and stocked trout.

ALSO WORTH NOTING
West Fork of the San Gabriel River
The West Fork flows through a deeply incised canyon for 8½ miles, beginning at Cogswell Reservoir and ending at the San Gabriel main channel. The stream holds more than eight thousand trout per mile and is the only river in California with access platforms for the disabled in a wild trout area. The dry-fly action is terrific, but the fish are very picky and skittish.

From its mouth at the San Gabriel, the West Fork is stocked with fifteen thousand rainbows in the 7- to 10-inch range for a little more than a mile and a half. The wild trout catch-and-release area is from the second bridge above the mouth of the stream to the reservoir, about 5½ miles. Most of the fish are under 12 inches, but there are many 14- to 15-inchers in the water. Try to fish the West Fork on a weekday.

The San Gabriel is located about 30 miles from downtown Los Angeles in the Angeles National Forest. Take I-210 (Foothill Freeway) to Azusa. Drive north on Route 39 and pass the Rincon Fire Station. Park at the mouth of the West Fork. A $5 parking permit is required and can be bought at the entrance station or local stores.

Kern River
The Kern River is a freestone fishery that gets most of its water from high up in the Western Sierras and lower from Lake Isabella. The river holds stocked rainbows and wild rainbows, and wild browns. Fishing is best is in the pocket water, around big boulders and in the deep pools. Generally, the farther upstream you go, the larger the fish will be. There is good fishing above the dam to 7,000 feet, where you can catch native golden trout.

The Kern River is located northeast of Los Angeles, about 50 miles from Bakersfield. From Bakersfield, take Route 178 north to Lake Isabella; continue to the Lake Isabella Dam. Kern River Highway (Route 178) runs right along the river. Pull off on any side road and park. The river courses through a pretty canyon, so be prepared to hike a little.

For more information, contact Kern River Fly Fishers, P.O. Box 686, Bakersfield, CA 93302, or Buz's Fly Shop in Visalia (about 40 miles north of Bakersfield) at (559) 734-1151.

Streams of the Kern River Drainage

Streams in the Kern River drainage offer an opportunity to catch golden trout without making an overnight camping trip. Located in an isolated area at the southwestern tip of the Sierras, about four and a half hours northeast of Los Angeles (and two and a half hours from Kernville—the nearest lodging), the South Fork of the Kern River provides excellent angling. The South Fork, Salmon Creek, Trout Creek, Taylor Creek, and Fish Creek are full of brilliant little golden trout. They are all receptive to flies—if you approach with caution.

For more information, contact High Sierra Flyfisher at (760) 375-5810. For a map of the Sequoia National Forest, contact the Cannell Meadow Ranger District at (760) 376-3781. It's wise to take a four-wheel-drive vehicle into this area.

IF YOU GO

Piru Creek is located northwest of Los Angeles in the Angeles National Forest, some 40 miles from downtown. From I-5, take the Templin Highway turnoff, about 7 miles north of Castaic. Drive 5 miles north on the Templin Highway, past the Oak Flat Ranger Station, to Frenchman's Flats Campground. Parking is available at the gate.

Tackle Shops and Guides

These are in the Los Angeles metro area.

Bob Marriott's. Fullerton. (714) 525-1827.

End of the Line. La Verne. (909) 596-6515.

Fisherman's Spot. Burbank. (818) 785-7306.

Huber's Hackle Haven. Torrance. (310) 324-7748.

Malibu Fish'n Tackle. Thousand Oaks. (805) 496-7332.

Mike Scott's Hackle. Orange. Tackle and flies. (714) 998-9400.

Sport Chalet. Beverly Connection. (310) 657-3210.

Where to Stay and Where to Eat

Since Piru Creek is less than an hour from Los Angeles, I recommend staying and eating in the city.

RESOURCES

A map of Piru Creek's wild trout section, as well as other Southern California streams, is available from Reel Maps. (310) 822-1877. E-mail: ReelMaps@aol.com.

Cal Trout. 870 Market St., Suite 859, San Francisco, CA 94102. (415) 392-8887. A local trout conservation and information group.

Southern & Central California Atlas & Gazetteer. Yarmouth, ME: DeLorme Mapping Company. (207) 846-7000. www.delorme.com.

DEEP CREEK

Jim Matthews

Deep Creek is the best of a handful of streams and small rivers that drain the Transverse Mountains, which separate the coastal population centers from the parched deserts to the north and east of Los Angeles. Deep Creek flows off the north side of the San Bernardino Mountains and becomes the major tributary of the Mojave River. During wet winters, the Mojave flows far out into the desert, but during dry seasons and the heat of summer, the river's surface flow recedes farther and farther upstream, often sinking beneath the desert sand only a mile or two from where Deep Creek comes out of its wild canyon.

The Pacific Crest Trail (PCT) follows Deep Creek, usually staying high on the rim of the canyon, from its terminus in the Mojave upstream to Splinter's Cabin, which serves as the hub for fishing expeditions on this river. During cool, wet years, trout can be found all the way down to the Mojave River, but the Willow Creek confluence is usually considered the lower end of the trout habitat. Water temperatures usually get too warm in the summer below that point. Willow Creek is also the boundary for the special-regulations section; anglers are required to use artificial lures and barbless hooks from this point upstream to the headwaters in Little Green Valley. Anglers are allowed to creel two fish over 8 inches long in this stretch, but most regulars practice complete catch-and-release fishing.

AVOIDING SNAKES AND NUDITY

Angling friends who don't really like sharing Deep Creek with other fishermen are quick to point out the so-called drawbacks to fishing the stream. Everyone has a story of a 5-foot-long rattlesnake on the PCT or coiled up on the sand by one of the 150-foot-long pools. Many tell tales of shaggy motorcycle trail riders with suspected criminal backgrounds, and there are usually stories about coming upon nude sunbathers and swimmers on the big pools (although I have yet to figure out how finding near-mermaids on a trout river is going to scare anglers away).

All the stories are true. One spring, I actually was so intent on working up the bank to cast to a rising brown trout that I didn't notice what was slithering at my feet. When I finally looked down, I had a dozen baby

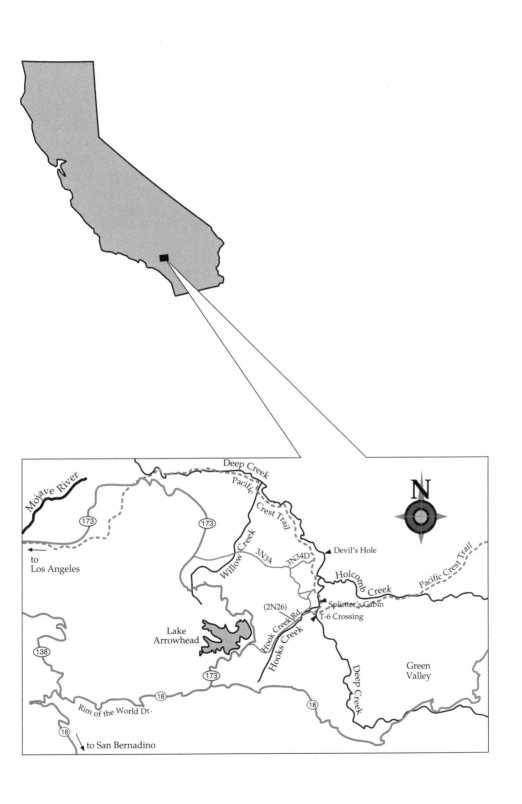

rattlesnakes around my waders, including one that had its tiny fangs buried in thick neoprene. None were bigger than healthy night crawlers, and when the one latched onto my waders let go, unable to penetrate the spongy material, I simply left the nest of snakes and tried to approach the trout from a different angle.

I have also met motorcyclists illegally riding the PCT and was stupid enough to say things before noticing they were packing heat. The nude swimmers are usually polite enough not to dive in while you are casting to working fish, preferring to watch the action from the rocks above, perhaps even helping direct your casts to moving fish.

Deep Creek is not a meadow stream. Along its entire length—from the headwaters, where ponderosa pine cling to the steep hillsides and dogwoods and sycamores crowd the banks in the canyon bottom, to its lower reaches on the margin of the Mojave Desert, where chaparral and creosote are the dominant shrubbery—the water plunges through a deep canyon filled with large boulders. The stream requires some athletic ability to fish.

ROPES AND CLIMBING GEAR

Don Stehsel, an avid Southern California fly fisherman and conservation activist, has been known to carry climbing ropes down the PCT, tie one end off, and rappel down steep hillsides into big pools that other anglers can't reach. Stehsel has a number of 18-inch browns to his credit from Deep Creek, most taken on deer hair mouse patterns at dusk.

Sheer rock faces can block movement up or down stretches of stream, requiring anglers to swim or make long climbs up, over, and back down to the water. In the summer, swimming is a viable option; it can become extremely hot in the canyon, and a dip is not unwelcome. In the late fall, when it is cool, and in the spring and early summer, when the water is rushing down the canyon, making swimming a potentially dangerous situation, climbing is in order.

Two of the best stretches of Deep Creek are the ones where you have to hike a bit to get away from other people. Upstream from Splinter's Cabin, it doesn't take more than about a quarter mile of rock-hopping to get away from most people. Here the stream is smaller and holds mostly 6-inch rainbows.

Downstream about a mile from Splinter's Cabin, Holcomb Creek joins Deep Creek in a huge pool. It's an easy walk down the PCT to reach this stretch, but the trail is close to the rim of the canyon, and you have to slip and slide down the steep hillside to the creek. It's worth it. There's excellent water above and below this juncture that doesn't get as much fishing pressure. This is also the stretch of water that seems to hold the most big browns, although rainbows have come to dominate the whole river in recent years.

HATCHES, FLIES, AND BEST TIMES TO FISH

Deep Creek is a rich stream. Its riffle stretches hold all of the common western mayflies, caddis, and stoneflies. While its big pools often get weed beds in the summer, there are fine hatches of stillwater mayflies and caddis (#20–#24). Damsels can also become important on windy days, and I've always used an ant pattern as a searching fly and sometimes don't change it through the day.

The trout generally are opportunistic feeders, and most anglers carry a selection of #14–#18 bushy dry flies—Humpies, Wulffs, and the like—for fishing the riffles. Imitations of ants, small mayflies, and caddis are best for dry-fly fishing on big pools. When the fish aren't rising, Hare's Ear Beadheads are very effective fished through the riffles or deeply below a strike indicator in the big pools.

I would be remiss in discussing hatches without talking about three major ones that I've had great success with over the years. In the spring, there's usually a tremendous hatch of ladybird beetles that find their way onto the water by the thousands. The beetles swarm all over the ground along the river. There are often windrows of beetles in eddies. The trout take the orange-and-black imitations leisurely all day long. Though I've been chided about the ethics of this, I've been known to pick up a handful of beetles from a swarm on the bank, go to the head of a pool, and feed the insects into the water until a number of fish were rising. No apologies.

Earlier in the spring, yellow stoneflies hatch in good numbers over a long period of time. It's usually the first major hatch after the winter, and snow can still be on the banks when it begins to come off. The flies are less than ½ inch long and very pale, colored like a faded piece of legal notebook paper. The water may still be cold, but the trout meet this early hatch with gusto.

In the heat of summer and early fall, the big pools crank out good evening spinner falls daily. The spinner is the dying stage of a tiny mayfly I have never identified. They are really tiny. A #24 is not too big, and I have a friend who ties a double spinner on a #20 hook, slightly offset. He says he does this so the flies don't appear to be perfectly in a straight line.

This is one of the few hatches where I have seen Deep Creek trout become very selective and refuse anything but a very small, very pale olive spentwing pattern. It's also the hatch that brings up the biggest trout in the river—not to feed on the tiny flies, but to eat the chubs that come to the surface for the mayflies. The big swirls that open up on Deep Creek these evenings are what keep most anglers coming back to this unique stream.

DEEP CREEK ACCESS

Take Route 18 to Route 173 at Lake Arrowhead, and go north on Route 173 around the south shore of the lake to Hook Creek Road, also shown as 3N34 on San Bernardino National Forest maps. Take a right on Hook

Creek Road. After 2.2 miles, the paved road will become 2N26, a forest service dirt road. Drive .9 mile and the dirt road will split; stay to your left and drive .2 mile. The road will split again. Take the right fork for .5 mile to Deep Creek at Splinter's Cabin parking lot. The road can be rough, but careful driving in a vehicle with decent clearance should get you to Splinter's.

ALSO WORTH NOTING
Santa Ana River
On the opposite side of the San Bernardino Mountains, the Santa Ana River flows out of the San Gorgonio Wilderness through a canyon unlike Deep Creek. Marked by beaver meadows in its upper reaches and tumbly pocket water in its lower reaches, it flows out of the mountains into an urban setting. This is fine brown trout water that gets little fishing pressure. Its wild fish have held up nicely under a five-fish, any-gear regulation. The Department of Fish and Game plants the water with rainbows (not so fondly called "puss-guts" by the wild trout devotees), and these draw the weekend crowds.

There is good fishing for browns from South Fork Campground on Route 38 downstream to Bear Creek. The best water is the unroaded stretch below Seven Oaks in the Filaree Flats area. A San Bernardino National Forest map or the *Southern and Central California Atlas & Gazetteer* makes navigation here a snap.

Bear Creek
A major tributary to the Santa Ana River, Bear Creek drains Big Bear Lake through a canyon that is less accessible and perhaps even more rugged than Deep Creek. Access is either via the long, steep Siberia Creek Trail behind the Snow Valley Ski Area just off Route 18, or from the Santa Ana River via bumpy, high-clearance forest service roads 1N09 and 1N64. I prefer to drive in and rock-hop into the canyon with a fly rod and a box of dry flies or an ultralight spinning rod and black and gold Panther Martins. The fish are not sophisticated.

Like the Santa Ana, Bear Creek is populated mostly with 6- to 13-inch brown trout, but a few bigger fish are in the deepest pools. Bear Creek has the same regulations as Deep Creek: artificial barbless flies or lures, a two-fish limit, with an 8-inch minimum size.

Bear Creek and the headwater portions of the Santa Ana River are reached by staying on I-10 past I-215 to Route 38 (Orange Street) in Redlands. Take Route 38 north into the national forest, and then take Seven Oaks Road down to the Santa Ana. This road leaves Route 38 to the north about 7 miles past Angelus Oaks, a small mountain community.

IF YOU GO
Deep Creek is about 80 miles east of Los Angeles. From Orange County, take Route 91 north to I-215 north. From Los Angeles, take Route 60 to Route 91 to I-215 north, or take I-10 east to San Bernardino and then travel north on I-215. From I-215, take Route 30 north and east to Route 18 (Waterman Avenue), and then travel north out of San Bernardino into the San Bernardino Mountains.

Tackle Shops and Guides
For fly and tackle shops in Los Angeles, see the previous section.

Charlie Bear's Custom Tackle. San Bernardino. Charlie "Bear" Palmer, proprietor. Though it's primarily a bass and striper saltwater shop, this is the closest shop to Deep Creek, and the staff usually knows what's happening on the fresh water. Moderate selection of flies and gear. (909) 886-9195.

Riverside Ski and Sport. Riverside. Bob Slamal, proprietor and Deep Creek guide. Full-service fly shop. Good knowledge of local streams. (909) 784-0205.

Where to Stay
This is part of the greater Los Angeles suburban sprawl, and there are thousands of places to stay within a couple hours of Deep Creek. If you don't wish to stay in metro Los Angeles, call the Lake Arrowhead Chamber of Commerce at (909) 337-3715 or the San Bernardino Chamber of Commerce at (909) 885-7515 for information.

Camping
San Bernardino National Forest. Four campgrounds are close to Deep Creek: North Shore, Dogwood, Crab Flats, and Green Valley. For reservations, call (800) 280-CAMP.

Santa Ana River. Four campgrounds along the river, if you intend to fish Bear Creek or the Santa Ana.

Where to Eat
Rosa Maria's. North San Bernardino. Wonderful home-cooked Mexican food for under $5. If you're coming back down Route 18 after a day of fishing, the first stoplight you come to is 40th Street. Turn right (west), and go two lights to Sierra Way; turn right (north), and go about a block.

The Thai Place. San Bernardino. Inexpensive, under $9. From Route 18, go west on 40th Street to Kendall Avenue (five lights from Route 18, 40th jogs south to meet Kendall), and turn right. Go about 2 miles (west) on Kendall, and turn into the little mall on the southeast corner of Kendall and University. You'll find the restaurant in the back corner of the complex. After eating, you can get back to I-215 by taking University south about 2 miles.

RESOURCES

San Bernardino National Forest map. This map, $4 at ranger stations, is the key to finding your way around easily.

Cal Trout. 870 Market St., Suite 859, San Francisco, CA 94102. (415) 392-8887. A local trout conservation and information group.

Southern & Central California Atlas & Gazetteer. Yarmouth, ME: DeLorme Mapping Company. (207) 846-7000. www.delorme.com.